DESIGNER POLITICS

Designer Politics

How Elections are Won

Margaret Scammell

Lecturer, School of Politics and Communication Studies
University of Liverpool

St. Martin's Press

First published in Great Britain 1995 by
MACMILLAN PRESS LTD
Houndmills, Basingstoke, Hampshire RG21 2XS
and London
Companies and representatives
throughout the world

A catalogue record for this book is available
from the British Library.

ISBN 0–333–58671–9 hardcover
ISBN 0–333–58672–7 paperback

10   9   8   7   6   5   4   3   2   1
04   03   02   01   00   99   98   97   96   95

Printed and bound in Great Britain by
Antony Rowe Ltd
Chippenham, Wiltshire

First published in the United States of America 1995 by
Scholarly and Reference Division,
ST. MARTIN'S PRESS, INC.,
175 Fifth Avenue,
New York, N.Y. 10010

ISBN 0–312–12317–5

Library of Congress Cataloging-in-Publication Data
Scammell, Margaret.
Designer politics : how elections are won / Margaret Scammell.
p. cm.
Includes bibliographical references and index.
ISBN 0–312–12317–5
1. Campaign management—Great Britain. 2. Electioneering—Great
Britain. 3. Elections—Great Britain. 4. Great Britain—Politics
and government—1979– . I. Title.
JN956.S3 1995
324.7'2'0941—dc20   94–24883
                                             CIP

For Jenks

Contents

List of Figures

List of Tables

List of Plates

Preface and Acknowledgements

'Does Britain need a Clinton?' – Lord Parkinson, *New Statesman and Society*, 23 September 1994.

Tony Blair, the 'British Clinton', greatly exercised Tory strategists in the months following his election as Labour leader in July 1994. 'If Blair turns out to be as good as he looks, we have a problem,' John Maples, Tory deputy chairman, warned in a top secret strategy paper, intended only for the Prime Minister's eyes. Embarrassingly for Maples and the Conservatives, the paper was leaked to the *Financial Times*.[1] Maples notoriously proposed a multi-pronged assault on the Labour leader: set loose the backbench Tory 'yobbos' to 'knock him about a bit'; set another team to operate 'more subtly' on Blair's changes of mind and 'huge' differences with his own party; and introduce legislation, such as identity cards and public service strike reballots, with the specific purpose of either splitting Blair from his party or exposing him as soft on crime and weak on trade unions.

The Maples paper, described by the *Financial Times* as 'rather more frank and perhaps cynical than the normal ministerial soundbite', captures much of the essence of marketing in modern British politics. It illustrates the key role of market research in party strategy: its conclusions were based on discussions with focus groups of working-class wavering Tories, whose support is vital for a fifth successive election victory. It demonstrates the importance to party strategy of political image. The standing of the parties on certain image dimensions, competence, unity, credibility, moderation and leadership, is thought crucial for success. Policy discussion is related, not to intrinsic merits or national interest, but to potential effects upon party images. And these images are relative; one party's loss is another's gain.

Tony Blair, according to the Maples research, is 'the only thing' Labour has going for it, besides the National Health Service. Hence, the logic of the particular proposals for attacking him. Crack Labour's main asset, test the moderate rhetoric to destruction, expose Labour's internal divisions and eventually the vacillating Tories should scurry back to the relative security of the devil they know.

Former Conservative chairman, Lord Parkinson, offered a more subtle approach when he proposed 'Does Britain need a Clinton?', as a potential campaigning slogan for the beleaguered Tories. Parkinson's question taps into widespread reservations about the new Labour leader's double-edged reputation as a 'media candidate'. Like Clinton, Blair looks good on television and is adept at soundbites which have a resonance across the usual party divide and a durability beyond the average political slogan. 'Tough on crime and tough on the causes of crime' and, latterly, 'a new, grown-up politics' are two examples. However, doubts remain that he has the experience to be a genuine national leader on the world stage, or the stature to carry with him internal party critics or to stand firm on matters of principle against a hostile media and the goading Tories. In short, is there authentic substance behind the admirable campaigning style?

Blair has made an impressive start. His first address as leader to the Labour Party conference was one of 'the great speeches of recent years', according to the respected *Guardian* commentator, Hugo Young (*Guardian*, 5 October 1994). Blair tackled head-on some of those concerns about his political courage. He volunteered the word 'socialism', banished from Labour rhetoric in recent years, to describe his brand of politics. He risked controversy with the demand that Labour modernise its constitution and abandon the Clause IV commitment to nationalisation. He argued the case for mainstream left-of-centre politics as desirable on its own terms, not simply because it is electorally pragmatic. 'There is no choice between being principled and unelectable; and electable and unprincipled. We have tortured ourselves with this foolishness for too long. We should win because of what we believe.'[2]

These are early days and, at the time of writing, it is too soon to offer judgement of Blair. Thus far he has had a relatively easy ride as the Conservatives have floundered in sexual and financial scandal and been torn asunder by internal divisions about Europe, VAT and privatisation. However, there are some indications that he is more than Labour's most media-friendly face. The signs from his conference performance were that marketing, with its sensitivity to public opinion and media presentation, will be important. But, perhaps rather like Margaret Thatcher, marketing will be harnessed to, rather than substituted for, a clear political project.

Labour's lesson of the 1992 general election was in the limitations of marketing and the difficulties of changing party images. For a while, at least, it seemed as though marketing was in retreat. Labour's team of advertising and media advisers, the Shadow Communications Agency (SCA), caught much of the backlash for defeat. The 'beautiful people', as John Prescott called them, needed to be brought to heel and they seemed to be, under John Smith's brief leadership. The SCA was disbanded and it seemed that the image-makers were to be put back in their place as hired consultants and *not* a central and independent power base. Meanwhile, the Tories have found themselves hoist by their own marketing petard. The VAT rises in the new government's first budget made a nonsense of Saatchi's 'Labour tax bombshell' election campaign. Major's trustworthiness, his great advantage over Neil Kinnock, was damaged, possibly irreparably. His post-election 'back to basics' family values campaign backfired amid the successive tales of Tory sleaze. Further weakened by the difficulties of uniting his party on Europe, Major's leadership has looked tenuous for more than a year and his government has so far failed spectacularly to reap the usual opinion poll rewards of an improving economy.

In the light of all this, what then can we say about the use of political marketing in contemporary Britain? First, marketing is entrenched in the modern political process. Blair may exercise stricter political control than previously over the image-makers, but he remains a Labour moderniser, attuned to the value of market research and the importance of presentation. The Maples report, prepared for the prime minister personally, confirms the continued importance of marketing to Tory strategy, despite the mixed, sometimes anti-marketing signals offered by Major. Second, marketing does *not* offer magic solutions for the winning of elections. It does not exist in a vacuum. The evidence from studies of British elections is that political images are not easily changed. Moreover, the best-laid plans can be buffeted by political events and will certainly be tested by political opponents. Even marketing that seems successful in the short term can recoil with dire consequences over the longer haul. Third, that the use of political marketing needs to be closely monitored. Much of the literature on political campaigning and politics and media generally claims that the marketing approach is actually or potentially subversive of the democratic process:[3] rational political debate is reduced to advertising soundbites, political image is becoming a matter of style and appearance, campaigning a matter of attacking opponents rather than promulgating policies and the whole process of electioneering and worse, governing, becoming a squalid enterprise, similar in conception and execution to commercial salesmanship.

There is an undeniable case for a close watching brief on the use of political marketing. However, I do not share the rather overwhelming pessimism of much of the literature in the field. The pages that follow will argue that many of the most damning criticisms are either simply not proven, or rely on a contrast with a mythical golden age of rational political debate. As already suggested, it is important also to remain sceptical about marketing's power to persuade. Voters' choices are made for the most part in the prosaic long-term, influenced more by socio-economic factors than any short-term campaigning wizardry. Moreover, marketing may bring real democratic benefits by improving two-way communications between voters and politicians and theoretically, at least, allowing both parties and voters to be better informed and make more rational choices.

ACKNOWLEDGEMENTS

This book owes much to the generous and considerate assistance of many friends, colleagues, journalists and individuals connected with the political parties. I thank them all.

I should like to thank everyone connected with Macmillan who has helped with this book, especially, Gráinne Twomey and my editor, Keith Povey. On a formal and practical note, I'm grateful for the copyright permissions of the polling organisations, Gallup, Harris and MORI. Thanks, too, to Register-MEAL for data on advertising expenditure and to the Central Office of Information.

There are a number of friends and colleagues to whom I owe a great deal and to whom special thanks are due. I am deeply grateful to Jane Falkingham, for her advice, support and computer wizardry. Special and warm thanks are due to the extraordinary Chris Moncrieff, who is as generous as he is ingenious and may be the only person in the world with more energy than Margaret Thatcher. I would be killed if I did not mention Millicent, so I have. This project started with an act of faith from Professor Tom Nossiter at the London School of Economics and his advice and resourcefulness ensured that this lady was not for turning. John Barnes, also at the LSE, and Dr Martin Harrop (University of Newcastle) also offered invaluable criticism and advice.

My family, above all my mother, Helen Scammell, supplied unstinting encouragement, despite sorely tested patience. Thanks are also due to Pat and Maldwyn Jenkins, whose faith never wavered and who helped in many practical ways. My greatest debt is to Lesley Jenkins, who has borne with this project from start to finish, offering constant moral and practical support, unfailingly good advice and inspiration. To her I owe far more than I could repay.

My friends, relatives and colleagues cannot be blamed for any errors or omissions that remain in this book, for which, of course, I'm happy to take responsibility.

MARGARET SCAMMELL

Notes

1   See Robert Preston 'Tories need "killer facts" to stop electoral death' *Financial Times*, 21 November 1994. John Maples, as well as Tory deputy chairman, is also chairman and chief executive of Saatchi & Saatchi Government Communications Worldwide.

2   Speech by Tony Blair, 4 October 1994, Labour Party Conference, Blackpool.

3   See, for example, Bob Franklin *Packaging Politics* London: Edward Arnold, 1994).

Introduction: Propaganda and Political Marketing

As those who aim at control of government come to regard mass persuasion as their central problem, then the specialist in mass persuasion will rise correspondingly in influence.

Stanley Kelley[1]

In the early 1980s, particularly on the Left, commercial 'marketing' was seen as taking a strong and potentially sinister grip on British politics. Lady Thatcher was regarded as central, both at a personal level and as populist leader. The 'marketing of Margaret' provided the common currency of political discussion: the Iron Lady image, the tabloid press cult of Maggie, the personal details of appearance and image, the deepening of her voice, the dental work, the change in style of dress and hair-do, and the copying of President Reagan-pioneered techniques, such as the use of the 'sincerity machine' autocue, photo-opportunities and 'sound-bites'. Thatcher was 'a willing instrument of all the latest wizardry of the political salesman', according to *Guardian* commentator Hugo Young.[2] The Labour Party's deputy leader, Roy Hattersley, attributed Thatcher's success to a ruthless exploitation of the murkier arts of image building.

> I remember just before the 1979 election talking to Jim Callaghan – I don't think I am giving away any secrets by telling you the story – and him saying, 'That woman's going to be packaged; they are going to decide what she ought to be and she is going to be that. I wouldn't do that.' And at the time I wasn't so sure that he was right to be so opposed to that sort of artifice. Seeing Mrs Thatcher now, I mean the guile of the voice production, I mean the guile of pretending that she is interested in things that she is palpably not interested in, the guile of associating herself unscrupulously with every popular cause, I have never seen such a politician in terms of unscrupulous association with things that seem likely to win her votes.[3]

1

Hattersley's criticism of Thatcher, made on BBC Radio 4 in 1985, does not exaggerate what was at that time a widely held view among her opponents. The twin themes of Thatcher as packaged politician and ruthless exploiter of right-wing populism recur in the left-of-centre journals of the 1980s.[4] This concern with Thatcher's image building spread wider than readily identifiable political opponents, however; the BBC's flagship, *Panorama*, broadcast 'The Marketing of Margaret' following the 1983 general election,[5] and Wendy Webster gave a feminist perspective of the marketing of the prime minister in *Not A Man To Match Her*.[6]

This notion of the 'marketed' Mrs Thatcher sits uneasily with the image of the strong, resolute, conviction politician which had taken root in public opinion, especially after the Falklands War. Indeed, by the end of her premiership, Thatcher had long since lost the mantle of political marketing leader to red rose Labour. Her stubborn refusal to budge on the hated poll tax is not explicable by any standard of concern with public opinion. As she moved to the Lords and became the leader of the Eurosceptic Tory right, so she wrapped herself ever more tightly in the clothes of the 'conviction politician', and was openly dismissive of John Major's much-publicised sensitivity to media criticism. Her Downing Street memoirs, 800 pages of undiluted self-belief, betray only tantalising glimpses of her debt to her image-makers.

Nevertheless political campaigning was transformed during the Thatcher decade and her contribution was fundamental. The hiring of Saatchi & Saatchi in 1978 as a full-time agency for a political party represented a quantum leap in the marketing of Margaret Thatcher and the Conservative Party. Originally sneered at by political opponents and mocked by satirists (Snatchi & Snatchi or Thaatchi & Thaatchi), the advertising agency's contribution came to be credited as vital to the Conservative victory in the 1979 general election. Philip Kleinman, chronicler of the Saatchi & Saatchi story, is more subtle:

> Paradoxically the company's prestige owed as much or more to the statements of its political clients' opponents as to anything said by the Tories. Labour Party people made much of the supposed 'packaging' of the Tories by advertising and

publicity professionals. Their victory was ascribed not to political factors but to the cleverness with which they had been 'sold' by Gordon Reece, their publicity chief, and the ad agency he had chosen. This line of argument, intended to belittle Mrs Thatcher, had one certain result, it elevated Saatchi & Saatchi to quasi-mythological status.[7]

Thatcher's faith in advertising extended most controversially beyond the purely party domain into the realm of government publicity. If advertising helped Thatcher, she more than repaid the debt: 'Thatcherism put advertising on the map' was the headline over a post-resignation assessment of Mrs Thatcher in the advertising trade magazine *Campaign*. According to *Campaign*'s story, the Thatcher era began with the 'most famous political advertising campaign of all time' and then witnessed the 'greatest ad bonanza in UK history', a boom fuelled in no small measure by government publicity departments:

> Even more so than the election advertising . . . it was the numerous privatisation campaigns which came to represent the definitive statement of Thatcherite populism. Beginning with British Telecom in 1984 and ending with Electricity's Frankenstein, they contributed to clouding the issue of quite what was and was not political advertising.[8]

Together with an ever increasing spend for the Central Office of Information, they helped the Government into first place ahead of Procter and Gamble as the country's heaviest advertiser. Advertising spending itself became a political issue.

Despite protestations at 'selling politics like soap', to borrow the over-worked pejorative description, the perceived success of marketing prompted Opposition politicians to follow suit. Martin Harrop puts it thus:

> The 1980s were pivotal years in the development of political marketing in Britain. When the Conservative Party hired Saatchi's in 1978, it was headline news. By the end of the 1980s it would have been just as big news if a major party had chosen not to use professional marketing expertise in an election.[9]

Marketing jargon entered the political lexicon. Peter Mandelson, Labour's communications director, talked of rebuilding the party's 'corporate identity', replacing the red flag with the red rose.[10] Labour, by acclaim of the national press, won the presentation battle at the 1987 general election and again in 1992. Mandelson, grandson of Herbert Morrison, Labour's post-war deputy prime minister, was acknowledged as a key figure behind the velvet revolution within the party machine and the driving force behind the reshaping of Labour's public image. To the Right and the Left, Mandelson was the new 'Machiavellian man'; a 'spin doctor' skilfully elevating shiny image over substance.[11]

Harrop suggests that the turning-point in this transformation from distaste to across-the-board adoption of 'political marketing' was the favourable reception of Labour's 1987 campaign.[12] No less important, in terms of winning the Left for marketing, was the Greater London Council's anti-abolition campaign of 1984/85, costing some £11 million including lobbying, public relations exercises, direct mail and advertising.[13] The 'Say No to No Say' advertising campaign helped transform the issue from minority interest to one where three-quarters of Londoners were opposed to the government's abolition policy. It seemed a clear demonstration of marketing power to influence public opinion, a perception that was only strengthened by subsequent government legislation to curb local authority spending on 'political publicity' through the Local Government Acts of 1986 and 1988.

By the end of the decade advertising and public relations were fully entrenched in political campaigns, even if there remained lingering suspicion in certain quarters as to its morality. The political media advisers, the advertisers and image-makers – Saatchi & Saatchi, (Sir) Bernard Ingham (Mrs Thatcher's press secretary), Peter Mandelson, and to a lesser extent (Sir) Tim Bell and Sir Gordon Reece, Michael Dobbs, Harvey Thomas, Philip Gould – had become, at the very least, minor stars in the political firmament whose names were probably as widely recognised as many of the Cabinet or Shadow Cabinet.

Charities, pressure groups – Friends of the Earth and Greenpeace, and trade unions – also climbed on the bandwagon. In 1970, for example, only one trade union, the TGWU, was listed in the annual round-up of advertising spending in Media Expenditure Analysis Limited's (MEAL) digests. In 1989, the TUC, NUR, NUT, Nalgo and the BMA, as well as the TGWU, all mounted advertising campaigns. Even Sussex University, the radical sixties alma mater of student chic, took advice from Saatchi about its corporate image,[14] and, in 1991, the Roman Catholic Church ran an advertising campaign in the national press directed at lapsed Catholics.

These then are the reasons which inspired the present volume. In a nutshell, they can be reduced to the common perception of the growing importance of 'marketing' in politics, and to the belief that the trend was pioneered by the Conservative Party. However it is obvious even from this preliminary discussion that 'political marketing' covers a multitude of activities, including advertising, public relations and, indeed, virtually any political activity concerned with image and persuasion. But what precisely is political marketing and what differentiates it from other forms of political communication?

PROPAGANDA AND POLITICAL MARKETING

'In the past 15 years a major change has occurred in the conduct of election campaigns,' Richard Rose wrote in 1967.[15] 'In efforts to influence voters candidates have increasingly relied upon mass media and experts in modern media techniques.' Rose describes the process now known as 'political marketing'. The term has entered into common parlance, particularly in the United States, as a convenient shorthand description of modern media techniques and expertise imported from the commercial world into political campaigns. As commonly used, political marketing is defined by the promotional techniques themselves. Viewed in this way, a candidate's political speech in a draughty, spartan hall would not be political marketing, but a rally complete with mood music, balloons, flags, laser light shows, eye-catching banners and backdrops, dry ice smoke, video screens and warm-up performers before the candidate's speech – all used in the British 1987 election campaign – would be political marketing. Similarly a door-to-door canvass may or may not be considered political marketing. If it is a simple canvass of voter intentions it would not be marketing. If it is a canvass designed to discover details of voters' views, hopes and anxieties which would then be banked on a computer database and lead to personal letters from the candidate, that would be marketing.

Used in this way 'political marketing' lacks specificity and ultimately boils down to a new title for the modern version of long-standing propaganda and campaigning activities. Techniques which now seem old-fashioned were once the leading edge of political communications. For example, Michael Foot's style of oratory and countrywide stump in 1983 were savaged as disastrously outmoded campaigning in the television era.[16] Yet when the technique was introduced to Britain, by Gladstone in his two Midlothian campaigns of 1879 and 1880, it was a sensational innovation which fearful critics called 'an influence of terrorism'.[17]

Examples of sometimes highly sophisticated 'marketing' can be traced back at least as far as the ancient Romans, whose mastery of spectacle and symbolism as propaganda has probably not been surpassed. Serge Chakotin, in his study of totalitarian propaganda, presents a description of a triumphal procession of the conquering Caesar which inspires awe even in the modern reader. The city streets and squares were garlanded, temples thrown open, incense burnt on the altars and trumpeters announced the coming of the procession. Behind the trumpeters marched the dignitaries; then rolled wagons laden with booty from the vanquished peoples, gold crowns, sculptures and symbols of victory. Following behind were the sacrifices to the gods, the bulls with gilded horns; then trudged the important prisoners bound in chains who were to be executed at the foot of the Capitol. Behind them came the hordes of captives and hostages; then the purple-robed lictors and bearers carrying vases of burning perfume. Singers and players of musical instruments announced the arrival of the victor's chariot. Caesar, crowned with a laurel wreath, rode in his chariot drawn by four white garlanded horses. Following Caesar were his sons and generals; then at last the ranks of soldiers, decorated with badges of honour, chanting their successes to the crowds. After it all there was a mammoth banquet.[18]

Nazi propagandists adapted the Roman techniques for stimulating crowds to excitement and awe. Hitler exploited spectacle, ceremony and ritual, the burning of incense, the use of coloured lights and candles, and groups of muscular young men in uniform marching to martial airs, which Hitler believed would stir the hearts of women.[19] The Nazis issued precise instructions for propaganda and one such document was entitled 'The Creation of Enthusiasm at a Meeting'.[20] Music was to be played continuously as people streamed into the hall which was to be decorated with flags, greenery and cloths bearing slogans and symbols. Hecklers were planted to incite the crowd into responding with a shout of 'yes' or 'no' at the interrupter. Mass affirmation of this sort 'acts like an electric shock' on the crowd, according to the instructions. The audience was urged to stand to sing songs before and after the speeches, which were always to be kept short, no more than 30 minutes. The audience were to be incited to revolutionary gesture, the cry of 'freedom' with clenched fist salute. Amusing sketches or symbolic tableaux were to be presented as light relief and, at the meeting's end, the audience was seen out with a spirited 'fighting' song. The stadium for Hitler's Nuremberg rallies was designed with microphones placed strategically among the crowd and wired to amplifiers behind the rostrum to magnify the cheers and chants of 'Sieg Heil'. The amplified volume encouraged greater excitement and enthusiasm among the audience, ultimately for the benefit of the newsreels.[21]

Many of these historic crowd stimulation techniques may be seen today at British political leaders' rallies: certainly the use of music, singing, symbols, slogans, flags, greenery and lighting was common at Mrs Thatcher's speeches to audiences of the faithful, although the more militaristic trappings were absent; and similarly for Kinnock, Major and John Smith. The question remains, then, does the term 'political marketing' denote any unique properties or contain any analytical value? The question is best answered by reference to the commercial world from which it has borrowed. The Chartered Institute of Marketing, the largest professional marketing management body in Europe, defines marketing as follows:

> those activities performed by individuals or organizations, whether profit or non-profit, that enable, facilitate, and encourage exchange to take place to the satisfaction of both parties.[22]

The 'marketing concept' is central to this definition in contemporary business practice; it is a consumer-oriented approach which 'puts the customer at the beginning rather than the end of the production-consumption cycle'.[23] This emphasis on the 'consumer', the voter, and the satisfaction of consumer wants, differentiates political marketing from earlier forms of political salesmanship: speech-making, advocacy, the packaging of a programme or even the use of commercially derived techniques. Nicholas O'Shaughnessy, in one of the few British academic studies of political marketing, makes the point:

> Marketing is . . . a derivative of what people seek in so far as this can be determined. It is not simply the attempt to persuade them to a point of view; therefore the election campaign conducted by the British Labour party in 1987, though it used media creatively, was not driven by any marketing concept: it was advertising devoid of the larger awareness that marketing brings, otherwise the party would have attended more to the popularity of the 'product', that is, its policies as well as its communications. The essence of marketing is reciprocity: 'consumers' themselves bring something to bear on the selling; they are not passive objects and the process is an interactive one.[24]

It is a common misconception that marketing equals advertising, or propaganda or image or brand-building, even though all these will almost certainly form part of the 'marketing mix'. Marketing's unique contribution is the strategic concern with what the market (electorate) wants and what it will bear. Although it is the razzle-dazzle of novel techniques which most capture the media's imagination, the strategic aspect of marketing is more fundamental, affecting goals, priorities, policies, candidate and party behaviour and organisation:

> Despite the growth of promotional activities in the 1980s, a party's overall strategy is still far more central to its electoral success. Effective promotion cannot counter a poor, or non-existent, strategy.[25]

This strategic concern to please the market-place, to tailor the product according to consumer taste, is political marketing's most serious threat to the democratic process, in the view of some critics (see below). It is also this element of reciprocity which separates political marketing from political propaganda, despite shared techniques of promotion. Because of this, as O'Shaughnessy argues, the similarities between the propagandist methods of Lenin and Hitler and American post-war presidents are superficial and ultimately misleading:

> In no sense did they [Lenin and Hitler] adopt a 'consumer' orientation or borrow techniques from business: they began with ideology and did not moderate it. Nor, of course, was marketing the description they themselves employed: the marketing approach has its roots in what people themselves say they want; totalitarians would tell them what was good for them. Totalitarian propaganda was insistent and continuous; the person living in such a society would breathe a permanent atmosphere of propaganda.[26]

Propaganda, especially in situations of state monopoly, tends to begin from the premise that the 'product' is sacrosanct, while public opinion is malleable and can be won over to the propagandist's cause. Political marketing starts from the other side of the communication equation and says that the product is malleable and may be changed according to 'consumer' wants. This is not to deny, of course, that propaganda, even the totalitarian variety, must pay some attention to public opinion, even where the state is prepared to devote enormous resources to coercion. Goebbels commissioned secret service reports to understand the public mood, and tailor Nazi appeals accordingly. At the same time, marketed politicians, even the most celebrated of 'media candidates', are rarely mere slaves to market research.

It is also true that the 'political marketing/Nazi propaganda' contrast ignores the historical context and in so doing exaggerates the differences. The consumer-oriented 'marketing concept' is a relatively new notion which only began to dominate commercial marketing thinking in the 1960s. Formerly marketing thinking had more in common with the propaganda approach, beginning with the product and relying on an aggressive sales force to shoulder the heavy burden of finding and persuading customers.[27] Much to the chagrin of advocates of the modern marketing concept, it has by no means been adopted universally in British commercial business practice even today:

Yet for the lip-service companies give to being market-oriented, it is remarkable how few of them have really taken on board the implications of that simple statement. The plain fact is that if even half the major (let alone the minor) companies in Britain understood and reacted to customers' needs as well as they should, the entire economy would be far stronger than it is now – and the Japanese would be trooping here to find out how it was done.[28]

Thus we should not be surprised if the real world furnishes few examples of purely consumer-led political candidates and parties. Doubtless there are politicians guided by no goal other than the attainment of popularity and power, but pure, naked ambition scarcely provides an adequate explanation of political behaviour. Even Ronald Reagan, who might be thought the ultimate media-packaged candidate, developed his policies from the basis of genuinely held political convictions, although there can be no doubt about the importance of opinion research both in shaping Reagan's election campaign strategy and his actions as president.[29] Indeed the ideologically committed American New Right is sometimes considered the principal agent behind the rise of modern political marketing.[30]

In reality, political marketing and its associated opinion research rarely picks the details of policies; rather the 'marketing approach' sets the parameters, suggests the stance and tone of policy, and recommends shifts of emphasis to play up or down parts of the already selected programme. Market analysis, for instance, helped persuade Mrs Thatcher to adopt a relatively restrained manifesto in 1983 and a more energetic and radical one in 1987. Tory market research also pinpointed specific areas which party policy needed to address – in 1987, education, the health service, unemployment and law and order – and recommended that new goals and ways of achieving them be announced.

In marked contrast, a consumer orientation did not inform the creation of the Labour Party's policy in 1987, although, later, marketing techniques were fundamental in the development of the communications strategy: to highlight the party's strong 'caring' issues and play down aspects considered electoral liabilities. Labour's pre-1987 approach might be dismissed in the commercial sphere as marketing misunderstood, as an example of 'bolt-on' marketing whereby a specialised customer-conscious media department is asked to remedy the lack of attention to consumer wants in the product itself. A 'bolt-on' marketing department may produce slight improvements in customer appreciation but cannot address critical areas where radical change and innovation are necessary.[31]

This partial use of marketing is a common feature of what the marketers call 'non-profit organisations' and indeed there is debate about whether marketing is appropriate for such organisations at all. All the major political parties share some characteristics common to non-profit organisations which complicate the use of marketing. The most important stems from the structure of typical non-profit organisations. Either by constitution or by accepted practice, members and/or volunteers expect to have a say in the setting of priorities, while the governing body may well be elected by the membership. Clearly this opens up the opportunity for much greater conflict about goals than in normal commercial companies where power devolves from ownership. Where members are in conflict the likely result will be a split, compromise and/or ambiguous objectives unless the organisation has a sufficiently strong leadership to impose a clear solution. Even where there is consensus about goals there may well be dispute about the means of achieving them. Since the purpose of marketing is to achieve an organisation's goals by providing consumer satisfaction, clearly any ambiguity about objectives makes marketing activity more difficult and less effective.[32]

Hence the Conservative Party with its strongly hierarchical and centralised structure which allows the wider membership few formal avenues for influencing policy is better placed than its rivals to implement effective marketing. The leadership's position is especially strong when in government, according to John Ramsden:

> When in office it is certainly correct to say that Conservative policy is to be found in whatever the then Conservative government is doing for there is no concept of a party policy distinct from the work of Conservative ministers, as there is on the Labour side.[33]

Arguably the leader's control of party organisation was strengthened under Mrs Thatcher, both by changes in the structure
of Conservative Central Office (CCO)[34] and by increased CCO
influence in the selection of constituency candidates.[35]

In the aftermath of its 1987 humiliation the Labour Party set
about restoring its electoral credibility in a manner that provides one of the clearest examples of political marketing in
British history. Detailed market research informed the Policy
Review which culminated in the abandonment of 'extremist'
commitments: unilateralism, nationalisation and a broad front
of public spending pledges with the accompanying threat of
income tax rises. Labour's embracing of the marketing concept was accompanied by a concentration of power in the
leadership and a lessening of the influence of the party conference. The leadership (the National Executive Committee)
assumed new powers to select by-election candidates and the
policy-making role of the party conference diminished. The
findings of the Policy Review were presented to party conferences in 1989 and 1990 as packages to be rejected or accepted
in their entirety, thus limiting the opportunities for effective
dissent on particular items. A new body, the Policy Forum, was
established in 1990 to provide 'rolling consultation' on policy
matters, reducing conference, in the eyes of critics, to the
status of a 'US-style convention where balloons will eventually
replace debates'.[36]

For Labour, political marketing has required a diminution
of internal party democracy in order to increase sensitivity to
the views of the electorate at large. Until the 1992 general
election defeat at least, the Labour membership generally
acquiesced rather than rejoiced in these changes, prepared to
lose some sovereignty as the price of electoral success. The
impact of political marketing on internal party organisation is
as yet hardly considered in Britain, but in the United States it
is cited as a major cause of the decline of the political parties.
There is another important historical reason which has impeded Labour's adoption of the marketing concept. Labour
has harboured a substantial element who believed that marketing and its associated techniques were inherently capitalis-
tic and thus intrinsically objectionable for a socialist party.
Although this view has rarely held sway over the post-war party
leadership, it has sometimes proved a barrier to the exploitation

of new presentational devices. One instance was the half-hearted compromise of 1983 when Johnny Wright's advertising agency was chosen not so much for its communications expertise as for its political credentials. Even then the agency's work was conducted under the suspicious eye of the campaign committee.[37]

Labour's moral qualms about marketing lingered into the early 1990s and are given most eloquent expression by the party's left wing. Veteran left-winger the late Eric Heffer provided a typical example when he gave vent in *The Guardian* to his rage at Labour's £500-a-ticket, fund-raising celebrity dinner at London's Park Lane Hotel:

> I'm not against rich people donating large sums if they so desire. Let them give generously. But for Labour to stage such an event at such a hotel is tantamount to slapping in the face those struggling to make ends meet, the unemployed, those facing redundancy, those living in poverty, and the homeless. I find it nauseating in the extreme . . . I thought the craven attitude of Labour's front bench over the Gulf war was bad enough; it was shameful. But this takes the biscuit . . . Labour is becoming totally bourgeois, and unless action is soon taken it will be too late.[38]

THE ETHICS OF POLITICAL MARKETING

The debate on political marketing could be encompassed under the heading: 'A force for good or evil?' The academic literature is concentrated, almost completely, in the United States and is, in the main, critical and suspicious of the phenomenon. Political marketing is only just entering the British arena as a subject for serious study; hitherto it was regarded largely as one of the less attractive aspects of American campaigning, which, it went almost without saying, would be undesirable here.[39]

The most important criticisms of political marketing fall into two broad areas: that political marketing is destroying the function of leadership within a democracy, replacing statesmen with telegenic candidates willing to sacrifice principle to opinion polls; and that political marketing increases the weapons at the disposal of an unscrupulous power-seeker to

manipulate and mislead the audience. One of the most influential American critics is Larry Sabato, a campaign staff member in several dozen US campaigns. He equated the triumph
of political marketing in the USA with the rise of the corps of
professional political consultants who have become, on occasions, as important as the candidates they serve.[40] The political
consultant corps were responsible for encouraging, if not caus-
ing, a litany of evils in the American body politic:

> Political professionals and their techniques have helped
> homogenize American politics, added signficantly to cam-
> paign costs, lengthened campaigns and narrowed the focus
> of elections. Consultants have emphasised personality and
> gimmickry over issues, often exploiting emotional and nega-
> tive themes rather than encouraging rational discussion. They
> have sought candidates who fit their technologies more than
> the requirements of office and have given an extra boost to
> candidates who are more skilled at electioneering than gov-
> erning. They have encouraged candidates' own worst in-
> stincts to blow with the prevailing winds of public opinion.
> Consultants have even consciously increased non-voting on
> occasion and meddled in the politics of other countries.[41]

The political consultants are cited both as an effect and cause
of fundamental changes in American politics, most notably
the decline of the party system. The rise of the corps of political consultants is closely associated with two changes, both
believed to have loosened the grip of party machinery: first,
changes in campaign finance methods; and, second, the institution of presidential primary contests to replace the previous
method of candidate selection by the party bosses.[42]

Sidney Blumenthal (1982) argues that the art of governing
is being turned increasingly into a 'permanent campaign'. With
the disintegration of party loyalties, the function of leadership
had become dominated by the constant engineering of consent among an increasingly fickle electorate. The distinction
between governing and campaigning had become blurred and
political consultants drawn into the inner sanctum of government.[43] Another influential American scholar, Dan Nimmo,
has a yet more scathing assessment of the political consultants,
the 'mercenaries' as he called them:

In screening potential candidates the mercenaries have given a new dimension to the notion of availability; the marketable candidate is selected on the basis of his brand name, his capacity to trigger an emotional response from electors, his skill in using mass media, and his ability to 'project'. Analysis of social problems and issues yields to parroting of themes; televised debates between contenders produce meaningless confrontations rather than rational discussion.[44]

The election of Ronald Reagan was seen as the nadir of this depressingly downward trend. Reagan, as candidate for governor in California, was so inept on the details of policy that a team of academicians were hired to summarise state problems, with suggested solutions on a set of index cards. Reagan, the former Hollywood actor, would memorise the lines to be repeated in public and at press conferences, a technique he employed throughout his presidency.[45]

Reagan's two successful presidential campaigns and his strategy while in the White House owed more to the use of sophisticated opinion research than had those of any previous incumbent. Roland Perry, in *The Programming of the President*, gives a detailed description of the Political Information System (PINS) which pollster Richard Wirthlin developed for Reagan to guide his campaign strategy and tactics. PINS' successor, Political Agenda Control System (PACS), was also developed by Wirthlin to guide Reagan's actions as president.[46] A crucial element of the PINS and PACS systems was a predictive facility which enabled it to anticipate public response to alternative courses of action. Allegedly, and most notoriously, PACS helped persuade Reagan to adopt an aggressive stance towards Libya. Wirthlin's colleague, Richard Beal, has said that the decision to shoot down Libyan airforce jets over the Bay of Sirte (19 August 1981) was a 'pre-scripted event' to boost the President's popularity and encourage Congressional support for a build-up of military forces.[47] According to Beal, 'Reagan knew the confrontation was coming and so did his men, right to the fighters in the F14s' (on board the US Navy aircraft carrier *Nimitz*). The next day, Reagan, wearing a peaked cap captioned 'Commander-in-Chief', was shown on television aboard the aircraft carrier *Constellation* witnessing a demonstration of US Navy air power off the Californian coast.

POLITICAL MARKETING AND DEMOCRACY

The Reagan example seemed to confirm the nightmare of the critics of political marketing that governance was being reduced to a series of actions designed and pre-tested according to public opinion. A new form of populist democracy, indeed a 'mobocracy', was being created whereby leaders were being replaced by expert media performers willing to be delegates to ill-informed public opinion. The critics' fears are summarised by O'Shaughnessy:

> Usage – or abusage – of these marketing methods will make for a lack of political leadership in society and a lack of political courage, since they take as their reference point a servile rather than a directorial attitude towards public opinion.[48]

At the root of this kind of objection commonly lies a rarely explicit, elitist conception of democracy. It has a powerful ancestry: from Plato to Lenin political theorists have demanded a 'leading' or vanguard and educative role from leaders. The perceived threat of political marketing to the function of leadership replicates, in modern form, age-old concerns about democracy itself. Plato's ideal was the philosopher king because, for him, democracy creates poor leadership; according to Thucydides, democracy encourages the emergence of unscrupulous leaders who succeed by flattering the masses.

Nineteenth-century theorists, such as Burke, de Tocqueville and John Stuart Mill, all favoured versions of 'elite' democracy where those most able were selected to govern and were largely left to follow the dictates of their own consciences. This conception informed the development of representative democracies in Britain and the USA. The distrust of popular elections shows clearly in many of the US institutions adopted in the eighteenth century: the electoral college, selection of senators by state legislators, choice of candidates by legislative caucuses and a host of restrictions on the right to vote, until the advent of universal and equal suffrage in the twentieth century.

The importance of the leadership theme has continued with twentieth-century democratic theorists. Both Schumpeter and Robert Dahl argued that the Western democratic model does not give people the power to decide, rather it grants power of decision to representatives, who earn the right by virtue of the competitive struggle for the people's vote. Writing in the 1940s, Schumpeter argued that the paraphernalia of propaganda was an essential accompaniment to this competitive process:

> Party and machine politicians are simply the response to the fact that the electoral mass is incapable of action other than a stampede, and they constitute an attempt to regulate political competition exactly similar to the corresponding practices of a trade association. *The psycho-technics of party management and party advertising, slogans, marching tunes, are not accessories. They are the essence of politics*...[49] (Author's italics)

Ironically, elitist criticisms of political marketing locate the dangers at the opposite pole from objections in the 1930s and 1940s to totalitarian propaganda. Where once the concern was for the psychological rape of the malleable masses, it is now that the masses are reducing leadership to the lowest common denominator needed for majority support. The result is bland, timid politics, it is claimed, with candidates and parties forced to the centre ground of the political spectrum, picked for their personable qualities and discouraged from taking risks for fear of upsetting public opinion.

Thus the marketing concept is inimical to elite theories of democracy. However it is more suited to a now more fashionable and populist view of democracy, which Abramson *et al.* call 'plebiscitary democracy'.[50] According to this model, the aim of democracy is the satisfaction of the interests of individual citizens, and public interest is defined as the sum of individual interests. The goal of the democratic process, therefore, should be to bring ever closer the fit between public interest and public policy. Abramson *et al.* argue that US democracy, despite its representative character, has been driven by this goal since the time of the founding fathers. Inherent within the system then was the drive towards the plebiscitary model. This is manifested not only in the widening of the franchise but also in the strong individualist ethic incorporated within the electoral system: the act of voting itself is a secret, personal matter and the sum of individual votes decides electoral outcomes. The point is not that 'plebiscitary' democracy is without weaknesses; it places enormous faith in the good sense of the electorate and the quality of information from independent and inquiring media. The point is that the tide of democracy for the last 200 years has been running towards increasing popular influence on governments' behaviour.

For those who favour populist 'plebiscitary' versions of democracy, the marketing concept may possess intrinsic virtue precisely because, in principle, it makes politics more democratic. It improves the tools at the disposal of parties and candidates to be better informed, sensitive and responsive to the needs, wants and views of the electorate at large. Equally it both broadens and sharpens the politicians' communications arsenal, equipping them better to reach both the mass of the electorate and the individual voter.

The critical tide of academia against political marketing is beginning, if only just, to turn. Frank Luntz, a political consultant turned academic, argues:

> Pollsters and media consultants, working together, have become a positive force in campaigns, enabling their clients to be better heard and understood by the voters they seek to reach. If, for instance, a candidate's constituency is primarily interested in one or two issues, then it is crucial that the candidate know and address those particular issues. The two-way feedback between candidates and their constituents, even if conducted through a third party, contributes to maintaining a representative, democratic system.[51]

It is also argued that the sharper communication techniques implied by political marketing, for example direct mail or advertising, heighten the interest and awareness of voters who might otherwise shun dry debates, lengthy documentaries, dense pamphlets or manifestoes.[52] As Martin Harrop argues:

> In general, political marketing has improved the extent, quality and efficiency of communication between voters and parties. An advertisement which electors look at and understand contributes more to political education than a dreary statement of policy which no one reads. Market research allows politicians to base their strategies on firm information about the electorate rather than prejudice.[53]

The argument which will be developed throughout the succeeding chapters is that 'political marketing' provides a rational way for parties or candidates to behave in conditions of competitive mass democracy. In British politics the 'marketing concept' appears no more than the modern version of the long-standing desire for electoral credibility, now based on increasingly sophisticated and precise research techniques and a more disciplined approach to communications.

Flaubert was right: our ignorance of history makes us vilify our own age. Certainly British political history since the nineteenth-century advent of popular democracy suggests that our age is no *less* principled, no *more* trivial, no *less* concerned with issues and debate than previous generations. Possibly the quality of political conduct has improved because the mass of people are better educated and have a greater range of sources of information to draw on; and the media, especially television and radio, are as inquisitive and probably less deferential than at any time in modern history.[54]

However, despite the continuities, political marketing does add a new dimension: as the techniques of market research and market prediction become more 'scientific' and precise, the more influential marketing and marketing experts are likely to become within politics. The more refined and sophisticated the techniques of public relations and communications, the more specialists will be enlisted to advise politicians and parties. The tier of specialist communicators and marketers has never been greater in British politics, never better-known and arguably never more influential. This is a trend which is unlikely to diminish, despite fluctuations according to the personal taste of party leaders and managers. The consequences appear more far-reaching for Labour than for the Conservatives. The need for clear goals and the demands of disciplined communications imply a stronger leadership grip over the party as a whole and a diminution of the role of party conference. This trend has invested greater influence in the hands of unelected communications experts, most notably Peter Mandelson and the Shadow Communications Agency, than was granted to most of the elected members of the NEC. In a party with a tradition of an activist membership with relatively wide participation in policy making, these are not small matters. Political marketing did not invent the leaders' wish for tight control – Harold Wilson and James Callaghan simply by-passed the party machinery altogether when they found it too troublesome – but it certainly exacerbates the trend.

POLITICAL MARKETING AND THE MANIPULATION OF OPINION

Concerns with the manipulative powers of marketing are similar to the fears about the indoctrinating influence of totalitarian propaganda; they begin from the premise that people are vulnerable to skilful and unscrupulous use of communications. The main differences are that political marketing is regarded as *manipulative persuasion*, based on research into individual motivation, while totalitarian propaganda may be read as *coercive persuasion*, based on an understanding of crowd behaviour and monopolistic control of the media.

Most notoriously, political marketing manipulates images – much as commercial advertising – to create an illusion that the 'product' meets the desires or aspirations of the consumer. Image, rather than substance, appears to be central to the political marketer's art. As Pat Caddell, political consultant to President Jimmy Carter, observed: 'Too many good people have been defeated because they tried to substitute substance for style.'[55] In the view of critics such as Sabato and Nimmo (above), the emphasis on image, at best, trivialises political debate and, at worst, may mislead and deceive. Ronald Reagan once again provides the example. In the 1980 presidential election against the incumbent president, Carter, Reagan's pollsters found that a majority of American voters feared Reagan's hawkish defence posture. The solution was not to change his policy, but at the prompting of his pollsters he used the word 'peace' at least five times per speech. The ruse appeared to succeed in softening his image.[56]

There is no doubt that the importance of image is a fundamental tenet of the marketing approach, broadly defined. Motivational and attitudinal (qualitative) research, which the Conservatives pioneered in Britain in the 1980s, confirmed for the marketers the importance of image, rather than ideology or policy packages or individual issues in determining voters' choices. A clear demonstration of the weight placed on party images is offered in the Conservatives' strategy document for the 1987 election, the *Blue Book*. However image is a substantial concept for the political marketers, involving, crucially, the reputation, trustworthiness and credibility of the candidates or parties. This aspect is of far greater significance than attention to detail of appearance or dress or body language which provide the normal currency for much casual media discussion of the 'image-makers'. Martin Harrop, in his perceptive article on political marketing, argues that the importance of image is a major lesson that the marketers can offer political scientists locked into policy and consumer models of voting.[57]

Consumer models, such as that of Himmelweit *et al*,[58] suggest that voters seek parties with policy profiles closest to their own preferences. But this ignores the electors' concern with credibility and competence to carry out the promised policies. Policy models or even ideological models[59] are confronted with the paradox that Mrs Thatcher's policies were frequently less popular than Labour's, and that even after two terms the British public were not converted to Thatcherite free market ideology and a majority tended towards egalitarianism and redistribution of wealth from rich to poor.[60] Marketing offers a solution to these problems of applied political science because it conceives of political parties in a different way – as service organisations:

> What most clients want from service companies is not policies but results. As long as the investment manager produces a good return, who cares what the investment policy is? If the philosophy fails to deliver, sack the manager. So too with parties. Voters certainly want evidence of policies and the ability to execute them but the content of the policies is secondary and, for some voters, incidental. After all, if the policies do not work, voters can simply change the government. Indeed, there is no reason why voters should be expected to have policy preferences. Just as criminals do not need to know the law in order to select a good defence lawyer, so voters do not need a detailed knowledge of party manifestoes in order to judge which party would be best at governing the country.[61]

Harrop's point is well taken, even if the analogies are laced a little with hyperbole. The boom in both the United States and Britain in 'ethical' investment, for instance, suggests that consumers are increasingly interested in philosophy as well as results. However the perception of parties as services explains two basic facets of the marketing approach: the need for negative campaigns to attack the credibility of incumbents, and the lack in political marketing of attention to details of policy.

Judgment by results provides governments with an inbuilt advantage. They can stand on their record while the opposition can offer only promises. Political marketers, such as Sir Tim Bell, are convinced that governments lose elections rather than oppositions winning them and that the one really effective appeal in the opposition's armoury is 'time for a change'.[62] It is essential for oppositions to attack the government's record and undermine its credibility; hence negative campaigns are preferred to positive ones.

Political marketing is relatively unconcerned with the details of policy. The threat that it might take over the details of policy seems to have occurred only rarely, even in the United States. Kinnock's former press secretary, Patricia Hewitt, who observed the Michael Dukakis presidential campaign at close quarters, found that policies were not dictated by pollsters; rather policies were sidelined in favour of a communications approach which emphasised image:

> Dukakis had reams of policies but they had nothing to do with the election which was much more about values, positioning and symbolic attitudes. Was he competent? Was he trustworthy? Was he somebody the voters felt comfortable with?[63]

However marketers are greatly interested in issues whose importance lies not in their intrinsic merit but in their ability to affect the overall image of credibility and competence of the party. Reagan's pollster, Dick Wirthlin, argued:

> Campaign consultants, rather than blurring the contact between candidates and voters, may have enhanced it, because survey research enables the candidate and his associates to determine more precisely what drives the vote. Specifically, the voter was found in the late 1970s and early 1980s in many campaigns to build perceptions more rapidly through issues than through imagery alone.[64]

Economic management and defence, or peace and prosperity, are the issues which marketers believe most affect party images.[65] The party trusted best to deal competently with these 'bottom line' issues, which may vary over time, is the best placed for electoral victory. As we proceed through the general elections over the last decade and a half, poll data on questions of trust and confidence in the parties' ability to deal with key issues will be used as an important indicator of the success of campaigns.

In summary, then, image is a far more substantial concept than the mere psycho-technics of presentation. There is no doubt that political imagery, just as in commercial advertising, may be partial and at times deliberately misleading. But just as the easiest product to advertise is the best product, so it is easiest to promote the party or politician who is most credible. Advertising works best when it chimes with reality.

A NOTE ON SOURCES

The agonies and ecstasies of writing contemporary electoral history have been described elegantly by Dennis Kavanagh.[66] Chief among the joys is the opportunity to interview participants while their memories are still fresh and before the onset of retrospective wisdom. The main body of research relies heavily on interviews, mostly unstructured, with politicians, campaign managers, press officers, advertisers, pollsters and journalists. Well over a hundred formal and informal interviews have been conducted, many of which were granted on an unattributable basis. The studies of the 1987 and 1992 election campaigns also include access to private party documents and opinion polls.

Also invaluable to this research were press and television stories, published party literature and first-hand observation of party conferences (all the Conservative and Labour annual conferences from 1986 to 1990) and press briefings (all major London press conferences during the 1987 election and several in 1992).

The agonies are caused primarily by difficulties in documentation. One finds, for example, no shortage of Conservative Party and CCO insiders willing to be interviewed, but few will be quoted on the record. Labour sources, by and large, were probably less forthcoming but more willing to talk on the record. In order to protect the anonymity of sources, it has been necessary to blur their identities, although the location of the source is indicated as nearly as possible. Where permitted the interviews were taped. One also needs to be aware of vested interests and attempts to massage what is reported. The 1987 Conservative campaign, with its highly public internal rows, and Labour's 1992 campaign, with its bitter post-mortem, were minefields in this regard.

Finally, one of the agonies *and* ecstasies is that the subject changes in front of your eyes: the unexpected happens, ministers and party officers resign, new disclosures are made and memoirs published with impressive speed. Every effort has been made to keep what follows on top of the times.

1 Crusted Agent to Media Expert: The Changing Face of Campaigns

> With the growth of the mass media political comm,unciation has become an increasingly important element in the effective application of political power . . . What is needed now is a greater awareness of what is being done by those who occupy themselves in communicating messages of a political character with an intention to persuade. Politicians as well as the press need to be more rigorous in seeking out who are the people behind the campaigns and leagues and lobbies. Party organisations should also be scrutinised to see who is exercising power in what way and by what right.
>
> Lord Windlesham (1966)[1]

Even a cursory examination of political campaigning in the limited electoral democracy of the Victorian era offers parallels with modern-day activities and dispels any nostalgic idea that the past provides a state of grace from which modern campaigners have fallen. H.J. Hanham comments on the personalisation of elections around the formidable figures of the major party leaders, Gladstone and Disraeli, 'in much the same way as the Conservatives magnified the appeal of Sir Winston Churchill in 1945'.[2] Election campaigning issues were usually few, and frequently there was just one national topic, such as the abolition of income tax (1874) or Irish Home Rule (1886). The campaigning slogan, 'the cry', was handed down by party leaders to their followers.

A small body of professional election experts, in many respects similar to the modern political consultants of the United States, became established. One of the most celebrated was James Acland, who hired himself out to both Tory and Radical candidates, and whose motto was to win, never mind the expense; a 'defeat was the most expensive of all contests'.[3] Acland possessed an acute sense of the power of personality to win over voters. For example, Sir Robert Clifton, candidate for Nottingham, a devotee of the turf but a poor speaker on the more serious issues of politics, benefited from Acland's acumen:

> At the first meeting [Acland] placed a man in the back of the room and when the candidate halted, stammered and got into a muddle, the man cried out 'Damn politics, Sir Robert, tell us who will win the Derby'.[4]

If presidential-style and personality-focused campaigning were not the inventions of the television era, nor were emotive appeals to prejudice. Sir Henry Edwards at Beverley attempted to stir anti-Catholic sentiment against Gladstone: 'I hate these perverts – I don't want to have in this country a Roman Catholic Prime Minister. I don't say that Mr Gladstone is a Roman Catholic but he looks deuced like it.'[5]

Contemporary politicians have their favourite landmark dates – the moment of revelation when they realised that the practice of politics had been altered fundamentally by developments in the arts of communication. Most choose either 1959 or 1970. Joe Haines, political editor at the *Daily Mirror* and formerly Harold Wilson's press secretary at Number 10, picked the Tories' 1970 general election campaign. The Conservatives employed 'disturbingly effective' advertising techniques which brought 'politics into the gutter' and fundamentally changed the ground rules.[6] Sir Tim Bell, Mrs Thatcher's advertising adviser, pinpoints the 1957–9 period.[7] The Tories introduced novel features, most notably an extended advertising campaign prior to the electoral period itself, which provoked a chorus of disapproval the like of which was not seen again until Saatchi & Saatchi emerged on the scene in 1978.

We return to these campaigns later, but we begin with the inter-war decades because political and technological changes took place then which revolutionised the craft of political persuasion. A combination of factors pushed political leaders to use propaganda in ways that had not been considered before. The most significant of these were:

1   the impact of war and the need for conscription;
2   the mass franchise;
3   class conflict; and
4   developments in communications technology.

THE IMPACT OF WAR

War 'opened the eyes of the intelligent few to the possibilities of regimenting the modern mind'.[8] So wrote Edward L. Bernays, the nephew of Sigmund Freud and the founding father of American political advertising. Bernays believed that public relations was a branch of the social sciences and his book, *Public Opinion* (1923), set out the 'trickle down' theory of mass persuasion by first convincing the opinion leaders. He was recruited to the Committee on Public Information (CPI) which oversaw American propaganda during the First World War. The CPI, under the chairmanship of former newspaper editor George Creel, was commissioned to 'sell' the war to America. Creel claimed that it was a 'vast enterprise in salesmanship, the world's greatest adventure in advertising'.[9] There was no medium of appeal which the committee did not employ: the printed word, the spoken word, cable, wireless, the relatively new and massively popular motion picture, the poster and the signboard. At one point more than 150 000 men and women were employed in the service of the CPI, which came to be known as the Creel Committee.[10]

In scale and ambition, this was a propaganda effort the like of which had not been seen before. The swing in American public opinion towards support for the war was attributed in large measure to the success of the CPI's efforts. Market and audience research techniques were at this time relatively undeveloped and in their absence a belief in the potential omnipotence of propaganda took root. Harold Lasswell's seminal work, *Propaganda Technique in the World War* (1927), invested propaganda with awesome power:

> But when all allowances have been made, and all extravagant estimates pared to the bone, the fact remains that propaganda is one of the most powerful instrumentalities in the modern world. It has arisen to its present eminence in response to a complex of changed circumstances which have altered the nature of society . . . A new subtler instrument must weld thousands and even millions of human beings into one amalgamated mass of hate and will and hope. A new flame must burn out the canker of dissent and temper the steel of bellicose enthusiasm. The name of this new hammer and anvil of social solidarity is propaganda.[11]

In Britain, too, propaganda was employed on an unprecedented scale to assist the war effort. This was partly because, unlike the other major European powers, Britain did not have universal conscription, nor were the Liberal or Labour parties united behind the war effort. Britain declared war on 4 August 1914, after the Germans invaded Belgium, whose neutrality had been guaranteed by the Great Powers. Atrocity stories from Belgium signalled the first great propaganda blast of the war and succeeded in inspiring British sympathy, encouraging the enlistment of more than two million volunteers by September 1915. Horror stories of the 'Hun's' brutality, some based on real incidents but many without foundation, were also the core of propaganda efforts to entice the United States to join battle.

Lloyd George enlisted the press barons Lord Beaverbrook (Minister of Information) and Lord Northcliffe to take charge of propaganda overseas. Northcliffe took responsibility for propaganda to enemy countries and his team at Crewe House devised imaginative ways to shatter the morale of the enemy. One notorious example of Allied black propaganda was the German corpse factory story: the 'Hun' was said to be boiling the bodies of dead German soldiers for use as fats. The story was later exposed publicly as a lie, based on a deliberate mistranslation of the German word 'kadaver'.[12] Domestic propaganda was supplemented by strict censorship as the British government attempted to control the press with the Defence of the Realm Acts of 1914–15. The Acts led to the closure of some of the radical anti-war and anti-conscription papers such as the *Labour Leader*, organ of the Independent Labour Party, and *Forward*, the Glasgow socialist weekly. In addition, and more controversially, the offices of the Conservative newspaper, *The Globe*, were raided by police in November 1915 and all copies of two days' editions seized. There was no official reason given but it was believed to be because of the publication of stories critical of Lord Kitchener, the Secretary for War.

The House of Commons had been hostile to Beaverbrook's ministry and when the war ended there was no enthusiasm to prolong its life into peacetime. It was scrapped even though its wartime success was acknowledged. After the war there were many in Germany who credited Allied propaganda with a vital role in demoralising the Germans. Among these, most notably, was Hitler, who took to heart the British and American lesson that effective propaganda needed to be prepared by specialist media professionals.[13] Ironically the perceived potency of Allied black propaganda probably contributed to the climate of distaste and suspicion in the following years as the scale of invention and lies filtered into the realm of public knowledge. Ultimately this scepticism may have contributed to disbelief with regard to the genuine stories of atrocity in Hitler's Germany:

> The very success of the British propaganda efforts in 1914–18 proved to be a serious handicap in getting the world to accept the reality of what was happening in Nazi Germany and this created a disastrous delay in the public's awareness of the horrors of the concentration camps and other Nazi atrocities.[14]

The mood of distaste was also heightened, doubtless, by the Zinoviev Letter episode: the letter, allegedly sent by Zinoviev, chairman of the Comintern, to the British Comintern, urged acts of sedition to foment revolution. It was printed in the press four days before the general election of 25 October 1924. Although the truth of the matter is not known, it was believed by Labour leaders to have been a forgery planted in the press to incite fear about Labour's policy of better relations with Russia, and to ensure the return of a Conservative government.

THE EXTENSION OF THE FRANCHISE

Popular influence in politics reached new heights with the 1918 Representation of the People Act and the 1928 Equal Franchise Act which delivered the vote to almost all adults aged 21 and over. The multiplication of the electorate from less than eight million to nearly 29 million brought about a transformation in electioneering practice. The 'crusted election agent' was forced to rethink his old methods, tried and trusted in days when the electorate was smaller and susceptible to the influence of squire and parson. The printed word and the development of press relations became increasingly vital work for agents.

A handbook of electioneering practice published in 1922 warned that politics would now have to be organised on business-like lines and that the election agent should regard himself primarily as a salesman and expert in the art of publicity. He was advised to leave politics to the candidate. The book mocked the outcry against the 'modern ways' in terms which have familiar echoes.

> ... probably nothing has more fundamentally changed in the last 50 years than our domestic politics. Hence it has provided a theme for the most mournful threnodies in the lamentations of our modern Jeremiahs. Politics are supposed to have undergone a sad change for the worse. They are more sordid, more concerned with bread and butter, more dependent upon the whims of the millions who must be cozened by flamboyant oratory or frightened by cheap histrionics into giving their votes. It is a matter of counting noses rather than weighing heads.[15]

The Conservative Party organisation had been urged to establish a dedicated press department as early as 1911. A confidential inquiry, under the chairmanship of Viscount Chilston, suggested organisational changes which set up the framework for the modern Conservative Party.[16] Chilston's committee recommended upgrading Conservative Central Office, which should take over from the National Union responsibility for literature, speakers and publicity and be headed by a chairman of Cabinet rank. The National Union was to retain a consultative role and organise the annual conference.

Chilston was highly critical of the party's poor press relations and recommended the formation of a permanent press department to supply confidential information to editors and to furnish propaganda to the press.

> It is patent that some feeling exists amongst the Unionist Press that, while in the past they have done much for the Party, the Party has not assisted them sufficiently in their work. In many quarters it is asserted that the Unionist Press are treated with greater courtesy by the Radicals than by their own side.[17]

However a formal and separate press section was not established until the appointment as party chairman of John Colin

Campbell Davidson,[18] who had been briefly Lloyd George's private secretary. Davidson decided that propaganda should be given its own organisational chief and removed from the ambit of the principal agent. He persuaded a former civil servant, Sir Patrick Gower, to become the Conservative Party's first chief publicity officer. Gower, who had been working at Number 10 for the Labour Prime Minister, Ramsay MacDonald, remained at Central Office until April 1939 when he moved to the National Publicity Bureau, the propaganda organisation created for the National Government.

At the same time, Davidson also created the Conservative Research Department (CRD) and he recruited Major Sir Joseph Ball as its first director. The appointment of Ball reflected the continuing influence of wartime intelligence. Although Davidson eschewed the lies and exaggeration of black propaganda he happily engaged Ball in spy-like activities to gain information for the Conservatives.[19] Ball, a former MI5 agent, was a shadowy, sinister figure whose presence looms in many of the more mysterious dealings of the party while he was in charge of CRD during 1930–39. He was 'steeped in Service tradition, and has had as much experience as anyone I know in the seamy side of life and the handling of crooks', Davidson said of him.[20] Ball and Davidson ran their own secret intelligence service and their agents infiltrated Labour Party headquarters to secure reports on Labour's research into the political feeling in the country. And via an unofficial deal with Labour's printers, they managed to get advance 'pulls' of Labour's literature, thus enabling the Conservatives to publish counterblasts simultaneously. While director of the CRD, Ball's services were also used by Baldwin and then Chamberlain at Number 10 to liaise with the press and take lobby briefings. He acted as a go-between in secret talks with the Italian ambassador, Dino Grandi, in furtherance of Chamberlain's policy of appeasement.[21] The full extent of Ball's intriguing activities remains to be explored.

THE IMPACT OF CLASS CONFLICT

If parliament was reluctant to sanction official propaganda in peacetime, the authorities were anxious to maintain wartime

censorship against undesirable publicity concerning class conflict. Cinema was believed to be the most potent communications medium as it rapidly became massively popular,
especially among the working class. By 1921, London had 266
cinemas and, by 1938, 20 million cinema tickets were sold
every week.[22]

The British Board of Censors banned any film 'calculated to
foment social unrest'.[23] It was largely successful in keeping
subversive film off the screens at a time of widespread labour
turmoil in Europe and some of the most militant years in the
history of the British working class, from the growth of the
shops stewards movement to the General Strike of 1926. Moreover, while the Ministry of Information was formally dismantled, the government encouraged the growth of nominally
independent publicity apparatus. In 1919, in the midst of crippling railway strikes, Prime Minister Lloyd George's aide,
William Sutherland, established a propaganda organisation to
incite hostility against militant trade unionism.[24]

A former undercover agent, Sidney Walton, was appointed
to run this organisation with funds supplied by industrial
sources, primarily the Engineering Employers' Federation.
Under the aegis of Sutherland and Coalition chief whips Lord
Talbot and Captain Guest, and with the assistance of Conservative Central Office, it took over the propaganda functions of
wartime employer-funded front organisations, such as the British Empire League and the British Workers' League. Cabinet
papers suggest that Walton had access to private sources of
information from government, Special Branch and the Secret
Intelligence services. By 1922 Walton claimed that he could put
'authoritative signed articles' in more than 1200 newspapers
and journals.

Less secretively, Whitehall departments began to develop
formal information and publicity machinery. In 1936 Thomas
Jones, a confidant of Baldwin's who had also given public
relations assistance to Lloyd George, told the Institute of Public Administration of the 'professionalization' of government
publicity:

> Governments actively supply information by letter and leaflet
> to individual enquirers; by communications to organisations

for the use of their central office, their branches, their individual members; by books and pamphlets, by articles in the press sometimes signed by a Minister, sometimes anonymous; by broadcasts; by cinema films. Work of this type is increasingly in the hands of Public Relations or Press Officers of the various Ministries. Even Downing Street has now a trained journalist, a full-time officer, who maintains daily contact with the Press and does the work which used to fall to one of the Private Secretaries. In addition there are more systematic bodies whose business is not only to carry on directed or free research but to advise the public.[25]

In 1930 Downing Street was furnished with a full-time press officer, George Steward, a former Foreign Office news department official, who was to serve prime ministers MacDonald, Baldwin and Chamberlain until 1940. Steward, officially titled the Chief Press Liaison Officer of His Majesty's Government, was the forerunner of the prime minister's Press Secretary, whose power was to reach its zenith in the person of Bernard Ingham.

Overt government attention to publicity reached its interwar peak when the National Government of 1935 established the National Publicity Bureau as the first peacetime attempt to co-ordinate government's publicity.[26] In response to the propaganda offensives of the totalitarian regimes in Europe, government also increased its overseas publicity, enlisting the services of the BBC. Yet despite these innovations there was relatively little formal official apparatus for the management of publicity and the dissemination of propaganda.[27]

The Second World War brought the next tremendous boost to official propaganda with the wartime Ministry of Information, which saw a succession of heads, including Sir John Reith (formerly BBC director general) and Brendan Bracken (proprietor of the *Financial Times*). At the war's end, the newly elected Labour government consolidated pre-war trends: the Central Office of Information was established as a permanent peacetime version of the MoI, without censorship functions; the structures of departmental publicity were entrenched and the office of the prime minister's press secretary formally accepted (see Chapters 5 and 6).

THE IMPACT OF COMMUNICATIONS TECHNOLOGY

The momentous social and political changes of the inter-war period were accompanied by the dramatic developments in communications technology. The cheap and readily available press was probably still the king of mass communications but its crown was being disputed by new technologies of radio and cinema.

Political parties were starting to make positive use of the new technologies. Conservative leader Stanley Baldwin led the way. He was the first leader to understand how to exploit radio, developing a relaxed and direct broadcast style. The contrast with his rivals was clear in the 1924 election, for, while both the Liberal and Labour leaders (Asquith and MacDonald) used radio, neither adapted his style in the manner of Baldwin. Asquith took the microphone into public meetings and harangued the audience in the old-fashioned manner, while MacDonald walked about the platform as he spoke so that not all his speech was picked up by the fixed microphone.[28] Baldwin paid extraordinary attention to detail in the preparation of his seemingly informal radio broadcasts: for example, before one radio broadcast during the 1929 election he wrote to the BBC requesting information about the social composition of his likely audience and whether working men would listen at home or in the public house. His biographers, Middlemas and Barnes, do not underestimate Baldwin's radio skills: 'In an age when the sound of the Prime Minister's voice in a man's own home was still something of a miracle, his mastery of the new medium was a new and remarkable source of power . . .'[29]

In this golden dawn of commercial cinema, the newsreels quickly became a tremendously important source of information for a mass audience. Baldwin was as quick to see an opportunity here as he was in radio. He had his own set of media advisors, including Sir John Reith at the BBC and friendly film-makers such as Alexander Korda, and Campbell, Craig and Sanger of Movietone. With their advice, Baldwin capitalised on cinema to develop his image as a calm and collected leader. He began adapting to newsreel style in 1923 when the moving pictures were still silent and by 1930, with the advent of the talking newsreels, he was a skilled performer. He was, in the words of John Ramsden, Conservative Party historian, 'lionised' by the newsreels.[30]

The Conservative Party followed Baldwin's lead and started to make its own propaganda films, including a cartoon about Labour policy called Red Tape Farm. The commercial cinemas would not screen overt political propaganda so, encouraged by Tory chairman Davidson, the party started its own mobile picture show. The cinema vans were specially made for the Conservatives by the Thorneycrofts, a then famous shipbuilding concern, and by the 1931 election they had built up a fleet of 22 cinema vans which toured the country and drew audiences of around 2000 people a day.[31] This was popular but the audiences were far too small to make any signficant claims for influencing the electorate. Yet it is another of several examples during the inter-war period of the way in which the Conservatives were the first to see and seize opportunities offered by the new communications media. Their pioneering efforts were particularly striking because a strongly and widely held left-wing viewpoint of the early cinema was that it was the new opium of the masses. There was no holding back the progress of the new media, however, and by 1935 cinema was sufficiently entrenched in the political communications process, for guidelines to be introduced for equal coverage during elections.

Sound and vision were the most dramatic developments of the period but in other fields too there was evidence of a more 'business-like' attitude towards publicity and campaigning. In 1929 the Liberals broke new ground by using press advertisements, while both the Liberals and the Conservatives used posters. It is estimated that both these parties spent about £300 000 on the 1929 campaign, with about half the total devoted to publicity. The Conservative outpouring of literature and publicity at the 1929 election (for example, 'The Baldwin Budget', 'The Woman of Today and Tomorrow' and 24 issues of 'Daily Notes' for constituency workers) reached record proportions. The 1929 Party Conference report stated that 85 159 776 leaflets were distributed, together with 8 360 800 posters. By comparison, 36 million leaflets and pamphlets were distributed at the 1924 election.[32] A further indication of the professionalisation of party publicity was the use of the advertising agency,

Benson's, who suggested the slogan, 'Safety First', which, in the wake of the Tories' defeat, was heavily criticised.[33]

Davidson, rather than Baldwin, bore the brunt of Conservative complaints for the electoral defeat of 1929. Davidson drew three vital campaigning lessons which have survived as the accepted wisdom through to the Thatcher era:

1 start planning the campaign early, at least a year before the end of term, to allow elbow room for manoeuvre;
2 concentrate on the marginal seats;
3 implement unpopular measures early in the term.

THE POST-WAR ERA: FORCES FOR CHANGE

The post-Second World War decades have been relatively peaceful and prosperous and the political system has been stable. There have been no shocks to the system to compare with the impact of the First World War or the Russian Revolution. Post-war working-class militancy has rarely carried the kind of revolutionary undertones of the first quarter of the century. While there has been some tinkering with and extension of the franchise (notably lowering the age to 18 in 1969), the major transformations were all in place by 1928. Thus we should not expect to find the post-war engines of change in the social and political spheres. Instead the driving forces have been the spellbinding innovation in mass communications technology and the quasi-scientific development of business research methods.

Communications Technology

Television is the most obvious and significant new player. Television gained a mass audience in the 1950s and by 1959 some three-quarters of Britain's households had a black and white set. By the end of the 1980s, 97.2 per cent of households owned or rented a television; 46.2 per cent of all television-owning households had more than one set and 61 per cent owned or rented a video cassette recorder.[34]

Television is now clearly established as the most important source of world and national news for most of the population.[35] Its impact on voters, however, is less clear. Political scientists continue to debate the influence of television on viewers' political attitudes and voting behaviour. In the 1950s and early 1960s the notion of 'limited effects' was the predominant model, based on influential studies of voters in American elections in the 1940s. Media impact was summed up in three words: 'reinforcement not change'; that is, media served merely to bolster and conserve pre-existing attitudes. Joseph Klapper summarised the mechanisms underlying the thesis as: selective exposure, interpretation and recall of information.[36]

Since then most scholars acknowledge a greater significance for the media. Television has superseded discussion with friends, family and peer groups as the main vehicle of election information. According to more recent thinking, the media set the agenda, influencing what people think about, if not what they think; they also encourage people with views contrary to the media mainstream to keep quiet – the 'spiral of silence', in the words of Elizabeth Noelle-Neuman's theory.[37] Modern researchers agree that the media cannot be reduced to 'reinforcement', but there is no new consensus about precisely how powerful they are.

If political scholars have been riddled with doubt, politicians have lacked the time for theoretical speculation. Television has created a revolution in political campaigning: it has focused attention on the leaders, enormously increasing the importance of the national campaign and concentrating power further in the hands of central organizations. Symptoms and consequences of this include the diminishing significance of constituency campaigning, canvassing, local public meetings (which for the Conservative Party have all but disappeared) and, therefore, of the regional organisation and constituency agent her/himself. From 1959, which saw the first modern television election campaign, a succession of party leaders have felt that they won or lost because of television: Alec Douglas-Home, Harold Wilson and Edward Heath.

Television, however, is only the most obvious of the advances in communications. Information technology was beginning to impress itself by the 1987 election and, as will be argued in later chapters, computers have the potential to trigger a further revolution in political campaigning, perhaps turning the tide a little towards the constituency campaign and facilitating new techniques of communication such as personalised direct mail.

Market Research

Another enormous influence in the post-war era has been the growth and increasing reliability of business research methods. In 1923 Bernays urged politicians to use 'science' instead of instinct to understand and influence their audience. The science in question was the then fledgling practice of marketing or market research.[38] Marketing first emerged as a distinct branch of management in the United States and the earliest recorded references to business marketing research stem from America in the late nineteenth century.[39] In the early years of the twentieth century the growth of marketing research was closely connected to the rise of advertising and it was seen essentially as a tool to promote the efficacy of business propaganda.

The inter-war period saw pioneering efforts at market research in Britain: in 1937 Tom Harrison founded Mass Observation, which specialised in social surveys, and the same year the BBC started the Listener Research Department (later known as Audience Research, when television took off). Market research reached the age of maturity after 1945 and has grown to become an indispensible tool of business practice for virtually every major company and many minor ones, in the industrialised world. Sampling techniques and research designs have improved significantly as the discipline borrowed widely from statistics (probability, non-parametrics, multivariate analysis and so on), psychology (motivational research) and sociology (social classification).

Research falls broadly into two categories, qualitative and quantitative. The demonstrable and increasing accuracy of quantitative opinion polling since the 1930s has provided the bedrock of credibility for the whole marketing research edifice, 1970 and 1992 débâcles notwithstanding. But qualitative research, into consumers' underlying attitudes, emotional responses and motivations, became the vogue of the 1950s and 1960s. Its most common uses now are at the early stages of product development to identify desirable and undesirable features, to pre-test advertising copy, and to map out the areas of research for follow-up quantitative polling. The claims for qualitative work have become less grandiose over the years but its place in marketing research has not become any less important.

While market research boomed in business, it took a long time to be incorporated fully into political practice in Britain. It was not until the late 1950s and 1960s that opinion polling made much headway in British politics and even then it continued to be resisted or treated as an unwelcome visitor. George Hutchinson, chief publicity officer for the Conservatives at the 1964 election, gave expression to the rather haughty disdain of many 'serious' politicians: 'The duty of the political leader is to advocate what he believes to be right, not what the market researchers prescribe for immediate popularity.'[40] Since the early 1960s both major parties have engaged in regular polling, and polls, private and public, have mushroomed at election times. At the 1945 election there was only one political poll, Gallup. Since then the volume has expanded to saturation: in 1983 there were 47 nationwide polls taken during the election campaign; in the 1987 general election there were 73 national surveys – a record number of polls carried out by a record number of polling agencies.

Here again the impact of polling on the political behaviour of voters is a moot point among academics. And here again there is no doubt that it has altered the behaviour of political practitioners. Opinion research is the foundation upon which the marketing concept has been built in British politics.

PARTY PUBLICITY IN THE POST-WAR ERA

Labour's landslide in 1945 (see Table 1.1) came as an enormous shock to the Conservatives, although the Gallup poll since 1943 had given Labour a comfortable lead. With war leader Winston Churchill at the helm they had confidently expected triumph and they had waged a campaign heavily focused on his personality: 'HELP HIM finish the job' was a campaign slogan. It is typical of the Tories that when they are defeated they look to their party organisation. It is a much-noted Conservative tendency to blame failure on the party's inability or incompetence at putting across its message. It is almost unthinkable, as Lord Windlesham once ruefully remarked, that the problem might be that the electorate understood party policy only too well.[41] However self-criticism

Table 1.1　The general election of 5 July 1945

	Con	Lab	Lib	Other	Total
Seats					
At dissolution	398	166	18	33	615
After election	213	393	12	22	640
Votes					
% of total	39.8	48.3	9.1	2.8	100
1935–45 change	–13.9	+10.4	+2.7	+0.8	

Labour overall majority 146
Turnout 73.3%

has the positive effects of sharpening and shaking up party organisation. Hence the great reorganisations of the party structure have tended to occur in opposition. This pattern was repeated in the aftermath of the 1945 defeat.

Lord Woolton, the plummy-voiced wartime Minister of Food and a former Fabian, was appointed party chairman in 1946. He became, in the words of Conservative Party historian Robert Blake, the 'greatest of all Conservative party managers'.[42] Party organisation had been limited to care-and-maintenance during the war and Woolton set about fundamental transformations. He revived the Conservative Research Department, which was to enjoy its most energetic and influential period under the leadership of R.A. Butler. He expanded the newly-formed Conservative Political Centre as the forum for the political education of party activists. He encouraged the growth of the Young Conservatives and extended the work of the Advisory Committee on Local Government.

Butler and the CRD were responsible for party policy, while Woolton concentrated his efforts on increasing membership, fund-raising and propaganda:

He was determined to make the party spend and not hoard. He adopted a seemingly paradoxical technique. He deliberately resolved to over-spend on publicity, propaganda etc., and thus force the local party organisation to raise the necessary funds. At the same time he decided to cut off one of their traditional sources, the heavy personal subscriptions through which in some safe constituencies the member virtually bought his seat.[43]

In public the Conservatives were immensely critical of the Labour government's Central Office of Information but in private Lord Woolton set about examining the new propaganda techniques. Woolton appointed Toby O'Brien as chief information officer at Conservative Central Office, a post that had been somewhat neglected since Patrick Gower left in 1939. O'Brien found much work to do. The party's publicity services had been criticised in a series of internal reports: the Mansell Committee of 1937, which especially drew attention to the old-fashioned use of film, the Butler–Topping Committee of 1941 and Topping's Organisation Review of 1944.[44]

O'Brien was struck by the absence of a concept of press and public relations. Press releases were dispatched to only a few select papers, usually by post. O'Brien moved swiftly to fill the vacuum and he later co-opted John Profumo to help rehearse Conservative leaders due to appear on radio and BBC's emerging television service. Just as importantly, the staffs of the 12 Tory area agents were increased to include permanent press officers.[45] O'Brien, the general director Stephen Pierssene, and Lord Woolton's personal assistant, Mark Chapman Walker, together ran the Tactical Staff Committee, whose existence was not officially acknowledged. The committee acted as a sort of propaganda guerrilla group, tracking enemy vulnerable spots and planning Conservative publicity tactics. Some of the committee's schemes would slip comfortably into the category of 'dirty tricks'. For example, agents were asked to supply the names of hecklers who were to be briefed with questions researched by the CRD and then despatched to cause havoc at Labour public meetings.[46] In another instance, the committee considered employing an intelligence officer 'of the ex-private detective type for obtaining useful information'.[47]

The committee kept a close eye on the newly-established government information apparatus and maintained a barrage of questions about the alleged misuse of government funds on publicity and lavish hospitality. It attempted to publicise all instances which connected government propaganda in any way with communist causes: it ordered photographs of the Communisty Party Bookshop van at one of its frequent visits to the offices of the Central Coal Board and it complained of government advertisements being placed in the communist *Daily Worker.*[48] Additionally it discussed ideas, for Conservative posters to run nationally in 1948 in (incorrect) anticipation of a general election the following year, and for advance publicity to focus attention on party political broadcasts; and it issued instructions to all party speakers to concentrate on a single theme, which the committee established weekly. Lord Woolton, who toyed with the idea of changing the Conservative Party's name, instructed Tory speakers never to use the name 'Labour' with its innocent connotations of honest toil. Instead they should substitute the more doctrinaire 'Socialist', a practice that was maintained into the late 1950s, when it was discovered that some voters thought 'Labour' and 'Socialist' were different parties.[49]

H.G. Nicholas, in the Nuffield study of the 1950 general election, notes that both major parties entered the campaign at a pitch of preparedness then unequalled in the history of British politics. The parties had become 'addicted to planned electioneering', he commented.[50] Each had unparalleled central command of activities in the field:

> The campaign maps studded with flags, before which each party manager was photographed in his office, did indeed indicate to an unprecedented degree troop movements controlled from a headquarters, and troops, moreover, who were regulars, in training, temperament and conditions of service.[51]

To a far greater extent than today it was a land war between armies of agents; the Conservatives claimed 428 fully qualified agents (compared to 300 in 1987), Labour had 279. Television was in its infancy and these were early days in the techniques of TV image making. Prime Minister Attlee conducted his national tour in his family car with Mrs Attlee at the wheel. The Attlee equivalent of photo-opportunities was roadside stops during which Mrs Attlee would take out her knitting and Mr Attlee would do the crossword.

A further, unwitting illustration of the relative amateurishness of the times is given in Lord Charles Hill's autobiography, *Both Sides of the Hill.* Hill was later made a Tory minister responsible for information services, and later still Harold Wilson appointed him chairman of the BBC. However he made his fame as a young man through his 'flying doctor' radio shows and because of this experience Lord Woolton asked him to make a Tory party political broadcast in 1950. Hill was left entirely alone to produce the broadcast as he saw fit, with the one proviso that he showed Woolton the script before it went out. Hill cites the story as an example of Tory party common sense and efficiency in matters of publicity. If praise and publicity are any guide, Hill's folksy talk on the NHS thoroughly vindicated Woolton's judgment.[52]

The First 'Modern' Campaign: the General Election of 1959

Woolton's attempts at modernisation did not bring victory in 1950 but since Labour's huge majority was whittled down to single figures the result was hailed as something of a success. Woolton remained in charge for the victories of October 1951, when the Tories gained a majority of 17, and May 1955, when they increased their majority to 54 seats. He left in July and was succeeded by (Lord) Oliver Poole, who had sat as a Conservative MP for Oswestry in 1945–50. Poole remained as either chairman or deputy chairman until 1963 and it was he who 'in the period 1957–59 . . . developed a pattern of political communication that was to become a standard model in British politics,' according to Lord Windlesham.[53]

Poole hired the advertising agency Colman, Prentis & Varley (CPV) to launch the first sustained political advertising campaign outside an election period. It was under Poole that the Tories first began to use market research in a systematic way to target their campaigns. He helped set up the Liaison Committee, a more wide-ranging but equally confidential successor to the Tactical Staff Committee, which established a regular forum for advice on the presentation of government policy and forms of propaganda. Poole was also responsible for setting up the Special Group, an idea he borrowed from the USA, for the express purpose of aiding the prime minister's own media relations.

What marked out Lord Poole so distinctively was not just his keen business brain, which understood very well the importance of marketing. It was also his enthusiasm and success in carrying out these reorganisations while the Conservatives were in power. The post of deputy chairman was actually recreated especially for Poole by Harold Macmillan; the party had not had a deputy chairman since the Marquis of Linlithgow, in 1924–6. After the Suez crisis and the resignation of Eden, Macmillan wanted a colourful character to head the party organisation and his choice was Viscount Hailsham. But Hailsham did not have Poole's interest in the techniques of political marketing, so Macmillan persuaded Poole to stay as deputy chairman (a post senior to vice chairman) to continue to run the party machine.

Poole deliberately chose experts from outside the party to run its advertising campaigns, even though there would have been volunteer expertise within the ranks. Colman Prentis and Varley supplied the Tories with copywriters, artists and media planners. Nielsen and National Opinion Polls were used for surveys. The research pointed to an avenue of opportunity for the Tories; it showed that a majority of younger people, in the 25–40 age bracket, regarded themselves as 'middle class'.[54] Since Labour was strongly identified with the working class, there was a clear chance of shifting younger voters' allegiance. The Tories set about doing this in a way which was then unique. Starting in the autumn of 1957 they launched a sustained campaign of press advertisements, which was novel on two counts: first, that the advertising was in newspapers as well as the more familiar posters, and second, that it was a lengthy, unified campaign by the party of government well in advance of the dissolution of parliament. The campaign's target was to win the new 'middle class' by presenting the Conservatives as the party of the whole nation. The campaign, created by CPV's Geoffrey Tucker, showed people not usually imagined as typical Tories: housewives, skilled and unskilled workers, technicians and clerical workers and celebrities such as England's cricket captain, Colin Cowdrey. It used the slogan, 'You're looking at a Conservative'. The campaign lasted from the autumn of 1957 to September 1959, split into two distinct pre-campaign phases, and it cost nearly £500 000.

The success of political advertising is always debatable. However the Tories achieved their highest poll ratings at about the same time as the advertising campaign could reasonably be expected to make most impact.[55] The advertisements were reintroduced into the election campaign proper with one change. The slogan was changed and set in lurid black on magenta Day-Glo: 'Life is better with the Conservatives. Don't let Labour ruin it.' The campaign raised questions concerning the morality of using highly-paid, professional motivational persuaders. In the phrase that was to become a hardy annual of campaign vocabulary, critics protested at the 'Americanisation' of British politics. The words of Labour's Alice Bacon, a member of the party's 1959 campaign committee, reflected the views of many: 'We do not want British political life to become a battle between two publicity agencies of Madison Avenue,' she told the House of Commons.[56]

Colman Prentis and Varley were at pains to point out that they had no influence, nor wanted any, on Tory party policy. They worked from a much tighter brief than they would normally accept from a commercial client. Their role was restricted to advertising and advice on how to use the media. The agency's disclaimer is treated sceptically by Lord Windlesham:

> It is difficult to think of circumstances in which the presentation of a political message . . . prepared by a professional agency did not have some effect on the policy of the party or on what the public believe policy to be.[57]

Another Poole innovation which deserves a closer look was the Special Group, which he established specifically to assist the prime minister with his speeches and liaison with the media. Poole recruited Nigel Lawson, then City editor on the *Sunday Telegraph*, and Eldon Griffiths, managing editor at *Newsweek*. The Special Group was put together for Macmillan in the summer of 1963 but after Macmillan resigned in the autumn it was inherited by the new leader Sir Alec Douglas Home. With the change of leader, Poole's own position in the party organisation changed once more.

Poole's energy in reshaping the party's attitude towards communications was important, but his ability to implement change was also a comment on the political climate in the leading factions of the party. Harold Macmillan was the consummate consensus politician. He led the party at a time when the intellectual climate was beguiled by 'the end of ideology' theory and a prevailing belief that electoral success depended upon capturing the centre ground:

The whole process of the politics of support in the mass electorate – drawing up programmes and manifestoes, canvassing, distributing propaganda and holding mass meetings – was increasingly viewed as similar to the marketing campaign of a firm.[58]

The Tory Bow Group, formed in 1951, helped spread the new Conservative, technocratic, anti-ideology outlook of the party. It was believed that economic prosperity and the welfare state had permanently undermined the old class politics and shifted the ground of the debate. Enoch Powell believes that if you are looking for the roots of modern marketing in politics you need go no further than Harold Macmillan.[59] While this outlook permitted the growth of rational electioneering, it constrained that development along fairly gentlemanly lines. Macmillan's opening speech of the 1959 election campaign included this phrase: 'Let us remember we are not enemies'.[60] Macmillan's tone, warm almost to the point of friendliness, contrasts sharply with the campaigning style of Thatcher, who tended to cast Labour opponents as beyond the pale of democratic politics.

Labour deliberately shunned a 'time for a change' strategy of attack on the government's record. It did not respond to the Tory's 1957–9 advertising blitz; there was no one in its press and publicity department with any professional public relations experience; and, fundamentally, it had moral reservations about the use of political advertising. In the party leader Gaitskell's view, 'the whole thing was somehow false'. Labour waged a positive campaign aimed at getting its own vote out; it promoted its own economic programme, launching a series of policy documents which were largely ignored by press and public.[61]

Labour's advertising campaign consisted of pamphlets and posters costing a total of some £103 000 – less than one-quarter of the Tories' bill. It did not use national daily papers for advertising until May 1963. Yet, for all that, the 1959 campaign contained signs that the party was sharpening its publicity organisation. The general secretary, Morgan Phillips, initiated the morning press briefings – a tactic now taken for granted by all major parties. Labour's television party election broadcasts (PEBs), considered, slick and polished, won praise in even the Tory press for outshining the Conservative efforts.

1959: the First 'Television' Election

1959 can lay claim to being the first true television election. Anthony Eden, advised by his press secretary William Clark, a former BBC presenter, had broken new ground with his television broadcasts in the 1955 campaign. He was arguably the first party leader to enlist the services of a specialist television adviser, Ronald Gillet, from the US.[62] However there are a number of reasons why 1959 stands out.

First, television was now reaching at least three-quarters of the population, compared to about half in 1955. Second, the rules of political broadcasting had been transformed from the early days of extreme caution and reverence. The BBC had observed a 14-day rule, under which it did not discuss any matter certain, or even likely, to be raised in the Commons during the next two weeks. There was also a ban on election reporting, so that in the 1955 election the only television coverage of the campaign was the PEBs. The advent of the commercial rival, ITV, altered the picture. ITV reported the Rochdale by-election in 1957, and thereafter the BBC abandoned the 14-day rule and both channels covered the 1959 campaign. The BBC's *Panorama*, fronted by Richard Dimbleby, was revamped into a hard-hitting current affairs programme, frequently reaching an audience of about eight million. Independent Television News (ITN), determined to break the cosy BBC/government relationship, hired (Sir) Robin Day, gained a reputation for tough questioning and abandoned the BBC practice of presenting ministers with an advance list of questions. Thus 1959 presented a substantially new media environment for the politicians, although as yet, and this is an important qualification, the party leaders were not subjected to the programme-length interviews which were to become features of later campaigns.

Macmillan, although he was to complain of the camera's 'hot, probing eye' and said that he never dared watch one of his own television performances, proved a skilful exploiter of the medium. On 31 August 1959, only days before he called the election, Macmillan staged an exclusive 'live' spectacular for the BBC. He invited the cameras into the Number 10 state drawing room to film a self-congratulatory and rehearsed 20-minute 'chat' on first-name terms between himself and the

visiting President Eisenhower. 'The first account from the viewers seems to be – enthusiastic,' Macmillan noted in his diary
that night.[63]

Ironically Labour, with their polished PEBs, seemed the more
accomplished television performers during the campaign. Tony
Wedgewood Benn produced a secret briefing which suggested
a linked series of PEBs, in a news format with a 'presenter'
introducing themes and party speakers. The words 'there now
follows an election broadcast' were an 'audience killer,' wrote
Benn, and viewers' attention would have to be grabbed immediately by the use of strong music and pictures: 'Suppose we
decide our theme is to be the "Land and the People". Then
the opening film sequence should be an atomic power station
under construction, seen across fields of waving corn. And our
music should be Jerusalem, sung by a Welsh choir.'[64]

The Conservatives' PEBs, by contrast, seemed stilted and
stiff until the final broadcast which featured Macmillan alone
talking to camera. At the instigation of Lord Poole, Macmillan
was tutored for the task by Norman Collins, a powerful figure
in commercial television and chairman of ATV. Collins decided that Macmillan's authoritative, military bearing would
be seen at best advantage if he conducted his broadcast standing up. Collins rehearsed the Prime Minister and he recorded
the PEB in advance, which was then highly unusual. According
to Edward Heath it transformed the campaign:

> It really was a most remarkable broadcast. Harold Macmillan
> was completely relaxed. The most dramatic part was when
> he walked over to a vast globe and he just turned it round
> and the whole world just revolved as people watched him.
> And he said, 'let me tell you what I am going to do about
> the rest of the world'. Dramatic. It changed everything.[65]

The election was held on 8 October 1959 and the Conservatives romped home with a majority of 100 seats.

1964: the First 'Rational' Election

The 1964 campaign is another landmark on the marketing
route. For the first time *both* major parties hired the services of
professional pollsters and publicists. Opinion research was
incorporated into campaign planning to an unprecedented

degree. However this time Labour was the leader in the field. For Richard Rose, Labour's 1964 campaign provided an object lesson in rational electioneering; it showed what could be achieved by using marketing research and a rational application of the results.[66] Compared to Labour, the Tories' publicity seemed 'oddly old-fashioned', according to the Nuffield general election study.[67]

The years between 1959 and 1964 transformed the fortunes of the Labour and Conservative Parties. The Tories' 1959 landslide, their third consecutive victory, plunged Labour into crisis and sowed doubts, similar to those that followed their 1987 failure, that the party could ever regain office. The party was ideologically split between those who felt that it should remain true to socialist principles and await patiently the moment for power (Richard Crossman, for example) and those who felt it should adapt and shed its old class-conscious image (Anthony Crosland led this group).

However by late 1963 both parties had new leaders and their fortunes were reversed. It was Labour looking united, competent and confident while the Tories were scandal-hit and split over their leadership. The observation that defeat is good for the soul of the party organisation had proved accurate again, this time to Labour's benefit. The party reviewed its organisation and planning and worked to build up an election campaign fund which reached £755 000 by May 1964, compared with a total election spend of £186 000 five years earlier.

Crosland's supporters commissioned pollster Mark Abrams to investigate why voters had deserted Labour and he produced a report in 1960 under the title 'Must Labour Lose?'[68] Abrams counselled that 'a party which values its own survival must follow as well as lead', yet the party had neglected the study of its own voters' motivations.[69] Abrams was recruited into a small publicity team of public relations (PR) and advertising specialists run by former journalist John Harris, Labour's head of press and publicity since 1962. Abrams' 'survey research was exploited continuously in a manner quite unprecedented in this country'.[70] His research was used to select issues for advertisements and posters, to test their impact on the audience and to assess reaction to Labour's leaders and to PEBs.

His research findings showed similarities to Poole's NOP surveys in the 1950s. About one-third of the electorate could be categorised as 'floating'; class-based voting was on the decline; more people perceived themselves as middle class. However Harold Wilson was seen as a significant asset, far more popular than the aristocrat Sir Alec Douglas-Home, and Labour was preferred on many bread-and-butter domestic issues, most importantly housing. This led to a campaign aimed at 'floating voters'. Traditionally Labour had concentrated on mobilising its own vote and, since floaters were spread across society, this strategy forced Labour away from a class-based campaign. 'Science', 'technology', 'meritocracy' and 'dynamism' were the key words in the image of the new classless Labour Party, personified by its leader, Wilson. Their slogan, 'Let's Go with Labour', emphasised the theme, while Wilson's amiable visage appeared on virtually all Labour Party posters.

Television offered Wilson new opportunities to bypass the mainly hostile press. In the comfort of their own living rooms people could see that the Labour leader was 'an ordinary decent chap', and would not be fooled whatever the poisonous propaganda in the Tory press.[71] Wilson was uniquely equipped for television, in the opinion of Sir Robin Day.[72] He was a witty platform speaker, he was relatively young at 48 and was to become the youngest prime minister of the century, and he had studied the techniques of successful television performance. Wilson made no secret of his admiration for John Kennedy's television style in the 1960 presidential election, and he consciously set out to copy parts of it. He and his aide and confidante, Marcia Williams, studied Kennedy's speeches and they borrowed the ideas of 'soundbites' (although that particular term was not then in vogue), relaxed presentation in front of the cameras and the theme of youthful dynamism. Despite his private preference for Havana cigars, Wilson smoked a pipe during television performances. This seemingly trivial device, adopted mainly to stop his hand clenching into an aggressive fist, became an integral part of Wilson's studied 'ordinary man' image, with his Gannex raincoat and his classless Yorkshire accent.

He also introduced another new element from the USA, American-style showbiz political rallies, a device that was revived under Thatcher and copied by Neil Kinnock. Ever alert to the political advantages of exploiting popular culture, Wilson presented the Beatles with an award on behalf of the Variety

Club of Great Britain and he began the 1964 election campaign with a glamorous rally at the Empire Pool, Wembley. It combined the traditions of Labour politics, the Welsh Male Voice Choir and colliery brass bands, with Pakistani dancers, African drummers, Humphrey Lyttelton's jazz band and performances from Vanessa Redgrave and the actor Harry H. Corbett, who played the pro-Labour rag-and-bone man in the popular comedy programme *Steptoe and Son.*

1964: the Conservative Campaign

The Conservatives spent about £1.2 million on propaganda between May 1963 and September 1964, the month before the election. It was one of the three most expensive Tory campaigns, together with 1935 and 1987. Such a costly defeat was ripe for criticism, particularly as it is a near-truism of politics that the winning party has waged a good campaign and the loser a poor one. With plenty of hindsight (Sir) Geoffrey Pattie, then a Conservative councillor, wrote in the Bow Group magazine *Crossbow* that the Tories campaigned on the wrong things for the wrong reasons.[73]

Another widely shared verdict was that something had gone drastically wrong with the product. Macmillan had slipped from his Supermac status of 1959, and the party, much like Mrs Thatcher's before her downfall, seemed prone to error, had dipped in the polls and internal discontent festered. Minister for War John Profumo resigned in June 1963 in the midst of one of the great post-war scandals. Ill-health forced Macmillan to resign in October that year and there followed a scrap for the succession at the party conference. Colonel Arthur Varley, of Colman, Prentis & Varley, pleaded the adman's impossible task caught in the midst of all this:

> Slap in the middle of chaos no party can make proper slogans . . . I mean, we can't plug a leader just now. We don't even know who he's going to be . . . We haven't any specific activity to advertise. So we're just advertising activity in general . . . Mind you, it's tricky trying to advertise a product if you don't really know what the product is.[74]

The basic building-blocks of a rational campaign were in place, however. In March 1960 the Tories set up a Psephology Group and the party has polled regularly ever since. However the value of polling depends on how it is used by the politicians and there continued to be resistance. A new chief publicity officer, George Hutchinson, an ex-lobby correspondent with the *Evening Standard*, was appointed in 1961. Hutchinson represented something of the Tory intellectual backlash against Poole's marketing razzmatazz. He believed that an over-reliance on opinion polls interfered with a politician's duty to follow his own conscience. There is some evidence of a quarrel between Hutchinson and Lord Poole about campaign strategy.[75] Poole managed to assert his views with some difficulty early in 1964 and he seconded Roger Pemberton from CPV to work with Hutchinson. Poole commissioned a huge NOP survey, with a 10 000 sample, which reported in January 1964. It suggested that Hutchinson's campaigning themes of modernisation and Europe had not been successful, that the new prime minister, Sir Alec Douglas-Home, was not well known and that the issue of most interest to the electorate was the standard of living.[76] Poole and Pemberton devised a second phase of pre-election campaigning which concentrated on Home's integrity and the Tory team versus the one-man campaign of Wilson.

With the polls against them the Tories decided against a spring election in 1964 and this allowed a third phase of publicity around the theme of prosperity. The tactics nearly worked. Labour had spent heavily on publicity in 1963 and the spring of 1964 and were not willing or able to maintain the expenditure into the autumn. Gallup polls showed the Tories steadily gaining ground on Labour: in May Labour held an 11-point advantage (50–39 per cent); by September the lead had narrowed to three points (47–44). When the election came Labour squeaked in with only a five-seat majority (Table 1.2). Labour appeared to take the lead in rational electioneering in 1964 – only to lose it again at the end of the decade. By 1974 Labour was running an election campaign which Joe Haines described half-seriously as one man and his dog – Wilson, the man, and Haines, his dog:

> Harold had a new suit and a couple of coats for the campaign. We had a valet go round with him and before he made a speech or went on TV his valet would bring out this new coat. We had a backdrop which said Vote Labour and

Table 1.2 The general election of 15 October 1964

	Con	Lab	Lib	Other	Total
Seats					
At dissolution	360	261	7	2	630
After election	304	317	9	–	630
Votes					
% of total	43.4	44.1	11.2	1.3	100
1959–64 change	–6.0	+0.3	+5.3	+0.4	

Labour overall majority 5
Turnout 77.1%

we had a young man go round and make sure the cameras were pointing in the right direction. We had Stanley Baker make a film for us. Everyone was happy until the bill came in for £1000 and then everyone had a fit of the vapours.[77]

The lessons which endured from the 1964 general election had less to do with the rational application of market research and more to do with exploitation of television and the projection of the leader's image. These resulted in presidential campaigns which were built almost entirely around the party leader. This was true especially for Labour under Wilson and Callaghan, but also for Heath. In this respect Thatcher bucked the trend somewhat: her picture and name were to be invoked rarely if at all in party-paid publicity and her appearances on television and in party broadcasts deliberately limited.

The Marketing of Edward Heath

Heath was the first Conservative leader to be elected by a ballot of MPs when he took over from Home in August 1965. He immediately initiated a major review of Conservative policy; it was probably the most rigorous policy review ever carried out by the Conservative Party, but it culminated in its second-worst defeat in half a century. The Tories' share of the vote dropped to 41.9 per cent, the lowest since 1945, and Labour won a majority of 96 seats. In the aftermath of defeat the Conservative organisation was revamped once again. Anthony

Barber was appointed chairman in 1967. The office of general director, established since 1931, was abolished. The holder of the post was restyled Director of Organisation in charge of agents and constituency campaigning. The Director of Organisation (Sir Richard Webster) was effectively downgraded to an equal footing with the three other directors, of publicity, the Conservative Research Department (CRD) and the Conservative Political Centre (CPC). This reflected the diminishing role of constituency campaigning in the party's thinking; it was still considered tremendously important, of course, but was no longer the master key to winning elections. As we move into the Thatcher era the director of organisation had less relative importance still in the heirarchy of campaign planning.

The former director of CRD, (Lord) Michael Fraser, became deputy director, in charge of the entire professional party organisation from 1964 to 1975. The intention was to provide greater co-ordination of all the parts of the organisation. In this it succeeded and, by happy chance, according to Fraser, the period 1966–70 was one of the few occasions when all the directors were exactly the right people for the job.[78] As soon as he became deputy chairman, Fraser tried to capture Geoffrey Tucker as publicity director, having admired his work on CPV's 1957–9 advertising campaign for the Tories. However Tucker had moved to Young & Rubicam, for whom he was working in Italy, and he did not become available until 1968. In the period from 1961 to 1968 a series of publicity officers had revolved through Central Office: Ronald Simms, George Hutchinson, Gerald O'Brien, Roger Pemberton and J.R. Rathbone. Tucker has never achieved the public acclaim of, for example Sir Tim Bell in the Thatcher era. Arguably he was as influential as any advertising expert has been in a Conservative campaign. His presence continued to be felt even after he left Central Office following the 1970 election. He continued to offer advice and expertise during the 1974 election and he was to be the link man between Young & Rubicam and Downing Street in 1986–7.

The Conservative team prepared a television-centred campaign around Heath for the 1970 election. The PEBs, in particular, alarmed the Labour leaders. Joe Haines recalls how they were taken by surprise in an election they expected to win with some comfort but did not. Haines identifies the 1970 campaign as the birth of modern political marketing:

I would have said that the development of modern marketing in politics began with Tony Barber in 1970. We were
outraged by the party political broadcasts, but although
we were outraged I would say we were disturbed by their
effectiveness.

In early 1970 we had a showing at No. 10 of the advertisements used by President Johnson. Because they were commercials we knew that they were not for us. We were aware
of what was happening but we didn't do anything about it.
We wanted a serious approach and the Tories were moving
to commercial presentation.[79]

Labour's 1970 approach was labelled the 'Do-it-yourself' campaign. Harold Wilson ran the campaign from Downing Street
and the party organisation in Transport House was frequently
left in the dark and rarely consulted. Wilson ran essentially a
presidential campaign. He had his own team of advisors, including the party's chief publicity officer, Will Camp, and
politics lecturer (Lord) Bernard Donoughue, who analysed
private polls, and Haines. Wilson ran a 'walkabout' campaign,
usually accompanied by Mrs Wilson, to emphasise his family
status and ease among ordinary folk, and to contrast with
Heath's bachelorhood and awkwardness. Haines later described
it as a disastrous campaign, yet at the time the polls put Labour ahead and media commentators said that Wilson was
following a 'brilliant, effective strategy' while poor Mr Heath
was stumbling along facing near-certain defeat.[80]

However, and perhaps in the afterglow of victory, Heath's
television campaign came to be seen as the most sophisticated
yet. Planning began early in 1969 in a committee known as the
'Thursday Group' for the simple reason that it met on Thursday mornings. It consisted initially of Barber, Fraser, Tucker,
Brendan Sewill of the CRD, Jim Garrett, a commercial film
producer, John Lindsey, of CCO's television department, and
key parliamentary party representatives, Willie Whitelaw, the
chief whip and Geoffrey Johnson-Smith, then MP for East
Grinstead and a former BBC reporter. The key man in this
group was Tucker. 'Geoffrey Tucker had dinned into all of us
his conviction that the election would be won or lost on television,' noted Douglas Hurd, who was then Heath's political
secretary.[81] As the election approached, Tucker recruited more
expert help: (Sir) Gordon Reece from television, film director

Bryan Forbes and Barry Day, from the advertising agency, McCann Erickson.

The Tory campaign team wanted to heighten Heath's profile and show him in a warmer, or in advertising parlance, 'sexier' light. But their best laid plans were sometimes sabotaged by the leader who either did not want, or did not know how, to play ball. They organised a 50-seater aeroplane for his tour, with the intention of selling 40 seats to the press. They thus ensured close proximity between Heath and the journalists in the hope that this would foster a better relationship. However things did not go completely to plan:

> Had Heath used each flight to talk at length with his passengers it might have been different. But he remained a generally remote figure at the front of the aircraft, dealing with paper work, preparing his speeches and relaxing occasionally by listening to music on earphones. It was not long before comments were appearing in the press about the sheer futility of flying to cities which could be reached faster by train.[82]

A weekend sailing trip early in the campaign offered glorious potential for what later became known as a photo-opportunity, especially as Heath's crew included an attractive young woman. The press duly arrived and on cue asked if there was any romance in the relationship. 'Ridiculous,' Heath replied, adding with a total lack of chivalrous humour, 'she's only the cook.'[83] Halfway through the campaign Tucker changed tactics and planned a series of Wilson-style, meet-the-people walkabouts. But again as an attempt to humanise Heath's remote image they were not always successful. Heath had no flair for small talk and his attempts at friendly conversation tended to sound 'rather like an orderly officer asking for complaints from the other ranks,' as one newspaper put it.[84] As James Prior noted in his memoirs, 'how wrong we were to think up these gimmicks for Ted. They always turned sour.'[85]

The one unqualified success of the Conservative TV campaign was the election broadcasts which shook up the old staid party political formula and so shocked the Labour Party. Barry Day believed they broke new ground:

> The first deliberate attempt to apply some of the relevant lessons of US experience and therefore . . . the first conscious

effort to use the established techniques of commercial marketing on the British political scene came in 1970 on behalf of the Conservative Party.[86]

The Thursday Group treated the PEBs, five 10-minute slots, as a co-ordinated series in which to tell the Tory Story. The timing for the PEBs was agreed for 10p.m. simultaneously on BBC and ITV and this could not have suited the Tories better. The idea, rather similar to the Tony Benn broadcasts in 1959, was to mimic the *News at Ten* format with Johnson-Smith and Christopher Chataway as anchormen reading short newsy snippets which attacked the Labour record. The format included 'commercial breaks' which were repeated in successive PEBs:

> We couldn't buy commercials but there was nothing that said we couldn't put them into our own programmes – the party political broadcasts.
>
> The essence of a TV commercial is its single-minded simplicity. One commercial showed a £1 note – shades of Wilson's 'pound in your pocket' – being brutally attacked by a pair of scissors. As each segment was snipped away, a voice-over stated the date and depleted value of the pound, ending with the inescapable fact that the continuation of Labour policies would lead to the ten-bob pound.
>
> Another showed a woman's hand taking a block of ice from a domestic fridge. Embedded in the ice was a frozen wage packet. Labour gave it to you last time. Vote for them and you'll get it again – in the family economy size.[87]

The Tory campaign team called it the 'Shopping Basket Election', convinced that the issues of prices and wages would decide the outcome. As the campaign progressed and the polls still looked gloomy, they decided to target attention towards the working-class housewife. 'She'd never had it so bad,' as Day put it. One PEB included an interview with a working-class woman, Sylvia, and her 'unprompted' complaints: 'the knife went in when Sylvia declared that, although her husband would probably vote Labour again because of his family voting tradition, she most certainly would not'.[88]

Because the Tories came from behind in the polls to win the election, 1970 seems to present itself as one of the few examples of a campaign making a decisive impact. Most polls gave Labour a lead of between 2 and 7 per cent in late May

Table 1.3 The general election of 18 June 1970

	Con	Lab	Lib	Other	Total
Seats					
At dissolution	264	346	13	7	630
After election	330	287	6	7	630
Votes					
% of total	46.4	43.0	7.5	3.1	
% change 1966–70	+4.5	–4.9	–1.0	+1.4	

Conservative overall majority 30
Turnout 72.0%

when the election was called, but the Tories emerged with a lead of more than 3 per cent in the voting figures (see Table 1.3). But the polls were notoriously off-target in 1970. Only one organisation, ORC, which incidentally conducted private polls for the Conservatives, predicted a Tory victory and even then its final forecast projected a slender 1 per cent lead. There was substantial variation in the other polls: Gallup and Marplan's final surveys gave Labour leads of 7 and 8.7 per cent, respectively. Apart from ORC, only Harris was remotely close. The polls' poor performances have been explained by a number of factors, varying from methodological error to a last-minute swing to the Conservatives – an almost exact forerunner of the post-1992 poll debate.[89] The errors compound the normal difficulties of assessing the impact of a campaign. The 1970 campaign was the last innovative electioneering until Thatcher took over the reins of the Tory party. Once in power, Heath tended to neglect publicity matters. Barry Day complained:

> It is all too easy for the party that wins an election to feel itself 'sanctified' by winning and becoming government. Too easy to forget what got it there and to lose some of its *political* edge, to allow itself to be shut off from certain realities that it understood perfectly well on the way to winning. What a party does in government is also legitimately *party* political ammunition too when an election comes around.
> If any conventional advertiser *stopped* advertising when he

had a brand leader on the market, his competitors would think he was mad. And they would have a point.

Advertising does not work properly on an *ad hoc* basis. Anyone who thinks it does is really saying they don't believe in advertising. The Tory party forgot a lot of things by 1974 that it had learned in 1970. It stopped putting its case. (Author's emphasis)[90]

The February 1974 election, prompted by the miners' strike, resulted inconclusively in a Labour minority government. The Tories' campaign was notable mostly for its clumsiness and the mishandling of the 'who governs?' theme. The October 1974 election brought Labour an overall majority of three. The most striking feature of these campaigns was the rise of the Liberals, up nearly 12 per cent to some 19 per cent of the vote. The Conservatives' share of the vote slumped at the October poll to its lowest point of the century.

2 The Rise of Thatcher: Political Marketing's Quantum Leap

> The papers are full of Margaret Thatcher. She has lent herself with grace and charm to every piece of photographer's gimmickry, but don't we all when the prize is big enough?
>
> Barbara Castle, *The Castle Diaries 1974–76*,
> 5 February 1975

Margaret Thatcher was elected leader of the Conservative Party on 11 February 1975. Her election, as first woman leader of a major British political party, was an outcome that few predicted even a few months previously. The Conservative Party had been in open disarray since its ignominious defeat a year previously in the 'Who governs?' general election of February 1974. Norman Tebbit's autobiography, *Upwardly Mobile*, makes no attempt to hide the humiliation many right-wing Tories felt at Heath's policy U-turns, electoral tactics and unsuccessful attempt to cobble together a coalition with the Liberals.[1] Mrs Thatcher, however, was few people's ideal candidate for the leadership. Patrick Cosgrave, then of the *Spectator* and later a part-time writer for Mrs Thatcher and her biographer, was one of the first to champion her cause in an article soon after the February 1974 general election. Thatcher was apparently embarrassed at the suggestion.[2] Her own loyalty was to Sir Keith Joseph, and she did not believe that a woman leader would be acceptable to the party. 'I don't see it happening in my time,' she said in an oft-cited answer to a reporter from the *Liverpool Daily Post* in June 1974.

Joseph withdrew from the leadership race in November 1974, and on the same day as he told Thatcher of his decision she sought an audience with Heath and informed him of her intention to stand.[3] Even then few took her candidacy seriously. She was relatively inexperienced, her only Cabinet experience was as a somewhat unpopular Education Secretary, she had no particularly high reputation for dazzling performance in the

60

House of Commons, nor any great popularity with backbench MPs, with whom she rarely mixed. Her campaign only picked up momentum in January 1975 after the right's favoured candidate, Edward Du Cann, refused to put himself forward, and Airey Neave, the unofficial campaign manager of the right, switched his attentions to Thatcher.

Thatcher was to govern for more than 11 years, enjoying for most of that time a reputation as a strong and resolute prime minister, so it is instructive to recall just how unstatesmanlike she appeared as a leadership candidate. 'She epitomised to many the shrill Home Counties woman,' according to Wapshott and Brock.[4] 'You can't mean the blonde from North Finchley in those bloody stupid hats,' was the reaction from Fleet Street colleagues to columnist Jean Rook's prediction in 1974 that Thatcher would become PM.[5] To anyone north of the Trent she might as well have come from Mars; she was 'limited, bossy, self-righteous and self-complacent', according to Woodrow Wyatt (*Sunday Mirror*, 9 February 1975), who converted into a Thatcher admirer in later years. As Education Secretary in Heath's government she had become 'THE MOST UNPOPU-LAR WOMAN IN BRITAIN' (*The Sun*, 25 November 1971) and was long remembered as the Milk Snatcher for restricting free school milk. The search to develop an image both suitably authoritative and feminine was not resolved until she became the Iron Lady.

It has been common speculation that Mrs Thatcher's sex, her realisation of both its disadvantages and potential advantages, and the knowledge that her appearance would attract far more comment than her male rivals, was a significant incentive to pay more than usual attention to presentation. Max Atkinson (1988) suggests that the humming exercises she eventually took to deepen her voice, under the guidance of a tutor at the National Theatre, were a rational response to a real problem. According to Atkinson, women have a specific public speaking handicap caused by the length of female vocal chords and the higher pitch of the female voice:

> Pitch can pose problems for all public speakers, whatever their sex, because it tends to rise when a speaker is nervous or speaks louder than usual, both of which are likely to happen in oratory. For women, however, the problem is

more acute because the natural pitch of their voices has a higher starting-point than is the case for men, and therefore cannot rise as far before reaching a level at which it sounds excessively 'shrill'. This might not matter were it not for the fact that high-pitched vocalizations tend to be strongly associated with emotional or irrational outbursts . . .[6]

Not especially experienced or comfortable in front of the television cameras, it was equally rational for her to enlist the advice of television experts.[7] Moreover Gordon Reece suggested that women in general are more receptive to cosmetic advice, and therefore better clients for the image-maker.[8] However, the gender factor should not be overplayed because clearly it would be ridiculous to suggest that there is something uniquely feminine about political concern with presentation and appearance. Self-evidently, it is not a function of gender: Bill Clinton, George Bush, Ronald Reagan and Harold Wilson are just four modern male examples of the preoccupation with appearance and body language.

Barbara Castle's diary references to Thatcher, a large proportion of which refer to image, offer sharp insight into Thatcher's use of 'femininity' as a marketing asset. She notes that, while the newly-elected Thatcher was flexing her leadership muscle by sacking Michael Wolff, Heath's former adviser, from Conservative Central Office, she was simultaneously projecting a soft, feminine image on television: 'our people tell me that Margaret's party political broadcast last night was such a sweetly calculated bit of femininity it was nauseating'.[9]

Before her election as leader, Thatcher turned to (Sir) Gordon Reece for media advice. Reece was a freelance television producer, whose experience spanned ITN and religious programmes, as well as the Dave Allen, Bruce Forsyth and Eamonn Andrews shows. He had been part of Heath's Thursday Group of media consultants in 1970, when Thatcher's inept camera style scuppered a planned party election broadcast. Advertising professional Barry Day, also a part of the Thursday team, recalled:

In 1970 she was filmed in a park, where she was surrounded by kids going up and down slides screaming. Margaret looked extremely out of touch. She was saying, 'I believe you should have a choice for your children,' and gave the impression she hoped they wouldn't be sick all over her dress. She was very ill at ease with the camera and the children: it was amateur night. But she was clever enough to ask for help. Margaret wanted to learn while most of the rest of the senior Tories wished television would just go away.[10]

Reece rendered his services to the Tories again in 1974 and worked with Thatcher on her PEBs, which this time were proficient enough to be broadcast. In February 1975 he took leave from his job at EMI to assist Thatcher's leadership campaign; together with BBC presenter Cliff Michelmore, he had formed a cassette company which was taken over by EMI.[11] Newspapers commented on the fact that the formerly stiff Thatcher appeared more confident and relaxed on television and Reece was attributed with most of the credit.[12] Reece was also credited with the shrewd decision to keep her off a *Panorama* programme which had invited all the second-ballot Tory leadership candidates to present their views. Instead she gave full access to her Flood Street home for a profile by Granada's *World in Action* which was transmitted on the same evening as *Panorama.* According to one of her campaign team, *World in Action* was worth 20 votes for her.[13]

Reece's contribution to her election was seen as significant, although its importance should be set beside Neave's campaign which was certainly the decisive influence. All accounts of the leadership struggle credit Neave's strategy and tactics for her surprise victory. But Reece came to be seen as something of a Svengali to Mrs Thatcher. He was credited not only with helping her television appearances but also with changing her image, altering her hairstyle and clothes, and encouraging her to develop a deeper, slower, more authoritative voice. The view of his key role in moulding her appearance has survived even into sober portraits of Thatcher, such as Hugo Young's biography. Reece has rarely spoken publicly about his working relationship with Mrs Thatcher, but has denied influence on her dress or hairstyle:

Privately, however, he was deeply offended by the image of himself as Mrs Thatcher's private Norman Hartnell, 'mincing around with a strategic powder puff', as the *Telegraph* put it. He had not redone her hair; she had done that herself advised by people more expert than he was. Nor had he softened her voice. What he *had* done was to urge her to act naturally, relax more in front of the cameras, follow her own political instincts. He had certainly schooled her in speaking to the microphone, getting her to slow down and talk more deliberately . . . 'It was really straightforward editing stuff,' says one of the people involved. 'He corrected her as a director would correct any performer, making her redo things, showing her how to act in front of the camera.'[14]

Reece's personal style contributed to his own growing reputation in Fleet Street. Slight, dapper, kitted out in well-cut suits, always adorned with a watch-chain and matching ties and handkerchief, he was rarely seen without a cigar and had a well-reported taste for drinking only expensive champagne.[15] Reece was born in Liverpool in 1930, the son of a car salesman. He went to a Roman Catholic school, where one of his seniors was Norman St John Stevas, who apparently once reported him to the headmaster for alleged atheism. However Reece confesses himself a devout Catholic and has reportedly forecast a religious revival: 'religion is the coming thing, people are ready for it'.[16] He studied law at Cambridge, worked on provincial newspapers, including the *Liverpool Daily Post*, before breaking into television in the 1960s. Hugo Young notes of him that, as a putative Svengali, Reece appeared surprisingly nervy and insecure:

> He once confided to me that he had been the recipient of that rarest of contrivances, a Thatcher joke. 'If we lose the election I may be sacked,' she told him in the spring of 1978. 'But you will be shot.'[17]

David Boddy, director of communications at Conservative Central Office during 1981–83, casts Reece's influence over Mrs Thatcher in a more mundane light. His most important role in the 1983 election campaign was as cheerleader, Boddy suggested. 'He kept her cheerful, which was very important but he did not do much apart from that. He told her it was all going splendidly.'[18] Reece's most enduring work came at Conservative Central Office (CCO) which was reorganised following Mrs Thatcher's assumption of the leadership mantle.

REVAMPING PARTY PUBLICITY

Mireille Babaz (1977) noted that the great part of British political campaigning escaped the control of the marketing experts: Party Election Broadcasts (PEBs), canvassing, election addresses, manifestoes, election tours, press conferences and party conferences were all handled by the politicians directly or by party activists. The professional advertisers' input was restricted to press advertising, posters, leaflets and technical advice on the use of television.[19] The period from 1978, marked by the appointment of Reece, witnessed the spreading influence of media and presentation experts. Ten years later publicity experts were closely involved in research, formulating overall electoral strategy within which the manifesto would fit, planning election tours, party and press conference themes and presentation, and party political broadcasts. This transformation was pioneered by the Conservatives. Mrs Thatcher's personal interest in presentation provided the springboard, but Gordon Reece's appointment was the key. Later appointments, of Harvey Thomas (presentation) and Christopher Lawson (marketing) at CCO, advanced the process, as we shall see.

Gordon Reece was appointed Director of Publicity in March 1978 and one of his first decisions, and his most important, was to hire Saatchi & Saatchi. The Conservatives had engaged the services of advertising agencies before, of course, the most celebrated liaison being with Colman, Prentis & Varley, which had run the first major political advertising campaign outside an election campaign proper in 1957/58. However, for the 1970 election and subsequently, Heath had preferred to seek individual help from volunteers. While their work had been considered strong and influential in 1970 it was not deemed as effective in the two losing campaigns of 1974. Reece believed the volunteer approach carried with it inherent pitfalls: the lines of command were more easily blurred, and there was a tendency for a well-meaning group to turn into an unwieldy committee:

> I've always thought the committee approach to running a political campaign is a very bad idea. One of the reasons is that they're all chiefs and there isn't a single Indian there.

And when you end up trying to get rid of someone it's the Battle of Hastings, because he resigns in a huff and you have to explain it to the newspapers and it becomes a major cause célèbre. If you've got an agency, you simply tell the managing director to change a chap because you don't get on with him and he is changed.[20]

THE SAATCHI CONNECTION

Reece sought a British agency, which ruled out most of the London shops at that time. He wanted one sufficiently established to have a reputation but ambitious enough to be hungry. He approached Saatchis, told them that he had two agencies in mind for the Tory account, and asked them if they were interested. Maurice Saatchi responded, 'We would like it very much; and we are all Conservatives.'[21] In fact, Reece had pretty much decided on Saatchis. He considered briefly Masius Wynne-Williams, but their creative reputation did not run as high as Saatchis.

The name of Saatchi first came to public attention with the 'pregnant man' poster for the Health Education Council (HEC) in 1970.[22] Saatchi & Saatchi had only just come into existence as a full agency; until 1970 it was a partnership, Cramer Saatchi, with Ross Cramer and Charles Saatchi. The partnership had won the then not insubstantial £100 000 anti-smoking campaign from the HEC, and the HEC then sought to take on Cramer Saatchi as its full-time agency. This contract, together with the 'Jaffa' brands account for the Citrus Marketing Broad of Israel, was transforming Cramer Saatchi from a consultancy into a fully-fledged, if small, advertising agency. Cramer did not want to be part of just another of the many small agencies in London, and he left to become a freelance director of television commercials. Charles brought in his younger brother Maurice, who had graduated from the London School of Economics and had been working as a junior executive for Michael Heseltine's Haymarket publishing company. Charles Saatchi was 27, and Maurice 25, when they registered Saatchi & Saatchi and Company in August 1970. Among their backers were Mary Quant and Michael Heseltine, although the latter link did not survive long.

The new agency began with four working directors who were all to become renowned characters in the advertising world: the Saatchi brothers, John Hegarty (who was later to found his own agency, Bartle Bogle and Hegarty) and Tim Bell, who was hired from Geers Gross agency to be Saatchi's media director. Saatchi & Saatchi's first offices were in the West End's Golden Square, and they started out with five copywriters, of whom Jeremy Sinclair would become closely involved with the Conservative campaigns. The agency's growing reputation was built not only on the quality of its 'creative' advertising, although indeed that was admired, but also through the public relations efforts of Charles Saatchi on his company's behalf. Journalist Philip Kleinman describes how the 'pregnant man' advertisement, picturing an apparently heavily pregnant young man over the caption 'Would you be more careful if it was you that got pregnant?', was milked for publicity value:

> Even today, when asked their opinion of the Saatchi's group's creative record, many advertisers mention the 'pregnant man', a commercially insignificant item produced by a small agency many years ago. It is doubtful whether the ad did anything to reduce the rate of illegitimate births, which was the objective of the client organisation. There is no doubt whatever that it did a wonderful job of selling Saatchi & Saatchi.[23]

The Saatchi empire began quietly enough with the acquisition of a number of small agencies: E.G. Dawes (Manchester), Notley Advertising and George J. Smith. Then in 1975 they merged with Compton UK Partners, a publicly-quoted advertising group whose main operating division was the London agency, Garland-Compton. The group ranked as the eleventh biggest agency in the country when the Saatchis made an audacious offer which allowed them to take control of the larger company. By 1976, the new agency, Saatchi & Saatchi Garland-Compton, ranked seventh in the annual billings league table of agencies. Both by absolute size and creative reputation it was growing. By 1978 a survey of client companies voted it the most creative agency.[24]

At the time Gordon Reece approached them, neither of the Saatchi brothers was politically active nor had any particularly

strong political preferences. Tim Bell, however, was an active
Conservative who had canvassed for Iain Macleod, Reginald
Maudling and Margaret Thatcher, although he had not met
her. He had also worked for Colman, Prentis and Varley during 1961–3, while they still had the Tory account. Ironically
Bell was the most cautious of the three at the prospect of
being so closely linked with the Conservatives:

> I knew perfectly well it would fall to me to run the business
> because Charles and Maurice didn't handle accounts. I reck-
> oned it would be tremendously disruptive and I didn't think
> it was worth any money. I was just vaguely negative about the
> whole thing, but they were extremely enthusiastic, particu-
> larly because Gordon Reece was asking us to take on the
> account without our even having to make a pitch.[25]

Although it was the name of Saatchi & Saatchi which profited
out of its association with the Conservatives, in reality the brothers rarely met Mrs Thatcher or indeed anyone from Conservative Central Office outside election time. According to Fallon's
account, Charles Saatchi made a point of not meeting clients
and he did not make an exception for Mrs Thatcher.[26] As Bell
predicted, the regular running of the account was left to him,
although Charles Saatchi helped Jeremy Sinclair and Bell with
the creative work. At first Bell's relations with CCO were much
as though it was any normal commercial client:

> The Tories were good clients in the beginning because they
> let the professionals get on with it. They were better than
> business clients because in those days they hadn't learned
> how to be bad clients. They employed professionals and let
> them do their job. Mrs Thatcher took the view that com-
> munication was important. She wrote me a letter saying that
> people will say there is something immoral about using an
> advertising agency in this way. She has got past the stage of
> whether it should or shouldn't happen. The fact is it does.[27]

The Saatchis were asked to take control of all advertising,
posters, press and broadcasting, including party broadcasts,
and were also asked to develop a communications strategy.
They were given access to virtually any piece of party policy or
research they requested.[28]

Bell was briefed by the party chairman, Lord Thorneycroft, that an election was likely that autumn, 1978, and warned that summertime in general, especially when the weather is good, tended to boost the popularity of the government. Thorneycroft, therefore, wanted an aggressive campaign to run from mid-summer.[29] The Saatchi team went to work on their new account much as they would any other; its first task was to research consumers' emotional reaction to the 'product' and then to reduce the client's objectives and most logical appeals to their simplest elements. Bell produced a presentation for Thorneycroft and Reece which, he believed, differentiated the Conservative from Labour at a fundamental, emotional level.[30] A vote for the Conservatives stood for freedom, opportunity, choice, individual responsibility and the creation of wealth. A vote for Labour was a vote for collectivism: restricted opportunity, controlled choice and the redistribution of wealth.

> The notion was that if you asked people what a vote for the Tories means, they would snap out with an answer which in some ways reflects these associations. We were not talking about incomes policies, or tax cuts, or industrial relations legislation, or public expenditure. We were talking about the emotional meaning of a Conservative vote.[31]

According to Bell, this presentation provided the basic communications strategy for the campaign of that year running into the following year's election. This emphasis on voters' emotional reactions led Saatchi to concentrate on the tone of the advertising, because tone would probably be its single most important feature:

> We wanted a tone which was warm, confident, non-divisive – and exciting . . . 'Warmth' just means talking with people rather than to them. The Conservative Party has long been perceived as a cold and unsympathetic party. This needed to be changed. 'Confidence', on the other hand, was an attribute we worked to re-create. Looking at the research over the previous twenty years we found that the Conservative Party had lost its position as the party ranked by the electorate as the most competent and confident. It was, therefore, essential for us to talk in a confident tone as though we knew that Conservative policies would work.

'Non-divisive', because a national appeal does actually reach further and deeper than a party appeal . . . 'Exciting', because we felt that politics had become unbelievably tedious and boring. Here after all was an election which could result in Britain's first woman Prime Minister. That was a rather exciting thought and we thought it would not hurt to make the whole approach exciting.[32]

Saatchi's stress on the general emotional appeal, rather than particular policy aspects, led them to engage more heavily in qualitative, motivational research rather than quantitative surveys. Saatchi imported qualitative marketing research direct from the commercial world: unlike quantitative research it does not attempt to produce statistically measurable results. It relies on focus group discussion and in-depth interviews with voters in target groups. In the commercial field it is used widely at the stage of product development to gain an early indication of consumer reactions. In advertising, it is frequently used to test copy before it is released. Saatchi tested campaign ideas on small discussion groups which were filmed 'so that we could read the faces as well as the words'.[33]

The extensive use of qualitative surveys was one of the major contributions the agency offered to Conservative campaigning. One of CCO's in-house polling advisers identified the use and sophistication of qualitative research as the most significant change he had seen in his years of service with the party.[34] The party, hitherto, had relied almost entirely on quantitative polling, even for research into the image dimensions of the party's standing in the electorate. The greater reliance on focus groups simultaneously increased the importance of the Saatchis, who had effective control over the qualitative analysis.

THE PRE-CAMPAIGN

Saatchi's first public work for the Tories was a party political broadcast (PPB) in the spring of 1978. PPBs rejoiced in a terminally dull reputation and had an impressive capacity for losing audiences.[35] Saatchi tried to stir interest with advertisements in the tabloid press, teasing that if you missed television at 9 o'clock that night you might regret it for the rest of your life. Apart from the extravagance of the claim, the use of advertisements in this way, to publicise future publicity, was new and audacious in British politics. The Saatchis have used the technique again and in different ways, most notably to draw attention to the 1986 party conference theme, The Next Moves Forward.

The PPB itself was scripted by Jeremy Sinclair and showed an image of Britain going backwards: commuters were seen walking backwards over Waterloo Bridge, Stephenson's Rocket thundered backwards and so on. An actor's voice spoke the lines:

> This country was once the finest nation on earth. We were famous for our freedom, justice and fair play. Our inventions brought the world out of the Middle Ages to industrial prosperity. Today we are famous for discouraging people from getting to the top. Famous for not rewarding skill, talent and effort. In a word, Britain is going backward.

Saatchi's work on the PPBs was groundbreaking in that the script was written by the advertisers and approved by the politicians; normally broadcasts had been scripted by the politicians and the professionals brought in afterwards to spice up presentation. Reece persuaded Lord Thorneycroft and Mrs Thatcher that the professional communicators should be entrusted with the message.[36]

Whatever the audience effect of this broadcast, it certainly ruffled Labour. Edward Booth-Clibborn, chairman of the Designers and Art Directors' Association (D&ADA), was head of a team of volunteers helping Labour which submitted a strategy document warning that Saatchi had changed the ground rules:

> We had said to the party: look, the name of the game has changed. You can no longer cut to a picture of a lathe every time you talk about industrial relations or to an old-age pensioner every time you talk about a caring, sharing society. Those days have gone. You have to start thinking about the approach used in Tory PPBs and you must borrow some of their techniques. At the very least, you must

acknowledge that the Conservative broadcasts are going to condition people to expect different things from party political broadcasts.[37]

The Saatchis welcomed Labour's objections to their commercial approach, because it drew more attention to their work. Their first PPB has probably been long forgotten, yet one Saatchi pre-campaign poster, 'Labour isn't working', remains the most memorable political advertising carried out by the agency. It depicted a queue snaking into the distance outside an unemployment office under the banner 'Labour isn't working'. The pay-off line, 'Britain's better off with the Conservatives' had echoes of their 1959 winning slogan, 'Life's Better with the Conservatives', a variation of which was to be used again in the 1987 campaign. It was posted on only about 20 sites nationally but the protest it provoked was probably worth millions to the Conservatives in free advertising. It was the summer 'silly season' for newspapers and the story made front page news; moreover it was so closely identified with the Saatchis that it became a kind of strap-head on many subsequent articles about the election campaign. Denis Healey complained that the dole queue was a fraud made up in reality of Saatchi employees. Saatchi denied it but Bell later revealed that they were Young Conservatives from South Hendon.[38]

Bell has since called 'Labour isn't working' one of the most effective political posters in history.[39] Again, as with virtually all publicity, it is impossible to estimate with any precision its effect on voters. However Labour did not make headway in the polls over the summer. By September they were between 2 and 7 points behind the Conservatives and Callaghan decided against an autumn election.[40] His decision was cheered at CCO where Gordon Reece believed it was a triumph for the summer campaign.[41]

The verdict of Willie Whitelaw's memoirs, that Callaghan had surrendered his best opportunity of victory, has become the orthodoxy.[42] Certainly Labour went ahead of the Conservatives in October and November according to Gallup polls and they also fared well in the Berwick by-election. However from December the Tories took a lead which they did not relinquish, as is shown by Table 2.1.

Table 2.1　Voting intention, Oct. 1978–May 1979

	Con	Lab	Lib	Other
Oct. 1978	42	47	7	3
Nov.	43	48	6	3
Dec.	48	42	6	3
Jan. 1979	49	41	6	3
Feb.	53	33	11	3
March	51	37	8	3
April	50	40	8	2
May	43	41	13	2

Source: Gallup.[43]

THE WINTER OF DISCONTENT AND ITS IMPACT

In November 1978, Ford workers breached the government's pay policy and opened the floodgates to a series of disputes: in early 1979 as many as one and a half million workers were at times on strike against the government's pay policy. Donoughue, policy adviser to Callaghan, believes that the strikes were squarely responsible for Labour's defeat in May 1979. It was the result of a series of self-inflicted wounds and had very little to do with the Conservative Opposition, whom Donoughue dismissed as ineffectual:

> The Conservative Opposition never inflicted any serious damage on the Government during 1974–79. Although Labour was in a parliamentary minority throughout most of the time, nobody in No 10 ever worried about the attacks from the Conservative Party opposite. Mr Callaghan certainly always dominated Mrs Thatcher in the Commons, even at the end when he fatalistically seemed to accept imminent defeat.[44]

For Tony Benn and the Labour left wing, the government lost because the leadership deserted its political base; it clung on to power with Tory policies that were close to being anti-working class.[45] However, from both left and right wings of the party, the view took root that Labour's defeat resulted from self-inflicted wounds.

The weapon was handed to them but the Conservatives did not fail to capitalise on the Winter of Discontent and the images of the uncollected refuse piled high in the streets, of health workers picketing hospitals and grave diggers refusing to bury the dead. On 17 January 1979 Mrs Thatcher did a straight-to-camera party broadcast, a complete change of style since Saatchis' involvement, and one which for the first time was not scripted by the agency. She used the broadcast to announce new proposals for trade union law reform, including no-strike agreements in essential industries and the taxation of supplementary benefits for strikers. Mrs Thatcher's own standing and her party's popularity improved as public resentment of the strikes increased.[46]

Moreover the Winter of Discontent provided a golden opportunity for the Tories to reach a vital group of target voters, the skilled workers or C2 social group, who had suffered an erosion of traditional pay differentials during the years of the Social Contract. Saatchi research indicated that tax cuts and a return to free collective bargaining would prove powerful incentives for this group.[47] Saatchi placed a double-spread advertisement in all the popular daily papers. Under the headline in bold capitals, 'WHY EVERY TRADE UNIONIST SHOULD CONSIDER VOTING CONSERVATIVE', it was a highly unusual advertisement in that two pages were devoted to text and argument. It presented a well-argued case that the 'working man' had fared better in years of Tory rule, 'the average worker has been 10 times better off with the Conservatives'.

The copy won advertising awards and is a fine example of the Saatchis' 'emotional' approach in action. It assaulted the gut feeling that the Labour Party was the natural home for the 'working man'; it adopted a confident and non-divisive tone – Labour was well-intentioned but destined to fail because of its class war philosophy; and it attempted warmth – the working man was better off *with* the Conservatives, not *under* Conservative government; trade unionists wanted better social services, schools, housing and freedom from government interference in pay bargaining, all Conservative ideals.[48] The drive for the skilled worker vote was followed up in a party political broadcast, again advertised with a teaser in the popular press: 'Trade Unionists. Confront your television at 9.00 tonight.'

As the winter deepened, the Saatchis tried to catch the mood of the electorate it believed was tired of a government clinging to office by its fingertips. They ran a poster: 'CHEER UP! LABOUR CAN'T HANG ON FOR EVER. Britain's better off with the Conservatives.' According to Bell, this was a classic example of good communication, expressing a serious message in a 'simple, amusing and involving way'.[49]

The end of the Labour administration was signalled in March following the collapse of the government's devolution plans for Wales and Scotland. Thatcher tabled a motion of no confidence which won by a single vote on the night of 28 March. It was the first time since the Second World War that a government had fallen on a censure motion.

THE 1979 GENERAL ELECTION

The Conservative Manifesto

When Thatcher moved into Downing Street she was perceived widely as the most right-wing leader of the most right-wing Conservative government since the war.[50] Yet the 1979 Conservative Manifesto demonstrated 'surprising sogginess', to borrow the words of political commentator Hugo Young.[51] It appeared a continuation and compromise with the policies of Heath, although it avoided the relative abundance of detail and specifics of Heath's manifestoes.

It drew heavily on two mid-term strategy documents: *The Right Approach* (1976) and *The Right Approach to the Economy* (1977). The first, written by Chris Patten and Angus Maude of the Research Department, emphasised balance and cautious realism and value for public money, and early drafts were checked with Heath.[52] The second was scarcely less consensual, although reflecting the importance newly ascribed to the money supply. It sought compromise between the radical and moderate wings of the party on incomes policies; it disapproved of statutory control but did not rule out a pay policy. It was committed to reforms of the law on picketing, the closed shop and strikers' rights to benefits, but embraced some of the consensual, corporatist notions which were later seen as the antithesis of Thatcherism. Hence it promised open discussion with employers and unions on the government's economic objectives. Privatisation, which after ten years of government became the single most distinctive Thatcherite policy, was mentioned only in the commitment to denationalise (as it was then termed) National Freight.

Veteran election-watchers Butler and Kavanagh were struck by the 'divergence between image and substance', between the rhetoric which made Thatcher appear as the most ideological, right-wing, aggressive post-war leader, and the actions which demonstrated the durability of the R.A. Butler One Nation group thinking.[53] The contrast between the tough talk and the more compromising reality was explained in terms of the tension between her free-market instincts, on the one hand, and her natural tactical caution, on the other.[54] The combination of tough talk and pragmatic action was thus a compromise.

However her particular mixture of strong leadership and economic prudence exactly matched a strategic analysis of the opinion polls. Crewe and Sarlvik's analysis of British Election Study data concluded that the Conservative Party's optimal appeal would 'combine moderation on the conventional bread-and-butter issues with a firm reassertion of traditional values on the more exotic authoritarian–populist issues'.[55] Crime and immigration, two issues about which Thatcher adopted a particularly firm tone, found the electorate well to the right of the ideological middle ground.

There was thus no contradiction, or even irony, about the dual perception of Thatcher on the eve of the election: on the one hand as the Iron Lady; on the other, the marketed, packaged politician. It would be stretching the point to suggest that 'marketing' dictated her deliberate stance as a tough leader. Doubtless this suited her instincts, but it also matched perfectly the Conservatives' market research. In the words of one of her Downing Street aides, Mrs Thatcher studied the polls with more care than any previous leader.[56] Biographers Wapshott and Brock suggested that Mrs Thatcher's controversial public statement early in 1978 about immigrants swamping the indigenous population was not at all a spontaneous remark, but rather a calculated response to the polls which had been discussed in Shadow Cabinet.[57]

Campaign Strategy

The general election was called for 3 May and the Conservatives entered the contest needing to gain at least 34 seats for an absolute majority. They had been ahead in the polls since December (see Table 2.1 above) and entered the campaign proper well on course for victory with a 10-point lead over Labour (50 per cent – 40 per cent). The expectation that they would win, barring unforeseen catastrophe, shaped the campaign strategy. It was a holding operation, designed to minimise the chances of mistakes, and to capitalise on the disenchantment with Labour. Thus, even though the period from dissolution to polling day, five weeks, was exceptionally long, the Conservatives restricted themselves to a relatively short and late campaign, not starting any substantial electioneering publicity until just two-and-a-half weeks before polling day. They did not launch their manifesto until 11 April, fully one week after Labour had unveiled theirs, and Mr Callaghan had already spent a week speech-making around the country before Mrs Thatcher's tour got under way. They were to repeat the pattern of late and short campaigns in the 1983 and 1987 elections.

The Leaders' Campaigns

The notion of 'Margaret the Marketed' took a firm grip during the course of the 1979 election campaign. To many observers the election seemed more of a media event and less of a political argument than previous polls. Thatcher's campaign 'moved closer to American techniques of packaging a presidential candidate and projecting an image than had ever been seen before in Britain', according to *Panorama* reporter Michael Cockerell, who has been the most prominent of the journalistic investigators into the marketing methods of British politicians.[58] A variety of observers agreed with his verdict. Adam Raphael of the *Observer* penned an article, 'The Selling of Maggie', during the height of the campaign (22 April) drawing attention to the role and influence of Gordon Reece. Butler and Kavanagh noted the increasing frequency of snide journalistic comments about the stage-managed pseudo-events of the Thatcher campaign.[59]

Ironically Callaghan conducted a campaign that was more truly presidential in the sense that it was the leader's personal team, rather than the party organisation, which was the dominant force.[60] The entire Labour campaign revolved around Callaghan, whose popularity advantage over Thatcher was treated as Labour's most significant electoral asset. He ran his campaign from Downing Street with a small group of advisers and speech-writers, and the Labour party organisation at Transport House was effectively bypassed. He enlisted volunteer media expertise from Edward Booth-Clibborn and Tim Delaney to prepare advertisements and PEBs, sometimes to the dismay of party officials at Transport House.

For all the presidential parallels of his campaign structure, Callaghan nevertheless scorned the American-style gimmickry of the Thatcher campaign. In marked contrast, he did not appear to make any special efforts to please the cameras:

> Callaghan would often exclude the cameras altogether from his meetings with the faithful in Labour committee rooms. Alternatively he would insist on silent filming, with the boom mikes left outside. 'Jim's style was to treat his tour as a private affair between himself and the electorate, making no concession to the television-age razzamatazz adopted by the publicity men at Conservative Central Office,' said Michael Sullivan, the BBC reporter assigned to follow Callaghan. 'It's not my style,' the Prime Minister would say as he turned down yet another plea from the cameramen for an interesting picture, 'if I do, I'll seem as phoney as she does'.[61]

However behind Thatcher's apparently gimmicky presentational techniques was deadly serious purpose. The problem facing the Tory campaign managers was that Thatcher entered the race as an electoral weakness. Her personal rating in the polls was some seven points below Callaghan's.[62] She was relatively inexperienced against the far more authoritative personality of the prime minister. She did not cut a sympathetic dash even among many Tory supporters. The associate editor of the *Sunday Telegraph*, Peregrine Worsthorne, for instance, found her inflexible and intolerant and contrary to the Conservative traditions.[63] Labour campaign leaders marked her as a weakness and potentially their best hope. The unusually lengthy campaign period was partly a political tactic: it would give

Thatcher plenty of rope to hang herself and plenty of time to lose her speech-making voice, or her nerve, or to perpetrate an exploitably extremist gaffe.[64] Callaghan had used his ministerial broadcast of 29 March not only to announce the election but also to sow the seeds of fear at the prospect of a right-wing Tory government 'tearing everything up by the roots'.

Anticipating the personal pressure that was likely to be placed on Thatcher's shoulders, both by Labour and by the media, it was a rational Tory response to seek a relatively quiet, short-run, safety first operation designed to hang on to the overall lead they had. Apart from the candidates' rally, she made only 12 campaign speeches, compared to Callaghan's 20. She set a deliberately 'non-divisive' tone in her reply to Callaghan's ministerial broadcast, which she made on 2 April, a few days later than originally planned because of the death of Airey Neave. 'Mr Callaghan tried to frighten you with a picture of the Conservatives tearing everything up by the roots. But we are the party of tradition. Paying your way is not tearing things up by the roots. Paying your way is good husbandry . . .' In this campaign, as in all previous ones since 1959, television was the dominant medium. Since her campaign to become leader of the party, Thatcher had taken advice from Gordon Reece about appearances on television. Reece had commissioned polls after her early broadcasts which showed that many people found her too shrill, austere, school-marmish and aggressive, although she also came across as sincere. He advised her to appear on certain programmes and avoid others, drawing up an 'enemies' list' of interviewers whose combative approach might entice Mrs Thatcher into responding too aggressively. He also suggested broadening the range of outlets, for example, *Jim'll Fix It*, in 1977 (and the *Jimmy Young Show* and *Desert Island Discs* on radio) to reach the Tory target audience of housewives and skilled workers.[65]

Reece's sharp sense of the importance of appearance and image stemmed partly from his expertise as a television director and partly from his knowledge of the 1976 Carter–Ford USA presidential contest which he had studied at close quarters. Reece imported from the USA the concept of the 'photo-opportunity': placing the candidate in 'telegenic' backgrounds, with the aim of providing novel pictures for the cameras in settings designed to enhance the image of the candidate. Thus the Thatcher tour was calculated to place Mrs Thatcher in environments where she would seem warm and womanly, making off-the-cuff remarks picked up by the boom mike and mixing easily with ordinary people. Her tour took in Leicester, where she cut her own dress pattern in a factory; she had her heart and lungs tested on a monitoring machine in Milton Keynes; she donned white overalls and hat to coat chocolates at Bournville; and most famously she cuddled a new-born calf for 15 minutes on a farm in Suffolk.

Reece advised that a minute's coverage on the television news was worth virtually the whole of a current affairs interview, advice which she took to heart, according to her admiring biographer Patrick Cosgrave.[66] When reporters, assigned to her tour, complained that they were being squeezed out in favour of the photographers at yet another photo-opportunity, she replied: 'It's not for me, it's for the cameramen, they are the most important people on this campaign.'[67] The pains Reece took to present the desired image were evident in his attitude towards the television climax of the campaign, Granada's *The Great Debate*, which featured the three party leaders taking questions from voters from the marginal Lancashire constituency of Bolton East, which had been a bell-wether of British politics, falling to the winning side in each election since 1950. Each leader's session was filmed separately. Reece held prior discussions with the producer about the lighting, the set, the height of the chair and the camera angles, seeking to ensure that it would concentrate on Thatcher's 'good' left side.[68]

Reece's advice was also of central importance in one of the minor sensations of the relatively quiet campaign, when Thatcher turned down the offer of a televised debate with Callaghan. Traditionally these presidential-style debates had been refused by the prime minister. But this time, with Labour behind in the polls, Downing Street press officers indicated to LWT's *Weekend World* that Callaghan would accept. News of his acceptance leaked to the *Daily Mirror*, which put pressure on Thatcher to take him on or appear frightened. Reportedly Thatcher was inclined to accept but was eventually persuaded against by Reece, Thorneycroft and Whitelaw. With the Tories comfortably ahead in the polls, it would be an unnecessary risk. A minor slip of the tongue could cause great damage.

Table 2.2   The general election of 3 May 1979

	Con	Lab	Lib	Other
Seats	339	269	11	16
% vote	43.9	36.9	13.8	5.4
% change since Oct. 74	+8.1	−2.3	−4.5	−1.3
Turnout 76%				

And, as we see again and again, elimination of risk is the guiding principle of political marketers.

Butler and Kavanagh summed up Mrs Thatcher's campaign as a judicious blend of pragmatism and radicalism. Certainly she appeared sensitive to presentational advice, willing to run a short campaign, to back down from direct television confrontation with Callaghan, tailoring speeches in keeping with strategy and conducting her tour for the benefit of the cameras. She was not the first leader to accede to photographers' demands, as Barbara Castle's comment at the head of this chapter readily admits. However the marketing aspects appeared more glaring for Mrs Thatcher than for her predecessors. This was partly because of the contrast between her style and Heath's almost superior attitude towards presentation;[69] perhaps it was also because she was up against Callaghan, who made repeated public points about the phoneyness of selling politics like soap. However it is also true that Reece took far greater pains than was then normal to control the images which would be beamed out to the public.

The Impact of the Election Campaign

The Conservatives won the general election on 3 May 1979 by 43 seats (Table 2.2), yet in the eyes of several commentators Callaghan waged the better campaign. The pro-Conservative *Economist* observed:

> She [Mrs Thatcher] has emerged as a leader uncertain under pressure and she has yet to demonstrate an ability to inspire great confidence or affection among the uncommitted voters, let alone among those who voted against her. Her shadow

cabinet did not come through strongly when pitted against an experienced, self-confident Labour cabinet.[70]

It is not unusual for press columnists to express a view of the campaign at odds with the electorate's vote; this was also the case in 1959, 1970, February 1974 and, later, 1987 and 1992, for instance.

It is notoriously difficult to judge the effectiveness of one party's campaign in isolation from all the other factors: long-term trends, the other parties' efforts, major news stories, incalculable mood swings and so on. However analysis of the polls throughout the campaign produces a slightly complicated picture of mixed success for the Tories.

On a straightforward share of the vote, the Tories lost ground during the campaign, their lead dropping from ten to seven points over the course of the five weeks.[71] Moreover Mrs Thatcher's own rating fared poorly. She started the campaign seven points behind the prime minister and by the end she trailed by 19 points. She was the only one of the three leaders whose rating declined throughout the campaign: a Gallup poll at the end of April showed Callaghan up from 40 per cent to 44 per cent; David Steel improved from 14 per cent to 22 per cent; Thatcher fell from 33 per cent to 25 per cent. Only 56 per cent of Conservative supporters thought she would make the best prime minister, while fully 43 per cent of them thought Callaghan better suited. Compared with Callaghan she was seen as less experienced, more extreme, more condescending and less in touch with ordinary people. Gender may have been a further handicap; the same Gallup poll found that respondents much preferred Heath as leader.

It would seem an obvious conclusion from this that Thatcher's own campaign was a failure. The weaknesses which Conservative Party campaign managers identified at the start remained the ones that damaged her ratings at the end. With the benefit of hindsight, it may well be that the electorate simply did not like Mrs Thatcher then and they have not since, despite admiring several leadership qualities. It is instructive to recall that in three of the ratings (extreme, condescending, out-of-touch) Thatcher continued to fare poorly throughout her premiership, even when her rating as a capable prime minister was high. This suggests that these categories are not relevant to voting decisions. Indeed in normal circumstances it seems that the leader is not a strong direct influence on the vote at all. According to ITN's Harris exit poll, only 5 per cent of Tory voters mentioned the party leader as a reason for their vote, compared to 62 per cent party policy and 23 per cent party loyalty. The salience of the leader was low even for Labour who pinned their entire campaign around Callaghan. Only 10 per cent of Labour supporters mentioned the party leader, compared to 49 per cent party policy and 29 per cent party loyalty.[72] Thus Labour clearly 'won' the leadership battle, but it proved to be relatively inconsequential terrain. Nevertheless Tory strategists were clearly wise to run a short campaign and restrict Mrs Thatcher's appearances. Given her unpopularity by comparison with Callaghan, a higher campaign profile would hardly have improved Tory chances.

A second measure of campaign effectiveness concerns issues: did the parties campaign on the issues most likely to affect voters' decisions and did they succeed in shifting opinion? By this measure the Conservatives fared well. In both the longer-term pre-campaign and the campaign proper the Conservatives outperformed Labour on the issues which voters rated the most important. The ITN exit poll found that the top issues in the 1979 election were as follows:[73]

1   prices/cost of living (31 per cent),
2   taxation (16 per cent),
3   law and order (14 per cent),
4   trade unions (13 per cent),
5   unemployment (13 per cent).

A panel study conducted by MORI tracked the longer-term and short-term change in voters attitudes on the major issues. From Table 2.3 it seems both parties made gains in the major issues during the campaign itself, but it is the Conservative long-term improvement which is most impressive. The Tories' most spectacular improvement comes in prices and law and order, two of the three most important issues. MORI figures do not provide a long-term comparison for taxation, although it does show that the Tories entered the campaign carrying a hefty 24 point advantage. Surprisingly, however, Labour still held the lead on the question of industrial relations, despite Tory gains during the Winter of Discontent.

Table 2.3   Changes in voters' attitudes towards major issues
during the 1978–9 election campaign

Issue and party rated best	Change				
	Aug. 78	Apr. 4/6	May 4/6	Long-term	Campaign
Prices					
Con	31	36	44	+13	+8
Lab	40	33	39	−1	+6
Con advantage	−9	+3	+5	+14	+2
Taxation					
Con	n/a	48	54	n/a	+6
Lab	n/a	24	28	n/a	+4
Con advantage	n/a	24	26	n/a	+2
Law and order					
Con	42	49	58	+16	+9
Lab	24	19	19	−5	0
Con advantage	+18	+30	+39	+21	+9
Ind. relations; strikes					
Con	32	35	39	+7	+4
Lab	41	36	41	0	+5
Con advantage	−9	−1	−2	+7	−1
Unemployment					
Con	36	37	42	+6	+5
Lab	29	28	36	+7	+8
Con advantage	+7	+9	+6	−1	−3

Note: Long-term = Aug. 78–May 79; campaign = 4/6 April–4/6 May.
Source: MORI, *British Public Opinion: General Election 1979.*

A further means of assessing campaign effectiveness is to
examine the voting behaviour of the target voters by comparison with the national trend. MORI's analysis of the polls indicated that the Conservatives had two spectacular successes:[74]
among 18–24-year-olds the Tory vote increased 18 points, from
24 per cent in 1974 to 42 per cent in 1979 and the C2 (skilled
worker) vote rose 15 points from 26 to 41 per cent (see Table
2.4). The first-time and skilled voter constituencies between
them accounted for about 41 per cent of the electorate. In

Table 2.4 Target voters, 1974–9

	Women (52%)			Men (48%)			18–24 yrs (14%)		
	1974	*1979*	*Change*	*1974*	*1979*	*Change*	*1974*	*1979*	*Change*
Con	39	47	+8	32	43	+11	24	42	+18
Lab	38	35	−3	43	40	−3	42	41	−1
Lib	20	15	−5	18	13	−5	27	12	−15
Con lead	+1	+12		−11	+3		−18	+1	

	TU members (23%)			Skilled working class (27%)		
	1974	*1979*	*Change*	*1974*	*1979*	*Change*
Con	23	33	+10	26	41	+15
Lab	55	51	−4	49	41	−8
Lib	16	13	−3	20	15	−5
Con lead	−32	−18		−23	0	

Source: MORI.

both cases the improvement in the target group vote was more than double the national increase of 8 per cent. In both cases the Tories clawed back a considerable Labour advantage to rate neck-and-neck. The 18–24-year-old vote showed easily the largest increase of any age category, although the Tory vote improved across all age ranges. The Tories also managed increases across all social classes, but the rise in the skilled worker (C2) vote was easily the most significant. Their middle class vote (ABC1) increased three points (56–59), and the semi-skilled (DE) vote moved up 12 points (22–34). The increase in the women's vote, at 8 per cent, was exactly the same as the national trend and, therefore, cannot be claimed as successful targeting. Moreover the increase in the male vote was greater, up 11 points from 32 to 43 per cent. The Conservatives could be satisfied with their inroads into the trade unionist vote up ten points from 23 to 33 per cent, although this remained one of the few categories which still preferred Labour. None of this analysis can prove the decisive influence of the Tory campaign; the Winter of Discontent will almost certainly claim the more powerful influence. It may have been also that there was a major change in the national mood. One Conservative polling adviser believed, for instance, that the electorate were simply ripe for radical change. 'If the leadership elections had gone the other way, had Heath beaten Thatcher and Benn beaten Callaghan, I think people would still have voted for the radical option. People desperately wanted change.'[75] Callaghan has also put forward the mood shift theory, although, of course, he had a vested interest in blaming factors other than the Winter of Discontent. He told Donoughue: 'You know there are times, perhaps once every thirty years, when there is a sea-change in politics. It does not matter what you say or do. There is a shift in what the public wants and what it approves of. I suspect there is now such a sea-change – and it is for Mrs Thatcher.'[76]

However there can be no doubt that the Conservatives ran a rational campaign. They geared their campaign to winning the election (rather than individual arguments); they sought to aim at the most winnable voters and tailored their communications efforts accordingly. They were handed the weapon of the Winter of Discontent and they made the most ot it. They were also aware of their own weaknesses and attempted to minimise them. Thus the assessment that Labour 'won' the campaign may boil down to the fact that Callaghan was the more impressive figure; but his advantage was not sufficient to win back ground lost during the Winter of Discontent.

SUMMARY

Mrs Thatcher, as leader of the party, brought a greater commitment and willingness to improve presentation. Certainly the contrast between Thatcher and Heath was marked, and became more so during Thatcher's premiership. Where Heath essentially used media advisers primarily for the electoral campaign and then dropped them, Thatcher maintained Saatchi on contract and paid close attention to opinion polls.

The 1978–9 period represents a landmark in the use of marketing in British politics. It witnessed the expansion of the sphere of media experts to include the development of communications strategy, overall co-ordination of publicity material and control of party political and election broadcasts. The importance of these, seemingly limited, steps should not be underestimated. Their significance comes into clearer focus in comparison with the Labour communications effort where the team of volunteer media experts, reporting to Callaghan, struggled with Transport House over control of party broadcasts and press advertising. In the opinion of one volunteer, Tim Delaney, the organisational structure was such that it was not possible to implement a co-ordinated communictions strategy.[77]

The Saatchis were also to have longer-term strategic significance, primarily because of their championing of qualitative polling. This was a major change at CCO, and it signalled a direct lift from the commercial world of attempts to understand and exploit emotional motivations. The exploitation of emotions is an old political trick, in evidence since orators first engaged in rhetoric. What appeared new about the Saatchis was the rather candid attempt to operate at the level of gut feelings in a more systematic way, using survey methods to this end. They brought a clear understanding that voters needed to be wooed on their own emotional territory, and not preached to, or 'educated' or argued with. The clarity of their approach enabled them to develop propaganda that was sometimes startling in its simplicity:

> What advertising people bring to politics is that they simplify it. People will not understand complicated political messages. People understand simple messages like: are you going to cut taxes or not? What advertising people do is to look at it in a very simple way. Politicians don't actually want to be specific because they don't know what they want to do, or whether they can do it, or whether people will like it.[78]

But the Saatchi approach did not bear out the fears of critics that the use of marketing in politics results in increasingly negative campaigns. Saatchi made no bones about the need to attack Labour; but by common consent the campaign was not the bitter one anticipated and the use of negative appeals did not strike commentators as particularly aggressive.[79]

3 Marketing Triumphant: Falklands Fallout

Thatcher's progress to the 1983 election landslide and, seemingly, complete dominance of the political scene could not have been predicted in the early months of her tenure. The government's 'honeymoon' with the voters quickly began to wane. Inflation soared, aided by the doubling of VAT in Chancellor Howe's June 1979 budget, and so too did unemployment, climbing to more than 2.5 million by April 1981.[1] The Social Democratic Party, launched in March 1981, threatened to break the mould of British politics with two sensational by-election results, culminating in Shirley Williams' win at Crosby in November. Opinion polls in the autumn of 1981 showed Thatcher as the least popular prime minister in modern British history: only 25 per cent of the public were satisfied with her performance and 62 per cent dissatisfied, according to Gallup. In December, the Tories trailed the SDP/Liberal Alliance by 27 per cent (23–50 per cent).[2]

By (almost) common consent, the Falklands War transformed Thatcher's fortunes.[3] By early April 1982 the three parties were all around 30–33 per cent, with the Alliance slightly ahead; by the end of the war the Tories had established a 20 per cent lead. Thatcher's approval rating soared from 34 per cent in March 1982, the month preceding the Argentinian invasion, to 51 per cent in June, when the islands were recaptured. From then until the general election in June the following year her approval rating did not dip below 44 per cent.

THE FALKLANDS FACTOR

This surge in popular esteem placed Thatcher in a position of unassailable command over her party and a previously cautious, suspicious, Heathite, 'wet' Cabinet.[4] Denis Healey called her 'Ted Heath in drag', so weak had she seemed within her first Cabinet, stocked with Heath's most prominent supporters.[5] Healey noted: 'In December 1980 Michael Heseltine told me that there was a group in Cabinet, with Christopher Soames, Peter Carrington, Peter Thorneycroft and Quintin Hailsham at its core, which could always impose an effective veto on her wilfulness.'[6] Before the war started Thatcher had already made her first moves to sponge up the 'wets', removing Norman St John-Stevas, then Gilmour and Soames, moving Prior to Northern Ireland and bringing in Cecil Parkinson as party chairman (September 1981). However her total dominance was not assured until the Falklands victory.

More than any other single event, the Falklands entrenched Thatcher's image as the iron and resolute leader. She began to be portrayed by supporters, and satirised by opponents, as the true heir to Winston Churchill. Paul Johnson, one-time editor of the *New Statesman* turned fulsome admirer of Thatcher, compared her leadership during the conflict to the 'gigantic and leonine spirit' of Winston Churchill.[7] A few weeks after the 1983 general election she was presented in Washington with the Winston Churchill Foundation Award, given to her with the citation that, like Churchill, she was known for 'courage, conviction, determination and willpower'.[8] The Churchillian mantle was bestowed and received without any apparent embarrassment, despite the extraordinary comparison of the Second World War and the battle for hitherto little-known islands in the South Atlantic (two months from invasion to recapture), a conflict whose global significance was characterised by Alexander Haig, then US Secretary of State, as like two bald men fighting over a comb.

Thatcher had long presented herself as the conviction politician, of course. She had embraced with pride the 'Iron Lady' title conferred by the Soviet Union; and in one of her most famous party conference speeches (October 1980) she had set herself squarely against 'soft' economic options, the Heath-like U-turn, with the line written for her by playright Sir Ronald Millar: 'U-turn if you want to, the lady's not for turning'.[9] But Thatcher's iron image was not truly forged until the Falklands. Enoch Powell posed the question at the outbreak of hostilities: 'In the next week or two the House, the nation and the Right Honourable Lady herself will learn of what metal she is made.'[10] Speaking at the end of the war, Powell congratulated her:

A report has now been received from the public analyst . . . It shows that the substance under test consists of ferrous matter of the highest quality. It is of exceptional tensile strength, resistant to wear and tear and stress, and may be used with advantage for all national purposes.[11]

Thatcher's reply is less often quoted. 'I agree with every word he says,' she said, without, according to her constituency agent, betraying a shred of modesty.[12]

Denis Healey later assessed the importance of the Falklands for Thatcher in terms with which it would be difficult to disagree:

It was the Falklands War which first established Mrs Thatcher both at home and abroad as a powerful national leader who must command respect, if not affection . . . It would be churlish to deny that she deserved respect, not least because she knew that her conduct often inspired in a large minority of British people the sort of personal hatred which most politicians find difficult to bear.[13]

The Falklands also saw the development of the regal image of Thatcher, almost as a rival to the Queen. On the weekend that the British Task Force set sail from Portsmouth, Mrs Thatcher told the BBC and ITN news, 'There is no possibility of defeat,' paraphrasing the words of Queen Victoria which Winston Churchill had kept on his desk throughout the Second World War. In *Not A Man To Match Her*, Wendy Webster tracks the various images of Thatcher, in Dame Edna-esque terms, from housewife to superstar, and she too locates the Falklands as the defining impetus for the 'regal' Thatcher:

Her increasingly regal bearing and performance were noted in the months after victory, and the comparison with the Queen was fostered by the way in which the Falklands victory parade was organised – an absent Queen, and Mrs Thatcher herself presiding over the trooping of the Falklands soldiers.[14]

Thatcher's exploitation of the political and public relations gains associated with her status as a victorious war leader was noted with distaste by some critics. David Owen was distressed at the way she milked partisan advantage despite enjoying cross-party support during the conflict. She:

began to talk as though the outcome was not so much an achievement of our armed forces as a triumph for the Conservative party. It left a very bad taste in the mouth when the march past in a ceremony arranged by the Lord Mayor of London was taken by her and not the Queen or another member of the Royal Family. In my opinion her behaviour after the victory was too self-regarding and too party political and partisan.[15]

She began to harness the 'spirit of the South Atlantic' to the Thatcherite vision of Great Britain, explicitly and directly summoning the spirit which defeated aggression in the Falklands to tackle aggression (that is, militant trade unionism) at home. Speaking shortly after the war to a Conservative rally, she could not have made the point more plainly:

> The battle of the South Atlantic was not won by ignoring the dangers or denying the risks. It was achieved by men and women who had no illusions about the difficulties. They faced them squarely and were determined to overcome. This is increasingly the mood of Britain. And that's why the rail strike won't do.
>
> We are no longer prepared to jeopardize our future just to defend manning practices agreed in 1919 when steam engines plied the tracks of the Grand Central Railway and the motor car had not yet taken over from the horse.
>
> What has indeed happened is that now once again Britain is not prepared to be pushed around. We have ceased to be a nation in retreat. We have instead a new-found confidence – born in the economic battles at home and tested and found true 8000 miles away.[16]

The Falklands Factor was exploited not just for the party's purposes but also for the enhancement of Mrs Thatcher's personal image. Former *Panorama* journalist Michael Cockerell suggested that Thatcher made skilful use of television deadlines to announce personally and dramatically good news to the nation:

> On June 14, Downing Street imposed a complete news blackout on reporters in the Falklands – for nine hours they were unable to file any story to London. In the middle of News

at Ten, Mrs Thatcher stood up in the Commons to announce that white flags were flying in Port Stanley.[17]

The Conservative party conference in October 1982 emphasised the point: the platform was decked in battleship grey, the conference slogan was 'The Resolute Approach', the widow of Col. 'H'. Jones VC, hero of Goose Green, was given a seat on the platform alongside the prime minister, other Cabinet ministers were urged to go easy on references to the Falklands to maximise the impact for the prime minister's oration at the climax of the conference.

The Falklands War and Public Relations

Thatcher's opinion poll gains from the war, and the hero-worship accorded her in the pro-Tory, tabloid press,[18] suggest a public relations, as well as military triumph. Opinion polls showed that the population at large was a great deal less than gung-ho initially at the prospect of war. Some 49 per cent did not think the Falklands worth the loss of British soldiers' lives, according to MORI. Only 44 per cent did think the islands sufficiently important.[19] Public opinion changed with the re-capture of South Georgia (25 April): 58 per cent thought that British sovereignty was worth British lives. The figure dipped slightly, to 53 per cent, at the time of the sinking of the *Belgrano*, but rose again to 62 per cent at the end of May.

Robert Worcester suggests that the pattern of the polls was predictable; in the early stages of both Suez and Vietnam there was strong domestic support for the government and the prosecution of the war.[20] However some commentators, especially on the Left, began to view the transformation of public opinion as a victory for the darker arts of propaganda. Thatcher was accused of employing the oldest trick in the book – military adventure abroad – to divert attention from troubles at home. At the furthest extreme, Labour backbencher Tam Dalyell put the most damaging interpretation on her conduct of the Falklands:

> The charge is not that Mrs Thatcher manipulated Galtieri into a military adventure against the Falklands. It is that, given the knowledge of a likely attack on the Falklands, the Prime Minister was quite content to let the situation run

and, by seeming inaction, to lure the Argentines on to the punch. A little war, deemed to be righteous by public opinion, might restore the domestic political fortunes of a Prime Minister who sat lower in the opinion polls than any Prime Minister had done since political polling began.[21]

Dalyell's thesis seems conspiratorial to a fault. Mistake and misjudgement seems a more likely explanation than Dalyell's calculated ploy to 'lure the Argentines on to the punch' – a breathtakingly high-risk strategy. The invasion could have caused a crisis for her government; indeed it did at first and the Foreign Secretary, Lord Carrington, resigned amid stern criticism of the government. There was also every possibility of severe British casualties, with the prospect that public support would soon dwindle.

More commonly, if less dramatically, Thatcher is accused of media manipulation through censorship, misinformation (especially over the Peruvian peace proposals and the sinking of the *Belgrano*) and skilful, and not always subtle, handling of the press.[22] Journalists, particularly at the BBC, were put under public pressure by Mrs Thatcher and some of her party to behave in a patriotic (that is, *biased*) manner. The BBC, carrying film from Argentina of the grieving relatives of the *Belgrano* dead, outraged Tory MP Robert Adley. The Corporation was becoming 'General Galtieri's fifth column,' he said.[23] Michael Cockerell made a report for *Panorama* about parliamentary misgivings at the looming battle. He estimated that about a fifth of Tory MPs had reservations. The programme also included an interview with Argentina's UN representative. 'That night the BBC switchboard lit up with complaints and John Cole was advised by a government whip to wear his steel helmet when he ventured into the MPs' Lobby. "Sure enough the flak from the Tory right-wingers was fierce," says Cole.'[24] Mrs Thatcher, at Prime Minister's Question Time the following day, expressed dismay that some BBC programmes were failing to 'put the case for our country' with 'sufficient vigour'. The chairman of the BBC had given assurances that the Corporation could not be neutral as between Britain and an enemy and 'I hope his words will be heeded by the many who have responsibility for standing up for our Task Force, our boys, our people and the cause of democracy.'[25]

The prime minister's attitude was conveyed into her press secretary's lobby briefings. Bernard Ingham, while claiming he kept the lid on government anger against the media, has made no secret of his irritation with journalists who saw their function as neutral, even when the nation was at war.[26] The restrained and placid styles of John Major and his press secretary, Gus O'Donnell, during the Gulf War provided stark contrast.[27]

According to the Glasgow University Media Group, media deference, whether caused by patriotic bias or capitulation to pressure, played a significant public relations role in legitimising the escalation of the conflict into open warfare. Television faithfully followed the official line that the British were not to blame for the failure of the peace negotiations: 'This country's government was very largely reported as "urgently pursuing peace" and as using the Task Force as a "back-up" for diplomatic efforts.'[28] Similarly television news tended to blame Argentinian 'intransigence' for the failure of the Peruvian peace plan,[29] which was vital for maintaining public support for the war: 'our analysis suggests it is not clear that a majority of the population desired the escalation of military conflict, and it is even less certain that they would have supported "government policy" on this, if they had been better informed as to what that policy was.'[30]

From the political marketing point of view, however, there was something curiously old-fashioned about the government public relations of the Falklands War. Having been given a taste of smart advertising copy, photo-opportunities and attention to the smallest details on the television set, the Falklands took a plunge backwards into tight censorship and suspicion of the press. By common accord, the MoD's reaction as the Task Force put to sea was to restrict media access, impose censorship and deliver only the bare essentials of information. There was a hard core of belief within military circles that media coverage was responsible for the collapse in American public morale during the Vietnam War, and they did not intend taking similar risks in the Falklands.[31] The Navy initially refused to carry any journalists with them until the MoD's public relations department persuaded them to take ten. The number was eventually increased to 28 following the direct intervention of Bernard Ingham.[32]

Censorship was applied strictly in the theatre of battle. No pictures of casualties during the land fighting were sent back to Britain until after the final ceasefire. Still pictures were allowed back but at a speed determined by the MoD and dependent on content. Post-Falklands criticism of the government and MoD information system was so great that the Commons Defence Committee set up an inquiry. Its report commented on the MoD censorship of pictures: 'Was it just by chance that the celebrated picture of a San Carlos villager offering a Marine a cup of tea achieved such instant currency, whilst others such as the one of the HMS *Antelope* exploding suffered considerable delays?'[33]

Copy from journalists with the Task Force had to pass through screens of MoD censorship. The ITN told the Defence Committee that stories were sometimes vetted through six layers: the local military authority (Falklands), MoD press officer (London), MoD director of public relations, the Chief Information Officer, the Clearing Committee and the Secretary of State.[34] The BBC reporter in the Falklands, Brian Hanrahan, was told to remove a phrase from his story describing the cries of British soldiers trapped at Bluff Cove; Michael Nicholson of the ITN attempted to prefix his reports with the word 'censored', but that too was censored.[35] In London, Ian McDonald, an assistant secretary who ran the MoD PR department, suspended all unattributable briefings on the grounds of security, much to the chagrin of the defence correspondents' lobby and to the anger of Ingham, who argued that 'the last thing you do in a crisis is withdraw your service to the media'.[36]

Ingham's autobiography describes the 'battle' between the press secretary and Sir Frank Cooper, permanent under secretary at the MoD, over control of war information.[37] Ingham was alarmed at the absence of a professional press officer as Chief of Public Relations at the MoD. Neville Taylor, then at the DHSS, later to become Director General of the Central Office of Information, was due to move into the post and Ingham managed to speed up the transfer when the Falklands crisis broke. 'The next problem left me convinced that the Ministry of Defence had gone barmy,' Ingham said. When Taylor arrived, he was informed that he was in charge of everything but the Falklands.[38] Ironically the MoD's reticence increased the importance of Ingham, who maintained his normal lobby briefings at Number 10. Cooper complained, in scarcely coded language, that Downing Street was giving journalists too much information and putting servicemen's lives at risk. There were disagreements over, among other things, Ingham's premature hints about the recapture of Goose Green and about the release of information concerning British casualties.

Sir Frank Cooper's distaste at Ingham's activities was later made public:

> the aim now is the management of the media with a very much higher degree of control from Number 10 Downing Street and with the connivance of a part of the media. There is now public relations – which I would define as biased information. I suggest that the post of Chief Information Officer at Number 10 Downing Street is in fact a political job in a party sense and is not a job which it is proper for a civil servant to fill . . .[39]

It is a quote that tends to be aired when criticisms are made of Ingham, but, from the evidence of the Defence Committee report and other accounts, it seems that it was Ingham who played the journalists' friend, squeezing more access from a reluctant MoD. There can be little doubt that Ingham calculated the kind of risks to be run by offering journalists more information. His duty as press secretary was plain: 'to maintain public support for the government's conduct of the war'.[40] He surely would not have fought for better media access if he believed that the overall result would be poor publicity for the government.

ITN evidence to the Defence Committee suggests that Ingham was a shrewd judge. ITN complained at the MoD's tardiness and reluctant attitude, because 'great opportunities were missed for the positive projection of the single-minded energy and determination by the British people in their support of the Task Force'.[41]

Party Publicity Machinery

Cecil Parkinson, as party chairman, presided over the most innovative change at Central Office, the establishment of the Marketing Department under the direction of Sir Christopher Lawson. It was the first marketing department in any major

British political party and the title was chosen with some care to help promote and reflect the kind of business-like efficiency which Parkinson hoped to foster. According to David Boddy, then at the CCO press office: 'The choice of the name was deliberate. I recall two or three meetings about the choice of the name because it would set a particular tone, which it most certainly did.'[42]

Lawson, an RAF pilot during the Second World War, had long experience of marketing in the commercial sector. He worked for Procter and Gamble and later for the chocolate giant, Mars Inc., USA, becoming president of Mars Snackmaster, USA, from 1977 until he joined Central Office. He had offered his expertise to CCO before Parkinson took over, but by coincidence he was also an old friend of Parkinson's. He, Parkinson and Norman Tebbit had all been constituency officers in Hemel Hempstead – the Hemel Hempstead Mafia, they were sometimes called at CCO. Lawson's commercial background provided material for the headline writers: 'The man from Mars'. Indeed his appointment, title and role provoked the familiar concern that politics was being sold like any commercial product.[43]

Lawson's marketing department had overall responsibility for the communications strategy for the general election. To this end it liaised with Saatchi & Saatchi, and oversaw advertising and PPBs. It also monitored and commissioned survey research, a task which until then had fallen within the ambit of the Conservative Research Department (CRD). This period witnessed the decline in importance of the CRD, which before Thatcher's time had been the major engine for the development of Tory policy. Formally independent right-wing think tanks – such as the Centre for Policy Studies and the Adam Smith Institute – effectively took over CRD's traditional role and CRD became reduced to an adjunct to the publicity department.

Lawson also had overall charge of the ME29 computer which was installed in CCO in December 1982 in order to experiment with direct mail. This period saw the introduction of direct mail into British politics. Lawson admired the US Republican party's use of direct mail and his intention was to use it for fund-raising, at which it had proved so effective in the USA, and also to reach key voters in critical seats. Over the winter of 1982/83 personalised letters, signed by the chairman, were sent out to some 83 000 people in 50 constituencies. The response rate of 10 per cent satisfied the department but the funds raised recouped only two-thirds of the cost.[44] However, direct mail and computers were in their British infancy in this period and it was not until 1983–7 that they were to play a significant role in election campaigning.

The establishment of the Marketing Department was part of wider changes in the publicity machinery of the party, some made through choice, some forced through resignation. The director of communications, Gordon Reece, left CCO after the election, taking with him much credit for that victory. He went to California where he worked for Armand Hammer's Occidental Petroleum. He left with agreement to return occasionally to provide advice for Mrs Thatcher and was employed by CCO to co-ordinate the 1983 campaign. Gordon Reece's remit had given him overall control of all publicity and he had taken responsibility for liaison with the advertising agency and market research companies. After he left his functions at CCO were divided.

He was succeeded in name in 1980 by a stop-gap appointment, Sir Harry Boyne, former political editor of the *Daily Telegraph* and former chairman of the Lobby. David Boddy, a young New Zealand-born journalist, who had worked in the Tory press office since 1976, was appointed Boyne's deputy.

> Sir Harry was quite elderly and must have been about 70; I was very young, about 27. I was described as Harry's arms and legs. That proceeded for a year, it was a holding operation and not very much happened. When Cecil was appointed chairman it was time for a review.[45]

As a result of the review, marketing, including research, was to be quite separate from press and public relations. Sir Harry stayed for two years at CCO but, when he left, his successor, David Boddy, took the title, not of Director of Communications, but of Director of Press and Public Relations:

> it was very obvious to me that the function of director of communications had at least two aspects, two special sorts of skills. One was press and PR, particularly the relationship between the parliamentary Lobby and the party, and the

handling of the media on a day-to-day basis. The second was marketing skills, with a lot of emphasis on market research. I didn't feel I had the necessary training on that, nor did I feel that one man had the time to do two diverse functions.[46]

Boddy remained in charge of the CCO press office until he resigned in January 1983 following a heated disagreement with Mrs Thatcher during an election strategy meeting. Boddy's account of the row contains similarities to the more famous argument between Thatcher and Michael Dobbs at a Chequers strategy meeting in the next parliament.

On January 5 Mrs Thatcher called a meeting at Chequers with key people from the party to discuss the election campaign. Parkinson, Lawson, Cropper [CRD] and myself had put together an extensive brief and proposals as to how the election should be run. We had done this without the consultation of Saatchi & Saatchi, who were back on board at that stage to do the PPBs. However, Saatchi people were there. Tim Bell led them and Gordon Reece also appeared at the meeting.

That which I had to present to the PM was unfavourably received. One of my indelible memories of politics is the way in which my colleagues abandoned me in the face of adversity. The primary issue over which we fell out was breakfast TV and how it should be used. We knew breakfast TV would be a factor that we had to deal with. I felt that breakfast TV could be used as the vehicle for establishing the line at the opposition parties' press conferences. It would have let us set the political tone for the day. It was probably just the day, but it ended that the PM and I had a considerable difference of opinion over that and several other things.[47]

Boddy's relations with Mrs Thatcher were restored at the 1983 election when she asked him back to work as a paid consultant and accompany her on her election tours. In March 1983 he was replaced as head of the press department by Anthony Shrimsley, former editor of Sir James Goldsmith's short-lived glossy news weekly *Now*.

Presentation: the Role of Harvey Thomas

Harvey Thomas makes the bold claim for himself that he has changed the face of political presentation in the UK;[48] and a comparison of the presentation of party rallies and conferences during the 1980s does, indeed, demonstrate substantial changes. This first became apparent at the 1982 post-Falklands Conservative Party conference. The stage scenery behind the speakers' platform was larger and more dramatic. Relatively simple backcloths bearing the conference slogan were replaced by theatre-style flies, colour-coordinated (battleship grey at the post-Falklands conference), with the party logo and conference slogans writ large. Care was taken to isolate the speaker's rostrum from the rest of the platform to ensure that television pictures would focus on only the speaker and the slogan behind, in order to minimise distractions for the television viewer.

The cluttered, distracting platform was a 'bugbear' for Thomas, which he struggled to bring under control:

> Generally there are too many bodies on stage and it may be your job to thin them out. I've fought this problem for years at political conferences and gradually we've been able to improve the situation. If you compare the platform parties of the middle and late eighties with those of 1979, the effect is quite noticeable. We've not managed to clear the speaker's part of the platform as entirely as the Americans do, but at least we've managed to create a decent space around the speaker. We set the tone at the Tory conferences and the other parties have followed suit.[49]

The 1982 conference also saw the Conservative conference debut for the Head Up Display Unit, known as the 'sincerity machine'. Pioneered by Ronald Reagan, it allows the speaker to read his/her text from unobstrusive, transparent perspex screens, thus creating the illusion that the orator is speaking without notes. From then on, Thatcher rarely spoke in public without the aid of this technology.[50] At the same conference Thomas introduced another technique, the electronic adjustable-height lectern. It is lowered while debates are taking place from the floor, thus allowing the audience a clear view of the platform, and it is raised to the appropriate level as each platform speaker holds the stage. 'It took me three years to convince politicians to use this "monster",' he said.[51]

Thomas's conference and rally sets became noticeably bolder in the use of lighting, colour, greenery, video screens, laser beams and other ambience-inducing paraphernalia, from the time that he was first engaged as a consultant to the party in 1978. He learned his craft in the Billy Graham Evangelistic Association which he joined in 1960, directing many of Graham's international crusades and conferences. Appalled at what he perceived as the decline of the British nation, he approached Gordon Reece in 1978, offered his services and was hired on a consultant basis.[52]

Thomas adopted a crusading attitude towards improving political presentation within the party, which struck him then as amateurish and naive:

> When the 1979 election was called, I asked to be introduced to the person who set up and organised their conferences and rallies. 'What do you mean set up?' I was asked. 'Well,' I said, 'who co-ordinates the presentation, liaises with the media, sets up the stage, the sound, the lights, speech rehearsal, all the TV arrangements?' 'Oh,' I was told, 'there's always someone who puts out a microphone'. 'Right,' I said, 'lead me to it.' And that's how our relationship, which has seen three general elections, ten annual conferences, many by-elections, campaigns, rallies, meetings, speeches, broadcasts and special events began.[53]

His work was geared to creating the appropriate atmosphere, because, he believed, *image* wins people's hearts, and the winning of hearts is the necessary precursor to the winning of minds – a lesson learned from the Billy Graham crusades. Small, seemingly trivial, details are crucial to the building of the perfect atmosphere. An example of this was the seating arrangements for the audience at rallies. On the eve of Thatcher's address to the 1989 Blackpool Tory conference, Thomas and aides discussed whether to remove a couple of hundred chairs from the Empress Ballroom floor, thus forcing more people to stand to reinforce the impression of a packed, excited crowd.[54]

Because of the importance of image, television is clearly the prime medium for politicians, according to Thomas, who in the years following 1983 was consulted by Tory MPs and candidates on their TV styles and appearance. 'People get their minds going from the newspapers and their hearts moving from TV. And we win the heart first, then the mind.'[55] It is a candid acknowledgement that his work is directed to the stirring of emotions, much as Tim Bell professed in his assessment of Saatchi's contribution to the 1979 victory. Image is, indeed, so important that politics can sometimes get in the way, according to Thomas. He cites the example of a glamorous rally in Paris for the 1988 presidential candidate Jacques Chirac:

> Politics were allowed to intrude too much: in fact they spoiled the rally. Chirac had to be seen to be making concessions to his defeated rival Le Barre [sic] in order to get Le Barre's support for the run-off against Mitterrand. So both men were given almost equal prominence and Le Barre virtually killed off any audience interest with a heavy speech.
>
> Chirac didn't even know where to go while Le Barre was speaking on an empty white platform with no chairs, and when it was his turn to speak he had no chance of a good clean start because he had to shake hands with Le Barre as they passed on the stairs. It was a study in how not to do it and it cost Chirac dear.[56]

However, even after 10 years of Thomas's best efforts, he did not think that the Conservative Party had taken on board fully the lessons of the importance of image: 'The Conservative Party in this country has been hindered by the concept that winning the argument means winning the people. The Socialists have historically been better at going for the gut-level reaction.'[57]

THE 1983 GENERAL ELECTION

Of Mrs Thatcher's three general election victories, the 1983 campaign was the most assured. The Conservatives went ahead in the opinion polls in May 1982 and maintained a comfortable lead over Labour and the Alliance for the entire year preceding the announcement of the election on 9 May 1983. From the turn of the year, Gallup monthly average polls showed the party fortunes indicated in Table 3.1. Thus the Tories entered the election race with the enormous cushion of an 18

Table 3.1   Monthly average polls, 1983(%)

1983	Con	Lab	Alliance
Jan.	44	31	22
Feb.	43	32	22
March	39	28	29
April	40	35	22
May	49	31	17

Source: Gallup.

Table 3.2   The general election of 9 June 1983

	Con	Lab	Alliance	Other	Total
Seats					
At dissolution	336	240	42	17	635
After election	397	209	23	21	650
Votes					
% of total	42.4	27.6	25.4	4.6	100
1979–83 change	−1.5	−9.3	+11.6	−0.8	

point lead over Labour. By polling day, the Tories' share had slipped but they still managed a 15 point lead over Labour because the opposition vote divided between Labour and the Alliance. With the opposition vote split, the Tories romped to a landslide 144 seat majority (see Table 3.2), the biggest winning margin since 1945. The massive majority should not be allowed to mask the decline in Tory vote share, from 43.9 per cent (1979) to 42.4 per cent on a reduced voter turnout (76 per cent in 1979, 73 per cent in 1983). This is a significant factor in the ultimate assessment of the success of the Tory campaign.

Campaign Strategy

Conservative strategy focused on the themes of continuity, leadership and economic 'realism'. The government's main weaknesses were an uncaring image, unemployment, which was a post-war record at more than 3 million, and the health service. Inflation, which with unemployment was the other economic bugbear in the first years of the government, had been brought under control, from a peak of about 18 per cent in 1980 down to 5 per cent in 1983.

The theme of continuity was essentially a call to the electorate for more time to complete the task of turning the British economy round. This dovetailed with the theme of economic realism: qualitative research suggested that people had lowered expectations of the role of government in the economy. Saatchi's presentation at Chequers urged that the party should encourage this 'realistic' view of politics.[58] Leadership was the Conservatives' trump card. Thatcher's pedigree as a strong and respected leader was by now well established, and this would contrast sharply with Labour and Michael Foot, in particular, but also with Roy Jenkins and David Steel of the Alliance. The leadership qualities associated with Mrs Thatcher since the Falklands continued to give her a commanding advantage over the other party leaders. According to a MORI poll (12 May 1983) which asked who would make the best prime minister, Mrs Thatcher scored 47 per cent, David Steel 19 per cent, Michael Foot 15 per cent, and Roy Jenkins 7 per cent.

The Tories' qualitative surveys in preparation for the campaign strategy, some 18 months before the election, brought to light a crucial discovery about voters' attitudes towards unemployment, which most people rated as the number one problem facing the country. According to David Boddy:

> Most people put unemployment as the most important issue affecting the country but it was only number six as an issue which affected their voting intention. People didn't blame government wholly, it was more the result of world conditions and partly the previous Labour government. So we used the line of shared blame.[59]

Party spokesmen argued that employment was not the responsibility of government; it was largely the result of world conditions and workers pricing themselves out of the market. Tory spokesmen also drew attention to the Manpower Services Commission's (MSC) various training schemes and, from 1982 onwards, the MSC under the new leadership of (Lord) David

Young, mounted a major advertising campaign for which Saatchis were the main agency. In the service of the party (rather than the government) Saatchis devised an aggressive communications campaign to deal with unemployment and developed a line first used at the 1979 election to attack Labour. Every Conservative election broadcast emphasised that 'every Labour government there has ever been' had increased unemployment.

Manifesto

Despite speculation about a radical, right-wing Conservative programme, the manifesto emphasised continuity and contained little that promised a great leap forward towards the anti-state new right. 'Extravagant commitments were few, and lunges forward in the new radicalism were hardly adumbrated at all,' commented Hugo Young.[60] The sober tone seemed surprising, partly because of the steely rhetoric of Mrs Thatcher's public speeches in which she continued to call for the banishing of socialism. She told the Scottish Conservative Conference at the start of the election campaign: 'This is a historic election. For the choice facing the nation is between two totally different ways of life. And what a prize we have to fight for: no less than the chance to banish from our land the dark, divisive clouds of marxist socialism.'[61]

The anodyne manifesto was surprising also because of the way the party had set about drawing it up. In the late summer of 1982 Sir Geoffrey Howe had invited some 70 people, including MPs, academics and party activists, to sit on nine policy groups on matters ranging from inner cities and family life to tax and trade unions. This was an unusually wide canvass of opinion for the Conservative party in government and helped fuel speculation that a radical manifesto was being contemplated.[62] The policy groups were told to report by March 1983. However their work had little impact on the manifesto, which was drafted under the auspices of Howe, Parkinson and Ferdinand Mount, the head of Thatcher's Policy Unit at Number 10. Lady Thatcher's memoirs all but wash her hands of the 'uninspiring' document, for which she blames Howe's excessive caution. However, she admits the tactical sense of a tame manifesto and thus, once again, the manifesto reflected precisely the approach recommended by the campaign strategists, in this instance, continuity.

In marked contrast, however, the Labour manifesto was far less prudent. Peter Shore called it the 'longest suicide note in history'.[63] It committed a Labour government to leave the EEC, adopt a non-nuclear defence, renationalise privatised assets and reinstitute the 'corporatist', tripartite approach to economic management and pay deals. It became apparent during the campaign that the manifesto lacked the whole-hearted consent of the party leadership, as Nick Grant, the Labour Party, director of publicity, conceded: 'Without this Labour lacked the necessary determination to win – and without this determination, the organisational discipline which is essential to any election campaign never materialised.'[64] Thus from the start Labour was hamstrung by divisions over its policy. Moreover its manifesto was seized upon as a powerful campaigning tool for the Conservatives. CCO bought copies in bulk and distributed them to the constituences[65] and Mrs Thatcher regularly displayed it at her rallies. Saatchis' election campaign advertising capitalised on the fear of Labour extremism: 'Like your manifesto, comrade,' ran the headline over a newspaper advertisement, which then checked off a list of 11 identical commitments in the Labour and Communist Party manifestoes.

Labour 'extremism' was a significant feature of this period. The party's post-mortem following its 1979 defeat had seen a strengthening of the Left, under the leadership of Tony Benn, arguing that Labour's defeat was due to Wilson/Callaghan's betrayal of socialist principles.[66] Benn's bid for the deputy leadership of the party signalled the start of the 'loony left' coverage by the Tory tabloid papers, led by the *Sun*. The 'loony left' stories, arguably more persistently savage than anything previously seen in the post-war period, focused most notoriously on Benn himself, but also on 'Red Ken' Livingstone, leader of the GLC, and Bermondsey by-election candidate, Peter Tatchell.[67] The aggressive coverage provided a ready-made scapegoat at the inevitable 'why Labour lost' post-mortems.

The Prime Minister's Campaign

'There is a myth about the Conservative campaign in 1983,' Cecil Parkinson remarked at a post-election conference on political communication, 'a myth nurtured if not created by the the post-election *Panorama* programme on "The marketing of Margaret". The myth is that we built our campaign around the skilful presentation of the Prime Minister and in doing so avoided discussion of the issues.'[68] The *Panorama* reporter was Michael Cockerell, who was impressed by the 'meticulous' planning of the Tory presentation 'right down to the colour of the curtains at the press conferences. Light blue for the relaxed mood, dark blue for the more resolute approach.'[69]

Cockerell reported that Thatcher had become the first major British party leader to have her own campaign song, in imitation of American presidential candidates. Specially written by her speechwriter and playwright Sir Ronald Miller it ran:

> Who do we want, who do we need?
> It is a leader who is bound to succeed
> Maggie Thatcher, just Maggie for me
> These British isles have found a fighter
> With the coolest of styles
> No other politician comes within miles,
> Two three four, Thatcher, Thatcher, Thatcher
> Not a man around to match her

Tapes of the song were distributed to the constituency association for use at local meetings and it was sung at the Young Conservative rally at Wembley on the weekend before polling day. The rally, staged by Harvey Thomas, was a ticket-only event for 'Britain's youth, strong and free'. It was 'one of the most remarkable political events ever staged in Britain', said Cockerell, and it deployed many of the innovations which Thatcher's publicity advisers had brought to electioneering.[70] Comedians Bob Monkhouse and Jimmy Tarbuck played master of ceremonies to an assemblage of sporting and show business celebrities: swimmer Sharron Davis, snooker star Steve Davis, wrestler Mick McManus, singer Lynsey De Paul, Fred Trueman, Nanette Newman and Kenny Everett, who notoriously urged the cheering audience to kick away Michael Foot's stick and to bomb Russia. With the crowd suitably warmed up, bedecked with balloons, streamers, and many adorned with 'I love Maggie' T-shirts and badges, the full band struck up and Thatcher entered the stage to a five-minute ovation.

Cockerell did not make direct comparisons with Nazi propaganda, yet it is difficult not to spot some similarities by implication: especially in the appeal to youth and the use of robust music and entertainment to engender excitement. 'Could Labour have organised a rally like this?' Mrs Thatcher put the rhetorical question to her audience. 'In the old days, perhaps, but not now. For they are the party of yesterday. Tomorrow is ours.'

Cast in the sober light of hindsight, the rally was of relatively minor importance. It borrowed heavily from American presidential rallies, much as Harold Wilson had, using music and celebrities, to establish an enthusiastic audience and veil the leader in an ambience of popularity. But it did not signal the start of a new style of barnstorming campaigning for Mrs Thatcher. Despite the presentational tricks and gimmicks, she never developed a reputation as a great orator and unlike Wilson her rallies and public speeches were relatively rare. Even within the context of general election campaigns, Mrs Thatcher relied on public speeches far less than her opponents or her predecessor, Edward Heath. She made only six set-piece speeches during the three-week campaign, easily the fewest for a major party leader in post-war campaigns. A number of other factors were more important in Tory marketing of the campaign: the timing and scheduling of the election (for example, to coincide with the world leaders' summit in Williamsberg), the role of market research in shaping the manifesto, press and television interviews, and photo-opportunities.

However the Wembley rally gained enormous publicity, was, by British standards, elaborate and brazen in its harnessing of showbiz to politics, and it came at the climax of the most media-oriented campaign yet seen, in the opinion of seasoned observers.[71] It remains one of the few memorable events in a campaign summed up as boring, too long, too one-sided and lacking in real debate.[72] For these reasons it almost certainly played an important role in entrenching a perception of 'Margaret the marketed product'. It was also one of the presentational tools which the Labour Party adopted under Neil Kinnock, who was to hold his own showbiz-infested rallies, most infamously the Sheffield Rally during the 1992 campaign.

Mrs Thatcher's personal campaign tour also established the model which Kinnock and others were to follow. In repetition of the 1979 campaign her tour was arranged primarily for the cameras, so much so that the writing journalists complained at the absence of opportunity for interviews and hard questions. They composed their own campaign song, 'Maggie, Maggie, give us an interview, Your not speaking is making us all feel blue.'[73]

Advertising and Party Election Broadcasts

The 1983 campaign was marked by a profusion of press advertising, some half of it placed, not by the parties, but by unions, the GLC and assorted pressure groups. Analysis for Butler and Kavanagh's general election study found that 201 advertisements were placed: the ratio of Conservative to Labour advertising was 2.5:1. But the Conservative quantitative advantage was negated by the bulk of anti-Conservative advertising from unions and other groups. The Alliance did not run any national press advertising at all.[74] The most prolific pressure groups were NALGO, British Telecommunications Union Committee and the GLC, which between them ran a total of 38 advertisements all opposing the Conservatives or aspects of Conservative policy. Aims of Industry, the fund-raising support group for the Conservatives, ran nine, CND and the Nuclear Weapons 'Freeze' campaign ran ten.

Saatchi advertising had a lower profile in the Conservative campaign than in 1979. This time the agency was not asked to run a substantial pre-election campaign. According to Cecil Parkinson, this was for tactical reasons because a major campaign would have generated a pre-election scare.

So we restricted ourselves to very limited advertising in the local elections and as a result we spent far less in the run-up than either Labour or the Alliance. Indeed we spent much less in the run-up this time than we did in Opposition before the 1979 contest. And there is a limit to how much you can spend in the three weeks of the campaign without putting people off. If voters had come across double-page spreads of Conservative advertising every time they opened their newspapers, it would not have been long before someone would have told them they were being bought. The whole exercise would have become counter-productive, to use Harold Wilson's favourite phrase. So I took the decision not to spend a penny on newspaper advertising after the final Sunday of the campaign. Contrary to myth, 1983 was really a very economical election for the Conservative Party.[75]

Nevertheless Saatchi's' spend in the campaign proper heavily outweighed that of Wright & Partners for the Labour Party. Pinto-Duschinsky estimated that some £2.5 million, 70 per cent of Conservative central campaign expenditure, went on advertising. By contrast, advertising took only about half (£0.9 million) of Labour's central spending.[76]

There were no real innovations in the parties' advertising campaigns. Saatchi's style largely repeated formulas developed five years previously: simple, single messages, 'warm' and down-to-earth in tone, and directed at the gut reactions of voters. As in 1978/79, its commercials were primarily negative, directed at attacking Labour (not the Alliance). There was no single piece of work which achieved the notoriety of 'Labour isn't working', although Labour's advertising consultant Johnny Wright described Saatchi's 'Like your manifesto, comrade' as brilliant.[77]

Mrs Thatcher cancelled a three-page advertisement scheduled for the final Sunday before polling day, which the Saatchi camp believed was their best work: it compared the three parties' programmes with a blank page for the Alliance. The 'grocer's daughter didn't like paying so much for blank paper,' according to one senior party official.[78] Mrs Thatcher vetoed on grounds of taste another Saatchi piece which displayed a picture of Michael Foot complete with walking stick over the caption that 'this pensioner would fare better under a Conservative government'. The prime minister also vetoed the 'Grantham tape', a biographical party broadcast of Mrs Thatcher which Bell had modelled on a 'fantastic' campaign commercial for Gerald Ford in the 1976 presidential election. According to Bell, Mrs Thatcher believed the party would object to its presidential style.[79] Thus the innovation of the US-style, leader's 'biog' broadcast was left to Labour and Hugh Hudson's 'Kinnock' in 1987.

For the first time at a general election, broadcasters did not transmit PEBs simultaneously on all the channels. BBC1 and ITV continued simultaneous broadcasts, but PEBs were staggered on the other three channels, BBC2 and the new television entrants Channel 4 and its Welsh sister S4C. The growth in popularity of video recorders, by then owned in some 15 per cent of households, also offered a further threat to the reach of PEBs.[80] Thus parties could be less assured of a 'captive' audience.

The allocation of PEBs was decided, as usual, by the Committee for Political Broadcasting, which was composed of IBA and BBC representatives in negotiation with party officials. The Conservative and Labour parties were each awarded five 10-minute slots and the Alliance four 10-minute broadcasts. However, Parkinson decided unilaterally and somewhat controversially to shorten the Tory PEBs and none ran to the full 10 minutes allotted. His decision caught even Saatchis by surprise. The agency had prepared a standard 10-minute programme and were required to do some hurried eleventh-hour cutting when they discovered that the party had booked five minutes only.[81] Saatchis escaped another potential embarrassment when they discovered that a hospital ward in Tower Hamlets, which they planned to hire for a film sequence illustrating the government's caring attitude towards health care, had been closed five months earlier amid considerable public outcry.

A striking feature of the Saatchi broadcasts was the relatively small part played directly by the politicians. Mrs Thatcher actually spoke in only one, the last, and in the others only Parkinson, Tebbit and Heseltine appeared briefly. Instead anonymous voice-overs and actors were used to put across the Conservative message. 'This was surely the smallest part that a Prime Minister has ever taken in election series,' commented Martin Harrison.[82] Harrison's account of broadcasting at the election noted that Labour stole much of their PEB style from Saatchi, despite protestations of distaste at the agency's flip commercialism:

> While they took up all their time [that is, 10-minute broadcasts] and used their politicians much more prominently, they exploited the same kind of rapidly-cut sequences as the Conservatives, displaying comparable statistical versatility to savage the government's record on employment and the welfare services – at times the two series looked like a fight to the death between VTR editors. The pace was almost as

fast as with the Conservatives and, since the programmes were longer, the cumulative effect was even more cramped and breathless. The overloading was compounded by the competition among senior politicians for a place in the sun, with an eye to a post-election leadership contest. Effective electioneering was secondary. One programme had no fewer than nine participlants.[83]

The Alliance series was markedly more ambitious than the solo efforts of the Liberal party at previous elections, and reflected the Alliance's need to establish the credibility of its potentially confusing two-man leadership.[84]

The PEB battle did not impress commentators. The legendary US anchorman Walter Cronkite said they ranged from the 'terrible to the barely tolerable'.[85] Martin Harrison gave his dismissive assessment thus: 'For all the parties' complaints about being trivialised by snippety news, their own programmes were more fragmented than the most breathless news bulletin.'[86]

The Campaign in Retrospect: its Impact

In the wake of the landslide on 9 June, the Tory campaign entered mythology as one of the best, if not the best, Conservative election campaigns ever, and the Labour campaign the worst. Certainly the Tory campaign seemed smooth enough. Butler and Kavanagh were struck with how closely the Tories managed to follow pre-election strategy and how completely Labour failed to follow theirs.[87] The Conservative campaign, from ministerial speeches and interviews to the campaign advertising, all harmonised around the preselected themes and issues, which had been decided, at least in principle, as early as January 1983. In a campaign relatively free of outside incident and major news competition, the Conservatives did not feel the need to make a single change in their pre-arranged schedule of morning press conferences.

However the Tories were never really tested in this election as Labour's campaign imploded with the shock of its own internal contradictions. Labour's divisions, culminating in the SDP breakaway of several of its leader members, were not completely healed and its campaign was conspicuous for the absence of planning, according to the party's publicity director, Nick

Grant.[88] Labour did not begin to conduct opinion research until January 1983 and continued to be deeply suspicious of its results, according to Grant.

The party overcame its distaste of Saatchi sufficiently to hire its own agency, Wright & Partners, in February 1983. It was a distinct break from the past practice of relying on volunteers. However the agency was hired too late to draw up a specific general election campaign. Its 'Think Positive, Vote Labour' campaign, geared essentially to the local elections in May, was extended into the general campaign. Moreover, in contrast with the relatively trim line of command in the Conservative organisation, Wright's work went through two tiers of approval: an advisory group of advertising volunteers and the Campaign Committee. It was an unwieldy structure, prone to delays, and reflected Labour's continued suspicion of commercialism. To the chagrin of both Grant and Johnny Wright, the Campaign Committee placed ideological considerations higher than a rational assessment of electoral considerations. For example, the committee vetoed the placement of any advertising in the *Sun*, although the paper was popular among Labour's target voters of the skilled working class.

In Grant's view, Labour's disaster in 1983 came partly because the party had not yet understood the 'need to develop political marketing as part of the science of communication in the multi-media society... The disaster of 1983 has played a major part in changing the party's view, although there remain a few sceptics.'[89]

Opinion polls during the course of the election accord with the verdict of a disastrous Labour campaign, and confirm that this was Thatcher's finest hour glory.

The Harris 1983 election exit poll (Table 3.3) confirmed Thatcher's standing as the most impressive leader. Voters were asked, 'Regardless of how you voted today, which of the party leaders do you think came across best during the campaign?' These polls also confirm the Conservative campaign strategists' assessment of the opposition parties leadership weaknesses. Michael Foot, who in the judgement of Butler and Kavanagh ran the least 'modern' campaign since Clement Attlee,[90] failed to impress a majority of even Labour supporters. He ran an old-style campaign of addressing rallies and 'pressing the flesh', his oratory was rambling and discursive, frequently wandering

Table 3.3   Leaders' images, 1983

	All %	Con %	Lab %	Alliance %
Thatcher	47	84	19	17
Foot	14	1	46	2
Jenkins	2	1	2	5
Steel	38	15	33	77

Source: Harris ITN exit poll, 9 June 1983.

from the text of prepared speech handouts, and his schedule not geared to photo-opportunities. Robert Fox, the BBC commentator who followed his campaign for the BBC, reported that Foot was 'out-Saatchied at every turn'.[91] Jenkins, styled the 'Prime Minister designate' by the Alliance, fared even worse. To the displeasure of Jenkins, Steel asked him to ditch the label to enable Steel to take a stronger leadership profile. Jenkins refused.[92]

Thatcher also maintained a commanding lead in voters' perceptions of the most capable leader and ability to deal with a crisis. A MORI poll for the *Sunday Times* in May 1983 found that 62 per cent of the sample rated Mrs Thatcher good in a crisis (Foot 9 per cent, Jenkins 14 per cent, Steel 17 per cent); 62 per cent also rated her a capable leader (Foot 21 per cent, Jenkins 26 per cent, Steel 53 per cent).

Issues

Analysis of the issues also suggests a strong Conservative performance. According to the Harris exit poll, the top issues which people took into account when deciding how to vote were those shown in Table 3.4.

The first point to note is that, although unemployment remained clearly the most important issue nationally, it ranked relatively low in the priorities of Conservative voters. This confirmed the party's private pre-campaign research which suggested that, while unemployment was clearly a political problem, it was not necessarily an electoral problem. Voters in the Tory heartlands of the south and midlands of England had suffered

Table 3.4   The major issues, 1983

	All %	Con %	Lab %	Alliance %
Unemployment	48	22	74	60
Prices	24	36	15	16
Disarmament	18	16	20	19
Economy	16	24	6	15
Defence	14	22	4	13
NHS	13	5	21	16

Source: Harris ITN exit poll, 9 June 1983.

less from the recession than those in the north. Consequently unemployment was lower and had less direct impact on the voting decisions of Tory target voters.

Moreover a MORI panel study for the *Sunday Times* shows that the Conservative standing on most of the top issues actually improved during the campaign (see Table 3.5). The MORI panel studies also showed a substantial Tory lead on taxation and on industrial relations and strikes. On taxation the campaign improved the Tory standing by nine points (34–43) while Labour drifted by two points (26–24); on industrial relations, the Conservatives improved five points (33–38) and Labour moved just one point (35–34).

SUMMARY

These were glory years for Mrs Thatcher, dominant in her Cabinet, adored by her party, lionised by the tabloid Tory press. The 'marketing of Margaret' began to be seen as a major contributor to these achievements. Yet, despite the magnitude of the Conservative victory, the 1983 election cannot compare with its predecessor as a landmark in the development of political marketing. It continued and maintained the lessons of 1979: to conduct market research carefully, to assess the public mood and design a strategy around that, and limit manifesto commitments according to it, to minimise risks and to harmonise all the major parts of the communications campaign

Table 3.5   Campaign impact on major issues, 1983

I am going to read out a list of problems facing Britain today. I would like you to tell me whether you think the Conservative Party, the Labour Party or the Liberal/SDP Alliance has the best policies on each problem?

	Panel I %	*Panel IV* %	*Change* %
Unemployment			
Con	20	27	+7
Lab	40	31	−9
Alliance	13	19	+6
Inflation			
Con	55	58	+3
Lab	19	20	+1
Alliance	8	12	+4
Disarmament			
Con	43	48	+5
Lab	24	21	−3
Alliance	9	15	+6
Defence			
Con	49	53	+4
Lab	22	19	−3
Alliance	8	14	+6

Source: MORI *Sunday Times* panels I & IV, 21 April and 2 June. (MORI did not ask a separate question on the economy.)

around tested themes. The major innovations had come before the election in the experiments with direct mail and Harvey Thomas's overhaul of rallies and conference presentation.

However 1983 did prove a pivotal point in Labour thinking on political marketing. In the four years that followed, Labour communications organisers paid the Tories the ultimate compliment of copying many of their presentational techniques, though not yet the more fundamental contribution of political marketing proper to the shaping of the policy product itself.

4 Towards the Permanent Campaign: the 1987 Election

By 1987 there was an air of invincibility and inevitability about the Conservatives. Yet the Tories only edged ahead in the polls in the early months of 1987, some six months before the election. Despite the massive 144-seat majority, the 1983–7 parliament was punctuated by a series of crises for the government and for Mrs Thatcher personally. The first major challenge arose with the miners' strike of 1984/85. There can be little doubt that the government's determination to win the strike entrenched the public image of Mrs Thatcher as a tough and resolute leader, yet there appeared to be scant reward in terms of popular support. Norman Tebbit noted somewhat ruefully in his memoirs:

> It is a pity that the Government made almost no political gain from one of the most important political events of my time in politics. Governments had walked in fear of a coal strike for decades. Ted Heath had destroyed his own Government, but it was the miners who delivered the *coup de grâce* in 1974. Margaret Thatcher's government had broken not just a strike but a spell. Parliament had regained its sovereignty ... I doubt if any other Prime Minister would have had the courage to win a coal strike, yet within weeks of that victory we suffered heavy losses in the local elections and the polls showed us in third place. No wonder the government's friends bemoaned our poor communications.[1]

At the end of 1985 and the beginning of 1986 came Thatcher's most serious personal crisis of the parliament with the eruption of the Westland Affair and the Cabinet resignations of first Michael Heseltine and then (Sir) Leon Brittan. At its climax Mrs Thatcher's own future as party leader seemed in doubt. Her vulnerability only increased with the third crisis, the American bombing of Tripoli by aircraft from British bases. Unpopular according to the polls, Mrs Thatcher's staunch support for the Americans was not unanimously shared by her Cabinet and damaging stories of internal division emerged.[2]

In the wake of Westland and the Libya bombing, the Conservatives trailed in public opinion and for much of 1986 they were running third in both their own and public polls. The nadir was reached in the week 26 March–1 April, when the Conservatives trailed Labour by 13.5 points (Conservatives 27 per cent, Labour 40.5 per cent, Alliance 31 per cent), according to Gallup polls for CCO.[3] They continued to lag behind Labour throughout the summer. By the end of September the Tories had recovered somewhat to around 33 per cent but were still behind Labour by a monthly average of 4 points. In other words, another Conservative landslide, far from being inevitable, did not even look likely some nine months before the election. The Tories believe that their campaign from the autumn of 1986, beginning with the October Party Conference at Bournemouth, was crucial. From then on the Tories recovered in the polls, to be neck and neck with Labour at 41 per cent by December.

Strategic planning began at the time of both the government's and Mrs Thatcher's lowest poll ratings, when Michael Dobbs, seconded to CCO from Saatchis and John Sharkey of Saatchis presented the results of a major qualitative survey to Mrs Thatcher at a meeting at Chequers on 13 April 1986. The meeting was called to bring Mrs Thatcher the results of a research study called *Life In Britain*. The research was conducted by BJM Research Associates who had carried out similar survey work for the Tories before the 1983 election. It was conducted in the normal commercial marketing way, through meetings of nine groups of about 12 people from target demographic sectors (one group of pensioners, two groups of under-25s, the rest floating voters in the 25–45 age range). The meetings, handled by market research experts, last typically for up to three hours and are designed to be relaxed gatherings, with snacks and alcohol, and people are encouraged to give vent to their gut feelings.

It is commonly agreed, and accepted by CCO sources, that the results deeply upset Mrs Thatcher. She was thought to have become more extreme, and it was said that both she and the party had lost their identification with the basic values of the voters. They were seen as stumbling along from crisis to crisis with no clear aims, no sense of direction and no clear leadership. The party traditionally rated poorly in the handling of unemployment but now it was also thought incompetent on the other 'caring' issues of education and the Health Service.

Rodney Tyler in *Campaign!* describes the April meeting in colourful terms as Dobbs confronted the prime minister with the news that she had become an electoral liability – the 'That Bloody Woman' factor.[4] Butler and Kavanagh suggest that she began to take more interest in the Young & Rubicam's Values and Lifestyle (VALS) research at that time because it was presenting a less unflattering personal portrait of her.[5] Be that as it may, Dobbs and Saatchis' analysis of the focus group research provided the foundations of the Tory campaign and equally importantly it set the parameters for a dynamic and radical manifesto. A senior Central Office official remarked:

> It seems to me to be quite paradoxical that, although you may find in various bits and pieces that have been published that the party leadership took great exception to what was being said about its problems in the spring of 1986, in the autumn of 1986 it totally welcomed the solutions that the research recommended.[6]

The key decision was to 'relaunch' – the commercial marketing term is used by Tory officials – the party at the Conservative conference in Bournemouth in the first week of October. The major task was to win back dissatisfied Tory supporters who had been drifting to the Alliance by combating the 'boredom factor', the 'time for a change' feeling that the government had gone on too long, was running out of steam and no longer appearing united around clear aims.

Planning for the conference began six months in advance and involved Saatchi more closely than in any previous conference. CCO and Saatchi agreed upon a theme and slogan – The Next Moves Forward (sometimes appearing as the Next Move Forward) – and market-tested it to see if it was the appropriate answer to the question that wavering supporters had most in mind. They then set about ensuring that the conference became a detailed platform for re-emphasising the slogan. Previous conference slogans have been coined purely for the event and forgotten shortly afterwards. But The Next Moves

Forward was intended as the campaigning slogan which would take the party through the election.

A Saatchi man closely involved in the campaign explained the agency's role:

> We had to make the slogan work very hard indeed and we did that in a number of ways. First we advertised. The ads were not particularly for mass consumption but they were the best possible way of letting opinion formers know what we wanted. We talked to the press and we laundered the slogan very heavily beforehand. We crammed the conference hall and the hotel full of leaflets and posters. We also went to every Cabinet minister or his representative to explain what was so important about the conference and help him understand what role he could play in it. This consisted of two things: perhaps offering a brief outline of how what he wanted to say could be fitted into The Next Move Forward and, indeed, the agency offered a few paragraphs of how this might be done. We also agreed with them the policy pronouncements they wanted to emphasise and we prepared promotional literature to support it, which helped it fit into the Next Move Forward. It would be wrong to say, however, that Saatchis controlled the conference. They didn't.[7]

This degree of agency involvement in a party conference was unprecedented and reflected the long association and bonds of trust between the party leadership and the Saatchis, emphasised by the key role entrusted to Dobbs at CCO.

The Tory election campaign started with that conference. That was part of the plan and it required a steady nerve to stick to it because Central Office was coming under pressure to relaunch earlier in the summer to improve their poor polling rating. Central Office managers refused, partly because they did not feel the party was yet ready to sustain a campaign and it would be worse to start something that frittered away uselessly than have nothing at all, and partly because they feared it would look like an imitation of Labour's summer Freedom and Fairness campaign.

Both the Tories and Labour identify the conference as the turning-point in Conservative fortunes. The Tories went into the conference trailing Labour by 6 per cent and recovered steadily thereafter. Labour's communication director Peter Mandelson pinpointed it as one of the main reasons for the decline in Labour's support.

> Our support gradually slipped for two reasons. First, the Conservative success in launching the government as a caring, united administration. In my view it had everything to do with that conference and very little to do with the election itself. Secondly, in the first quarter of 1987 the rekindling of two Labour weaknesses, defence and extremism.[8]

Perhaps even more significantly, the *Life in Britain* research was also a vital factor which persuaded Mrs Thatcher to adopt a radical manifesto. As John Sharkey put it, tactfully:

> What was required was new targets for her phenomenal energies. The research had identified the current principal areas of public concern: unemployment, the health service, education and law and order. We said that new goals had to be set within each of these – and the ways for achieving them be announced.[9]

This was the third consecutive example of Mrs Thatcher, despite her image as a conviction politician, tailoring her programme to the parameters established by market research. The significance of this point should not be underrated, even though the advertisers and marketing consultants do not claim any input into the details of the policy which eventually resulted. A Downing Street aide confirmed the importance of the research:

> It was a very strong spur and the Prime Minister spent a large part of 1987 pushing through policies in Cabinet to get them to a stage for inclusion in the manifesto: education, rent reform, housing and the community charge. She was driving like mad, aware that she was determined to have a radical manifesto, very concerned not to have a manifesto which was inert and would expose her to the charge that she had run out of ideas. She wanted to have more ideas than the opposition parties, which in fact she did.[10]

Party leaders and officials were later to set great store in the 'radical manifesto' as an election winner, because it enabled them to counter effectively the 'time for a change' challenge.

Ironically this marketing solution, embraced because of the problems of 1986/87, also contained the seeds of Mrs Thatcher's eventual downfall: radical policies adopted then, in health, education and, most notably, the poll tax, helped create the crisis of popularity and leadership which led to her resignation in November 1990.

THE BLUE WAR BOOK

By Christmas 1986, CCO was able to present to Mrs Thatcher a detailed election planning document, the *Blue Book*, sometimes known as the *War Book*. It was the first time in the memory of CCO officials that all the details of preparation had been brought together at such an early stage. Previously *War Books* were put together piecemeal as the various Central Office departments worked out the details of their campaigns.

The *Blue Book* offers a rare insight into the campaigning and communications strategies of the Conservative Party, all the more intriguing for the fact that, more than any other party, the Tories tend to guard jealously their campaign secrets. One important qualification should be noted, however. The details quoted here and in other published accounts come from the *December draft* of the *Blue Book*, which was the first draft. It is likely that there were some alterations to strategy in the aftermath of Rosie Barnes' shock SDP gain from Labour at the Greenwich by-election in February 1987. The *Blue Book* clearly locates Labour as the main strategic opponent and does not yet mention the 'Doomsday Scenario', that is, the Conservative calculations of the electoral implications if the Labour vote collapsed. The final draft of the *Blue Book* almost certainly paid far greater attention to the Alliance threat.

The *Blue Book* was about 100 pages, drafted by Dobbs and prepared personally for Thatcher. Its plans were made on the assumption that June or October/November 1987 would be the likely election date, although it could be adapted if necessary. It set out the grounds of battle, the order of battle, precampaign activity, the election campaign and timetable options. Under the strategic theme 'Britain Moving Forward' it listed the Conservatives' unique selling points as leadership, direction, success, vision and patriotism. It stressed that *party image* would be more important than any issue and argued that the strength of the 'moving forward' theme was that it would contrast with backward-looking Labour and the great weakness of the Alliance, its lack of direction and unity.

> It is vital that we establish a clear contrast between us and other parties, because we believe that the clearer the choice which is facing the electorate, the more their basically conservative instincts and values will be reflected in Conservative votes . . . Moreover we believe that the best means of squeezing the Alliance is to concentrate the voters' minds on a clear choice between the two major parties rather than presenting them with a confused 'middle of the road muddle'.

It also argued that the Tories needed to be specific about their plans 'because we believe the electorate will be in a more questioning mood than 1983 in the aftermath of the Falklands. This can be made an advantage as it would once again contrast very starkly with the Labour Party, which has difficulty in agreeing on policies which are acceptable to both its warring factions and the electorate.'

Labour's weaknesses were perceptions that it was too extreme, dependent on the trade unions and too divided. Moreover Kinnock was a significant handicap. 'Importantly, Mr Kinnock is not seen as a popular leader; he is inexperienced and weak and we assume that his recent US trip will have reconfirmed this view.' Elsewhere in the book, Kinnock is described as the most 'intellectually lightweight' Labour leader in modern times. However Labour seemed to have recovered some support in the C1 and C2 social groups and was polling solidly in the mid- to high 30 per cent range – a base which might prove difficult to reduce, according to the *Blue Book*. The Alliance weakness was that its support was still based heavily on dissatisfaction with the other two parties. 'We conclude that the best single means of combating the Alliance is through generating positive support for our own party's policies.'

The document predicted correctly that Labour's campaign would concentrate on the 'caring' issues on which the Tories were vulnerable. 'However, they have not yet proved to be trumps and it is difficult to see how they can dramatically improve their attack in these areas . . .' It warned that the greatest danger to the Conservatives might be complacency (echoes

of 1983). The aims of the Tory campaign should be to recon-
cile individual responsibility with caring, stability with change,
and raise the profile of defence, taxation, inflation and trade
union reform. 'While issues are generally less important than
the overall view of government, defence and taxation are crucial. The Conservatives have a clear and unique position on
both. The opposition is entirely divided on both.' The weak
issues were likely to be health, education and pensions. Significantly unemployment was not mentioned in the *Blue Book* and,
since this is unlikely to have been an oversight, it must be
supposed that CCO no longer deemed unemployment a major liability.

The strategy for attacking Labour was to press for details of
their policies; tie in the leadership with the extremists; and
put personal pressure on Kinnock. The Alliance was to be
treated as irrelevant and the main battle against them would
be conducted at the local level, where more often than not
they were the main opponent to a Tory incumbent. The document also predicted a more presidential campaign than ever,
'partly because of your position as Europe's senior statesman,
partly because Mr Kinnock has . . . apparently laid plans for a
presidential-style campaign and partly because the media finds
such a campaign easier to report'. It urged Mrs Thatcher not
to try to develop a soft image, but to play to her strengths of
leadership, strength and experience. The role of the prime
minister was to become *the* trigger of the rows about strategy
which were to erupt during the campaign.

The *Blue Book* was discussed at the first formal strategy
meeting of the campaign on 8 January 1987. Present were Mrs
Thatcher, Tebbit, Dobbs, Robin Harris (Conservative Research
Department), Peter Morrison (deputy chairman), Stephen
Sherbourne, political secretary at Number 10, and the party
treasurer, Lord McAlpine. A further meeting was held at Downing Street on 15 April at which all the main strategy recommendations of the *Blue Book* were accepted. On 24 April
Maurice Saatchi and John Sharkey, the agency's man in charge
of the Tory account, showed the prime minister the portfolio
of advertisements for the campaign. She requested them to be
more positive, and by the weekend of 2–3 May they had produced a revised package which she approved.

All aspects of the campaign under Central Office control

were well in hand and all that remained was for Mrs Thatcher to pick the date. The decisive moment came after the local elections in May; the Central Office computer analysis projected a national election victory by 98 seats. At a Chequers meeting to discuss the local results, Tebbit tempered the computer's enthusiasm, however, and predicted victory by 50 or 60 seats.[11] The following Monday, 11 May, Mrs Thatcher named 11 June as polling day.

ORGANISING FOR BATTLE

Norman Tebbit had been appointed chairman in September 1985, replacing John Selwyn Gummer, chairman since 1983. By tradition the chairman is supported by a clutch of vice chairmen (five in 1987), normally MPs, who are given specific responsibilities, such as candidate or women's organisation. There were also two deputy chairmen during the 1983–7 parliament: novelist Jeffrey Archer, until his resignation in connection with a prostitute scandal, and Peter Morrison, MP for Chester, who was appointed in September 1986 to be Tebbit's deputy. For the campaign Morrison was made CCO's chief 'trouble-shooter' in administration and personnel matters.

Beneath the strata at the top, CCO employed about 180 staff whose principal departments were headed by five directors: Director of Organisation (Sir Anthony Garner), Director of Campaigning (John Lacey), Director of Conservative Research Department (Robin Harris), Director of Special Services, formerly the Marketing Department (Sir Christopher Lawson) and Director of the Conservative Political Centre (David Knapp). There was one other major department, communications, which operated without a director after Harvey Thomas moved sideways in August 1986 to become Director of Presentation and Promotion. The role of director of communications was more or less split between Norman Tebbit and Michael Dobbs, with former *Mirror* reporter John Desborough, the Chief Information Officer, in charge of press.

Director of Communications – the Central Failure?

Given the importance generally attributed to the national television campaign, and the kudos accorded to a former holder of the post (Sir Gordon Reece), it seems astonishing that the Conservatives should have entered an election campaign without a communications director. Tebbit singled out the absence as the biggest single weakness of the Tory campaign and the cause of many of its problems.[12] 'Not having a director was not a problem up to the election but once the election started it was a nightmare,' said a senior campaign official. 'Because there was no one person co-ordinating communications it created a lot of internal problems which would have been possible to solve.'[13]

Reasons for the failure to appoint a communications director go to the heart of the differences which were later to emerge in the factions vying for control of the Conservative campaign. According to the Tebbit/Dobbs camp the main blame lies with Mrs Thatcher and it is still a mystery why she refused Tebbit's choice. Tebbit and Dobbs began looking for a new communications director in the middle of 1986 and were hoping for a Gordon Reece look-alike, a respected figure in the communications world. Reece was, in fact, offered the job in the spring of 1986 but he declined. By the end of the summer, Dobbs had identified more than 20 people from which a Central Office committee produced a short list. Michael Mander, whose experience was mainly in newspapers, was selected and offered the job subject to the prime minister's approval. She turned him down.

Mrs Thatcher's apparent obstinacy is cast in a different light in an account given by one of her personal campaign aides:

> Norman Tebbit and Michael Dobbs have convinced themselves that the Prime Minister was being obdurate in some way. The reality was that the organisation of Central Office was at fault, although this was not entirely the fault of Norman Tebbit. Communications is really an all-embracing job but you had bits of the machinery parcelled out among different people. Part of it was done by Harvey Thomas, then you had Desborough brought in by Norman to handle the press, then you had Michael Dobbs doing something indefinable. What they had done was taken the empire of communications, carved it up and then said they wanted a big man to run it. No big man wanted it because it was too small. Then they find a small man to run what is left of the empire and the PM says this is too big a job for a small man.

Give me a big man. This is what happened. It is as simple as that. But Michael [Dobbs] and Norman are convinced that the PM, for reasons which of course are unfathomable, refused to give them the director they wanted.

However the end result was that none of the people heading the communications department had any direct experience of working with television, in contrast with Labour, who had former *Weekend World* producer, Peter Mandelson, leading their operation.

Special Services Department

This department carried out the most innovative work of the Tory campaign – the implementation of new technology and direct mail. Sir Christopher Lawson and Dobbs were in charge of the Tories' massive direct mail campaign which sent out about eight million letters to target voters. The main target groups were young householders and about five million shareholders, but also included were farmers, headmasters, power workers, lecturers, trade associations, first-time voters (about 450 000 of them), council house buyers (about 100 000), private health scheme members, people with incomes over £20 000, health service doctors and nurses, the Institute of Directors and the CBI.[14]

Central Office began testing direct mail in August 1986 with advice from CCN Systems, one of the country's leading direct mail organisations. CCN uses 'Mosaic' geo-demographic classification system to identify the recipients of mailings. Dobbs looked closely at the American, German, Australian and Canadian experience of political direct mail and found nothing that was directly transferable. In the end the Tories relied heavily on the share registers and developed their own classification system with advice from CCN.

Despite the disparaging label of 'junk mail', direct mail was at that time the fastest growing sector of the British advertising industry. By 1984 it had become the UK's third largest mass medium, behind television and print. It had long been used in US politics, most notably as a fund-raising tool. Richard Vigurie is commonly regarded as the instigator of US political direct mail, which he started using in 1965 for the right-wing Young

Americans for Freedom. The SDP pioneered its use in Britain and the Tories first used it before the 1983 election, but they quickly abandoned it amid a great deal of internal disagreement. Campaign managers in the constituencies felt that a centrally organised direct mail campaign cut across their independence of action and reduced their ability to raise funds. It was argued that funds raised for the central organisation through direct mail merely reduced the sums contributed to the local associations. This debate is still not resolved within the party although party managers have no doubt that direct mail is a powerful communications tool.

From 1986 the Tories used direct mail personalised letters primarily as a communications tool, to attract votes and recruit members. The privatisations, particularly of British Telecom and British Gas, gave them a readily identifiable market for the pilot schemes. Its success, 'the most successful direct mail campaign in British politics', according to Tebbit,[15] spurred the massive direct mail campaign which culminated in mailings of one million per month from the beginning of 1987 to May. The first mailing to 10 000 British Telecom shareholders, at a cost of about 30p a shot, produced a response rate of almost 10 per cent, bringing in some £10 000 in contributions. Other letters went out to shareholders in Jaguar, British Gas, company directors as well as the target groups. The party also capitalised on Nigel Lawson's budget, preparing a million letters to go out to shareholders and homeowners explaining how they would benefit from the government's economic proposals. When the direct mail campaign finished, it had brought in some 35 000 new members.[16]

The scale of the mailings was prompted partly by CCO's assessment of biased political reporting on television. CCO, at Tebbit's initiative, had started to monitor television programmes for anti-Tory bias. Tebbit's loudly proclaimed criticism of the BBC's coverage of the American raid on Libya was only one example, and CCO concluded that television was likely to be against them in the election campaign. The Conservatives were by no means alone in the direct mail campaigns. Labour claimed to have raised about £400 000 through their campaign, overseen by Steve Billcliffe.[17] The SDP too had built up a bank of 90 000 donators and supporters.

The Special Services department was also in charge of the

Table 4.1   State of the parties, 1983–7

	May 1983		May 1987
	Votes	*Share (%)*	*Seats*
Con	13 012 315	42.4	393
Lab	8 456 934	27.6	208
Alliance	7 780 949	25.4	27
Others	1 420 938	4.6	22

CCO computers. Central Office used an ICL ME29 mainframe computer with a capacity double that of their 1983 machine. Banked on it were the names of about a quarter of a million supporters who had donated money or responded favourably to questions. At the same time constituencies were encouraged to use computers and were urged to buy ICLs or Apricots, in order to be compatible with Central Office. By the election there were slightly fewer than 300 computers in the constituencies. A large number of these were cheaper models such as the Amstrad PCW, BBC and the Sinclair Spectrum.

THE TARGET

The Conservatives entered the 1987 General Election campaign holding a working majority of 135 seats (Table 4.1). Of equal significance, given the workings of the British first-past-the-post (FPTP) system, the Tories held an 185-seat advantage over Labour.[18]

Looking at the arithmetic, the Conservatives were comfortably placed. They could afford to lose 67 seats (a swing against the government of about 6.5 per cent) and would still have an absolute majority of one. The target for the Tories then was to 'hold what we have' and try to keep most of the seats they won last time. They proved remarkably successful both at hanging on to their seats and maintaining the Conservative share of the vote.

Labour needed a swing against the Tories of 11 per cent to achieve a bare majority, something that has never been achieved since the landslide in 1945. They needed to win 117 seats over and above their 1983 total for an absolute majority. Even to become the largest single party they would need a swing of 8.6 per cent to gain an extra 94 seats. They had to overturn substantial majorities in the hostile south and recapture the decisive battlegrounds in the Midlands to be sure of outright power. To a considerable degree, they needed to buck the regional trends.[19] Their prospects were not enhanced by the boundary changes prior to the 1983 election which cost them some ten seats.[20] The Alliance had no realistic chance of forming a majority government. They did hope, however, that they might win more votes than Labour and thus start establishing themselves as the major opposition. Overhauling the Labour vote was the Alliance target.[21]

The task of dislodging the Conservatives looked daunting, if not impossible. However there was a consensus among politicans and commentators that this would be a closer ride than 1983. This was partly because the Conservatives only began to show a winning lead in the polls in early 1987, whereas they had held a larger lead for more than a year in 1983. Peter Riddell, then political editor of the *Financial Times*, argued that this difference:

> could be crucial within a campaign. With a decline in public commitment to particular parties, not only are the voters more volatile in their preferences but a higher proportion make up their minds during the course of the campaign itself. For instance, in 1983 Tory and Labour support both fell by about 4 percentage points during the campaign to the Alliance's benefit. This is more than double the average change in each party's vote in the month up to polling day in 1970.[22]

A second crucial factor was the stronger starting position of the Alliance and a belief, shared by all the parties, that the Alliance were well placed to break through and become the second largest party. The tortuous complexities of the way in while a strong Alliance showing might affect the party arrangement of seats in a new parliament taxed not only the pundits (in particular Peter Kellner, regular columnist in the *New Statesman*): CCO also calculated the result of a collapse in the Labour vote, the 'Doomsday Scenario'. This possibility and the consequent threat from the Alliance played an increasingly dominant part in Conservative strategic thinking as the election came closer and Labour languished ever more poorly in the polls.[23]

Tactical Seats

In early 1986 the Tories analysed each constituency and came up with a target list of 110 seats which would decide the election. This was pruned to 72 'critical' constituencies needed to ensure a solid Conservative victory by at least 50–60 seats.

Norman Tebbit and his chief-of-staff Dobbs took a decision early on to keep the critical seats campaign as tightly controlled as possible. They were fearful of the tendency for the critical seat list to snowball because everyone wants to be included. With limited time and resources, they were anxious not to spread the butter too thinly. For that reason, as much as the fear of giving their enemies useful information, the critical seat list had to be kept a closely guarded secret. 'We didn't boast or brag about what we had done because everybody would have wanted to be treated this way,' said a CCO official.[24]

Stewart Newman was urged out of his retirement home in Bermuda to be full-time critical seats co-ordinator. Party vice-chairmen Hal Miller and (Sir) Tom Arnold were responsible for the regional co-ordination of the tactical seats. The detailed audit of each constituency was carried out in conjunction with the professional agents, regional organisers, National Union and MPs. The seats were then divided into seven categories:

Category One 286 safe Conservative seats – here the basic minimum requirement of safety was a majority of 5000 plus.
Category Two There were 13 seats in this category. These were apparently safe Tory seats, but were endangered because of potential problems, such as a retiring incumbent, unpopular MP or weak local association.
Category Three Vulnerable seats – the ones the Conservatives had to hold for a majority of 50 plus seats, which was the minimum Tory target. There were 59 seats in group three.
Category Four Conservative seats regarded as more vulnerable than category three. These were 'bonus' seats, because they would bring a majority over 50.
Categories Five, Six and Seven These were opposition-held seats and were split according to the chances of Tory victory.

CCO concentrated on categories two, three and four. Constituencies were not told explicitly which category they were in, to avoid unnecessary problems, but most resources were poured into Categories Two and Three – the 'Critical 72' – and relatively little was done for category four seats. The Critical 72 had to have an agent, an office, a secretary, proper office equipment including an electric typewriter, duplicating machine and a computer where possible. Not all were encouraged to use computers because it would have stretched local resources too far, but the vast majority did and they were taught, and where necessary, pressured into using them for campaigning purposes. Central Office made it plain that they wanted computers used for detailed canvassing and local direct mail. Constituencies would be told, for instance, to send mail-outs to first time voters at a certain time.

Central Office provided funding for improvements in all the Category Two and Three seats, although 100 per cent grants were given only exceptionally. CCO also subsidised the *In Touch* newsletter[25] and distributed free lists of the names and addresses of council house buyers and first-time voters for local direct mail campaigns. Additionally the target seats were encouraged to use telephone canvassing in the last seven days before polling. The technique had been first introduced and developed at by-elections late in the 1983–7 parliament.[26]

Tom Arnold's own seat, Hazel Grove, was a Category Three tactical seat and a Conservative/Alliance marginal. Arnold felt that the most important help he received from CCO was financial:

> What we needed most was financial help with the postage because it's no good anyone talking about direct mail campaigns unless we can get the stuff out. My association was already fully stretched.
>
> At the turn of 1986/87, for example, we sent out a questionnaire to selected households. It contained a franked envelope to send back to me and there was a list of 17 issues such as defence, environment, law and order, education, and I asked people to tick off the various boxes. I wrote back personally to everyone who replied, setting out the party's policies and making some of my own comments. That was a very successful exercise with a response rate of about 12 per cent which I consider good. Now, postage involved in

that exercise was beyond our local budget because I sent out several thousand questionnaires. We also needed more secretarial help in the office and I was able to get money for another secretary.[27]

Arnold noted that the usefulness of CCO aid depended largely on the efficiency of the local association. 'If a candidate knows what he wants and doesn't make impossible demands in terms of time and money, then CCO can provide valuable, indeed vital, assistance. If the candidate doesn't know then it's very difficult for this place [CCO] to respond with the precision that is required.'

NATIONAL COMMUNICATIONS CAMPAIGN

The communications campaign proved to be the Achilles' heel of the Tory planning and, virtually from day one, things started to go wrong. As the campaign wore on, the sideshow developed of rows and rifts within CCO, between Tebbit, his chief-of-staff Dobbs, and Saatchi & Saatchi, all ranged on one side, and Mrs Thatcher, former Saatchi man (Sir) Tim Bell and Lord Young on the other, with Young & Rubicam chairman, John Banks, and former Conservative communications head, Geoffrey Tucker, also involved.

The day after polling day, *The Times* ran the story of 'Project Blue' – how Young & Rubicam had effectively taken over from Saatchi midway through the campaign. The week after the election, the BBC's *Panorama* reported that 'much blood was spilled on the Central Office carpets' on Wobbly Thursday – 4 June – the day that the *Daily Telegraph*'s Gallup poll showed the Tory lead cut to just four points over Labour. *Panorama*'s report that Thatcher 'effectively dispensed with Saatchi & Saatchi' and put her own personal team in charge led to the threat of a libel suit from Saatchi. The BBC paid £1000 to the NSPCC by way of apology.

Television

In 1987 British television devoted more than 200 hours of programmes entirely or substantially to the election,[28] and election coverage dominated the news bulletins in the five weeks up to polling day. This was the greatest volume of election broadcasting to date. The saturation coverage, much grumbled at by viewers, was compounded by breakfast television which made its first full-scale entrance into an election campaign.[29]

Television greatly extends its political coverage at election time and the real beauty for politicians is that the 'fairness rules' render TV uniquely vulnerable.[30] While no special restrictions fetter press editorial freedom, TV is legally obliged to be impartial and editorialising is forbidden. Until 1992, at least, the amount of coverage each party received was in accordance with guidelines laid down by the Committee for Political Broadcasting. This committee, composed of broadcasters and party representatives, allocates the number of party election broadcasts (PEBs) to each party, and until 1992, this ratio determined the amount of news coverage the parties could expect – the 'tot' as it was called. The 'tot' system led to what *The Economist* called 'bizarre stop-watching – the drawing up of second-for-second lists to make sure the parties get equal air time on the news whether or not they have done anything worth reporting'.[31]

On this occasion the committee decided on a 5:5:5 allocation, five PEBs each for the three major parties with the crucial spin-off that they would each get equal air time in news coverage. There was no objection at all from the Tories to the Alliance request for equal airtime, perhaps because they miscalculated that the Alliance would direct most of their attack against Labour. In the event the Alliance turned most of their fire on the Tories, which meant that for every minute of Tory coverage they felt they got two minutes of opposition attack.[32]

All the major parties mounted media-monitoring operations, which included checking with a stopwatch the amount of time each party got on news bulletins, as well as watching for signs of bias or opportunities to respond quickly to breaking news. Steve Robin, the CCO press officer, was in charge of the Tory media monitoring operation. Within the Conservative leadership there had been a view held over period of at least a year that television news and current affairs was biased against the government. Norman Tebbit had publicly complained about the BBC's coverage of the Libya bombing raid, and had established a media-watch campaign at CCO to track incidents of bias.[33]

However, during the campaign itself, the campaign managers took a decision not to make formal protests. They reasoned that any complaint would become a news issue in itself and they could not be sure of support even from the sectors of the press normally favourable to them.[34] By contrast, Labour's communication managers had adopted a policy of deliberate grumbling. Patricia Hewitt, press secretary to Neil Kinnock, believed it was especially important keep television journalists 'on their toes', by keeping them constantly aware that everything they said was being closely watched:

> Basically television gave us a very good ride and we didn't complain a lot during the campaign. But there was one occasion early on concerning Neil's very first speech, the 'thousand generations' speech. The speech was made in the morning and the 1pm BBC news made a reference to his voice, although he had not had trouble with his voice for months. I rang up and complained because we weren't going to have a story that Neil was losing his voice at the very beginning of the campaign. No way. They changed the commentary for the evening news.[35]

Whatever concerns the partisans may have had, however, viewers generally found television impartial. According to a BBC/IBA survey, 70 per cent of the TV audience felt the election coverage was fair.[36]

The parties' performances on television were the single strongest reason for the post-election verdict – generally shared among the media pundits – that Labour had run the better campaign. A MORI poll found that Labour made the more favourable impression both in TV interviews and in general coverage.[37] It should be noted, however, that Labour's campaign impressed scarcely more than the Alliance, when the Alliance by the admission of its own campaign co-ordinator John Pardoe, ran a wretched campaign.[38] Moreover the Tories were successful in pushing defence to the top of the news bulletin agenda. Martin Harrison's analysis[39] found that defence was the foremost issue in election news coverage. Importantly it was not only a strong issue for the Tories; it was also given as one of major reasons for not voting Labour (see below).

Yet no one, least of all the Conservative camp, would claim

that the Tories had waged a good TV campaign. Without a communications director, responsibilities were split: the chief whip, John Wakeham was to allocate the Cabinet team for various TV appearances and Lord Young was put in charge of Mrs Thatcher's tour. Former Downing Street press officer Christine Wall was recruited to accompany Mrs Thatcher and advise on her television appearances.[40] Wakeham decided to appear on a BBC *Election Call* himself, although as chief whip he had not given an interview for four years. His inept performance caused Mrs Thatcher to remark, 'Wakeham's a total disaster,' according to Lord Young's account.[41] As a result, Young and Tebbit, together with Wakeham, were asked to take joint charge of television appearances.

The Leader's Tour

Mrs Thatcher's carefully arranged tours with their purposefully-created photo-opportunities were a feature of the previous two elections. In 1987, Conservative campaign circles regarded the leader's tour as a serious weakness and a major reason why the campaign looked poor on television. Tebbit admitted this later. Quoting the Conservative campaign strategy document (Blue Book) he said: ' "The PM's tours – these are essentially for the media. We suggest it should have a distinct theme which is compatible with the tone of the campaign. We suggest it should be Regeneration." . . . It never happened.'[42]

The tour was taken away from Central Office control and given to Lord Young, whom Mrs Thatcher had asked to take on the job in March 1987. It is not surprising, therefore, that Tebbit and his supporters should be eager to highlight its failings. One CCO campaign manager complained that the details of the tour were not completed until late in the day and were not properly thought through, partly because of the extra-tight security arrangements which the police wanted to enforce, mindful of the Brighton bomb; but it was also due to a failure of leadership:

I don't think David Young ever really had proper control. Essentially it was taken over by herself and therefore until she gave the go ahead nothing could be done in Central Office. All we did was the bus – which was itself a world

beater and Roger Boaden deserves credit. We'd had an involved discussion in early January about the PM's tour and
transport, because the transport you use affects the kind of
tour you can arrange. We had to commit expenditure to the
bus despite the fact that at a very late stage we had no
permission from Downing Street. It was a very expensive
operation, a purpose-built bus designed to give maximum
security with all the latest in new technology devices. You
are talking about many tens of thousands of pounds.[43]

The upshot was a tour that seemed disjointed, unlike Kinnock's
which was neatly co-ordinated with the theme the Labour leaders had developed at the morning press conferences. As Rodney
Tyler noted:

in its first full week, the tour managed to visit an East Midlands school on a Bank Holiday, and Wales during Wakes
Weeks when most of the factories were closed and then hold
three events in one constituency in the West Country. It had
taken only two days to antagonise the travelling press and
build up resentment which was fuelled the following day
when, on a visit to a guide dogs training centre, a briefing
of reporters was finally arranged, only for them to be told
high-handedly that it was 'off the record'; when most of
them walked out, the official line was swiftly changed.[44]

Party Election Broadcasts

Hugh Hudson's 'presidential' PEB for Kinnock was the outstanding piece of work in this category, and was certainly one
of the highlights, if not *the* highlight, of the Labour campaign.
The Conservative broadcasts suffered, as did their whole communications campaign, from the internal arguments over strategy. At the end of the first week of the campaign proper, the
Tories changed tack to raise the profile of Mrs Thatcher and
to run a more aggressive campaign than originally envisaged,
because the manifesto had run into problems and it had became clear that Labour, not the Alliance, were posing the more
serious challenge. The rather grudging compromise showed
itself most particularly in the third PEB, which in the words of
Lord Young, was 'two entirely separate films'.[45] A campaign

official close to Tebbit considered it the Conservatives' poorest piece of publicity and nowhere near as good as a PEB that Saatchis had already prepared. The official said: 'In defence of Saatchis, given the muddle that we the client presented them with, they did produce some very good and effective advertising and I thought ours was much more effective than the Labour Party.'[46]

The Press

It might be tempting to imagine that because the Tories get the most favourable press they also have the most sophisticated press relations machinery. This was certainly not the case in 1987. The party's press campaign got off on a poor footing with the first full-scale press conference – the launch of the manifesto. With the start scheduled for 11am, the conference room at CCO, Smith Square, was packed, hot and airless by 10.30 and was clearly too small for the numbers trying to squeeze in. Journalists were, in writer Terry Coleman's words, 'brawling' to get in.[47] CCO set up an overflow room with video and microphone links, but since it was next to the kitchen, the smell of frying fat and noise of vegetables being chopped up made it unpopular with journalists. A measure of the state of disorganisation was that a photographer from the staunchly Tory *Daily Express* had to battle with a security guard to enter the press conference. It was not an auspicious way to start the campaign but not untypical of what was to follow. For efficiency and easy availability of press releases and speeches, and answers to queries the Tory organisation was less impressive than either Labour or the Alliance. This was true despite the fact that CCO had topped up its complement of eight full-time press officers with 15 temporary helpers and kept the press office open 24 hours a day.

In keeping with the practice of recent elections, the Tories did not start daily press conferences until three weeks before polling – later than either the Alliance or Labour. They had intended, much like Labour, to set the tone for the day at the press conference and then follow the theme through with the leader's tour, photo-opportunities and speeches. However, almost from the beginning, things went wrong. A Central Office senior official explained:

Right from the start we discovered that, although we may
have set the press conference theme for the day, it was almost unilaterally hi-jacked [by Mrs Thatcher] while the press
conference was going on. It started on Day One after the
press conference was supposed to have been finished. We
wanted it to end at 10am so we could get on with the day's
programme but she would not accept that. If there were
questions put to her by journalists she would answer them.

I can't remember the theme for Day One [Mrs Thatcher's
first conference following the manifesto launch] but it ended
up being education, which the day's activities hadn't been
designed to meet. There was some confusion where we were
saying something at the press conference which was not
quite what the manifesto was saying. Basically, we spent 48
hours struggling to try to clarify the situation.[48]

The early press conferences saw the Tories get in a muddle
over a few of their manifesto pledges, notably education and
housing. John Sharkey, Saatchis' Conservative account director, admitted that the manifesto, which was to have been the
major launching pad for a positive Tory campaign, 'caused a
lot of problems even among our own supporters, particularly
the proposals for schools'.[49]

However the Tories could still count on the bulk of the
British press; six of the ten national daily papers, accounting
for 71 per cent of the total national newspaper circulation,
campaigned for a Conservative victory.[50] Two, *The Guardian*
and *Daily Mirror*, supported Labour; one, *Today*, supported the
Alliance, and one, *The Independent*, remained strictly neutral.
The Tory-supporting tabloid newspapers devoted large proportions of their election coverage to knocking Labour: 73 per
cent of the *Sun's* election stories were 'knocking' copy – general incompetence of Labour, Labour and extremism, Labour
and lesbians and gays and so on – 54 per cent of the *Daily Mail*
and 46 per cent of the *Daily Star*.[51]

There are some members of the Conservative campaign team
who believe that the press is more important than television,
in the sense that the press sets the agenda which television
then follows. Lead stories in the national press (18 May–11
June 1987) were dominated by opinion polls followed by defence, scandal and smear stories, and then party strategy and

prospects. Taxation was fifth in the list, followed by health and education.[52] By comparison, the most common election stories on television news were, in order, defence, unemployment, education, NHS, the economy, attacks, counter-attacks and praise.[53] It should be noted, however, that different criteria may been used for establishing the categories of stories on television and in the press.

There are two blindingly clear examples of the press coming to the Tories' aid during the campaign. The first is in the reporting of Kinnock's interview with David Frost on TV-am's *David Frost on Sunday* on 24 May. It was journalists who spotted the potential in Kinnock's answer to a question about pitting British soldiers against the nuclear weapons of an enemy. In truth, Kinnock's waffled answer was far from clear but in three of the following day's papers – the *Express*, *Telegraph*, *Today* – it was construed as a 'dad's army' faith in guerilla warfare to beat the enemy. The story ran for most of the week, spurred on by Kinnock's replies to follow-up questions. Arguably this story helped pin defence more firmly in the headlines than any of the campaign tactics and techniques employed by CCO.

The second occasion followed Mrs Thatcher's press conference blunder on Wobbly Thursday (4 June) when she said she used private health care in order to 'go on the day I want, at the time I want, with the doctor I want'. Labour seized this and used it in their advertising and speeches. The following Tuesday the *Sun* took the heat out of Labour's attack when it revealed that Denis Healey's wife had had a private hip operation. Healey made matters worse by shouting angrily on a TV-am interview with Anne Diamond, thus giving the story even greater prominence.

Advertising

The Conservatives took 217 pages of advertising in the national daily and Sunday newspapers during the campaign, a threefold increase on its 67 pages in the 1983 campaign. Labour took 102 pages, almost four times more than in 1983, when its total was only 27. The vast bulk of the Tory spend was concentrated into the four days before polling. The late burst was not pre-planned, and indeed there is some dispute over who authorised it, with both Tebbit and Lord Young claiming the credit.

Tebbit explained that the Tories were afraid that Labour was planning a last-week advertising blitz:

> Whether such a campaign would have been directly effective or not, there was no doubt in my mind that a heavy press advertising campaign would have demoralised our party workers. For us it was imperative that the Labour Party should not be seen to be leading us in press advertising in the final week.[54]

He said that the late advertising blast was one of the only two major changes to the campaign plan, the other being that the anticipated challenge of the Alliance did not emerge so material prepared to deal with them, including a whole advertising package, was not used. Lord Young, in his memoirs, however, says that he had to persuade Tebbit to agree the unprecedented scale of the advertising:

> I said, 'Come on Norman, let's have three pages every single day, Sunday through to Thursday – don't worry about the cost because I've spoken to Alistair [Lord McAlpine – the party treasurer] and there's plenty of money' . . . I then went to find Alistair to tell him how much of his funds I had committed, as I had not agreed anything with him. He agreed right away. Better to be the party in power with an overdraft than a rich opposition, that was always his motto . . .[55]

The Tory press advertising was designed to coincide with the themes of the PEBs. Early advertisements included a two-page spread with mugshots of 'left-wing' Labour candidates with the caption: 'So this is the new Militant-free Labour Party'. Mid-campaign advertisements included probably the most memorable of the four weeks, a picture of a soldier in surrender pose beside the bold capitals caption: 'LABOUR'S POLICY ON ARMS'. Another ran a full-page picture of a violent picket line scene with a quote from Kinnock: 'Secondary picketing . . . is a right that should be enjoyed.'

In the last week the Tories' advertising blitz (that word is used by friend and foe alike) ran three full pages in every national newspaper daily from the final Sunday until polling day. It included eight separate advertisements all featuring heavy, mostly huge, bold capitals on a plain white background with short captions detailing Tory achievements followed by a much smaller type, lower-case caption on Labour's failures. At the bottom of each ran the slogan which echoed the Tories' 1959 campaign call: 'Britain is great again. Don't let Labour wreck it. Vote Conservative.' The themes were lowest inflation for nearly 20 years, lowest income tax for nearly 50 years, unemployment falling faster than any country in Europe, health service spending up by 31 per cent more than inflation, nurses pay up 30 per cent above inflation, fewest strikes for 50 years; the final one had just the slogan on it: 'Britain is great again. Don't let Labour wreck it. Vote Conservative.'

Central Campaign Costs

The Conservatives spent some £9 million on the election campaign, compared to £3.8 million in 1983. The cost of the final four-day advertising blitz alone was about £3 million. The total advertising bill was £6.4 million – up from £2.6 million in the 1983 campaign – an increase of 106 per cent in real terms.[56] Funds raised over 1986–7 were about £8.9 million and it seems that Central Office was prepared to spend well beyond its means during the campaign. According to Pinto-Duschinsky:

> This was partly on the presumption that donors would be persuaded to give more generously when they saw how heavily the party was spending on its advertising and that, even if the money was not raised, it was better to go into deficit than to risk losing the election. In the words of one senior Conservative official: 'I'd hate to be the [official] who balanced the books and lost the election.'[57]

Pinto-Duschinsky estimated that 1987 was the third most expensive campaign for the Tories, 1935 and 1964 being more costly in real terms. The most striking feature this time was the concentration of the spending, all the advertising being packed into the last three weeks, whereas the earlier campaigns had spread the spending over the months, or years, before the announcement of an election.

Although Labour significantly increased its advertising spend compared with 1983, it was still heavily outspent by the Conservatives (see Table 4.2). Ratios of Conservative:Labour:Alliance spending under Mrs Thatcher's three elections as prime minister were: 12:7:1 in 1979; 12:7:6 in 1983; and 12:6:3 in 1987.

Table 4.2   Central campaign expenditure, 1987 (£000)

			Con	Lab
Grants to constituencies			137	388
Advertising	Press	4523		
	Posters			
	& leafs	1834		
			6357	2175
PEBs (production costs)			366	143
Opinion research			219	148
Leader's tour & meetings			417	233
Publications			714	269
Staff & admin costs			818	838
TOTAL			9028	4194

Source: Pinto-Duschinsky (1989). (Figures exclude local campaign spending.)

So even though this was the most expensive Labour campaign ever, at some £4 million, the Tories still managed to increase their advantage. Pinto-Duschinsky estimated the cost of the Alliance campaign at £2.7–3.1 million. Cost per vote, excluding subsidies in kind – such as the free air time for PEBs – worked out at 83p per vote for the Conservatives, 62p for Labour and 37–42p for the Alliance. He concluded:

> In my view, its advertising, though not decisive, was useful to the Conservative campaign. It enabled the party strongly to reinforce the messages, particularly about the Conservatives' economic record and the way Labour would threaten it, that were also being made in the party's press conferences and in Mrs Thatcher's speeches. If this assessment is correct, the election was probably influenced by the financial superiority of Conservative Central Office.[58]

A Mass-Observation poll conducted in the days following the election supports the conclusion that Tory advertising may have been effective. Some 41 per cent of their sample thought that the Conservatives ran the best press and poster advertisements, nearly twice as many who favoured Labour's efforts (24 per cent).

THE CAMPAIGN IN RETROSPECT

The 1987 election was another milestone for political marketing for a number of reasons:

1   It reinforced the tendency prevalent since Margaret Thatcher had become leader for the party to rely on marketing experts to shape the campaign and set the parameters for the manifesto.
2   It produced hard evidence of a relatively new development in British political campaigning: a conscious and co-ordinated pre-campaign (Conservative) which was almost certainly far more significant than the campaign itself and which adds weight to the belief that 'permanent campaigns' are the future of modern politics.
3   It saw the development and first significant use of campaigning techniques and technology which will surely become increasingly important in future elections, in particular the use of computers, direct mail and telephone canvassing. These innovations may slow the post-war tendency to ever greater reliance on the mass media at the expense of doorstep electioneering and personal contact with voters.
4   The four weeks of the campaign proper were among the most costly ever; some £12 million was spent by the Conservatives, about £4 million by Labour and about £2 million by the Alliance. The last five days saw the heaviest concentration of party political advertising in British history.
5   The pre-campaign witnessed heavily increased use of government advertising with significant party political implications. The period 1983–7 saw a spectacular increase in government advertising in support of controversial economic and social policy. Publicly neither the government nor anybody else for that matter paid much attention before 1987 to the party political effect of the government advertising campaigns. Only the marketing press gave much prominence to stories of the government having become the second biggest advertising spender in the nation, behind Unilever. Total spending for the financial year to April 1987 was some £90 million, more than three times the

Table 4.3   The general election of 11 June 1987

	Con	*Lab*	*Alliance*	*Other*	*Total*
Seats					
At dissolution	393	208	27	22	650
After election	376	229	22	23	650
Votes					
% of total	42.2	30.8	22.6	4.4	100
1983–7 change	–0.2	+3.2	–2.8	–0.2	

Conservative overall majority 102
Turnout 75.3%

Central Office of Information advertising spend in the previous year. Some was unarguably neutral information, but much, like the £38 million Manpower Services Commission campaign on training and Restart, and the £34 million British Gas flotation campaign, had a clear public relations element.

Many assorted and sometimes contradictory verdicts have been returned on the 1987 election: the campaign changed nothing, it was dull and lacking in any real political argument, it was one of the most media-conscious ever, it was the most carefully stage-managed, Labour 'won' the campaign even though they lost the election, it was a worse result for Labour than the 1983 débâcle, the Tories triumphed despite their lacklustre campaign . . . and so on. The first verdict gets to the crux of the matter.

The Campaign Made No Difference to the Outcome

Despite all the money spent, all the advertising, all the careful planning, stage management and media hype, there was scarcely any change, in seats or share of the vote, compared with either the 1983 general election result or the average of the major polls in the six months up to May 1987 (Table 4.3). Compared with 1983 Labour improved slightly, the Alliance declined slightly and the Conservatives stayed rock solid, winning by a landslide exceeding even their own expectations. The change over the six month average of polls up to May is even less: Conservative, no change; Labour -1 per cent; the Alliance -1 per cent. Ivor Crewe, writing a post-election analysis in *The Guardian*, summed it up:

> Britain's most expensive, media-saturated campaign appears to have had the smallest net impact on party support for decades. The BBC TV/Gallup election survey revealed an electorate whose mind had been firmly set. Fully 81 per cent of respondents claimed to have decided their vote before the campaign began, a higher percentage than for any election since 1966.[59]

So what difference, if any, can be accounted for by the campaigning activities of the parties?

The pre-campaign
Party managers point to the importance of the pre-campaign: the party conference, the relaunch of the Conservative government as a dynamic, united, forward-looking administration, the massive direct mail effort making use of the party's privatisation and taxation policies and the concerted attacks on Labour's main weakness of 'extremism'. Additionally there was the use of government publicity to provide images of an active and dynamic government.

It is highly likely that pre-campaign activities are now more important than the four-week, official campaign itself. Yet the academic study of elections has been slow to respond and the vast bulk of scholarly research into party campaigning is concerned almost exclusively with the three or four weeks of the campaign proper (for example, the Nuffield general election series and the more recent Crewe and Harrop political communication series). This preoccupation has continued despite the general consensus that the campaign proper usually has only a slight or marginal impact on voters. The temptation has been to seek explanations of electoral outcomes outside campaigns, in the long-term sweep of historical, political and sociodemographic change. The tendency in the context of the 1987 election was to see Conservative victory as the more or less inevitable outcome of non-campaign factors.

However, in the opinion of Conservative campaign managers, the result was far from inevitable: the government had been in severe political trouble after the Westland, Libya bombing and British Leyland affairs. Ministers resigned from the sinking ship, the prime minister looked increasingly vulnerable and out of touch and the party languished behind Labour in the opinion polls for virtually the whole of 1986. The Conservative transformation to seemingly invincible favourites by early 1987 cannot, of course, constitute proof of the party's pre-campaign marketing success. However the pre-campaign activity was a factor considered important by both Conservative and Labour campaign managers, and as yet it has received little or no academic attention. One would expect pre-election campaigns and mid-term campaigns[60] to play an increasingly important part, especially if, as many claim, the traditional bonds of party identification are eroding and voters are becoming more volatile and possibly more open to political persuasion.[61]

The margins of victory: national versus local factors
At a second level, the campaign is seen as having made a vital contribution, not so much to the result, but to the margin of victory and defeat. The Tories believe the campaign made the difference between winning by a 40–50 seat majority or by a 100-seat majority. Precisely which facet of the campaign gets the credit depends on who is doing the talking. The public relations and advertising specialists believe it was the national campaign, including the party conferences and particularly the Conservatives' late advertising blast which was largely responsible. CCO campaign staff tend to believe it was the effort in the key marginal constituencies, the local campaign, that made the difference.

Advertisers, such as Tim Bell, who was brought in late and controversially to advise the Tory campaign, believe that the last ten days before polling were crucial. The decisive factors were the Tories' late advertising blitz aimed squarely at 'fear and greed'; Mrs Thatcher's own commanding form; the withering away of the Labour campaign in the last week; and the complete disaster of the Alliance campaign from start to finish.[62] Paul Medlicott, who toured with David Steel as the Liberal leader's press aide, also gives credit to the Tories' late advertising surge:

> I was very impressed with the way the Tories simply outblasted Labour in the last few days. It was something like four to

one. The Tories had a miserable campaign apart from two things which won them the election. One was Norman Tebbit's exercise in writing before the campaign to British Telecom shareholders in targeted constituencies and the other was the huge blitz in the last few days which made Labour look like they were going to pinch all your pennies. Very well done, a real appeal to greed and fear. Brilliant and horrible.[63]

The 'constituency campaign' theory is supported *prima facie* by the successful results in the critical marginals, many of which stayed Tory despite regional swings to Labour. The Conservatives held or regained all but 15 of their 72 critical seats and in 47 of these (65 per cent) they achieved a share of the vote higher than the Tory regional average. However while local factors, particularly new incumbency, had a noticeable impact, the claims for successful Tory targeting seem exaggerated. After controlling for the incumbency effect, the CCO-directed target seat campaign appears to have been worth no more than about 250 votes on average.[64]

Even though the result appeared miserable, Labour campaigners believed their campaign achieved their major goal, which was to stave off the Alliance and establish themselves clearly as the opposition party with the only realistic prospect of defeating the Tories. Despite a flutter of poll-induced excitement around Wobbly Thursday (4 June), no one, including Labour campaigners themselves, really expected Labour to win. Their most optimistic target was to cut the Tory majority to about 30–40 seats.

For obvious reasons, Labour did not broadcast this before the election. A year after the election, the Labour leadership had still not publicly admitted their limited aspirations. But Philip Gould, head of the Labour Party's Shadow Communications Agency which developed its advertising campaign, made it abundantly clear in a letter to the marketing magazine *Campaign*:

One of the penalties of the success of the Labour campaign is that people, understandably, have forgotten how different Labour's prospects looked at the beginning of the election.

In the first week of the campaign, an average of opinion polls had the Labour Party at 28 per cent and the Alliance at 27 per cent . . . Many experienced pundits saw it as only a matter of time before the Alliance managed to overtake Labour as the main opposition party . . . By polling day Labour had gained an additional four per cent of the popular vote, the first time in recent history that Labour has increased its share during the course of an election campaign. Conversely, the Alliance lost four per cent, Labour widening a one per cent lead over the Alliance to nine per cent during a four-week campaign.

. . . Demonstrably, the Labour campaign made a decisive difference, not just in attitudes, not just in votes, but in helping to shape a political map in which the Labour party is firmly identified as the only possible alternative party of government to the Tories. The real measure of the campaign's success in this general election, will be Labour's success at the next.[65]

Did Labour 'Win' the Campaign?

Considering the enormity of the Conservative victory this particular point of view has an extraordinary number of adherents and, perhaps most surprising, it has survived the sobering passage of a few years. Lady Thatcher's memoirs pay somewhat graceless tribute to Labour's superior communications[66] and there are some even within the Conservative camp who would probably still agree with Patricia Hewitt and Peter Mandelson, that the election result 'does not alter the basic judgment that Labour's campaign was one of the most effective pieces of disciplined communications of modern British politics'.[67]

Any number of examples can be plucked from the election-time press to sing the praises of the Labour campaign in comparison with a Conservative effort which seemed 'disorganised and strangely hesitant' according to *The Independent* (12 June 1987). The highlights were probably Hugh Hudson's 'Kinnock' PEB which was said to have boosted the Labour leader's rating by 16 per cent,[68] and the disciplined communications operation which ensured that the party determinedly pursued its own 'people's agenda' of the caring issues, concentrating on one theme throughout each day.

Tim Bell paid a high compliment to Labour's efforts when he tried to recruit Mandelson into his own agency after the

Table 4.4   Leaders' images, 1987

Q. Who do you think would make the most capable Prime Minister –
Mrs Thatcher, Mr Kinnock, Mr Steel or Mr Owen?

	12–14 May %	20–21 May %	27–28 May %	3–4 June %	Change %
Mrs Thatcher	46	46	45	45	–1
Mr Kinnock	21	24	26	27	+6
Mr Steel	10	9	9	8	–2
Mr Owen	13	12	13	13	0
No opinion	11	9	7	7	–4

Source: MORI.

election.[69] However there is virtually no hard evidence that
Labour's campaign was more effective. According to MORI
surveys, it raised the standing of Kinnock, although he still
finished well below Mrs Thatcher as the most capable prime
minister (see Table 4.4 above); and according to Harris Observer polls it went a long way to dispelling the image of Labour as too divided (see Table 4.5 below). It raised the profile
of Labour's favoured 'caring' issues – unemployment, health,
education – but it did not do the Tories any real damage on
these, their vulnerable issues. It hardly dented the Conservatives' rating on the question, 'which party to you trust most to
deal with . . .'. Nor did it raise Labour's own rating. Indeed the
Tories finished neck-and-neck with Labour on two of the three
issues, unemployment and education (see Tables 4.6 and 4.7
below).

The four-week campaign saw very little movement in the
polls of any statistical significance on any major issue or image
dimension. One of the few areas that did move was defence,
a major problem area for Labour. As a reason for not voting
Labour it jumped 12 points (35–47) becoming the single biggest block to Labour (Table 4.5). To this extent the Conservatives can claim some success. By contrast, Labour's attacks
on the Conservatives missed the mark. The major reasons
for not voting Conservative (too extreme, don't like leader,

Table 4.5   Negative images, 1987

Q. Looking at the list, which would you say are the two main reasons why you don't intend to vote Conservative?

Too extreme	22	20	22	25	+3
Don't like leader	37	38	40	37	0
Not caring	54	54	60	55	+1
Time for change	31	34	25	27	−4
Defence policy	15	17	16	17	+2
None of these	5	7	6	8	+3 ·
Don't know	12	8	10	8	−4

Q. Looking at this list, which would you say are the two main reasons why you don't intend to vote Labour?

Too extreme	29	30	28	31	+2
Don't like leader	24	25	22	21	−3
Too divided	38	34	30	27	−11
Will damage economy	41	41	38	40	−1
Defence	35	34	45	47	+12
None of these	3	6	5	7	+4
Don't know	11	10	10	6	−5

Q. Looking at this list, which would you say are the two main reasons why you don't intend to vote for the Liberal/SDP Alliance?

Leadership divided	44	44	42	46	+2
Waste of a vote	34	35	38	39	+5
Damage economy	13	11	11	9	−4
Too much like Labour Party	14	12	11	11	−3
Don't know what an Alliance govt would be like	46	44	42	46	0
None of these	8	12	9	11	+3
Don't know	11	12	13	8	−3

Source: Harris.

Table 4.6   Key issues, 1987

Q. Which two or three issues will be most important to you in helping you decide which party to vote for at the general election?

Unemployment	45	51	51	51	+6
NHS/health	32	37	39	42	+10
Education	26	35	42	44	+18
Defence	16	19	29	27	+11
Law & order	14	17	19	18	+4

Source: MORI.

not caring, time for a change and so on) remained virtually unmoved.

Leaving aside for the minute the sheer weight of the result, it is a plausible reading from the opinion polls that the Conservative campaign was more effective – especially on defence – than Labour's. Despite the poor reviews of its television presentation, the movement of the polls during the campaign suggests that the Conservative strategy as laid down in the *Blue Book* was largely correct. Judging by the polls the party waged a rational campaign, pitching its efforts and energies into the issues and image dimensions most likely to further the Conservative vote and undermine the opposition's. Its predictions proved accurate that Labour's major thrust would be on the caring issues and, perhaps more importantly, that this attack would be unlikely to gain much ground. By contrast, the Conservative's favoured issues, particularly the economy and defence, appear to be capable of making a real difference to the vote. In a post-election report to Labour's ruling NEC, Larry Whitty, the party's general secretary, admitted that Tory PEBs and advertising on these issues 'undoubtedly did us damage'.[70]

It is worth dwelling a little on the economy because this was a major plank of the Conservative campaign, but was virtually ignored in the Labour publicity effort.[71] Economic optimism, the standard of living and general perceptions of prosperity are usually considered key factors which influence voters – a theory which continues to impress Tory campaigners. John Curtice found a marked increase in economic optimism between 1985

Table 4.7   Party images, 1987: trustworthiness

Q. Which party, Conservative, Labour or the Liberal/SDP Alliance, do you most trust to make the right decisions on:

	13–14 May %	20–21 May %	27–28 May %	3–4 June %	Change
Unemployment					
Conservative	32	30	33	35	+3
Labour	35	36	38	33	–2
Alliance	16	15	14	15	–1
Don't know	17	19	15	17	0
Health service					
Conservative	30	29	n/a	28	–2
Labour	40	41	n/a	41	+1
Alliance	16	15	n/a	15	–1
Don't know	14	15	n/a	15	+1
Defence					
Conservative	51	48	51	53	+2
Labour	20	21	23	19	–1
Alliance	13	13	13	13	0
Don't know	16	18	13	15	–1
Law & order					
Conservative	46	44	42	44	–2
Labour	22	25	28	23	+1
Alliance	14	12	12	13	–1
Don't know	18	19	18	21	+3
Education					
Conservative	36	35	33	33	–3
Labour	31	32	37	34	+3
Alliance	17	15	16	17	0
Don't know	16	18	14	15	–1

Source: Harris.

and 1986 and observed a link between this and the Conservatives' improved polling performance. His analysis discovered that:

> a governing party can appeal successfully to voters whose values are different from their own, on the basis of improving economic indications. Changes in evaluations of the economy can apparently produce a rise or fall in the level of support for a party from those of *all* ideological persuasions. We may thus have a clue as to why the Conservative Party won the June 1987 election even when the electorate had been moving away from it ideologically.[72] (Curtice's italics)

Party campaigners from all sides agree that the economy is the vital battleground for persuading voters, yet Labour strategists decided to steer clear of economic messages during the campaign. Advice from the Australian Labour Party suggested that a government would be virtually unassailable if a majority of voters had confidence in its economic performance. According to Patricia Hewitt, then press secretary to Neil Kinnock:

> The Australian Labour Party and their researchers have a nice way of illustrating this:
>
> Economic plus
>
> _____
>
> Battleground
>
> _____
>
> Economic minus
>
> What they say is that if the government is above the top line, it doesn't matter what the opposition does, the government will win. If the opposition are below the bottom line on credibility, then it doesn't matter what the government does even if it is in the middle, it will not lose. It is when both parties are in the middle that you have got a battle.
>
> In 1987 the government was above the top line and we were below the bottom line so defeat was likely. We didn't see it quite like that then, but that was what was actually going on. Most people in work had enjoyed substantial increases in their income and in the value of their property. Why vote against the government that had delivered that? What we finally decided to do was to play to our strengths,

the social issues, and although there was some stuff on the economy, it was very much a social issues campaign.[73]

Thus, strategically the Conservatives were better placed for battle, and Labour reduced to fighting on territory that promised little reward. The view that Labour won the campaign seems a superficial assessment, perhaps based purely on the slickness of certain television images and the campaigning verve of Neil Kinnock. The campaign did not increase the Labour vote share compared to the six month average of polls up to May, nor did it do any discernible damage to the Tories. Moreover apparent success in winning votes from the Alliance may have been due as much to Alliance confusions and failures as to the Labour campaign. The single unequivocal achievement of the Labour campaign was to save Kinnock's position as party leader. Arguably the 1987 failure was even more devastating than 1983 because Labour had fewer fig leaves to spare their blushes, no Falklands Factor or Michael Foot handicap, for instance. In the aftermath of such a humiliation one might have expected a serious challenge to Kinnock's leadership, yet none emerged until, in 1988, a reluctant Tony Benn put in a bid that was easily crushed.

The Tories Won in Spite of Their Campaign

There are two main reasons for this view. The first is that Labour and Kinnock came over much more strongly on television. The second is the astonishing leaks from Downing Street and CCO of personality clashes between Tebbit, Thatcher and Lord Young, rows over strategy, panic attacks on Wobbly Thursday and the battle of the advertising agencies for the prime minister's ear. For a nation accustomed in recent elections to seeing united, slick, polished Conservative campaigns, it was a highly newsworthy spectacle.

Successful Tory election campaigns have been criticised before. In 1959 in particular, Labour's campaign won all the praise, yet the Conservatives won by a landslide. In 1970 Harold Wilson's mingle-with-the-people campaign was a roaring success according to contemporary press reports, yet Heath won with a 30-seat majority and was eventually assessed as having waged the most sophisticated television campaign yet seen.

One might have expected that the passing of time would have taken the gloss off Labour's effort and favoured the 1987 Tory campaign with a kinder verdict. A major reason why that has not happened is Rodney Tyler's book, *Campaign!*, which first revealed the extent of the divisions and panic in the Tory camp. Since then Lord Young, brought into CCO to run Mrs Thatcher's tour, has published his memoirs, and they so closely match Tyler's version that it is hard to escape the conclusion that Young or people close to him must have been Tyler's main sources. Fuel to the fire was added by two other accounts, one from Norman Tebbit and another emanating from the agency Young & Rubicam via *The Times*.

It emerged that there were rows over strategy, which was changed during the four weeks; lines of responsibility were blurred; 'closet' campaigns were waged; and Mrs Thatcher was personally unhappy and felt insecure at the way the campaign was managed. All this is common ground; however the details of the story are greatly in dispute. Three separate explanations have been aired of events within the Tory campaign, reflecting the three separate camps that vied for control of strategy.

'Project Blue'
This first came to public notice in *The Times* on 13 June 1987, two days after the election. The story claimed that the advertising agency Young & Rubicam effectively took over the campaign from Saatchi & Saatchi and 'rescued' the Tory strategy. The leading protagonists here were Young & Rubicam's chairman, John Banks, and the agency's consultant, Geoffrey Tucker, who had been Tory publicity director for Heath's victory in 1970 and who was also involved less formally in 1974. They were said to have the ear of Lord Whitelaw and Chief Whip John Wakeham.

According to *The Times*, the agency had been feeding research to Downing Street regularly for about a year before the election. The claim is that Young & Rubicam's qualitative research, known as VALs (values and lifestyles), showed the Tories in potentially deep trouble by Wobbly Thursday. Mr Kinnock's campaign was proving successful and Conservative support soft and slipping. Banks presented their research to the prime minister and effectively changed the Tory campaign strategy to one of 'don't let Labour ruin everything'.

An aide to Mrs Thatcher confirmed that the prime minister was interested in Young & Rubicam's research but said that agency's input had been blown out of proportion, partly at its prodding, and partly by Norman Tebbit, who felt that the interference was a slur on CCO's efforts. Tebbit later claimed that he did not know Young & Rubicam's research was being funded by the party, and thought it a terrible waste of money which 'caused the Prime Minister unnecessary alarm and me considerable irritation'.[74]

According to the anonymous aide, Young & Rubicam were 'a very small bit of the jigsaw'. He said:

> This has been blown out of proportion in a way that is quite unbelievable. This PM and I would have thought any Prime Minister with any sense talks to people outside all the time. How else could they judge the quality of advice coming to them from their official advisers. To suggest that by speaking to anyone outside it somehow undermined the official opinion poll people or the official advertising people is a crazy way of looking at the world.[75]

'Beau Bell'

The title for this explanation is lifted from a marketing magazine review of Tyler's *Campaign!* which credits Tim Bell as the man mainly responsible for turning the lacklustre Tory campaign around and finishing it in a blaze of glory. Bell, former media director of Saatchi & Saatchi, had worked closely on the Tory account in the previous two elections and is a personal friend both of Lady Thatcher and her family and of Lord Young. Bell is a man of extraordinary personal charm and energy whose friendship with Lady Thatcher survived indiscretions one might have expected to be fatally wounding.[76] Her regard for him may be judged by his reward of a knighthood in the prime minister's resignation honours in 1990. Michael Dobbs and the Saatchi brothers Maurice and Charles, by stark contrast, were not honoured.

Bell is probably the closest British equivalent to the American political consultant and has worked on campaigns in Malta, Ghana, Venezuela, Colombia, post-Pinochet Chile and for F.W. de Klerk in the South African elections of 1994. He was twice involved with Reagan's campaigns, once as observer and then in 1980 as an adviser. Mrs Thatcher recommended his services to the National Coal Board chairman Ian MacGregor during the miners' strike of 1984/85 and he helped prepare advertising, organised regular briefings with editors and advised on MacGregor's TV presentation.[77] Bell also worked closely during the strike with David Hart, founder of the New Right ginger group, Committee for a Free Britain, whose lavish meetings, complete with free champagne, video screens and laser light displays were among the most popular of the Conservative conference fringe.[78] Since then his services have been enlisted by, among others, David Mellor after the story broke of his affair with actress Antonia de Sancha, and most infamously, by the Department of National Heritage, to advise on celebrations to commemorate the fiftieth anniversary of D-Day.

Bell left Saatchi after the 1983 election amid some acrimony that has never been fully explained publicly and went to the agency Lowe, Howard-Spink & Bell.[79] However he was held on a retainer, partly in case he was needed to help with Tory campaigns and, partly, to prevent him taking the Tory account with him. In the event, party chairman Norman Tebbit refused to allow him any official role in the campaign. A Central Office official said that Tebbit did not want Bell anywhere near the campaign because of rumours that the *Daily Mirror* was going to splash stories about Bell's private life and Tebbit did not want to risk a damaging distraction from the campaign.

But Bell did become involved as one of Mrs Thatcher's secret campaign team – 'the exiles' as they were known: Bell, former chairman Cecil Parkinson and Sir Gordon Reece. At first Bell's meetings with Mrs Thatcher, and with Lord Young with whom he mainly liaised, were kept secret from CCO. But from Wobbly Thursday he was brought out of hiding and helped openly in the preparation of election broadcasts and newspaper advertising. At that stage too Gordon Reece was handed an open role in the campaign to assist Mrs Thatcher with her television presentation.

Lord Young gives an extraordinary account of the panic, mainly his own, on the days of 3 and 4 June in the wake of unfavourable opinion polls on *Newsnight* and in the *Daily Telegraph*.[80] He instructed Bell to draw up an alternative advertising campaign for the last week and showed it to an approving Mrs Thatcher. The Tories were in danger of losing the election, Young believed, and Bell's advertising was vital to saving it. In a waiting room at Number 10, Young confronted first Norman Tebbit and then Maurice Saatchi, insisting that they follow Bell's advertising ideas:

> I got him [Tebbit] by the shoulders and said, 'Norman, listen to me, we're about to lose this f . . . ing election! You're going to go, I'm going to go, the whole thing is going to go. The entire election depends upon her doing fine performances for the next five days – she has got to be happy, we have got to do this.[81]

The Bell/Young axis were highly critical of Tebbit/CCO strategy. Bell thought that they were wrong to wage a mainly positive campaign and had paid too much attention to the Alliance threat. When Labour emerged strongly in the first week and the Alliance appeared in disarray, CCO did not know how to cope and lost the initiative. For Bell, Mrs Thatcher was always going to be the Tories' strongest campaigning card. Yet the CCO planners did not give her a high enough profile, did not know how to get the best out of her and had not allowed her closest campaigning friends (Bell, Reece and Parkinson) to be involved. Moreover the emphasis on a positive campaign was also misplaced. According to a member of the Bell camp, 'You have to approach people through fear and greed. People vote basically out of self-interest, and why shouldn't they?'[82]

Central Office
The third version of events is the one Tebbit has propounded and which has support in Butler and Kavanagh's *The British General Election of 1987*. It admits that there were conflicts and a variety of closet campaigns going on but argues that the basic strategy, as prepared by Tebbit and chief-of-staff Dobbs, remained intact.

It has never been openly stated by anyone, but it is a clear implication of this viewpoint, that the problems in the Tory campaign stemmed mainly from Mrs Thatcher: her surprising insecurity, her refusal to agree on the appointment of a communications director, her hesitancy in agreeing details of the campaign tour and willingness to allow outside advisers to change her mind and sow the seeds of general confusion in the Tory camp. This view of Mrs Thatcher is the polar opposite of the Bell/Young camp's. A former party official put it like this in the calmer months after the election:

> Mrs Thatcher had an awful campaign and a lot of people in the party saw it and didn't believe she would be able to go through another hard campaign. I think that's one of the main reasons why we've seen senior party members starting to jockey for position for a leadership battle.[83]

It is virtually impossible to say which is the definitive explanation, partly because the people most closely involved will not talk on the record. There is no shortage of people within Central Office and close to Downing Street willing to speak off the record and so, for students of the 1987 campaign, it boils down to best guesses and trust. But certain background features are common ground. The most important of these is that there was a rift between Thatcher and Tebbit during the course of 1986.

The first few months of the year were the worst for the Tories in the whole of the parliament with the Westland crisis, the resignations of Cabinet Ministers Heseltine and Brittan, the British Leyland controversy and the Libya bombing raid crisis. Butler and Kavanagh's summary puts it well:

> To understand the origins of the tensions between the two [Thatcher and Tebbit] it is essential to recall how vulnerable Mrs Thatcher felt in the wake of the Westland crisis. In February 1986 she learned that some of her more trusted senior ministers (and their wives) were talking of the need to replace her. Rightly or wrongly, she grew more convinced that Mr Tebbit regarded her as 'finished' and was using Central Office to advance his own claims to the succession. Henceforth, she looked with a jaundiced eye at the activities of Mr Tebbit, Central Office, and Saatchi & Saatchi . . .[84]

A CCO official close to Tebbit also gave credence to the Butler and Kavanagh summary. Tebbit, he said, remarked a few times that he wondered whether Mrs Thatcher would survive 1986.[85] Although in the approach to the election Mrs Thatcher and Tebbit patched up their differences, she continued to be concerned about the preparedness of Central Office. Her fears were doubtless heightened by the tendency, which the same

Central Office aide admits, of Tebbit and Dobbs to keep the details of the campaign planning close to their chests.

Mrs Thatcher decided to tackle the problem by removing some of the power from Mr Tebbit's control by putting Lord Young (then Employment Secretary) into Central Office with responsibility for her campaign tour, television appearances and the design and style of the manifesto. As a peer Lord Young could not possibly be a rival for leadership and therefore was entirely trustworthy. Moreover 'my friendship with Tim Bell would ensure that she would still be able to rely on his advice from time to time'.[86]

It is common knowledge, too, that some ten days into the campaign there were arguments over strategy. The Tory manifesto's pledges on schools and housing had caused confusion and controversy; Kinnock and Labour started strongly and were gaining ground in the polls. At this point the stories conflict. The Bell/Young camp wanted Mrs Thatcher to go on the attack against Labour and to raise her own profile. The version from the Central Office camp is different and deserves to be told, if only because it has not been up to now:

> In the middle of that second week, a view was expressed that Labour was making too much headway at our expense; that they were depicting the PM as uncaring – which we knew they would – and that therefore the PM should respond to this. She must respond in two ways; first by dealing with the health service issue, and secondly by giving herself a much higher profile. That was a major change in strategy and one which was 100 per cent wrong. It was essentially agreeing to fight the campaign on Labour's ground, on which we were very weak and had little hope of making a strong impression. It also put the PM in a weak position, maximising her use too early in the campaign and on entirely the wrong issues. There was for 48 hours quite a tussle and at the end a sort of compromise was reached and like all compromises it was unsatisfactory and it meant that for 48–72 hours the initiative was lost because we were arguing amongst ourselves.[87]

Arguments over strategy simmered again on Wobbly Thursday, when anxiety caused by the Gallup and *Newsnight* polls was exacerbated by rumours of more bad news in the next day's Marplan poll and research from Young & Rubicam which seemed to confirm the bad tidings. The Central Office view, and the one argued forcibly by Dobbs against Lord Young, was that it was absurd to change strategy on the basis of one discredited poll (*Newsnight*) and one other potentially rogue poll (Gallup). Nor was much trust placed in the value of the VALs research. The CCO source said:

> The whole of Thursday was spent with nobody knowing what was going on, from the PM down. The whole thing was resolved just like that on Thursday evening when we got the latest opinion polls. Far from seeing the whole campaign washed away, nothing had changed.

The campaign finished according to this view with all the various protagonists coming to more or less the same conclusion, which was to attack Labour, unleash the PM on a series of TV interviews and launch an appeal to their own supporters under the slogan which echoed 1959: 'Britain is great again. Don't let Labour wreck it.'

This then is how the Tory campaign, which in many respects was the most painstakingly prepared in Central Office memory, came to look disorganised and leaden in the few weeks before polling. One of the Central Office campaign managers admitted:

> Frankly, nobody could put their hands on their hearts and say that we managed the campaign very well. We didn't, we managed it rather poorly. We perhaps looked more like the Labour Party. We forgot some of the lessons we learned from the 1979 campaign. The 1983 campaign was pretty good, but then we were not tried and tested by the opposition. We made classic traditional mistakes of party management.[88]

There is more truth in the remark 'we perhaps looked more like the Labour party' than this source may realise. It may be applied with accuracy to the lack of unity in the leadership of the campaign and in this the 1987 election was surely extraordinary. We have seen Labour leaders, notably Wilson and Callaghan, running their campaigns from Downing Street, effectively bypassing the party machinery. However it is extremely rare for a Conservative prime minister to behave in this fashion. The reasons for the normal Conservative harmony are obvious: the leader makes the key appointments at CCO and has control over policy and the manifesto largely untrammelled by the intrusions of party conference decisions and wider party democracy. In the usual course of events CCO should be the leader's machine and there would be no need for the leader to organise separately. There were specific reasons, as suggested above, why Mrs Thatcher came to regard Tebbit's CCO with a wary eye. However, the 1987 campaign was a one-off. It has not set a pattern likely to be repeated in normal circumstances.

Without doubt Labour ran the more disciplined communications campaign and at times the Conservatives looked amateurish by comparison; Labour had out-Saatchi'd the Saatchis. Yet, for all that, the impact of marketing was greater on the Conservatives than on Labour: marketing research and strategy was incorporated into the Conservative political product and not simply into the communications campaign. The lesson for Labour, and one which it took to heart in the years following 1987, was set out with abundant clarity by the party's then pollster, Bob Worcester of MORI:

> To move from 32 per cent to 40 per cent will take more than being packaged like soap powder or dog food, and if Labour can't find the formula that people think will wash their clothes whiter than white then all the packaging in the world won't do the trick. And the Labour Party must find out what the dog will eat and not only looks good but tastes good too. There's an old saying in the market research business: there's no substitute for trying it out on the dog.[89]

1 'Labour isn't working', one of Saatchi's most memorable, and earliest, pieces of political advertising.

2 Mrs Thatcher, Britain's first woman prime minister, greets victory at the 1979 general election.

3 Mrs Thatcher with husband, Denis, on the steps of No. 10 Downing Street as she arrives for the first time to take up residence (May 1979).

4   The Falklands Factor: the Falklands victory transformed Mrs Thatcher's political prospects. Here, members of the Royal Hampshire Regiment, 'The Tigers', welcome the prime minister on her visit to Goose Green.

5   Thatcher's campaigns entrenched the photo-opportunity as a staple of electioneering. The calf-cuddling episode was one of the earliest and most notorious
photo-ops.

6   Mrs Thatcher milks the applause after her speech at the Conservative Party conference, October 1989. The party faithful called for '10 more years'. Just over a
year later, Mrs Thatcher was forced to resign.

7   John Major on his soap-box during the 1992 general election campaign.

8   The winning combination: 'honest John' and behind him Saatchi's 'taxbomb' poster. Many commentators believed that trust and taxes cost Labour the election.

9 The American slang in this 1992 Saatchi's poster needed to be translated for British reporters when the advertisement was first unveiled.

10 One of the few memorable posters of the 1987 general election.

DEFENCE.

CONSERVATIVE ☒   LABOUR

11   The Tories remain convinced that defence is a vote-winner for them.

12 The campaign tactics which worked for the Tories failed for the Republicans in 1992 despite help from Conservative Central Office. Instead Bill Clinton's victory set an example for the British Labour Party. Here, Bill and Hillary Clinton join John and Norma Major during ceremonies to commemorate the 50th anniversary of the D-Day Landings.

13 New Labour Party leader, Tony Blair, spent nearly £80 000 on his leadership election campaign.

5 Government Publicity: Managing the News

Nowhere in British politics during the 1980s was the use of marketing techniques more extensive or more contentious than in the field of government publicity. Government's relations with the media, particularly with television and the Westminster correspondents' lobby, and the allegedly improper use of the Number 10 Downing Street press office, became political issues during Mrs Thatcher's second administration. In her third term, the scale and nature of government advertising became matters of public debate and investigation by both the Public Accounts Committee and the Treasury and Civil Service Committee. In the period 1987–9 government advertising attracted more criticism, comment, controversy, parliamentary questions and debate, than at any time since the Second World War. More than 100 parliamentary questions were asked on the subject in the session 1987/88 alone.

The array of marketing tools available to a government was never before so dazzling. Government initiatives were launched with roadshows, publicity breakfasts, direct mail, teleconferences and glossy full-colour white papers; privatisations were preceded by 'awareness campaigns'; public relations experts developed 'cascading' strategies to maximise publicity for policy announcements; and increasingly sophisticated graphics and video shows became normal fare for departmental press conferences. But the more glamorous marketing techniques only reveal the tip of the iceberg of the government communications effort. Government publicity is vast and complex, covering several distinct areas: 'news management' and relations with the news media, official secrecy, freedom of information, government advertising campaigns, the civil service code of neutrality and the relationship between government publicity and party propaganda.

It is not possible here to offer an exhaustive account of government communications during Thatcher's period in office. We are concerned primarily with domestic communications and, therefore, the Foreign Office relations with the media are

165

outside the remit. There are also a number of domestic areas which we touch only at a tangent. If we take official secrecy as an example, the period under review provides plenty of material for further investigation: the trials of civil servants Clive Ponting and Sarah Tisdall for leaking information, arguably in the public interest; government's long-running attempt to ban Peter Wright's *Spycatcher*; and the introduction of new official secrets legislation.[1] Ministry of Defence publicity is another important area which is not dealt with here in any depth, although, of course, it was examined in connection with the Falklands War.[2] The frequently troubled relations between television and a succession of governments have also been addressed in more detail elsewhere.[3]

We have two primary concerns: the propriety of government publicity; and the use of marketing and public relations techniques by the government information services (GIS).

THE PROPRIETY OF GOVERNMENT PUBLICITY

Did the government/party relationship change during Thatcher's tenure and was there substance to criticisms that the GIS has became significantly 'politicised'? In other words, did the government information services become a tool of party propaganda? This is not a new question. Government propaganda has been a sensitive area throughout much of its history and certainly since the first department of information was established during the First World War. The Central Office of Information (COI), created in 1946, 'was born in an atmosphere of suspicion' on the part of the press and parliamentary opposition, according to a former director general of the COI, Sir Fife Clark: 'For some years after the end of the War and intermittently until the early 1950s mistrust of the information services in general and the COI as one of their agents was voiced by the parliamentary Opposition and newspapers.'[4]

The government publicity bill amounted to about six shillings per head of population in 1948, which in real terms was about the same, £4 a head, as in 1988. The post-war Labour administration's innovative use of publicity was on a scale unprecedented in peacetime and, at its peak in 1948, more than £5 million was spent on advertising and promotions alone, some £70 million in 1988 prices. Herbert Morrison, responsible for co-ordinating government information, warned a Cabinet committee that such a high level of spending could not escape public criticism.[5] Nor did it avoid the wrath of Fleet Street.

'Public Relations Officers,' asserted the *Daily Express*, 'became the the propaganda agents for the Party in power and with the best of intentions could never be anything else'. Readers of the *Daily Mail* were told that the government PRO system was a 'direct menace to one of our fundamental freedoms'.[6]

The extent of the attack on the publicity of Attlee's government is chronicled in William Crofts' *Coercion or Persuasion?* and one cannot help but be struck by similarities with Mrs Thatcher's golden age of advertising.

Labour government advertising in the mid-1970s also provoked controversy. In particular, the 1975 counter-inflation advertising campaign, contracted to Boase Massimi Pollitt (who later handled the GLC anti-abolition account), crossed the boundary into political propaganda, according to both the Opposition and the Independent Broadcasting Authority which objected to proposed TV commercials. Ross Barr, an advertising executive at BMP who worked on the counter-inflation account, recalled that Labour's campaign was 'more or less exactly what the [Thatcher] government is doing'.[7]

Government publicity is an inherently emotive commodity. The real difficulty lies in determining exactly where the boundary of propriety lies. At what point does government information stray into the territory of political propaganda? On closer inspection the question itself becomes, if not false, then too limited to provide a satisfactory understanding of the vexed relationship between party propaganda and government publicity. There is inevitably a convergence of party and government publicity. In contrast with local government, the propriety of central government publicity is bound by convention, not legislation, and the boundary separating propriety from impropriety is a narrow and frequently arcane definition of 'party political', which in practice has as much to do with public acceptability as principle. Whenever government publicity is used in the service of a controversial policy it is likely to be viewed by opponents of the government as party propaganda.

The machinery of government publicity, and indeed the civil service generally, largely supersedes party organisation when a party is in office. Policy making shifts to a great extent from the party to government: Cabinet committees, ministerial advisers, publicly funded think tanks and civil servants. Publicity, likewise, is largely taken over by the GIS, except for specifically and narrowly defined party matters and events. Harold Wilson explained the process:

> The prime minister's speeches on party occasions are not issued through the Government Information Service or No. 10 Press Office, though these have access to the material should they receive inquiries from the overseas press. This is essential, for the prime minister, being a composite being, political and administrative, cannot utter a word that is not that of the head of the British Government. For that reason they see, comment on and suggest revisions on speeches on party occasions, which are issued to the press by the Labour Party press Department.[8]

Government publicity cannot escape a party political element. The GIS is enlisted to explain, answer questions and disseminate information about the policies of the party in power. This, as various official guidelines for the GIS make clear, is one of the perquisites of government. The very nature of publicity – with its inherent element of advocacy – suggests strains on the Whitehall creed of political neutrality, possibly more than in any other sector of the civil service. The civil service recognises this difficulty and attempts to preserve the sanctity of its neutrality through the subtleties of definition – the difference between explanation and advocacy, for instance, and its code of professionalism – the ability to work for one party one day and do exactly the same job for a different party the next. The COI 1980 *Official Handbook for Government Information Officers* makes the point candidly in a section headed 'The Political Factor':

> Ministers are political animals. Civil servants are not. The Information Division can be the part of the Department where this situation creates the greatest difficulty. A Minister expects the Information Division to further the policies and objectives of the Government, and these policies may be the

subject of bitter political controversy in the country. By furthering the Departmental policies and objectives, therefore, the Information Officer is often also furthering the objectives of the political party in office. This is perfectly proper, and it is one of the perquisites of political office that the machinery of the Government Information Service is available in this way.

. . . He [the Information Officer] must be prepared to explain the reasons for the Government's actions and must establish a position for himself with the media where they understand that he is apart from the political battle, but is there to assist them to understand the policies of the Government in office just as he will in a few years' time assist them to understand the policies of the Opposition when they come to office. It is a difficult tightrope to walk. It can be done, and the experience of many years has shown that journalists have greater respect for the Civil Service Information Officer who has achieved it than for the committed political spokesman.

Allegations remained, however, that Thatcher's governments strained the publicity guidelines beyond the bounds of acceptability: that certain campaigns and ministers contravened the neutrality conventions, goverment campaigns too closely resembled Tory propaganda, the same advertising personnel were involved in both party and government publicity strategies, there was no acceptable justification for the vast sums lavished on commercials, and that the government attempted to squeeze too much partisan advantage out of its politically exclusive access to television advertising. Even if there was no technical breach, there remains a case that government revelled in the looseness of the conventions while resisting cross-party calls to administer to itself the same medicine it had given local government: stricter conventions backed by law.

There are a number of detailed allegations of impropriety of which the most important are the role of Sir Bernard Ingham, the Action for Jobs television advertising campaign, the poll tax and privatisation campaigns. We look at government advertising in the next chapter. Here we focus on Bernard Ingham and his alleged misuse of the parliamentary correspondents' lobby.

Ingham, as press secretary, undoubtedly had more influence than any of the other image-makers associated with Mrs Thatcher. He became more widely known than any previous press secretary, his activities the subject of more press and political comment, academic debate and controversy. This chapter examines the role of Bernard Ingham and questions whether his relatively high public profile reflected a genuine change and potentially sinister accretion of power, or whether he was simply performing the conventional tasks of the press secretary in an era of intense media interest.

GOVERNMENT INFORMATION SERVICE

The Whitehall department Chief Information Officer (or Head of Information) is in a unique position, according to the 1980 *Official Handbook for Government Information Officers*, which was the GIS bible throughout the 1980s:

> His work spans the whole range of departmental activities in a way matched only by that of the Permanent Secretary or the Minister. The Minister will look to him for daily contact and advice on the presentation of all Departmental policies. He is the chief spokesman for the Department as well as the chief adviser on information matters.
>
> It follows that he must ensure that his division is kept fully informed of all proposals, all policies, all decisions, all the awkward stories which will eventually become public and – even more important – those that the Department fondly hope will not become public. (They certainly will – probably at the most difficult moment.)
>
> No Chief Information Officer can hope to achieve this flow of vital information unless he has the trust and understanding of senior officials of the Permanent Secretary and, of course, Ministers . . . A Chief Information Officer must have the trust of the Principal Private Secretary and all the Private Office staff. Indeed he should be able to walk in and talk at any time (within reason) and to see the Minister regularly.

The breadth of departmental knowledge and extent of access place the head of information in a potentially powerful position within the Whitehall departmental heirarchy. He or she is able not only to oversee presentation but also to influence the minister and policy decisions. The interplay between policy and presentation has traditionally concerned scholars with respect to party activity. John Ramsden, in his seminal work on the making of Conservative Party policy, suggested that considerations of publicity had only the most marginal influence.[9] The tone of much academic writing suggests that the margin is precisely the rightful place for presentation. Governments, however, have tended to be less coy in admitting the publicity/policy nexus.

The information officers' handbook advises:

> The Information Division should never be regarded simply as the machinery for announcing decisions and issuing press notices. It should play a part in the formation of policy by reflecting public and media attitudes, and it should be consulted about timing, method and content of any press announcement before submissions are made to Ministers. Indeed all submissions to Ministers should carry a section on PR aspects contributed by the Chief Information Officer.

According to the handbook, the Information Division should be consulted in the preparation of green and white papers; and the Chief Information Officer should have the chance to comment on the draft and advise on public reaction and on methods of presentation.

The handbook is an invaluable resource for students of government publicity, indeed for students of any branch of public relations. It is admirably uncontaminated by civil service jargon and offers candid insights into the techniques of news management, relations with media and also relations between departments and Number 10. It advises officers to engage in the kind of news management techniques for which Bernard Ingham and the government was to be heavily criticised, for example: planted questions in the House of Commons, careful vetting of current affairs programmes and acute sensitivity to media deadlines.[10] But, curiously, the handbook is advanced by some of the same critics as the model of propriety and rectitude. 'I don't think anyone could have any complaints about it,' said an official of the Institution of Professional Civil Servants, whose members were to engage in a tussle with Ingham about the ethics of government publicity. The handbook, for example, advises information officers that 'the arranged Parliamentary Question is an invaluable method of putting right ill-informed criticism. It is not immediately obvious that the occasion has been "arranged", and the reply is likely to receive general coverage'.

The release of parliamentary papers should be coordinated with Number 10 in order to avoid bunching of important publications. Technically it is a breach of privilege to issue copies of parliamentary papers to the press before they are made available to MPs. However for many years 'it has been the practice to provide Confidential Final Revise (CFR) copies of Command Papers to lobby correspondents a certain time in advance of publication' under strict cover of embargo. The embargo system was severely curtailed by Bernard Ingham who was angered by journalists' tendency to seek Opposition comment before the publication date and make the reaction, rather than the government action, their main story.[11]

The handbook recommends advance planning with the BBC and ITN when a government announcement is due. Information officers are warned to pay attention to two points in particular: TV and radio interviews should *follow* the press briefing, which will operate as a 'good rehearsal for the more exacting television interview'; and second, ministers should avoid using on television statements they have made at unattributable press briefings. The Chief Information Officer should not hesitate to point out any 'unfortunate remark' made by the minister and should try to persuade broadcast reporters to retake questions or whole interviews if things go 'badly wrong'.

The sternest warnings are reserved for current affairs programmes, which are much more dangerous beasts for ministers than straight news bulletins. The handbook devotes a full six pages to advice: the producer is likely to be knowledgeable about the subject and approach the minister with a clear idea of what is wanted in the programme. 'The producer will be on the look out for drama and scandal. He will be seeking to make a name for himself as a fearless producer who refuses to be influenced by government propaganda. He may wish to put the Minister and the department in the pillory. He holds many trump cards in the game, because the editing of the film is in his hands . . .'.

The information officer must protect the minister's interests. The officer should make essential inquiries about the nature, date and time of the broadcast, the objectives, the other interviewees, the identity of the interviewer, the length of the interview, at what point in the programme the minister will appear and whether the interview will be split in segments. In the light of the answers, the information officer should weigh the pros and cons, based on his knowledge of the journalists involved and the track record of the programme; ministers are unlikely to accept direct confrontation with members of the Opposition or to discuss policy on television with backbenchers. If the programme is likely to be critical, the interview should be shown at the end. Once satisfied on these points, the officer must then seek clearance from Number 10. 'The key information already discussed must be passed to No. 10 together with any conditions already agreed with the producer. *No reply should be given to the producer until clearance is obtained from No.10. If No.10 turns down the proposal, the department should not indicate this to the producer.*' (Emphasis added.)

Permission from Number 10 is also required for interviews on radio programmes such as *World at One* and *The World Tonight*, which are 'in effect current affairs programmes and should be treated as such'. Although the handbook makes no mention, it is clear from Ingham's memoir that Radio 4's *Today* was also viewed in the same suspicious light.[12] Where an interview invitation is turned down, information officers should not be 'blackmailed into acceptance. The broadcasting authorities are required to maintain balance; it is worth reminding them that this is so and the refusal of a Minister to take part does not remove from them that legal requirement'. But good relations and give-and-take with the media are of the essence for the effective operation of the Information Division. Where relations are good, a producer is less likely to refuse a retake of a question if requested. However, 'if a producer of a particular magazine or current affairs programme consistently adopts aggressive and unhelpful attitudes, he will quickly find that this becomes known throughout Whitehall. He can expect little enthusiasm for his ideas and requests.'

Ingham's own view of television current affairs producers could scarcely have sunk lower; they were pretentious, precious and untrustworthy creatures who cloaked their base desires for high ratings and fat salaries in the mantle of responsibility to truth and public interest:

> When I retired from the Civil Service, I knew of no Departmental head in Her Majesty's Government who would trust current affairs producers further than he or she could throw them. It was impossible to have confidence in any agreement reached with them.[13]

The effect of the kind of methods outlined above has altered fundamentally the rules of engagement between the media and the government in the view of at least some journalists on the receiving end. Roger Bolton, who, as editor of the BBC's *Panorama* and then Thames Television's *This Week*, was involved in some of the most notorious TV clashes with government, wrote in 1986 of the politicians' 'PR offensive' and increasingly sophisticated understanding of journalists' deadlines, desires and constraints: the offer of the exclusive interview, Sunday interviews which generally ensure coverage in Monday's papers, press conferences on complicated matters timed close to news deadlines, refusal to take part in political discussions with junior opponents, and demands for separate interviews.[14]

Bolton viewed the PR offensive rather as an extension and broadening of practices employed by Harold Wilson. Even after the furious government reaction to his programme, *Death on the Rock*, Bolton remained convinced that Thatcher was little different from earlier prime ministers: 'she had just had longer at it with larger majorities than most . . .'.[15] However John Tusa, then managing director of the BBC World Service, found a qualitative and disquieting change. Where once government press officers saw their news management task in terms of channelling journalists' understanding, they were now encouraging ministers to to treat TV appearances as a marketing exercise, he argued. Quoting an unnamed broadcasting colleague, he said:

> 'Today, they see us as another outlet, more volatile but not dissimilar to the advertising slot.' The consequences which flow from this . . . are profound: 'A minister is encouraged to think of his time on a programme as a slot . . . there are demands for effective control of editing. It is as if the appearance belongs to the interviewee.' If a minister will appear

in segments, the demand is for each piece of interview preceding his or her own contribution to be read to him or her in advance. A smooth practitioner then inserts references to what has gone before, thus giving the impression of being in charge of the programme.

. . . in turning to the rival communicating arts of advertising for their salvation, they are in danger of distorting those media for their own purposes. They turn the form of a documentary programme – which broadcasters see as a means for the critical examination of issues and policies – into a vehicle for political persuasion.[16]

There is a startling contrast between Tusa's view of the smooth minister dictating terms and the handbook's vivid portrayal of the ambitious TV producer, red in tooth and claw, with the minister at his mercy. In one sense it epitomises the tension that has long existed between politicians and broadcasters. In another sense, Tusa identifies precisely the point of contemporary government communications effort. It *is* a marketing exercise within the definition of public relations as the management of communications between an organisation and its public. The organisation attempts to bathe itself in the most favourable light and makes the best use it can of the means of communication at its disposal.

Bernard Ingham made this point in his speech to the Guild of British Newspaper Editors:

If by news management you mean I seek to present the case for the policies and measures of the government I serve as effectively as possible, I plead guilty a thousand times – nay 10 000 times. I've been at it for all the governments I've served for 16 years. It is the aim of all organisations to present their best case to the world, consistent with their long-term credibility . . . If by news management you mean I try to avoid government's coming out with five major announcements on the same day – or worse on Budget Day, or even worse than that, on Bank Holiday Monday, I again plead guilty and there isn't an erstwhile news editor in this building who doesn't in his heart of hearts say, 'Thank God'.[17]

Tusa's complaint reflects a wider unease at government use of marketing techniques which goes to the heart of the issue. Is it right and proper that, at taxpayers' expense, the government may present its case with all the panache, sophistication and resources of a multinational enterprise? Is it right and proper that the GIS should commit itself wholeheartedly to the government of the day without restraint of a higher loyalty to the national interest? Bernard Ingham, to whom we turn next, leaves no room for doubt as to his opinion.

(SIR) BERNARD INGHAM, THE PRIME MINISTER'S PRESS SECRETARY

On the way out I talked to Joe Haines about Bernard Ingham. He said Bernard didn't like the Number 10 set-up, he didn't behave like a political press officer and was capable of creating terrible trouble if I got rid of him.

Tony Benn, *Against the Tide: Diaries 1973–76*,
18 November 1975

Given the furore that was later to engulf Ingham, particularly over his role in the Westland affair, there is a certain irony in Haines's rather cryptic comment that he was not a 'political' press officer. Yet equally it hints at Ingham's commitment to, and identification with, the civil service which is essential for an understanding of the way he developed his role as the prime minister's press secretary. Unlike Haines, he was not a political appointment and was not directly involved with specifically party occasions, such as conferences or election campaigns, although members of his staff have moved to Conservative Central Office.[18] Unlike Haines, Ingham identified closely with the GIS generally, as opposed to confining himself to prime ministerial concerns. He became Head of Profession in 1989, taking responsibility for appointments, training, co-ordination and, ultimately, for the ethical conduct of the service. This post gave him more influence over the totality of government publicity than Haines or, indeed, any other holder of the office of prime minister's press secretary.

The tension between his insistence that he was strictly a civil servant, performing a civil servant's job, and his universally acknowledged dedication to the prime minister lies at the heart of the many criticisms he was to face. Excessive commitment does not sit easily with a certain view of the civil service, one which has many adherents, that the service belongs to neither politicians nor officials but to the Crown and the nation.[19] Ingham, however, believed that his duties lay absolutely in the service of the government of the day and that it was dangerous to behave in any other fashion – to 'withhold the last ounce':

> I have never had much time for those civil servants who argue that their proper duty is to withhold that last ounce from the elected government lest they become over-committed. That, to me, could become a cover for withholding a bit more than an ounce, depending on your preferences . . . The only thing to be done in my view is to serve whomsoever you are landed with by the voters to the very best of your ability . . . I think my record shows that whether or not I had shared Mrs Thatcher's enthusiasm for sorting out a debilitated country I would have thrown my full weight behind her.[20]

Ingham's autobiography makes his position plain: his duty was not to the press, nor to an abstract concept of the nation, but completely to the prime minister and her government. In practice, this view was sometimes shocking. Anthony Bevins, then political editor of the *Independent*, has complained that Ingham refused to talk to him after Bevins broke ranks with the lobby collective briefing system. Bevins was astounded by the behaviour of this servant of the Crown who was 'paid to talk to me'.[21] For Ingham this was just not the case; he was not paid to talk to Bevins or indeed any other member of the media. He was paid to present the government in the best possible light and journalists with unhelpful attitudes – to quote the *Official Handbook* – could not expect much assistance. Those who chose to boycott Ingham's lobby briefings would not get private guidance: 'for I was simply not prepared to allow journalists to have it both ways: to boycott collective briefings but enjoy a personal service on exactly the same terms'.[22]

Ingham's abrasive style and infamous temper, scarcely in the mode expected from civil servants, contributed much to his notoriety. He has called himself Mrs Thatcher's personal Rottweiler[23] and admitted that a person of his temperament should probably not have been allowed within a mile of Number 10 – except to serve someone as 'straightforward' as Thatcher.[24]

Table 5.1   Post-Second World War press secretaries

Prime minister	Press secretary	Background
C.R. Attlee	Francis Williams	Journalist/civil servant
	Philip Jordan	Journalist/civil servant
	Reginald Bacon	Journalist/civil servant
W.S. Churchill	Fife Clark	Journalist/civil servant
A. Eden	William Clark	Journalist
	Alfred Richardson	Journalist/civil servant
H. Macmillan	Harold Evans	Journalist/civil servant
A. Douglas-Home	John Groves	Journalist/civil servant
H. Wilson	Trevor Lloyd-Hughes	Journalist
	Joe Haines	Journalist
E.G. Heath	Donald Maitland	Civil servant
	Robin Haydon	Civil Servant
H. Wilson	Joe Haines	Journalist
J. Callaghan	Tom McCaffrey	Civil servant
M. Thatcher	Henry James	Journalist/civil servant
	Bernard Ingham	Journalist/civil servant
John Major	Gus O'Donnell	Civil Servant
	Christopher Meyer	Civil Servant

There are numerous recorded examples of Ingham's un-diplomatic style, but there is no need to trawl the press clippings because the instances are clear and abundant in his autobiography, *Kill the Messenger*. It reveals an abiding hostility towards 'investigative' journalists, rooted apparently less in partisan grounds than in a kind of anti-intellectualism. They were a 'small effortlessly self-regarding clique', who set themselves apart from society as guardians of the common weal, but would not recognise anything common at five yards.[25] Bevins was an example; he had a 'built-in sneer, which is an instant slander on all Government press officers'.[26] Journalists whose intention was to 'take the mickey' out of Number 10 could expect little help: 'I am not aware that the rules of a free society require Number 10 to connive at its own ridicule.'[27]

Bernard Ingham became the sixteenth post-war holder of the title of Press Secretary, and the seventeenth all told (Table 5.1); George Steward, who was appointed to Number 10 in 1931, was the first. His background, like many before him, was in both journalism and the civil service.[28] While working as an industrial correspondent for the *Guardian* he was noted for his robust Labour views and in May 1965 he stood unsuccessfully as a candidate for Labour in the Moortown ward of Leeds council.

The depth of his Labour passions was revealed in a column he wrote for the *Leeds Weekly Citizen*, a local Labour journal. Under the pseudonym 'Albion', Ingham vented his spleen against the Tory press, the capitalists who 'worship only Mammon' and the Tory party which did not 'give a tinker's cuss' for the consequences of its policies on the 'under-employed, under-privileged muck-heap of the north'.[29]

He joined the Whitehall information service in 1967, working at the Prices and Incomes Board and then at the Department of Employment and Productivity, the Department of Employment and the Department of Energy, where he left the information service to become under secretary responsible for energy conservation and the 'Save It' campaign. He served such disparate ministers as Barbara Castle, Lord Carrington, Maurice Macmillan, Eric Varley and Tony Benn. The one he admired most, apart from Margaret Thatcher, was Barbara Castle:

> Barbara Castle prepared me for the big stuff. She, like Margaret Thatcher, was a substantial politician endowed with good looks, energy, fire, intelligence, power, determination and guts. And the greatest of these is guts . . . Both Barbara and Margaret were made of sterner stuff than their Parliamentary parties and the Cabinets of which they were members.[30]

He moved to Downing Street in November 1979, six months after Mrs Thatcher's election, and replaced Henry James, recently retired head of the COI, who had been appointed by Thatcher partly on the recommendation of the lobby.[31] Curiously Ingham did not know Thatcher at all, having met her once briefly over tea at a departmental gathering. More curiously still, given that his private Labour views were known to the civil service, he needed only a 20-minute interview to convince Thatcher of his fitness for the job. Sir Ian Bancroft, head of the civil service, recommended Ingham as the best press officer in Whitehall and she acted on his advice.[32]

Typically prime ministers appoint a press secretary they know and trust. Joe Haines advised Harold Wilson on press relations from 1969 both in and out of prime ministerial office; Sir Tom McCaffrey followed James Callaghan to Number 10 having worked for him at both the Home and Foreign Offices; and Ingham's successor, Gus O'Donnell, had served Major at the Treasury. Given his background, it is ironic that Ingham became one of Thatcher's most trusted advisers and the longest-serving of all the press secretaries. Of Thatcher's staff, only Charles Powell (whose brother Chris offers advertising expertise to the Labour Party) can compare with Ingham for length of service.[33]

The Post of Press Secretary

Ingham's book rehearses the main features and day-to-day duties of the post of press secretary: spokesman and intermediary with press and television, adviser on media relations, and co-ordinator of government information. These duties have remained much the same for all incumbents.[34]

Spokesman and intermediary
Thatcher relied on her press secretary to a greater extent than her predecessors for contact with the media. She rarely made herself available for general questions except on overseas trips. Snatched questions as she left or entered Number 10 went for the most part unanswered. She never, as prime minister, took a lobby briefing herself. A lobby correspondent source for this book recalled just one occasion when Thatcher agreed to meet the lobby, which was on her return from her trip to the Falklands in January 1983. She pulled out at the last minute for various reasons. Aeroplane flights to, and especially from, overseas visits provided one of the few opportunities for reporters to get close to the PM in a relatively unstructured and informal way.

It is highly unusual, possibly unique, for a post-war premier never to have taken a lobby briefing. Harold Wilson regularly took briefings during his first spell as prime minister.[35] When he felt that failed he tried to create a new relationship with a series of lunches with newspaper editors and chief political correspondents at Number 10 and Chequers. Following that,

Wilson tried the experiment that became known as the 'white commonwealth', holding fortnightly evening meetings at Number 10 with senior lobby correspondents. Heath began with a more circumspect relationship with the media although, for a short time, he tried on-the-record ministerial press conferences to which cameras were invited. James Callaghan also took lobby briefings periodically, although fairly infrequently, while he was PM.[36]

Formal interviews with Thatcher were vetted by Ingham. Newspapers, magazines and television programmes put in 'bids' and, if granted, there was usually a wait of several months before Downing Street picked its moment to set up the interview. The process was hastened at times of heightened difficulty for the government or Thatcher personally, notably after the resignation of Nigel Lawson as Chancellor in October 1989, when Thatcher gave a series of interviews to favoured journalists (for example, Jean Rook, *Daily Express*, and Brian Walden, London Weekend Television).

Once in Downing Street, Thatcher did not court journalists and with a few exceptions she did not enjoy their company, according to Ingham.[37] Media entrepreneurs, however, appeared more to her taste, notably Rupert Murdoch who was a Christmas guest at Chequers. She did not read the papers, except the front pages of the *Evening Standard* and the *Financial Times*, and she hated to watch herself on television. Ingham sometimes had to press her into the few interviews she did grant. Most post-war prime ministers have been wary, even contemptuous of the press. Lord Donoughue, political adviser to first Wilson and then Callaghan, found that Wilson's contempt for the press was only exceeded by Callaghan's.[38] Moreover, in his latter days at Number 10, Wilson's press secretary, Haines, abandoned lobby briefings altogether. But Mrs Thatcher distanced herself from the media to a greater extent than usual. She was also unusually sparing in her use of her other main conduit for direct media coverage, appearances in the Commons. Research by Patrick Dunleavy *et al.* (1990) found that Thatcher was the least active prime minister in the House of Commons since 1868. Apart from unavoidable twice-weekly sessions at the despatch box for Prime Minister's Questions, Thatcher rarely appeared. She all but abandoned the practice of interventions in debates: post-war PMs have made such interventions every 14 parliamentary days on average; Mrs Thatcher's average was one intervention every 110 days. She also made far less generous use of speeches or statements, making speeches every 49 days compared to the post-war average of every 24 days; she made statements, on average, every 25 parliamentary days compared to every 12. Her relatively infrequent speeches and statements were overwhelmingly about foreign affairs, especially overseas summits and conferences, or, more rarely, about matters of national security.[39]

This reticence shifted much of the weight of attention to her statements and interviews outside the House, over which Ingham provided vital advice, and to Ingham himself and his daily briefings. His unparalleled access to Mrs Thatcher made him become, by common consent, the single most important of all her various communications advisers. Writing in *Scotland on Sunday*, Bill Mackintosh encapsulated the general view of journalists:

> In some ways, he can be said to have created Mrs Thatcher's image. Through the economic troubles and the Falklands, especially, it was his language which the press used to describe – and actually to define – what Thatcherism was. That it became identifiable had much to do with Ingham.[40]

Ingham and Thatcher had good fortune in that Rupert Murdoch's growing empire tilted the political balance of the British press: for the whole of the post-war period until 1970, pro-Tory papers accounted for between 50 and 60 per cent of national circulation. Murdoch relaunched the once pro-Labour *Sun* as an ardently pro-Thatcher (rather than pro-Tory) paper and increased its circulation from 1.5 million (1970) to more than 4 million (1983). This alone was largely responsible for increasing the pro-Conservative share of circulation to 66 per cent in 1979 and 75 per cent in 1983.[41]

Equally, of course, Murdoch could also be grateful to Thatcher's government at crucial moments: in 1981 John Biffen, the trade secretary, declined to refer Murdoch's bid for *The Times* and *Sunday Times* to the Monopolies Commission; and the Broadcasting Act 1990 left Murdoch's Astra satellite channels exempt from cross-media ownership controls which limited newspaper proprietors to a maximum 20 per cent share of domestic TV companies.[42] Thatcher's good fortune also was that Ingham, by common accord of even his enemies, was a highly effective press spokesman. Lord Prior noted in 1986 that Thatcher had a marvellous press; she was the 'most adept Prime Minister at handling the right-wing press since the War'.[43] The compliment belonged, at least equally, to the prime minister's press secretary.

Adviser on media relations
The press secretary's role is similar to that of the departmental head of information writ large. He is required to give advice on on all matters affecting the presentation of government policy, the timing and manner of policy launches and government initiatives. There is no evidence to suggest that Ingham's involvement with government policy formulation stretched beyond the civil service bounds of probity, which confined him to considerations of presentation. However policies and presentation are closely linked and sometimes the latter may have the deciding influence. Ingham believed that his role included the protection of government's overall credibility and that sometimes meant scotching plans which implied a 'U-turn':

> If I felt the government's credibility was in danger of being undermined, it was my duty to say so. I did my duty, for example, when a compromise was proposed over trade union membership in the Government Communications Headquarters at Cheltenham where it had been banned after an industrial dispute. Union membership remains unacceptable.[44]

He also declares 'moving heaven and earth' to safeguard the future of ITN as a national news network to rival the BBC when government broadcasting proposals appeared to threaten it.[45] However Ingham's involvement with policy was nowhere near as extensive as that of Joe Haines, who made no bones about his political input with Harold Wilson nor of his close co-operation with Bernard Donoughue, who was head of the Number 10 Policy Unit.[46]

Co-ordination of government information services
The press secretary liaises with departmental press heads to ensure that government speaks with one voice and that the

various ministerial activities do not clash or invade each other's publicity space. To this end Ingham chaired a meeting of departmental heads of information (MIO – Meeting of Information Officers) every Monday, normally held at 5pm. Ingham took over the chair from (Lord) Angus Maude, paymaster general, during Mrs Thatcher's first term.

Historically there have been periodic clashes between Number 10 and various government departments. The Foreign Office acts independently of the GIS, while the Ministry of Defence, which has the largest GIS information office, was noted for its differences with Number 10 during the Falklands War. According to Sir Tom McCaffrey (Callaghan's press secretary) differences of opinion between Downing Street and the departments were quite usual in his day.

> Anyone who is an active information officer ought to be a pretty aggressive, thrusting, pushy type of character and if you can get away with something without telling Downing Street, you do. That's what I did. If Downing Street wanted to interfere with your plans you'd fight like anything and it is the strongest man who wins . . . I've made it sound as though there was tremendous conflict but it was rare that conflict ensued. Mostly it was done on a friendly basis because you were all batting on the same side.[47]

Indeed Ingham recalls being 'harassed' by McCaffrey when he (Ingham) was working for Benn at the Department of Energy.[48]

Ingham was not unique among press secretaries in holding the once-weekly meetings of chief information officers – Tom McCaffrey took MIOs and believed he attempted similar control over departmental publicity output.[49] However there is evidence to support the claim that the press secretary's influence over all government publicity reached its highest level since 1945 under Ingham.

His co-ordinating role was in many respects akin to the role played by ministers responsible for information in previous governments.[50] Macmillan's press secretary, Harold Evans, was supported by Cabinet ministers – first Dr Charles Hill and later F.W. Deedes – who handled the political side of public relations, prepared media strategy and linked with CCO. To a great extent, the minister sheltered Evans, a civil servant, from criticisms of political bias. However Ingham operated for long spells without the support of a 'minister of information'. Lord Whitelaw held the post from 1986 to 1987 but it was not formally filled again until May 1990 when John Wakeham, Energy Secretary, was given the clumsy title of 'Cabinet Minister responsible for co-ordinating the development of government publicity'. At other times, the Leader of the House (Pym and later Biffen) had formal responsibility for publicity; but, as Seymour-Ure notes: 'the ministerial role has generally been very insignificant. When critics say Ingham has been behaving like a minister they may indeed describe a role which ministers in the past have played.'[51]

Ingham's influence increased further when he was appointed head of profession for the GIS in February 1989, a role formerly filled by the director general of the COI. The title gave him formal powers to appoint senior press departmental (and Metropolitan Police) spokesmen and ultimate responsibility for ensuring that the GIS conformed to civil service standards of probity. The official explanation for his new powers lay in the changing status of the COI. It had been the centre of advice on propriety for government publicity until 1987–8, when it was 'untied' from the departments. Since the COI was being transformed into a profit-making executive agency, competing with the private sector for departmental accounts, it was deemed no longer appropriate for it also to be the centre of propriety. COI's proprietal functions went to the Cabinet Office and the title of head of profession was conferred upon Ingham. This explanation was never entirely satisfactory and the title reverted to the director general of the COI within weeks of Ingham leaving Downing Street.

Ingham was well aware of the criticism he was likely to face when he took the post: that his close association with Thatcher would compromise the neutrality of the GIS.[52] The information officers' union, the IPCS, did object in precisely these terms and, fearful that the GIS was becoming politicised, also proposed a code of ethics, which was turned down by Ingham.[53] However, even before his appointment to head of GIS, Bernard Ingham wielded influence over senior appointments. Several of Ingham's Number 10 deputies left Downing Street to become heads of information.[54] Ingham denies that these were his 'placemen and placewomen' and says that he made conscious efforts not to undermine the independence of heads of information.[55] However these appointments might well be considered to have increased Ingham's influence over the whole government publicity machine.

Ingham is given great credit for improving the status of the GIS. During the early 1980s morale was low, the GIS was facing cuts and professional press officers were distressed at the ascendancy among the top departmental information jobs of administrators rather than trained information officers. Neville Taylor, former director general of the COI, believed that Ingham had a 'chip on his shoulder' that professional information officers were not given the same respect as administrators within the civil service.[56] Ingham's eagerness to 'do my bit' for the information officers was a major reason for his wanting to become Head of Profession.[57] His colleagues in the GIS offer a glowing portrait of his contribution to the service, a view shared even by some who opposed his new powers. Elizabeth Jenkins, assisant secretary of IPCS, commented:

> We do not for a moment question Mr Ingham's personal commitment to the GIS, nor his professional skills, which are indeed impressive. We welcome his strengthening of the Information Officers' Management Unit and his proposals for training in the GIS. Indeed . . . he has set aside time to meet GIS members; something else which the IPCS has very much welcomed and which is particularly impressive in view of Mr Ingham's crowded time-table.[58]

Jenkins welcomed Ingham's crusade for professional press officers, rather than administrators, in top posts and she saluted Ingham's response to a Conservative Central Office initiative to hire private sector public relations professionals as 'minders' for the Home, Health and Education secretaries. The scheme was abandoned after a telephone call from Ingham to Kenneth Baker, chairman of the party. A letter from Ingham to departmental heads of information was sent to the press:

> As head of the Government Information Service, I telephoned Mr Kenneth Baker, Chancellor of the Duchy of Lancaster, this morning about the the reported appointment of public relations minders to three Cabinet ministers: Home

Secretary – Tim Bell; Kenneth Clarke – John Banks; John McGregor – Robin Wight.

I said I was doing so in response to serious concern which had been expressed to me by heads of information, especially as there seemed to be the possibility of further appointments. . . . The announcement of the appointments, made without any consultation with the heads of information concerned, was seen as a grave reflection on the competence of the GIS – indeed as an insult to it.

The GIS has and I am sure would continue to do its level best for the government of the day. But it was inevitably getting a lot of flak these days and this kind of episode would be damaging of its morale unless there was proper consultation and explanation. It was absolutely essential that ministers and Messrs Bell, Banks and Wight handled the GIS with kid gloves, given the circumstances of their appointment. Mr Baker regretted the publicity and said no announcement had been made. It had leaked out . . . I asked him to make it clear to all inquirers that these were party appointments and did not and were not intended to relect upon the competence and abilities of the GIS. Mr Baker agreed to do this.[59]

This was not the first time Ingham had shown his dislike of outside interference, whether from CCO or from personal admirers of Mrs Thatcher. A plan was mooted in the troubled aftermath of Westland for Tim Bell and Sir Gordon Reece to meet the PM at 8.50 every morning to go over her presentation. The plan was squashed by a combination of Ingham and Tebbit (party chairman).[60] A similar story was told by a journalist admirer of the prime minister who believed that her uncaring public image was caused partly by Ingham's abrasive style. He wrote to Thatcher in August 1986 suggesting that she should have a more visible spokesman in the manner of American presidents, and rely less heavily on unattributable briefings.

The riot was unbelievable. At the party conference I was taken aside by someone and told:'You do not know the trouble you've caused. There are people who will never forgive you.' It took about a month for the whole thing to dampen down.[61]

Ingham: Questions of Propriety

Ingham developed an unenviable reputation which, if correct, took him beyond the pale of civil service acceptablity. In his own words, 'rubbishing and leaking' became his hallmarks.[62] Most notoriously, he was said to have rubbished Cabinet Ministers Francis Pym, John Biffen and Sir Geoffrey Howe; and by allegedly authorising the leak of the Solicitor-General's letter in the Westland affair, he also rubbished Michael Heseltine. Cabinet ministers reportedly feared the 'black spot' from Ingham – an intimation in his lobby briefings that they were out of favour with the prime minister.[63]

Critics, both from the Conservative Party, the Opposition and media, accused him of unethical conduct, sometimes on the prime minister's behalf, sometimes for his own self-aggrandisement. Biffen, who believed himself a victim of the black spot, said of Ingham: 'He is not the sewage, only the sewer.'[64] Heath accused the prime minister of leaking through the Number 10 press office 'in a way which can only be described as corrupt . . . beyond not only the achievements but even the aspirations of any previous governments'.[65]

Labour MP Tam Dalyell was Ingham's most persistent critic – particularly over the Westland leak – and he argued that Ingham had perpetrated 'a whole litany of operations unbecoming to a civil servant'. In an adjournment debate in the House of Commons, he said:

> We are tonight not considering the role of a mere press secretary, but dealing with the position of a man who is an adviser on central decisions of government in Britain, and whose power has grown exponentially, along a geometric progression, with the years during which he has occupied the office . . . I do not think I exaggerate if I say that, with the arguable exception of Sir Robert Armstrong [Cabinet Secretary], Mr Bernard Ingham has evolved as the most important man making decisions in British politics. When I put this view to a senior Conservative Party privy councillor, he shook his head sadly and said he could not dissent.[66]

Ingham's autobiography addresses directly and at length all these allegations and he admits mistakes. He regretted using the words which rubbished Pym (likened to Mona Lott, 'It's being so cheerful as keeps me going') and Biffen (a 'semi-detached member of the Cabinet'). These comments were, he says, clumsy attempts to divert fierce questioning, dragged out of him by the lobby in full cry, and written up out of context to fit journalists' predetermined stories that Thatcher was preparing to dismiss the ministers from her Cabinet.[67] 'Mrs Thatcher never once asked – let alone instructed – me to criticize a Ministerial colleague in my dealings with journalists. Nor did she ever imply that I should do so.'[68] He denies wrongdoing in the Westland leak but admits partial error. He refused a Department of Trade and Industry (DTI) request for Downing Street to leak the Solicitor-General's letter to the Press Association and did not authorise Colette Bowe, DTI head of information, so to do. But:

> What I ought to have done – and regret to this day that I did not – was advise Colette Bowe, regardless of her Minister's permission, to have nothing to do with the ploy herself. It is on the basis of this failure that the DTI felt able to claim that I – and, indeed, Charles Powell – had accepted that the letter should be disclosed. It was at best tacit acceptance in the sense that I did not actively object to a Ministerial decision to disclose it.[69]

Ingham's slight of Sir Geoffrey Howe (that the post of deputy prime minister conferred on him in July 1989 was only 'a courtesy title') is widely held to have sowed the seeds of Howe's disenchantment which culminated in his resignation a year later, and ultimately Thatcher's downfall. The irony that Thatcher's faithful mouthpiece was an unwitting cause of her demise was not lost on Ingham: 'It might be argued that all else pales into insignificance.'[70] Again he denies any intentional slur; he was merely trying to correct an overblown impression in the lobby of Howe's new role.

> I had been confronted, mostly by John Cole, BBC, with the most remarkably upbeat account of what Sir Geoffrey Howe's role ... would entail. It somewhat enlarged that played by Willie Whitelaw. And no one would ever play a bigger role than Lord Whitelaw did in any government led by Mrs Thatcher ... to hear the Lobby talk, Mrs Thatcher was going out of business.[71]

Ingham's reputation as a rubbisher and a leaker may now be so firmly entrenched that it may prove difficult to shift. However, given the severity of his critics, one is struck by how *few*, rather than how many, specific incidents of impropriety are listed against him. They amount to no more than six or so, including the main ones discussed above, over his 11 years at Downing Street, when by common consent he was a more than usually forthcoming press secretary with an infamously quick temper. Robert Harris, his critical biographer, recalls his days as part of the Sunday lobby:

> The point about Bernard was that he was so aggressively opinionated, there was always the chance he would say something useable. God, how our hearts would slip into our boots on those Friday afternoons when we walked in to find he was not there and the lugubrious Mr Perks was sitting in his chair.[72]

It is difficult not to sympathise with Ingham's defence that half a dozen errors in some 30 000 briefings hardly constitutes damning evidence of impropriety.[73] It is probable that his notoriety was based as much on his blunt manner as on any specific incidents. Opinions about Ingham tend not to fall in the middle ground; journalists either found him a manipulating bully or would probably agree with Chris Moncrieff, the Press Association's respected lobby correspondent of some 20 years' standing, that he was 'the most straightforward and honest of all the press secretaries I've known at Number 10'.[74]

Clearly his uncompromising attitude was going to gain enemies. It also meant partiality: journalists with unhelpful attitudes would not get such a good service as others. This is normal in the wider world of commercial public relations, and it was probably typical of press relations for most prime ministers. Wilson's notorious 'white commonwealth' is one obvious example. Had Ingham been a political appointment, such as Haines, he might have been expected to behave in a partial manner and probably have encountered less criticism. However Ingham continued to protest that he and Mrs Thatcher were rock-solid guardians of civil service conventions.[75]

'Neutrality' in practice was akin to the lawyer's code of professionalism: all manner of tricks of the trade, consistent with the law, may be employed to put the client's case. Just as the lawyer will argue tomorrow for a new client, so will the press officer when the government changes. The difference, of course, was that the government had not changed for 11 years. Just as a lawyer who spent that amount of time on one cause might be thought partial, so too was Ingham. Neville Taylor feared that the neutrality of the GIS as a whole might be undermined by government's length of tenure; more and more civil servants were moving up the ladder without the disciplined experience of working for a government of a different colour.[76]

Neutrality was maintained formally in that Ingham stayed away from party conferences and election campaigns and maintained an arms'-length approach to Conservative Central Office. David Boddy, in charge of the CCO press office from 1981 to 1983, described his contact with Bernard Ingham thus:

> It was relatively formal although that is not quite the word because I find it difficult to be formal with Bernard. I would frequently let him know what I was planning to do. He would seldom let us know what he was planning to do. I would complain to him about his handling of the press. He would tell me I had no right. We had quite a degree of mutual respect. He would never volunteer any information to me, quite rightly.[77]

However Boddy ventured that Ingham became more 'political' as the years went on. The appointment of Christine Wall to CCO from Number 10 was regarded widely as a move to bring Ingham's influence to bear within the Conservative organisation. The *Mail on Sunday*'s political editor reported it as a sign that 'the theory of collusion between government press officers and Conservative party propaganda may have substance'.[78] A political reporter, and admirer of Ingham, said that he had noticed relatively recent (post-1987) signs of liaison between Ingham and the party and that Ingham had called him aside on a few occasions to brief him privately on stories that fell in the grey area where government and party matters meet.[79] Towards the end of Thatcher's tenure, during the leadership challenge, Ingham became virtually unconcerned about breaches of the rules: 'I was damned if I was going to desert Mrs Thatcher at this hour.'[80]

The political demands of the press secretary's post ensures a perilous course for the civil servant: if he becomes too closely involved with the party (as a party) he risks losing credibility as a civil servant and hence with his colleagues in the various departments and the press. On the other hand, a press secretary who stays cold-bloodedly neutral may not be of much use to the prime minister. Marcia Williams complained of the neutrality of Wilson's first press secretary, Trevor Lloyd-Hughes, ironically a journalist, not a civil servant, by trade. She said that he became 'more of a civil servant than the civil servants, and so impartial as to make his statements sometimes sound devoid of content'.[81] Wilson decided to appoint a 'political man' at Number 10, opting for Gerald Kaufman.

Ingham failed to negotiate the tightrope in that he became closely identified as 'Maggie's man' and, thereby, lost some credibility as a civil servant. That was certainly the view of Tam Dalyell, Heath and Biffen, the Labour Opposition and certain sections of the media. It is difficult to disagree with the conclusion of Colin Seymour-Ure, who argues that, if Ingham has been at fault, it is 'basically because the nature of the job will not bear the strain on one incumbent, strictly a civil servant, for 10 years'.[82]

With hindsight, the controversy about the 'political' nature of Ingham seems a storm in a very British teacup, which may seem scarcely understandable from an overseas standpoint. Elsewhere, for example, Australia, Canada and the United States, press secretaries are automatically partisan appointments.[83] Ironically, if the post of prime minister's press secretary had been a political appointment Bernard Ingham would not have been considered for the job.

THE LOBBY: A TOOL FOR NEWS MANIPULATION?

Some of them [newspaper correspondents] tend to depend so largely on official sources for information and to develop such obligations to the officals with whom they work, that they become mouthpieces of authority, taking their 'line' from the Minister or his officials and undertaking to hold up the news to suit the convenience of the Department.

They are known as 'trustworthy' by the Department with whom they work.

But a journalist's trust is not to any government Department but to the public. Some of these groups include men of ability and independent judgment who do in fact take their own line. Their presence does not alter the general principle that anything which ties newspapers too closely to official sources of news, or sets up obligations which may conflict with a newspaper's primary responsiblity to the public is a bad system and ought not to exist.[84]

Francis Williams (1946)

Williams, Attlee's press secretary, was writing of the potential evils the system of unattributable, collective briefings for specialist groups of journalists, of which the Westminster correspondents' lobby is the most notorious. Although more than 40 years old, his assessment provides the core argument which propelled the 1980s objectors to the lobby. His account 'has never been bettered', according to Peter Hennessy,[85] who was largely responsible for reviving the lobby debate. 'Revival' is the correct word because the lobby had its public detractors in the 1960s,[86] and again in the 1970s when Joe Haines jettisoned mass lobby briefings. Nevertheless the 1980s crisis of the lobby was particularly acute: three newspapers, *The Independent, Guardian* and *Scotsman*, opted out of the lobby briefing system, Labour and Alliance leaders promised to abandon it, and the lobby itself held two internal inquiries and produced two reports, the latter warning that the system was in danger of collapse.

The crisis of the lobby should be set in context of the public, parliamentary and media debate about government secrecy in general. The lobby, with its secret unattributable briefings, whose very existence were to be denied to outsiders, and its arcane practices (Celestial Blue was the lobby codename for Mrs Thatcher, Red Mantle for Kinnock) came to be seen as embodying all that was most clandestine and disturbing. The all-party Campaign for Freedom of Information (CFI), established in 1984 and numbering former top-ranking civil servants among its panel of advisers, embraced among its goals the reform of the lobby. In one of the most robust assaults upon the lobby system, Des Wilson, CFI's co-chairman, said it drew journalists into a conspiracy to influence public opinion:

What is worrying is that the energy and resources devoted to manipulation of the media, and to campaigns of misinformation, are far greater and far more damaging than ever before, and that the media, for all its ritual protests, and even with a few notable exceptions, allows itself to be manipulated with what I can only described as shocking ease.[87]

The argument clearly contains a double criticism: of the *briefer* for attempting to manipulate the news, and of *lobby journalists* for colluding in and perpetuating the system of their own deception. The concern here is specifically with the collective unattributable briefings given by the Number 10 press secretary. Other briefings, by the Leader of the House and the opposition leaders, have not aroused particular controversy. Nor have the other lobby privileges, such as access to the Members' Lobby and advance copies of parliamentary papers – confidential final revises – which continued to be enjoyed by correspondents who boycotted the press secretary briefings.

The Lobby: the Inquiries

The two lobby internal inquiries focused on whether briefings should be on or off the record and the form of attribution for the press secretary. The first inquiry was held in 1984 and reached its conclusions after meetings with Ingham, John Biffen (then Leader of the House), David Steel (then leader of the Liberals), David Owen (leader of the SDP) and Neil Kinnock.

Bernard Ingham met the committee on lobby practice on 7 November 1984 and, according to the minutes, he saw no problem with introducing on-the-record briefings for ministers:

He said Minister's briefings should be assumed to be on-the-record unless specified unattributable. But he warned there could be dangers in 'mixed' meetings. On-the-record lobbies would encourage him to get Ministers to see the Lobby regularly, especially during recesses.

But for his own daily briefings he did not think on-the-record attribution would work except on some occasions when he wished to knock down a story. The system would suffer because Ministers would complain he was becoming a personality. On attribution, he wanted this confined to 'government sources', and not more specific.

The committee met, with Owen and Steel, in Owen's room at the Commons on 15 November and found at first that the two leaders' opinions were opposed: Steel was anxious that non-attributable briefings should stay; Owen was enthusiastic for on-the-record briefings. Eventually they ageed a compromise, half on, half off the record.[88] It seems that Owen's enthusiasm eventually held sway because, in evidence to the second inquiry, Steel wrote to the lobby secretary telling him that, in the event of an Alliance government, it would scrap the lobby system.[89]

Steel still believed that off-the-record briefings had advantages for Opposition leaders, and that if all briefings were on the record journalists would be privy to less information. 'However, I am persuaded,' he continued, that the Alliance should 'set an example' to the present government. But, while the prime minister's press secretary should be identified, he felt it would wrong to name the Liberal press spokesman (then Jim Dumsday):

> I do not believe, and I know that Jim Dumsday agrees with me on this, that the new prominence of certain press spokesmen as named personalities in their own right is a helpful development, in that it tends to interpose another person between the press and the individual on whose behalf they speak. Therefore any information obtained should be attributed to a party spokesman rather than a named individual.

Neil Kinnock told the first inquiry that he favoured 'mixed' lobby briefings. The minute of this meeting is particularly brief, just two paragraphs, finishing with this curt comment: 'In passing Mr Kinnock said he did "not think the Lobby much good" because its value was to provide informally detailed background briefing and, for example in the miners' strike, this it had failed to do.'[90] The print unions' dispute with Murdoch's News International in 1986 brought Kinnock's relations with the lobby to a head. The Labour Party, committed to a policy of non-co-operation with Murdoch's papers, had to abandon lobby briefings as such. Technically, lobby briefings are held at the invitation of the lobby, which, according to its own rules, cannot prohibit any of its members from attending. A compromise was reached according to which Kinnock arranged meetings at his own office and thereby took control of the invitation list. However Kinnock's low estimation of the value of the lobby did not abate and even after the Wapping dispute was settled he did not resume the practice of regular weekly lobby briefings, although his deputy, Roy Hattersley, did attend occasionally.

The first report into lobby practice was short, an eight-point, two-page document, signed by its four-man working party: Glyn Mathias (Lobby chairman), David Healey (then Press Association and lobby secretary), John Lewis (then of the provincial press) and James Naughtie (then *Guardian*). It recommended on-the-record briefings with politicians where mutually agreed, but found no consensus on Downing Street spokesmen and therefore 'the present rules of non-attribution will apply'. It also decided that the 'aura of secrecy' about lobby practice was unnecessary and recommended that its existence and general workings should be open to public scrutiny.[91] Lobby journalists voted to keep the rules of non-attribution (67–55) but also voted for a more substantial inquiry into lobby practice (68–58).

The second Lobby Inquiry team comprised four men: Chris Moncrieff (lobby chairman), David Hughes (honorary secretary), Gordon Jackson (of the provincial press) and Peter Riddell (then *Financial Times*). They concluded that only a minority, albeit a substantial one, wanted to change the system completely.[92] The task facing the lobby was to establish 'a workable and sustainable system which does not provoke continual debilitating conflict'. It was committed to pressing for on-the-record information where 'practicable and agreed', although not at the risk of inhibiting the flow of information.

The move to the largely attributable briefings by the Labour and Alliance leaders after the 1984 Lobby inquiry worked successfully. We note that each of the opposition leaders now state [*sic*] they are committed to ending the present unattributable system of Downing Street briefings if they win office. But Tom McCaffrey reflects the scepticism of many participants in doubting whether this aspiration might prove realistic in practice. But clearly if any of these parties were in office after the next general election, the situation would have to be reconsidered.

The inquiry team defined its task as establishing the nature of unattributable briefings and enforcing the rules. The form of attribution acceptable to Bernard Ingham was 'government sources', which he felt was accurate because he was speaking on behalf of the whole government. The problem of enforcement was delicate; the lobby as a group, and through its elected committee, was a voluntary body. It did not formally decide who could be its members as accreditation to the lobby was by inclusion in the Serjeant at Arms' list.

> It is not a disciplinary body. It cannot take action against newspapers or any other bodies which do not attend briefings but which then use the information supplied at the briefings (for example via Press Association tapes) and attribute it to Mr Ingham and his staff. What they do is their own affair.
>
> However, those journalists accredited to be Lobby correspondents who do choose to attend unattributable briefings have an obligation to accept and abide by whatever rules are mutually agreed . . . It is clear that in the recent past some members have not done so, both by bending the rules themselves to the point of breaking and by supplying information to those who explicitly do not accept the rules. This situation cannot continue.

The report recommended: (1) a clarification and simplification of the rules which should be made public; (2) a written undertaking from lobby journalists to obey the rules; (3) exclusion of offenders until such time as they are prepared to give the undertaking; (4) reaffirmation of the lobby's commitment to on-the-record information where possible. The report warned that if lobby members did not accept tighter discipline it would 'almost certainly lead to the collapse of the system and probably some form of selective briefing which will damage the interests of the majority'. It also urged Downing Street to show restraint if the practice of non-attribution was not to be strained beyond endurance.

Lobby members voted on the recommendations in a manner likely to extend confusion because a substantial majority (54–31) voted against a system of written undertakings. Further, on recommendation three, the exclusion of offenders, the vote split down the middle (42–42). Thus the Lobby voted in favour of unattributable briefings but has left itself completely shorn of any procedure to enforce the rules. It has thereby created exactly the situation which the inquiry team tried to avoid and which will test the report's warnings of collapse.

The Lobby as a Tool of News Management: Conclusion

What then are we to make of the charge that the lobby briefing is a tool of news management for witting or unwitting lobby journalists? On the basis of submissions to the inquiry the case is far from proven. There are four likely important consequences of the abandonment of unattributable lobby briefings:

1 There seemed to be agreement across the board that on-the-record briefings would mean less information.
2 Reporters would be forced to rely more on individual contacts and sources to keep tabs on Cabinet and government activity. Lobby critics, particularly Peter Hennessy, and Tony Bevins, would welcome this as a move away from what they perceive as the crippling herd instinct of journalists.
3 Journalists working for the less glamorous sectors would find themselves at a disadvantage. It was no surprise that the regional press was amongst the strongest supporters of the existing lobby system because it would probably have the most to lose if it collapsed. In the words of Jon Hibbs, then chief political correspondent of Thomson Regional Newspapers, the lobby briefings are especially important 'to those of us in the provincial press who do not have the ministerial pulling power of the national newspapers and broadcasting organisations'.[93]
4 A system of selective unattributable briefings would replace the mass unattributable briefing. Former lobby chairman, David Rose, believed this would strengthen rather than reduce the power of the Number 10 press secretary.[94]

The critics of the lobby initiated the public discussion, and set the terms and tone of the debate. On closer inspection their case is less than compelling. The Lobby inquiries in themselves, the submissions and the votes suggest a body of men and women genuinely concerned to find the most appropriate means of conveying the maximum information to their readers and viewers. Moreover, in important respects, the case against the lobby appears to be a critique of a system that has not existed in practice for some years. For example, the strict secrecy demanded in the private and confidential *Notes on the Practice of Lobby Journalism* belongs to an earlier era.

Lobby briefings began regularly between the wars and at first members were urged to behave rather like a masonic brotherhood with secret vows, secret lunches and secret meetings. Guy Eden, the father of the modern lobby, described how new members were 'coached in the etiquette of the place'.[95] It seems the elite gentlemen's club atmosphere survived into the 1950s. Henry James, in his submission to the Inquiry, describes the almost seminar-like atmosphere of Harold Evans' briefings. Evans fine-tuned the art of 'thinking aloud' to let journalists into the thinking processes in policy development.

However from 1958 newspapers were allowed an 'alternate' member, a deputy for occasions when the number one was away, and by the late 1960s the lobby had expanded to about 110 members. It was up to 220 by the late 1980s. As the second Inquiry report notes, the lobby is both larger and more fluid, as journalists frequently work at Westminster for relatively short periods before moving on. Nor is its status quite as highly prized: 'It is no longer necessarily the pinnacle of a career,' according to the second report. These factors served to loosen the bonds of the brotherhood and peel away layers of mystique and secrecy well before the first report recommended opening procedures to public scutiny. Jon Hibbs was in the lobby for more than a year before he was even shown a copy of the rule book.[96] It is likely that the criticisms of Lobby practice, especially from Peter Hennessy and colleagues in *Sources Close to the Prime Minister*, encouraged the lobby to abandon formally any pretence of secrecy. But it also appears that this was merely formal recognition of existing practice, and there was no attempt at a rearguard action to defend the crumbling walls.

There has as yet been no serious study, involving a cross-check with information divulged at briefings and stories appearing in a sample of the media, which can either prove or disprove the contention that Lobby members' 'credulity' has made the system 'the Prime Minister's most useful tool for the political management of the news', to quote Cockerell *et al.*[97] It seems fair to say, from the evidence to the inquiries, that critics have over-estimated the importance of the lobby as a news management tool. Lobby briefings last on average about 20 minutes, twice a day, which should leave ample time for cross-checking of sources. Moreover the 'disinformation' content of these briefings may also have been exaggerated. Jon Hibbs's submission to the second inquiry casts them in a mundane light:

> Very soon after I arrived at Westminster I became sceptical of the value of Downing Street briefings. Contrary to all the horror stories about gullible Lobby fodder and official disinformation, they never seemed to provide any hard information worth repeating at all. Perhaps it is a chicken and egg situation: that Bernard can't trust today's expanded everchanging Lobby so he never tells it anything, so members are forced to make mountains out of molehills to justify going to it.[98]

In the light of this, then, how important is the matter of non-attribution? In practice it is not likely that a press secretary could make a habit of denying comments made unattributably. A press secretary who behaved in that way would soon lose credibility with journalists and therefore any power he may have had to influence their handling of the news. Ironically Ingham did not attempt to deny the comments which were cited against him as an abuse of the lobby system. The example of Ingham suggests that the other side of the lobby critics' coin, that the press passively regurgitate what they are told, does not ring true either. Joe Haines said that the lobby could no longer deliver its side of the bargain because if the story was good enough the source would not be sacred, and it was ever thus.

Finally lobby critics draw a subtle distinction between off-the-record comments to an individual reporter and mass unattributable briefings. None complain at journalists using anonymous sources on an individual basis, which is accepted as normal and even essential for the practice of journalism. Indeed a journalist's protection of an anonymous source is a cardinal rule and held to be fundamental for freedom of information. Instead, it is suggested the *mass* nature of the unattributable briefing adds an unhealthy or even sinister element, encouraging laziness, fostering the herd instinct and making reporters easier to manage. Anthony Bevins has waxed eloquent on this point, stressing that this is a complaint against journalism in general, of which the lobby is merely the worst example.[99]

Bevins's thesis has merit as a broad criticism of journalists in general. Many groups of specialist reporters hunt in packs, discuss stories, exchange ideas, work out the 'intro', to use the newspaper parlance. Lobby correspondents stand accused of this, and they in turn point an accusing finger at industrial correspondents. Nor is it a British ailment alone; Timothy Crouse has entertained generations of American journalism students with his descriptions of the 1972 presidential press corps in *The Boys on the Bus*, coining the phrase 'pack journalism' and 'thereby seeding half the questions we are still asked in college seminars and lecture halls', according to the *Washington Post*'s David Broder.[100] The pack journalism criticism will surely outlive the lobby controversy, which has all but disappeared in the post-Ingham years. Newspapers have returned to the lobby and problems of attribution evaporated as Ingham's successors, Gus O'Donnell and Christopher Meyer, took a more flexible approach.

6 Government Advertising: Information or Propaganda?

The Central Office of Information (COI) was and remains the channel for the vast bulk of government publicity expenditure. It was established in 1946 to provide a central government agency for the supply of paid-for publicity material, services and advice. It was a peacetime version of the wartime Ministry of Information, shorn of censorship and security duties and with a reduced propaganda commitment overseas.

At first the COI's activities bore the brunt of the Conservative Opposition's hostility to government publicity in the post-Second World War years. The Ministry of Information had been set up specifically as a propaganda machine for the war, and its retention into peacetime, albeit in modified form, evoked suspicion of Nazi-style opinion-moulding machinery. Since the difficult early days, however, the COI came to be accepted broadly unchanged by successive governments and by the mid-1980s it was cast virtually as a bulwark of probity against the propagandist ambitions of the Conservative government.

Mrs Thatcher's premiership wrought the most far-reaching changes in the COI since 1946. Created as the obligatory central organisation for virtually all government paid-for publicity, the COI was transformed into an agency competing with the private sector for departmental accounts for all manner of publicity expertise. Until 1984 the COI provided services on an 'allied service basis'; that is, it administered most departmental publicity budget at no charge. Since April 1984 departments have shouldered direct responsibility for their own publicity budgets and pay the COI for services rendered. In 1987 departments were 'untied' and were free to engage private sector companies for almost all publicity requirements, the main exception being advertising, where the COI's procurement muscle enabled it to negotiate substantial discounts. This has effectively downgraded the COI and increased the importance of departmental press and publicity offices. At the same time, the COI was required to break even year after year and was forced to become leaner in its quest to be more competitive. Staff numbers were pruned from 1283 in April 1979 to 583 at 31 March 1993.[1]

ADVERTISING

Typically advertising takes the biggest slice of COI spending (about 60–64 per cent in the late 1980s) and, being the most visible of communications techniques, it also provides the target for the most criticism. Opponents complain not merely at the cost and bias of government advertising but also its triviality, wastefulness and excursion into areas of human behaviour which should be no concern of government.[2] In the following pages we shall examine expenditure on advertising and the propriety of campaigns. It is enough here to offer a brief outline of the types of campaign undertaken.

Until the Conservatives took office in 1979 most government advertising campaigns fell under one of three headings: recruitment (particularly to the armed forces), social persuasion (such as Don't Drink and Drive, Watch Out, There's a Thief About, Keep Britain Tidy, Clunk Click Every Trip) and public information, usually to explain new legislation (for example, provisions for housing improvement grants, 'We'll give you up to £350 to modernise your home', or the introduction of decimal currency).[3] These broad headings also cover most of the advertising spend in the Thatcher years, with the one important exception of privatisation, which formed a new category.

The COI's involvement with privatisation advertising campaigns has varied. In fact it was not brought in on privatisation campaigns before 1986, when it carried out some detailed work for the British Gas flotation, but its involvement in subsequent privatisations has fluctuated considerably. Unlike government departments, nationalised corporations are not tied to the COI for advertising. There are also other public bodies which have never been required to use COI services, the two most notable being National Savings and the Scottish Office.

millions (£)

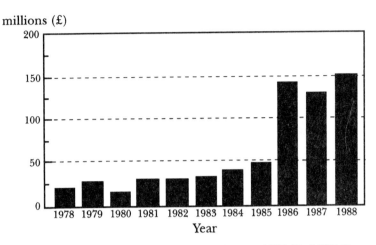

Figure 6.1   Total COI home expenditure, 1978/9–1988/9
Source: COI annual reports and government supply estimates.

THE SCALE OF GOVERNMENT PUBLICITY: EXPENDITURE

Spectacular growth in the scale of government publicity expenditure, particularly on television advertising, was the major trigger for renewed controversy in the latter half of the 1980s. The watershed year for government publicity spending was 1986, the year before the general election, which witnessed an enormous leap. From this date until 1993 Her Majesty's Government has featured among the top two or three annual advertisers with Procter & Gamble and Unilever. In cash terms, total COI spending on behalf of government departments soared from £68 million in 1985/86 to £162 million the following year, an increase of close to 150 per cent. The contrast is starker still if the figures are confined to domestic expenditure: up from £48 million in 1985/86 to £142 million in 1986/87, an increase of nearly 200 per cent (see Figure 6.1). COI spending on advertising alone trebled from under £30 million to close to £90 million.[4]

The increase is less dramatic if privatisation campaigns are included throughout the whole period. It should be remembered that 1986 was the first year COI had significant involvement with privatisation campaigns and the 1986/87 figure includes an item of £36 million for the Department of Energy, a 15-fold departmental increase, which is accounted for mainly by the British Gas flotation. Advertising industry monitor, Media Expenditure Analysis Limited (MEAL), includes pre-1986 privatisation spends in its government figures, and consequently registers a less dramatic rise, from £52 million in the calendar year 1985 to just over £80 million in 1986. Nevertheless, by any standard, government publicity expenditure climbed steeply. Moreover an increasing proportion of this spending was on television advertising and much of it on politically contentious programmes, such as the privatisations and schemes for the unemployed.

The sheer scale of government publicity, at the same time as the Local Government Acts of 1986 and 1988 were restraining 'propaganda on the rates' by local councils, seemed evidence of government's 'double standards'.[5] Government's own evidence to the Widdicombe Committee inquiry into Local Government 1985 was quoted back at them: 'The unregulated use by any public authority of highly developed media techniques, particularly for persuasive purposes with a strong political undertone, is perceived as a dangerous trend in a democratic society.'[6] Government, however, replied that its publicity was legitimate public information within the conventions of propriety and that, when adjustments were made for inflation, comparisons showed that the level of spending in the late 1980s was only just returning to levels of the early 1970s. The National Audit Office (NAO)'s 1989 report (*Publicity Services for Government Departments*) broadly supported both strands of this argument and found COI expenditure on a downward trend at constant prices from 1973 to 1983. However this argument is true only if privatisation advertising is excluded. MEAL data on advertising alone show that, even at constant prices, government's annual expenditure on advertising was usually £20 million higher in the mid- to late 1980s (see Figure 6.2). The NAO reached its conclusion by treating privatisation as a special case – that is, one-off expenditure.[7] For our purposes there is no good reason to exclude privatisations. Rather the reverse, because flotation advertising promoted controversial policy and conveyed enthusiastic messages about 'popular capitalism', a major and distinctive theme of Thatcher's programme. In this sense the British Gas campaign, in particular, was among the most 'political' of government advertising.

millions (£)

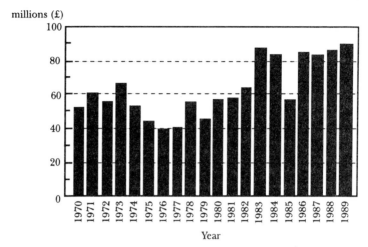

Year

Figure 6.2   Total advertising expenditure, 1970–89
(1987/8 prices)
Source: Register-MEAL.

The bulk of government advertising in the early 1970s went on campaigns that were not controversial in a party political sense: armed forces recruitment, and postal and telecommunications services. There were occasional one-off campaigns which generated some political criticism, particularly the Conservatives' energy crisis campaign of 1973–4, and Labour's counter-inflation campaign of 1975–6. But these were relatively minor campaigns compared to other sectors of government advertising.

The Thatcher era, by contrast, saw a marked increase in publicity expenditure in support of controversial policy. The privatisations start to show through in 1983/84 with British Telecom and then with the 'Tell Sid' British Gas campaign in 1986. Employment publicity picks up in spectacular fashion in 1986 and, thereafter, trade and industry initiatives, social security and latterly health reforms take increasingly significant chunks of the government publicity pie.

Looking at the period from 1970 on, there are clear trends over time: there was a marked increase in expenditure on advertising and a distinct shift from print to television; there was a marked shift in the proportions of spending from overseas to home publicity; and a substantial increase in both the absolute and proportionate amounts of spending in support of economic and social policy. On the other side of the coin, there was a concomitant decline in the proportions of spending on previously dominant domestic sectors, in particular recruitment to the armed forces.[8]

The Growth of Government Advertising

From 1983 onwards advertising expenditure is consistently and significantly higher than the preceding period, with the single exception of 1985 (Figure 6.2). The dip in 1985 may be accounted for primarily by the fact that there were no high-spending privatisations that year. British Aerospace and Britoil were sold in 1985 at a combined advertising cost of £6 million, compared to the £23 million estimated cost of the British Telecom sale the previous year.

Advertising also increased as a proportion of total COI publicity spending. In 1970, for instance, advertising accounted for about £5.5 million, which was about 44 per cent. The proportion decreased in the early years of the Thatcher government and was some 32 per cent in 1984/85. By the late 1980s the proportion had increased again to some 60 per cent. Privatisation advertising was the main motor driving this trend. A second engine was the increased use of the relatively more costly *television* advertising. In the calendar year 1970, television took only 25 per cent of total government advertising expenditure, according to MEAL. By 1988 it accounted for 56 per cent. It stayed between 46 and 50 per cent thereafter.

The Increasing Significance of Domestic Publicity

The COI's annual report and accounts for 1984/5 noted that the Foreign and Commonwealth Office was its biggest single client. The relative importance of overseas publicity has declined significantly since then. Overseas expenditure declined from 34 per cent of the COI publicity budget in 1984/5 to 14 per cent and less since 1987/8. Again privatisation may be one explanatory factor, but it by no means provides the whole story. As we are about to see, there have also been substantial advances by the health, social and economic related departments.

Table 6.1   Employment advertising expenditure, 1986

Campaign	Agency	Expenditure
Youth training	Saatchi & Saatchi	£8 192 000
Action for Jobs	Davidson Pearce	£6 102 000
Restart	Yellowhammer	£5 672 000

Source: MEAL.

The Growth of Economic and Social Publicity

Employment expenditure, through the Department of Employment, Manpower Services Commission and other training agencies, increased as a proportion of COI home spending from about 2 per cent in the years 1978–86 to 26 per cent in 1986–7, falling to a still substantial 20 per cent the following year. The jump in cash terms was from less than £1 million before 1985 to £6.4 million in 1985/6, to £37.2 million in 1986/7. MEAL assigns the increase to three campaigns (see Table 6.1). Note that the whole of Yellowhammer's 1986 Restart campaign was conducted on television, 67 per cent of the youth training campaign and 60 per cent of Action for Jobs.

There is no clear correlation between this expenditure and unemployment levels. The 1979–83 Thatcher government inherited unemployment of some 1.5 million and the number doubled by 1982. The official jobless total stayed at more than 3 million until 1987. The MEAL data shows a mini-peak of advertising in 1983, fuelled primarily by Saatchi & Saatchi's £3 million plus youth training and Youth Opportunities campaigns. After 1983, however, there was no real movement until 1986. The peaks in employment advertising, the timing of general elections (and the involvement of Saatchi & Saatchi) seem more than mere coincidence, a fact not lost on critics of government publicity.

Spending on health and social security has also increased markedly, both in absolute terms and as a proportion. Department of Health and Social Security spending lingered around the 2–3 per cent mark as a proportion of home expenditure from 1978 to 1984. In 1985 it increased sharply to 13 per cent. reaching a peak of 19 per cent the following year. Expenditure

Table 6.2   Health advertising expenditure, 1986

Campaign	Agency	Expenditure
AIDS information	TBWA	£2 266 000
Misuse of drugs	Yellowhammer	£1 200 000

Source: Register-MEAL.

doubled in 1987, although the proportion of total spending decreased because the COI took on responsibity for privatisation campaigns for the first time. The main motors of the 1986 health increase were non-party political, however: AIDS and drugs (Table 6.2). AIDS continued to be health's highest spender (£2.5 million in 1989), although nursing recruitment and government changes to the the family doctor practices increased in importance.

Social security publicity also burgeoned, especially in the late 1980s, in response to major reform of the social security system. The reform policy package was introduced in 1986 and advertising agency BSB Dorland were engaged to run a £3 649 000 campaign in 1988 (about 50 per cent of which was on television). The Family Credit campaign, switched to BMP DDB Needham, spent £3.2 million in 1989, 85 per cent of it on television commercials. Family Credit was another key target for opponents of government publicity, and it was also severely criticised in the NAO report for poor planning, poor targets and poor results.[9]

Trade and industry advertising also shows striking growth, reaching peaks in 1984 (the British Telecom flotation) and 1988. The 1988 peak was built on two major campaigns, according to that year's MEAL digest:

| Europe (1992) | DMB&B | £6 721 000 |
| Enterprise | WCRS | £9 805 000 |

Again the great weight of these campaigns was on television: 82 per cent in the case of the European single market campaign, 74 per cent of the enterprise initiatives campaign.

Altogether, health and social security, employment and trade and industry accounted for 17 per cent of COI's home publicity spend in 1979/80, the first full year of the first Thatcher government. In 1987–8 they accounted for 42 per cent.

Declining Importance of the Armed Forces

At the beginning of the 1970s the two dominant advertising sectors were the armed forces and postal services which together consumed more than 57 per cent of the total government spending or advertising. By 1988 they took less than 25 per cent between them. The decline is accounted for primarily by the striking reduction in the armed forces recruitment advertising (down at constant prices from about £18m in 1970 to about £5m in 1986 and 1987, according to MEAL). There are a number of reasons why the armed forces should have worked harder for recruits in the early 1970s: there was close to full employment and recruitment to the forces had dipped over 1967 and 1968. In addition, British troops had moved into Belfast in 1969 and it was necessary to ensure that recruitment did not decline as a result.

Advertising expenditure on postal services has actually increased in real terms since 1970, even though the service lost British Telecom in 1981. Nevertheless, its share of the government advertising cake has declined slightly. Figures 6.3 and 6.4 show the changing pattern of government advertising expenditure and graphically demonstrate the decline in the armed forces and increasing importance of employment, health and trade and industry.

The above analysis is based on advertising expenditure alone, but the trend shows through equally strongly also in COI home spending. Ministry of Defence expenditure took 53 per cent of the COI's home budget in 1969/70, 25 per cent in 1978/9 and 8 per cent in 1987/8.

Thus government's argument that its publicity spending had not increased in real terms since the early 1970s is misleading, ignoring spending on privatisation and obscuring the substantial switch from spending on matters of cross-party agreement to expenditure in support of controversial policy. Logically this trend might be expected. The Thatcher administrations undertook social and economic reforms which in their sweep and scope have exceeded any previous post-war government, with the exception of Attlee's 1945–51 Labour government.

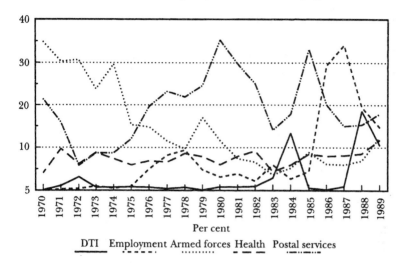

Figure 6.3 Advertising expenditure of selected sectors as a
proportion of total expenditure, 1970–89
Source: Register-MEAL.

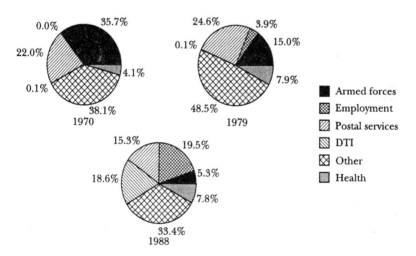

Figure 6.4 Changing pattern of advertising expenditure by
selected categories, 1970–88
Source: Register-MEAL.

New legislation inevitably requires publicity and the more contested the policy, the more controversial the publicity. Perhaps the fairest comparison of the Thatcher government may not be with the immediately preceding governments but with the post-war Labour administration.

The Lord Young Factor

Lord Young, a businessman who made his fortune in the construction industry, was called 'the man who has sold advertising to Whitehall' by advertising trade magazine *Campaign*.[10] The magazine claimed of him, and with some justification, that he blazed the trail for government advertising first at the Manpower Services Commission (MSC) and then the Department of Employment (DoE).

His spells at the MSC, DoE, and then Trade and Industry (DTI), were all accompanied by substantial increases in advertising and publicity. Lord Young, a director of the right-wing think-tank, the Centre for Policy Studies, during 1979–82, was appointed chairman of the MSC in 1982. The MSC's advertising doubled under his leadership from less than £2 million to £4.3 million in 1983. More than half of that went on Saatchis' youth opportunites and youth training campaigns. He was appointed Employment Secretary in 1985 and, as we have seen, the department's publicity spend snowballed in 1986. If we leave the MSC aside, DoE expenditure through the COI increased as follows:

1984/5	£283 000
1985/6	£997 000
1986/7	£14 767 000

The 'Lord Young factor' transferred to the DTI in 1987 when he became Secretary of State there. He presided over the relaunch of the DTI as the 'department for enterprise', a comprehensive attempt to create a new corporate image. Its publicity spending increased as follows:

1986/7	£1 785 000
1987/8	£11 248 000
1988/9	£31 276 000 (including Board of Trade)

If one ignores privatisation spending, government departmental publicity declined slightly over 1979–82 at constant prices, and during 1982–5 it was still below early 1970s levels. The steep upward climb stems from 1986 and spending by the DoE and MSC were major engines of growth. Lord Young's campaigns invariably attracted comment and controversy, both for the sums expended and the tone. He resigned from government in July 1989 and DTI spending fell by nearly half, to £16 million in 1989–90. The DoE's publicity spending through COI also dropped from its 1986–7 peak to £3.7 million in 1989–90, although it should be remembered that unemployment declined steadily to under 2 million by 1989.[11]

The significance of Lord Young should not be underestimated but there are two other factors which are probably major causes of the transformation from a relatively publicity-shy to a publicity-conscious government. One is clearly privatisation, and the key campaign here was the British Gas 'Tell Sid' advertising (see below). Secondly it is fair speculation to suggest that the Greater London Council (GLC)'s 1984 aggressive anti-abolition campaign impressed the government enormously. The legal curbs on local government publicity spending were prompted partly by the GLC campaign and government ministers cannot have helped but be impressed by the shift in public opinion in the capital in favour of retention of the GLC and its Labour leader Ken Livingstone.[12]

Government Publicity and General Elections

There is a pattern of increased spending either in the year before a general election or in the election year itself. COI data produced for the NAO report show such increases for every general election since 1964. The pattern appears to hold regardless of party in power or whether the analysis is in cash terms or at constant prices. It is also confirmed when the analysis is confined to advertising (see Figure 6.2). The increases are noticeable and significant for the election years 1966, 1970, 1983, 1987 and also for the years preceding elections, 1969, 1973, 1978 and 1986. Without any question the most striking leap is in 1986. For our purposes MEAL's 1983 rise should be discounted; it refers primarily to BT corporate image commercials before privatisation and telephone call stimulation campaigns, which were not likely to affect voters' perceptions of government. Without the British Telecom element the 1983 increase is relatively small.

It is also true that the spending patterns in the years after general elections are by no means consistent. Expenditure following elections decreased on three occasions, increased on two and stayed more or less the same after the 1983 election. One might expect the expenditure to decrease after the election if the primary purpose of the pre-election publicity had been to influence voting decisions.

CONVENTIONS ON PROPRIETY IN GOVERNMENT PUBLICITY

The propriety of government publicity services is decided by conventions based on precedent and practice and the long-standing Whitehall notion of 'neutrality'. These hold that the government information services should not anticipate the decisions of parliament or become involved in justifying government's proposals before parliament has approved the policy.

In practice it is impossible for GIS officers dealing with the press to avoid discussion of policy proposals which are likely to be precisely the issues generating political debate and controversy and therefore the very subjects of most interest to the media. However, by tradition, paid-for publicity is a different matter and the accepted rule is that money should not be spent on a controversial policy still under discussion. Former director general of the COI, Sir Fife Clark, drew the line between government information (about public policy) and party propaganda (about party policy) at the point of legislation:

> All government action may be said to spring from a political dynamic and philosophy and much of it from party manifestoes; but at what point does public policy emerge from the discussion process? This must sometimes be a matter for individual judgment, *but a basic convention has become established as governing COI production. It is that while legislation is in progress no money is spent on publicity material; but as soon as a new scheme has become the law of the land, then no matter how controversial it was in debates, and may still be in the country, or*

how small the majority by which it was passed the Government has a duty to make its details widely known.[13] (Emphasis added)

However the self-denying ordinance concerning pre-statute publicity has never been enforced with total rigidity. The post-war Labour government produced shortened 'popular' versions of some white papers, for example, on the proposals for National Insurance and the NHS. In 1953 the Conservative government issued for popular consumption a leaflet, 'Operation Rescue', which set out the government's housing and rental proposals before they had been debated in the House. Operation Rescue went beyond mere explanation of the proposed legislation and strayed into propaganda describing government's housing objectives generally, according to Marjorie Ogilvy-Webb, author of one of the few comprehensive accounts of the GIS.[14] The government, she said, took criticisms to heart and did not again provoke such allegations.

In 1971 Edward Heath's government printed $5\frac{1}{2}$ million copies of a popular version of the white paper on Britain's application to join the EEC. The COI also published leaflets and mounted an advertising campaign to draw attention to the leaflets. In 1976 the Labour government mounted a similar type of campaign, this time on devolution, with a popular version of the white paper available free at post offices and press advertising of its availability.

Thus there were precedents for the Thatcher governments' paid publicity on a number of policy proposals. They have provided booklets and leaflets, free on request, on policy proposals such as the Police and Criminal Evidence Bill (1983/4), bus policy (1984) and on the proposed privatisation of British Telecom (1983). Pamphlets on the NHS white paper proposals were also produced, advertised and distributed on request and through post offices. Most contentiously, the COI produced a leaflet, 'Paying for Local Government: The Need for Change', based on government proposals for the poll tax which were then only at the green paper stage.

A further convention started by Labour in 1950 and adhered to by successive governments was that publicity would be drastically curtailed in advance of a general election. From close of nomination until polling day there would be no advertising and the parties agreed not to make use of the COI library material in any electoral publicity. This convention has applied strictly only at general elections. Frank Dobson, then Shadow Leader of the Commons, called on the IBA to ban government advertising on television in advance of the European elections in 1989. The IBA replied that this was a matter for the government to decide. The convention, like all government information rules, is merely that, a convention with no statutory force, nor is it included in the IBA's Code of Advertising Standards and Practice.

Unlike local authorities, central government departments are not restricted by any specific legislation. The mechanism for ensuring that the conventions are enforced is government accountability to parliament for content and expenditure, with individual ministers responsible for the activities of their departments. The guidelines were not codified into written form until 1985, when a note by the Cabinet Office, 'Central Government Conventions on Publicity and Advertising', was submitted to the Widdicombe Committee, whose report led to legislation controlling local authority publicity spending in the Local Government Act 1986.

The Cabinet Office note lists the main conventions as follows: (1) subject matters should be ones in which government has direct and substantial responsibilities; (2) content, tone and presentation should not be party political. The treatment should be objective, not personalised, not contain political slogans and not directly attack (although it may respond to implicitly) opinions and policies of opposition parties and groups; (3) material on controversial matters should not be distributed unsolicited except where the information and directly affects the recipients' interests; and (4) costs should be justifiable. Notably the conventions make no reference, as did Sir Fife Clark, to legislation. Point (3) permits publicity on policy proposals, as opposed to policy enshrined in law. The key point here is that material should not be unsolicited (therefore ruling out advertising campaigns and house-to-house mailings) *except where the information directly affects the recipients' interests.*

The Treasury and Civil Service Committee remarked on the 'looseness' of the conventions, arguing that there 'may be a case' for reinforcing them, 'perhaps even by giving them statutory backing as with the codes of practice for local authorities under the Local Government Act'.[15] The Local Government Acts of 1986 and 1988 imposed a far stricter definition of propriety on town halls. Clause 27 of the 1988 Act forbids material which promotes a point of view on a matter of political controversy which is identifiable as the view of one party and not another. However the Treasury decided that statutory controls were unnecessary:

> Ministers are collectively committed to the conventions which were submitted to the Widdicombe Committee and placed in the Libraries of both Houses in 1985. And parliament can always require Ministers to justify their actions in individual cases in the usual way, a discipline that parliament cannot effectively apply in the local authority field.[16]

Propriety: the Scale of Government Advertising Expenditure

Nowhere is the 'looseness' of the conventions more apparent than on this issue. The one constraint on expenditure until 1989 was that 'costs should be justifiable'. In practice the boundaries of probity are set by public acceptability; historically parliamentary criticism has led to inquiries with the usual outcome of recommendations for the tightening of publicity budgets. This was the case for the Attlee Labour government which drastically cut its publicity spending following the French Committee recommendations; spending dropped from about £5½ million to £2 million.[17] The pattern of criticism, inquiry and recommendations to reduce spending was followed also in the case of the Thatcher government. Criticism in the House was followed by questions asked by the Treasury and Civil Service Committee and the Public Accounts Committee and an inquiry by the National Audit Office. The criticism reached its height in 1989 with the Opposition Day debate led by Frank Dobson, who could not better the *Daily Telegraph*'s 'expensive vote-catching' description of government publicity.[18]

Labour complained to Lord Thomson, head of the IBA, about both the scale and the tone of government commercials which, it was argued, breached the statutory ban on political advertisements on television.[19] The IBA responded that all government advertisements were carefully vetted for content. Overall it found less need to require changes of government than commercial advertisers.[20] However the IBA effectively withdrew from the volume argument, saying that its task lay in vetting the content of the commercials, not the volume.

> the content of Government advertising was subject to the same rules and scrutiny as that of other advertisers and the IBA sought at all times to interpret its rules fairly and with regard to precedent and legal advice. The volume of such advertising and expenditure on it were matters for Ministers and Parliament, not for the IBA.[21]

The IBA's controller of advertising, Frank Willis, accepted that the sheer bulk of government advertising may have 'secondary' cumulative party political effects, regardless of whether each individual commercial passed the propriety test. 'It does give the government an inside track,' but the same advantage will pass to the opposition when there is a change of government.[22]

Volume of spending, however, was top of the concerns of the Public Accounts Committee which initiated the National Audit Office inquiry in the spring of 1989. The NAO's brief was to investigate the value-for-money aspects of government publicity, and it largely cleared the government of charges of extravagant expenditure. It made a number of detailed recommendations for reducing costs, but mostly these were technical; for example, tying privatisation and National Savings advertising more closely to the COI to achieve greater bulk discounts; and squeezing rates of commission to advertising agencies. The COI emerged healthily, even triumphantly from the report after a turbulent decade in which its future had seemed threatened by a government with an inborn dislike of what it perceived as bloated, bureaucratic, centralised bodies. NAO criticisms were directed at inefficiencies in planning and buying in the privatisation and Family Credit campaigns, in which the COI played limited roles. The Public Accounts Committee closely followed the NAO's recommendations. It also urged a strengthening of the COI's advisory function to provide broader guidance and training to departments on campaign planning, implementation and advice on good practice.[23]

Some nine months before the NAO began its inquiry the Cabinet Office issued a supplementary set of publicity guidelines. The move, coupled with the transfer of proprietal advice from the COI to the Cabinet Office, was greeted with suspicion by Labour. The new guidelines, however, were reported in advertising trade magazine *Campaign* as a tightening of the rules. That seems the fair assessment. Certainly they offer far more specific guidance than the previous conventions. 'Image-building', whether on behalf of a minister or the government, was not acceptable. Ministers and departments were told not to hire public relations consultants, guidance which did not always chime with the wishes of Conservative Central Office (see section on the PM's press secretary, previous chapter). Indeed, this particular advice seems to have been ignored by Major's government.

The Cabinet Office also noted that 'it would be counter-productive if the level of spending on a public campaign impeded the communication of the message it is intended to convey by itself becoming a controversial issue'. It continued:

> It is no less crucial, if Government publicity is to remain acceptable within the conventions, that it avoids any doubts about its purpose. Government publicity should always be directed at informing the public even where it also has the objective of influencing the behaviour of individuals or particular groups. It is possible that in serving the public in this way a well-founded publicity campaign can redound to the political credit of the party in Government. This is by definition a natural consequence of political office and has been accepted as such by successive Governments. But it has equally been accepted that it must not be, or be believed to be, either the primary purpose or principal incidental purpose of a campaign.

The guidelines outlined a seven-point value-for-money (VFM) test which all government publicity proposals should pass. They noted that there is often a close link between propriety of the publicity campaign and value for money. They continued: 'The argument that it is a legitimate use of public money to promote the importance of better business performance through paid advertising depends crucially on its effect on behaviour.'

The tenor of the document implied criticism of Lord Young's DTI enterprise campaigns. Bernard Ingham has revealed that the DTI's advertising was the main cause of the reassessment of the guidelines, although he personally thought Young's campaign was not beyond the pale.[24] Despite the new strictures, however, there were few immediate signs of a reduction in total government advertising. Government's 1988–90 advertising spend was more than £98 million, a record,[25] which made government the nation's heaviest advertiser. The water and electricity privatisations kept the spending total high, although government estimates showed substantial cuts in certain departments, notably in the Lord Young's former territory at the Department of Employment, the DTI and the Training Agency (formerly the MSC). According to COI's figures, government's annual advertising expenditure did not fall significantly below £90 million until 1992–3 when, without any privatisations, it nearly halved to £47 million.[26]

Propriety: the Campaigns

Action for Jobs
Action for Jobs was the slogan given to the 1986–8 campaign to publicise the range of some 30 employment, training and enterprise schemes offered by government, such as Restart, Jobclubs, Jobsearch, Job Release, Job Splitting, YTS and Job Training Scheme. The 'Action' umbrella, however, did not cover any major new initiatives apart from Restart, which was introduced nationally in July 1986 and whose major thrust was to invite all long-term unemployed for in-depth counselling interviews. Lord Young has said that the point of Restart was 'to bring down the count', either by directing the unemployed towards government schemes or by scaring off the register people who were fraudulently claiming benefit while working in the 'black economy'.[27] Television advertising for Action for Jobs started in July 1986, reaching its height in October 1986 and February 1987. Three individual departmental schemes were all run under the Action logo: Restart, YTS and the Job Training Scheme.[28]

Of all the controversial government publicity, Action for Jobs was probably the most politically sensitive. Opinion polls showed that unemployment was consistently seen as the outstanding problem facing the nation over the period 1983–7. It was clearly perceived as a Conservative weakness and Saatchis had urged new policies to deal with it for the 1987 manifesto (see Chapter 4). Action for Jobs did not herald new policy, yet was still one of the most costly campaigns government waged in 1986. Only the Department of Energy, selling British Gas, spent more that year. The 'action' theme was later adopted by the Conservative Party in two campaigns: Action for Employment and Action for Inner Cities; and the 1987 Conservative Party conference was held under the banner slogan Action for the Third Term. During the election itself Conservative Central Office distributed the DoE's Action for Jobs pamphlet as campaigning material.[29] The Action advertising was cut drastically after the general election and dropped altogether in the spring of 1988.

BBC's *Panorama* analysed the choice of TV slots for the period from January until May 1987 and discovered the campaign was not weighted to audiences and areas of high unemployment, as might be expected, but was targeted more at high-income viewers in the south-east.[30] A DoE planning paper which was leaked to *Panorama* identified the primary target groups as 'influencers', especially senior managers, the City, local government, politicians, community groups, the media and professional advisers. The secondary target groups were the unemployed, their families, potential school leavers and careers advisers.

Panorama quoted Gallup polls which showed an improvement in the government's rating on the question of policies to deal with unemployment, up from 15 per cent in July 1986 to 30 per cent by the general election. Falling unemployment, due in part to Restart, was surely the most important factor, but there can be no doubt that the advertising imprinted Action for Jobs on the public consciousness. Lord Young quotes a MORI tracking survey (July 1986–April 1987) which found public awareness increased from 10 per cent to 56 per cent; among the unemployed it increased from 15 per cent to 74 per cent; among 18–24-year-olds from 12 per cent to 75 per cent. The unemployed and the young were the target groups but Lord Young was well aware of the wider public relations benefits: 'Of course, the rest of the population were now fully aware that the Government was tackling the problem of unemployment with full vigour!'[31]

The television advertising was the most contentious part of the campaign, but Action for Jobs also introduced some innovatory techniques: the Action for Jobs roadshow, with 'Jobs breakfasts' at which business people could meet ministers and be encouraged to participate in training schemes;[32] and the MSC collaboration with BBC Radio One on Action Special Week in the spring of 1987, which was heavily weighted to the description and explanation of the YTS and other government youth employment and training schemes. An Action Special booklet for school leavers, with an introduction by disc jockey Janice Long, was produced by the MSC.

It was campaigning of a new sort and, according to Neville Taylor who was COI director at the time, it was 'expensive, glossy and pushed the boundaries further than they had been pushed before'.[33] A political aide to Lord Young at the DoE explained the reasoning behind the campaign:

> The horrifying thing we discovered when we got to the department was that large numbers of people who were directly in the target groups for these schemes didn't know about them. One thing that Lord Young is determined about is that government has a job to communicate. It is no good turning out schemes that people don't know about. People didn't know about the Community Programme. They had a very bad image of YTS. The department ran 30 schemes and Lord Young wanted to ensure that the information was getting out ...
>
> Politically unemployment was very troublesome for a government which believed it had got the right economic policies for the country. We had to make people believe that we were doing all that could be done. We wanted to tell people that there were schemes there for them. We were there to help lubricate the labour market.[34]

According to this source, the campaign was a self-conscious marketing exercise for the department, and needed to be in order to raise morale at the department and to convince both business people and the unemployed of the attractiveness of the schemes and of the bouncy new professionalism of the DoE.

This was government publicity with a clear public relations and image-boosting – propagandist element. Yet it did not breach the, then unrevised, conventions of propriety. The National Audit Office found no case against it; and the NAO claimed that *Panorama* had given a misleading impression by isolating one burst of advertising taken out of context from a campaign directly mainly at the obvious target areas of high unemployment.[35] In evidence to the Public Accounts Committee, Mike Devereau, director general of the COI, also insisted that the campaign was fully within the guidelines. The purpose of the television advertising, he said, was to draw attention to the pamphlet, 'Action for Jobs: Opening More Doors'.[36]

Given the broadness of the conventions, which had not then been bolstered by the supplementary Cabinet Office guidance, it is difficult to maintain a case that there was a technical breach. The adoption by the Conservative Party of its 'action' slogan shows how much it impressed party leaders – but it came a year after the DoE campaign and may be a reason why the slogan was eventually dropped from official government publicity. The slickness of Action for Jobs, produced by three of the leading advertising agencies, can be defended on the grounds that government advertising needs to compete for attention and stand comparison with commercial advertising. Its deliberate appeal to opinion formers and the business community was part of the objective to pull in support from the private sector.

Thus there appears an answer on virtually every ground of complaint. Nevertheless this was clearly 'political' advertising in the more commonly understood sense of the word, and clearly meant as a public relations exercise for the government.

Poll tax
The replacement of the rates with the community charge, or poll tax, was heralded as the flagship legislation of Thatcher's third term. It was also arguably the most unpopular piece of legislation during her tenure in office. Thus it was to be expected that publicity for the poll tax would be controversial. Grounds for complaint were twofold: first, publicity material was published while the proposals were at the green paper stage, and second, the leaflet, 'The Community Charge: How It Will Work For You' was challenged legally as inaccurate.

Proposals for the poll tax were set out in the green paper, 'Paying for Local Government' (Cmnd 9714) which was published on 28 January 1986. At the same time the Department of Environment prepared a leaflet, 'Paying for Local Government: The Need for Change'. COI arranged for 100 000 copies to be printed at a cost of £16 200. By January 1988, 39 500 had been distributed.[37] The issue of concern was that public funds had been spent in support of policy proposals at such an early stage. Popular versions of white papers are not uncommon, but green papers are not yet statements of government policy, merely consultative documents on policy options.

The Treasury and Civil Service Committee raised the matter with Mike Devereau, who was then acting director general of the COI. Committee chairman Terence Higgins tried to pin down the point where the COI felt public expenditure was justified and he asked if it was a bill's second reading. Devereau replied that a large paid-for advertising campaign clearly could not be run until a bill received Royal Assent. But he believed the poll tax leaflets were within the spirit of the Widdicombe conventions which did not specify the point in the parliamentary process when paid-for publicity might become acceptable in certain circumstances. In answer to another member of the committee, Devereau explained:

> Indeed, in the case of the information that was issued concerning local government legislation, this was very much an attempt to deal with the volume of inquiries that the particular department was getting about the proposed changes, that rather than write thousands of letters it was thought cost effective to produce a leaflet. This is what the department chose to do.[38]

The committee accepted his argument but added a note of scepticism about the propriety:

> Given the looseness of the conventions, this is difficult to dispute . . . In view of recent disquiet our view is that there may be a case for attempting to reinforce the conventions . . . perhaps even by giving them statutory backing as with the codes of practice for local authorities under the Local Government Act 1986 which gave effect to the proposals of the Interim Report of the Widdicombe Committee.[39]

Poll tax publicity was destined for more controversy with the leaflet, 'The Community Charge: How It Will Work For You', which was delivered to 21 million households in the spring of 1989. The leaflet, in question-and-answer format, followed the passage of the Local Government Finance Act 1988, so there were no qualms about its timing, but the Association of

Metropolitan Authorities and a number of individual councils objected to what they alleged were omissions and misleading inaccuracies. Labour-controlled Greenwich Council won a High Court injunction in May forcing government to suspend delivery until the outcome of its legal challenge to the probity of the leaflet.

Greenwich Council chose to concentrate on one of a number of complaints about the leaflet: that it was misleading because it omitted all reference to the joint liability of spouses and cohabiting couples for each other's poll tax and thus did not accord with government publicity conventions. Lord Justice Woolf and Mr Justice Ian Kennedy dismissed the Greenwich call for a judicial review and their reasons show the difficulty in proving impropriety against government. They found that the court could only intervene if the document was 'fatally flawed' by distortion or omission. They accepted that the leaflet might be considered misleading by omission, although it was not literally inaccurate. However:

> In the absence of legislation, it was not the task of the courts to act as a critic or censor of information published by the government or anyone else. The courts only had the power to intervene in exceptional cases where it could be shown that the guidance or advice given by a government department misstated the law or if a publication was manifestly inaccurate or misleading.[40]

Privatisation

This was a new departure for government publicity. Government campaigns normally fall into the explanatory, exhortatory or recruitment categories. Privatisation, however, was an explicit sales task, more akin to a private sector commercial campaign, and it appears to have been bound by a different set of rules. It was geared to the unabashed, indeed jubilatory, selling of a government product, a nationalised industry, and by extension a (sometimes unpopular) government policy. Privatisation publicity also was organised differently from other campaigns, normally with specially created departmental task forces. COI was not always directly involved, not at all before 1986, and in varying degrees thereafter. Privatisations produced the costliest campaigns of the Thatcher years and employed

Table 6.3   Advertising costs of major privatisations, 1984–7

Amount of float	Company	Advertising expenditure	Date of float
£4bn	B Telecom	£25m	Nov. 1984
£550m	B Aerospace	£2.3m	May. 1985
£450m	Britoil	£3.5	Aug. 1985
£1.3bn	TSB	£10m	Sep. 1986
£5.4bn	British Gas	£34.5m	Dec. 1986
£900m	B Airways	£11m	Feb. 1987
£1.4bn	Rolls Royce	£4m	May. 1987
£1.2bn	BAA	£5.7m	July. 1987
£7.2bn	BP	£23m	Oct. 1987

Source: MEAL.[41]

the broadest range of marketing techniques. Awareness campaigns and image building, frowned upon in the revamped conventions for government departments, were requisite for privatisations. Additionally public relations consultants, then taboo for departments and ministers, were hired as standard.

Part of this difference is due to the fact that privatisation campaigns were regarded as somewhat out of the ordinary in terms of government publicity. They were specific one-off projects which did not fall within the usual domain of government information. Moreover nationalised industries have always been free to develop their own communications strategies and were never bound to use COI services. Costs for privatisation publicity typically were split between the sponsoring department and the denationalising industry. Total marketing expenses for the privatisations was estimated at £215 million up to 1989. British Gas (£40m), water (£40m) and electricity (£76m) between them took the lion's share.[42] Table 6.3 shows the advertising costs of the privatisations from 1984–87. The sales of British Telecom and the TSB had proved enormously successful, from government's point of view, in pulling in new investors. The share issues had been oversubscribed, offered few apparent risks and a healthy return on the investment. BT attracted some 2.3 million shareholders, many of whom were first-time buyers. But, as Alison Turner of the advertising agency Young & Rubicam noted, the scale of the British Gas operation set it in a 'league apart from other privatisations'. Its twin objectives were to raise substantially more in equity than BT and, equally important, to try to attract twice the number of individual investors, 4.5 million or more.[43] Young & Rubicam handled the flotation account and Turner was responsible for the 'Tell Sid' campaign, which was another quantum leap for government publicity. The agency won a certificate of commendation from the Institute of Practitioners in Advertising (1988 Advertising Effectiveness Awards) for 'Tell Sid'. Turner's account of the campaign provides candid insight into the agency's attempt not merely to sell British Gas, but effectively to sell the idea of popular capitalism. Turner explained:

> The strategy we developed to achieve these objectives was to encourage participation in 'The People's Share Offer'. We aimed to create a feeling of excitement consonant with a great national event, and to develop beyond this, a feeling that *everyone* would want to participate; people would be missing out on a unique opportunity if they did not participate ... To announce the share offer, and stimulate interest in it, the advertising used the analogy of the Jubilee beacons, and communicated that everyone, everywhere was invited to join in this national event.[44] (Emphasis in original)

The theme of the 'people's share offer' was developed through three phases of advertising. Two bursts of TV advertising, for example, featured pairs of people with similar job titles: conductors, builders, singers, drivers, riders and old Bill. The countdown phase (prior to the application deadline) 'reflected the way in which people behave in everyday life when talking and passing information to each other – in pubs, at bus-stops, at railway stations'. The creative linking device for the various episodes of advertising was the character Sid, who never actually appeared 'but was quickly understood as a metaphor for the general public'.

Young & Rubicam's qualitative research found that consumer response was consistently positive towards the advertising, according to Turner: it provided information, created a sense of involvement, build-up and urgency, was entertaining, communicated the idea that the flotation was truly for everyone and implied that everyone would be participating. Quantitative results also suggest success: awareness of the campaign reached 97 per cent, it attracted about 7 million inquiries and 4.6 million applications for shares, 2.2 million of these from first-time buyers. Said Turner:

> Financially, the British Gas share offer was four times over-subscribed, the retail clawback of shares from the financial institutions was thereby triggered, and the shares opened at a healthy but reasonable premium. All this for a stock which had been widely described as 'dull' in the City, and at a price (135p) at least 5p higher than the City had predicted; in terms of the final equity raised, this amounted to an additional £200 million.

In terms of value-for-money, then, the British Gas campaign clearly paid its way. Indeed, in a Commons debate, John Major, then Treasury Minister responsible for publicity expenditure, called it a 'good bargain'. It had helped government get a good price.

Moreover it was netted off against the sale proceeds and represented only a small percentage of those proceeds, 0.3 per cent in the case of British Telecom, 0.4 per cent for British Gas.[45]

In terms of propriety, however, the British Gas campaign was questionable. Young & Rubican's strategy, attempted, apparently with some success, to create the idea of a popular share offer in which everyone would want to participate. Yet the sale was opposed by both the Labour Party and the Alliance parties. Government publicity is not, nor ever has been, obliged to spell out opposition to government policy. But the implicit suggestion that there was no opposition, that everyone would want to participate, was surely misleading.

Moreover IBA rules insist that advertisers may not advocate the sale of shares without a disclaimer warning of the potential risks. All privatisation advertising has had to comply with this instruction, but it is arguable whether the risks were made sufficiently clear and the disclaimer sufficiently noticeable, especially when a deliberate attempt was being made to attract new investors. BT, TSB and British Gas were all sold in a bull market and there were quick profits there for the taking. The bubble burst, however, with the stock market crash of October

1987 and private investors who were already committed to BP shares were threatened with losses.

The British Gas campaign may be judged in all respects as a success for the government. Yet the example of BP reminds us that all the publicity resources at government's disposal cannot guarantee a favourable response. Water privatisation offers a further example with a campaign that was to prove more controversial than 'Tell Sid'. The water campaign first provoked criticism with its awareness and image-building TV, press and poster commercials which were run early in 1989 while the privatisation bill was in its committee stages in the Commons. The Water Authorities denied that the advertising was in any way connected to privatisation and it was not therefore a breach of the conventions. But, since this was the first time the Water Authorities had engaged in image advertising on television, the denial seems disingenuous.

The criticism took several forms, not just of propriety of the timing, but also of the content of the commercials, created by D'Arcy Masius Benton & Bowles, one of whose employees, Brendan Bruce, became director of communications at CCO in 1989. The water campaign was devised in three phases: first, to create positive images of water quality which had suffered in public esteem, second, to create positive attitudes towards the Water Authorities as efficient businesses, and third, to advertise the flotation and attract investors.[46] The first two phases were the most disliked by political opponents, nor did they win admirers in the trade press. Perhaps people were becoming more used to and more cynical about government advertising, because the water campaign, more than any other in the Thatcher era, provoked ridicule as much as concern.

Labour MP Brian Sedgemore described one roadside poster depicting a cloud and the caption underneath saying, 'This is the beginning of our production line'. Sedgemore continued:

> Millions of pounds of taxpayers' money is being spent on telling the public that water comes from rain – can anyone believe the perceptive abilities, the limits of the human intellect? – and that rain comes from clouds. Surely that is the grossest example of waste in the history of the world?[47]

MORI tracking polls also suggest that public enchantment with privatisation was on the wane: support for privatisation peaked in the summer of 1982 with 45 per cent in favour; it stayed at around 39 per cent until the spring of 1987 and then declined steadily to about 30 per cent in the summer of 1989.[48] It is not possible, of course, to conclude from this that the water campaign failed. It is possible, if unlikely, that attitudes might have become more hostile without the promotion. However it does indicate the limitations of advertising: it failed to reverse the trend running against privatisation, which was probably the single most distinctive policy of the Thatcher years.

A final point about water is included because it reveals some of the public relations tactics employed. Documents leaked to Friends of the Earth included a tactics paper drawn up by the PR firm Hill & Knowlton, which had been engaged by the Water Authorities Association to prepare corporate communications strategy in the run-in to flotation. Among its suggestions were a series of items on BBC programmes: an item for *Tomorrow's World* which was a story on how trout were used to monitor water quality; the 'training' of swimming celebrities such as Duncan Goodhew, David Wilkie and Sharron Davies who would then seek guest appearances on *Wogan* and breakfast TV; and the possible plant of promotional material on the soap opera *EastEnders*. Feature items on Radio 4's *Women's Hour* and *The Jimmy Young Programme* were also discussed. There was also, incidentally, a plan to run a wet T-shirt competition in the *Sun*.[49]

CONCLUSION

The period under review saw the transformation from relatively restrained government publicity in Margaret Thatcher's first term to the aggressive use of marketing techniques in support of social and economic policy from 1986 onwards. The contrast with immediate predecessors was not so much the amount of expenditure, because government had also been among the leading two or three national advertisers in the early 1970s, but in the use of publicity to promote controversial policy.

Such use is not unprecedented. The 1945–51 Labour government made extensive and expensive use of official communications machinery in a similar fashion. And, as with Labour then, this type of publicity almost inevitably strays into areas of party propaganda and strains the conventions of neutrality. Marjorie Ogilvy-Webb's 1960s account of the government information services points to a number of transgressions in the immediate post-war period, such as COI speakers being briefed with handouts from Labour Party headquarters, information officers accompanying ministers to party conferences, paid publicity which sometimes was over-enthusiastic about Labour achievements.[50] These she termed 'minor' infringements within a service generally dedicated to serving equally successive governments.

Similarly this analysis of the Thatcher governments has not found a substantial or sustainable case for the wholesale breach of conventions, as accepted over the years. Within a strict interpretation of the rules there does not appear to have been more than relatively minor breaches of the conventions. Moreover, under the spotlight of criticism, the rules were updated and strengthened. However, if there rules were not technically broken, the boundaries were certainly pushed forward: expenditure before legislation became almost the norm rather than the exception, and the use of costly publicity, especially television advertising, far more common. Government, at least certain sectors, appeared to become addicted to advertising and mass media campaigns – the 'megaphone solution', in the words of Conservative critic Digby Anderson.[51] Sir Donald Maitland, former press secretary to Edward Heath, appeared on *Panorama* (see above) voicing concern that Thatcher's government had pushed the rules: 'Certainly there has been a departure from previous practice which was more or less accepted on all sides.'

The most influential campaigns driving government publicity were Action for Jobs and the privatisations. Action for Jobs, in particular, showed how the application of imaginative marketing could breathe new life into essentially old government policies. Government made telling use of its politically exclusive access to television advertising to promote these policies and Lord Young, at least, was in no doubt that the Action for Jobs campaign was vital in removing unemployment from the electoral agenda.[52]

It is true that government was playing on a new field. The advertising industry, especially in Britain, and particularly

Saatchi & Saatchi, boomed in the late 1970s and 1980s. Slick and smart television advertising became an increasingly important mode of communication for the business sector and latterly for government as well. The whole machinery of marketing and public relations became more sophisticated and specialised. The Chartered Institute of Marketing noted in 1985 that the press was losing its share of the advertising cake to television 'steadily and comparatively rapidly'.[53] If government's messages were to be taken seriously it would also need to adopt these techniques.

Mrs Thatcher's exceptionally long tenure, with a large majority for much of the time, put stresses on the neutral tradition of the civil service as a whole, and on the information services in particular.[54] It also exposed the weakness of the publicity conventions which rely ultimately on the self-restraint of the party in power, which in turn may depend on the existence of a strong and vigilant Opposition. There is no other sanction against the government's publicity services.

With the departure of Thatcher and Ingham, the post of head of GIS returned to the director general of the COI, a move which has doubtless calmed some fears with regard to John Major's publicity regime. One is tempted to think that his mild manner would be less suited to the 'megaphone solution' than his predecessor. Government publicity has ceased to be such a controversial area and there has been no campaign to compare with the ambition of Action for Jobs or 'Tell Sid'. But the government publicity budget did not drop significantly until 1993, in the year following the general election. And, it should be remembered, the Thatcher government publicity machine did not break into full stride until its second term.

7 The Image-Makers Unbound: Marketing in the Post-Thatcher Era

Political presentation in Britain reached a new milestone in the post-Thatcher period ending in the April 1992 general election. This was the most 'professional' campaign in British post-war history in that all the main political parties adopted many of the techniques and disciplines associated with political marketing. Labour offered, after 1987, the most ostentatious example in post-war history of a party remodelling its product in line with market research. The Tories ran a consciously marketing-inspired 'branding' exercise to distance Major's party from Kinnock's. The Liberal Democrats, guided by the pressure group veteran Des Wilson, mounted a highly disciplined communications campaign, in total contrast to the muddled shambles of 1987.

In other ways, too, trends and tactics associated with political marketing were much in evidence: pre-campaigns were waged on all sides; advertising, especially on television via the PEBs, became a more prominent weapon in the political communications arsenal; the corps of media experts – spin doctors, advertisers, pollsters, designers and so on – both swelled in number and seemed to increase in influence on party behaviour.

The impression of a highly orchestrated campaign was compounded by the media coverage which, to an unprecedented extent, focused on campaign tactics and techniques. Journalists, under intense pressure from politicians and their press officers or 'spin doctors' for six months before the election, were sensitive as to their place at the centre of the agenda-setting battle. An International Press Institute report, 'Potholes on the Campaign Trail', laid bare the tricks of the spin doctors' trade: tight control of access to press conferences, ruthless suppression of supplementary questions, precedence given to TV journalists, attempts to 'spin' the journalists' interpretation of stories, judicious allocation of spokesmen for TV appearances and, less frequently, bullying of newsrooms.[1]

All this marked an intensification of trends, rather than the introduction of new techniques. The election of 1992 was *not* a ground-breaking political marketing exercise, in the way that 1959, 1964 and 1979 had been, but it was nonetheless the most intensely marketed or, in *Guardian* editor Peter Preston's words, 'the most cautious and orchestrated of elections'.[2]

Reflecting this, the image-makers' names, faces, arts and crafts featured more prominently on TV news than before. Both in the parties' behaviour and in the media coverage, Britain in the period 1991–2 appeared to have trudged ever further down the US presidential campaign route.[3] So far, in fact, that the usual transatlantic traffic was reversed by President George Bush in the autumn of 1992, when he called on assistance from Conservative Central Office and adopted the Tories' campaign themes of tax and trust.[4]

However, before exploring further the impact of marketing, a first and most important question must be asked. For all the planning and careful stage management, did the campaign have any influence on the vote?

DID THE CAMPAIGN MAKE ANY DIFFERENCE?

Clues offered by the election result can be interpreted quite differently, depending on whether one looks at share of vote or movement in seats. By share of vote there appears little change since 1987 (see Table 7.1). The Conservatives were remarkably successful in holding on to their 42 per cent or so share for the fourth successive election. Their lead over Labour decreased four points, but they maintained a 7.5 per cent advantage – the fourth election running when they were 7 per cent or more clear of the second party. The stability of the Tory vote must be a major source of concern for Labour strategists and suggests a basic failure of their campaign to increase dissatisfaction with the government.

Labour increased its vote by 3.6 percentage points (compared to 3.2 in 1987) but it was still the third worst result since the Second World War, bettering only 1983 and 1987. Labour's failure was all the more stark against a background of

Table 7.1   The general election of 9 April 1992

	Con	Lab	LibDem	Other	Total
Seats					
At dissolution	367	229	22	32	650
After election	336	271	20	24	651
Votes					
% of total	41.9	34.4	17.8	5.8	100
1987–92 change	−0.4	3.6	−4.8	1.6	

Conservative majority 21 (84 at dissolution)
Swing (Con to Lab) 1.9% (1.7% in 1987)
Turnout 77.7%

Table 7.2   Voting intentions, Nov. 1991–Feb. 1992

	Con	Lab	LibDem	Con lead over Lab
1991				
Nov.	40	42	15	−2
Dec.	38	44	14	−6
1992				
Jan.	42	39	16	+3
Feb.	39	40	18	−1

Source: MORI.

deep economic recession and opinion polls which had put them regularly, if only just, ahead of the Tories since the party conferences in October 1992. Labour was still holding a slight poll advantage (see Table 7.2) when Major fired the starting pistol on 11 March, 1992. Of the 54 mainstream national polls during the four weeks to 9 April, all but 12 put Labour ahead. On 29–30 March, Labour scored leads of six and seven points in three separate polls. Thus, if the polls are to be trusted at all, the conduct of the campaign may well have been decisive, to the advantage of the Tories. This was the view of a number of critics of the Labour campaign who believe the leadership threw the election away in the last nine days before polling.[5]

The problem, of course, is how far to trust the polls when they recorded their most spectacular failure since 1970. And, in an almost exact replica of 1970, there is considerable debate between those who argue that the polls were fooled by a last-minute surge to the Tories and those who think the polls got it wrong all along, and were consistently underestimating the Tories and overestimating Labour.

The Market Research Society's investigation into the discrepancy between the polls and the result estimated that the late surge contributed about three percentage points to the Tory lead.[6] Campaigners for both the Labour and Liberal Democrat parties agree that there was real slippage in the final week. Labour campaigners blame the issues of tax and a widespread distrust of Labour's ability to govern, a fear which only really emerged as the prospect of a Labour victory became tangible. Des Wilson believes that his party's support was drained by the Tory scare that a Liberal Democrat vote would let in Labour. Both views offer a back-handed compliment to the Tory campaign, for these were precisely the main thrusts of Tory propaganda.

The late surge theory is disputed by some political scientists and, unsurprisingly, Tory campaign managers.[7] John Wakeham, who helped chairman Chris Patten run the campaign, claimed that the Conservatives were always sure that they would remain in government;[8] and it is true that the Tories' pollsters, Harris, were tipping a 20-seat Conservative victory in early March.[9]

However CCO's view at the start of the campaign proper was that 39 seats were likely to go and a further 30 were too close to call.[10] The loss of the full 69 seats would have reduced the Conservatives to the largest party in a hung parliament, and this prospect must have loomed horribly large for even the most confident of Tories as the polls slipped away. Indeed the Tory victory was much less convincing if we examine seats – which after all is what decides the House of Commons – rather than national vote share. A relatively tiny movement of votes would have transformed the outcome. Just 2500 fewer votes (a swing of half a per cent) would have cost the Tories 11 seats and their overall majority in the House of Commons. The Conservatives won four seats with majorities of less than 100 votes; 21 seats were won with majorities of less than 1000, which could be wiped out by a paltry 1 per cent swing. Thus, even if the prospect of outright Labour power was remote, there was every possibility that the Conservatives would lose their majority.

This was easily the closest race since 1974, and probably not clearly decided until the eleventh-hour surge to the Tories. In these circumstances even small influences on the vote may have made a difference. Thus the campaign is of greater than usual signficance – not just the four-week campaign proper, but more importantly the long-term pre-campaign – because it is worth remembering that many commentators wrote Labour's obituary in 1987 and few then would have predicted the strength of Labour's challenge.

THE MARKETING EMBRACE

The Conservatives: the Wheel Turns?

At first sight it may seem that the Conservatives beat a retreat from political marketing in the period 1987–92. Mrs Thatcher's stubborn insistence on the poll tax is not explicable by any usual yardstick of popular opinion nor by her own former standards of pragmatism. Indeed, in Thatcher's final months, the political marketing wheel seemed to have turned full circle. Where once Labour leaders reacted with contumely and alarm to the the 'marketing of Margaret', by 1990 the Tories were accusing Labour of reducing politics to slick and phoney images. 'Labour behind the mask' was the thrust of the last full-scale communications assault on Labour under Thatcher's leadership.[11]

John Major inherited a Conservative Central Office organisation which looked far less fit and able to manage a campaign than at any time since 1975. Indeed this was the main reason why the Tories declined the option of a spring election in 1991. Seasoned architects of previous campaigns had either left after 1987 or were replaced in the inevitable upheaval when Major became leader: the Treasurer Lord McAlpine quit in June 1990; chief of staff, Michael Dobbs, and advertising agency Saatchi both left in 1987; the Director of Information, John Desborough, retired in the summer of 1989 and his successor, Christine Wall, left for Nestlé in November 1991. Harvey

Thomas, the presentation and stage-management supremo at CCO for the length of Mrs Thatcher's premiership, quit in May 1991, complaining that the party was neglecting core lessons of communications.[12]

Brendan Bruce, Director of Communications since March 1989 and the first occupier of that CCO problem spot since Sir Gordon Reece, left in January 1991. An advertising account director at D'Arcy Masius Benton & Bowles, Bruce had been vetted for the appointment by Sir Gordon, Bernard Ingham, Tim Bell and Lord Young.[13] He was closely associated with Bell, whose importance to party communications increased after the departure of Saatchi. In September 1990 Bruce recommended that, rather than hire a new agency, Bell should be put in overall control of communications with the power to recruit a variety of experts for specific tasks, along the lines of Philip Gould and Labour's Shadow Communications Agency. Bruce's recommendations were put on the back burner as the leadership election intervened, and, as usual, a new leader heralded change at CCO. The new party chairman, Chris Patten, rejected his plan. Patten did not want to give a leading role to Bell, who was too closely associated with Mrs Thatcher, and in January 1991 Bruce too was replaced.

Shaun Woodward, 32, a former researcher and producer on *That's Life, Panorama* and *Newsnight*, took over as Director of Communications. Married to Camilla Sainsbury, daughter of the government minister, Woodward had been selected for the Conservative approved candidates list but had never actually fought a parliamentary campaign. The CCO team presided over by Chris Patten was the youngest and politically the least experienced in memory; they were to be dismissed as the 'brat pack' and 'Patten's puppies' by the headline writers during the election, especially when it seemed to slipping from the Tories.

To make matters worse for Patten, CCO was in considerable debt when he took the helm: modernisation and rebuilding at Smith Square, new computer equipment and the expenses of the Euro-elections in June 1989 pushed the accumulated deficit up to £13 million by March 1991 and CCO's accounts recorded a loss of £5 million over that financial year.[14]

The party leadership also seemed less willing to 'market' itself than in its previous three campaigns. Major moved into

Number 10 in November 1990 with a pledge that 'the image-makers will not find me in their tutelage' and that he was perfectly content to remain 'the same plug-ugly as I always was on television'.[15]

Chris Patten was one of the main contributors to party policy during his period as Director of the Conservative Research Department (1974–9) and now, as chairman of the party, he seemed personally more interested in the details of policy and less in presentation than his predecessor, Kenneth Baker. 'Compared to Mr Baker, he spent less time in Central Office and more in Downing Street maintaining close contact with Mr Major and the Policy Unit,' say Butler and Kavanagh.[16]

Patten decided to cancel research conducted for CCO by Dr Richard Wirthlin, whose models of opinion analysis and prediction had been influential with Ronald Reagan. Wirthlin's link with CCO had built up informally over a number of years, but he was formally taken on during Baker's tenure and worked with the Tories' long-time pollsters, Harris. His methods were essentially qualitative, attempting to uncover voters' basic values and make connections from values to issues and political choice. His research found that the most important values to the electorate were, first, hope; second, security; and third, peace of mind. Presentations were put to Mrs Thatcher in September 1989 and twice in January 1990, but the research was never integrated into an overall communications strategy.[17]

However Wirthlin's work massively impressed Brendan Bruce and would probably have been more influential had Mrs Thatcher not resigned:

> Wirthlin's research methodology represents the most important advance in political communications of the last two decades. It provides the image-makers with the best possible guide to the effective presentation of policy, by creating a clear understanding of how voters make their choice of party . . . The party that first grasps the true importance of Wirthlin's work and applies it to the British political process will win an enormous advantage over their opponents and greatly increase their chances of gaining power.[18]

Shaun Woodward also felt that Wirthlin offered the clearest available analysis of voter motivation, enabling – the marketers' goal – sophisticated targeting of the electorate broken down into constituencies of interest.[19] But Wirthlin's results were not taken seriously by the politicians, and provoked the age-old fears of being manipulated by image-makers. Certainly Patten was not impressed; Wirthlin was expensive (about £1 million in 1990) at a time when CCO needed to prune costs and, besides, values research had its detractors. Michael Dobbs and Saatchi examined it briefly before 1987 but had not found any clear way of translating the results into a practical communications strategy. Thus, there is a prima facie case that the Tories had cooled towards political marketing, especially in comparison to Labour and the Shadow Communications Agency. However appearances are deceptive; the Tory communications strategy and tactics owed a great deal to the disciplines of political marketing, as much if not more than Labour's.

Conservative communications strategy was framed consciously as a 'branding' exercise, which, in the words of one party official, was not dissimilar to the way a chocolate manufacturer might approach a sales campaign. Woodward's team thought that packaging would be more important than at any of the elections under Mrs Thatcher, because the parties and policies were now almost indistinguishable to many of the electorate.

> Our problem was finding a real difference between the parties. Of course, if you ask the politicians they will cite a whole series of policy differences. But really to the average voter the parties seemed much the same; on Europe, defence, monetary policy and the Exchange Rate Mechanism, even on the unions Labour had accepted a great deal of government policy, and people no longer felt that the unions needed to be put in their place. So what we were confronted with was very much like a marketing exercise trying to establish differences between brands that were basically alike. The answer was obvious – packaging. From the packaging point of view the obvious difference was Major and Kinnock.[20]

According to standard marketing theory, the primary tool for product branding is advertising. It follows, therefore that the advertising agency would play a key role, and indeed, Saatchi & Saatchi were more intimately involved in strategy than in either 1983 or 1987. The importance of the Saatchis' role was underscored by the decision to base Maurice Saatchi at CCO for the duration of the campaign proper, the first time this had happened.

The Saatchis' reconnection with the Tories after the acrimonious split in 1987 was a shock to many at Smith Square – it seemed a 'barmy' decision, according to one source. Saatchi's reintegration was not smoothed by news that the agency had offered its services to Labour in the months before it regained the Tory account in March 1991. Kinnock's press secretary Julie Hall and Philip Gould were lunched at the Savoy by Saatchis' chairman, Bill Muirhead, and Michael Dobbs, then deputy chairman, according to a report deliberately leaked by Labour to coincide with Saatchi's first batch of advertisements for the Tories in 1991.[21]

Ironically Saatchi had not been on CCO's shortlist when Patten and Woodward began a trawl for a new agency in January 1991. Acting anonymously through a third party (Shandwick), agencies were invited to send in samples of recent brand product advertising, particularly aimed at C2s, with a media spend of £4–6 million.[22] Three shops caught the eye: WCRS, D'Arcy Masius Benton & Bowles (Brendan Bruce's former employers) and JWT. D'Arcy Masius were actually the first choice until they withdrew and Saatchi stepped in with a display of interest which impressed Woodward: 'Saatchi's got on because they were ravenous. If you had a meeting with Bill Muirhead, you couldn't get rid of him. If you gave him a list of impossible conditions, he made them possible.'[23] Saatchi had endured a turbulent few years since the previous election. After becoming briefly the world's largest advertising agency, mainly through mergers and acquisitions, the Saatchis found themselves badly overstretched in both Britain and the USA as the recession started to bite.[24] Doubtless their sliding fortunes whetted their appetite for the kind of free publicity that only a general election campaign can provide. In any event, the Saatchis were eager to take on the Tory account and prepared to offer a considerable period of grace before payment of their fees.

The agency offered crucial advice on repositioning the Conservatives. Since Thatcher's resignation, the party's image had become less clear. 'Caring' Mr Major was fighting on social issues territory which was solidly Labour's.[25] At the same time, the continued introduction of market disciplines into health and education alarmed the electorate in a way that Labour was quick to exploit, with the suggestion that the Tories wanted to privatise the NHS. Saatchi recommended that the Tories return to their traditional strength – economic management – combining this with a commitment to improving public services, as evidenced by the Citizens' Charter.

The Tories' campaign theme of 'trust' also owed a great deal to the marketers. Both publicly and privately, campaign managers credit Chris Patten with the decision to emphasise trust. About a year before the election Tory strategists were convinced that the election would be a contest between change (Labour) versus trust (Tory). In Woodward's words, 'trust was the political input'; Saatchi's contribution was the precise wording of the slogan – 'You can't trust Labour' – and the L-plate for Labour in the advertisements and posters. It is inconceivable, however, that the political input was not influenced by pollsters at Harris who had long incorporated questions of trust into their opinion polling design, with significant results. For example, about one year before the election Labour were scoring higher than the Tories as the better party to manage the economy. But when the question was changed to 'Who do you most trust to manage the economy?' the Conservatives were ahead.[26]

Harris qualitative surveys also discovered that 'trust' seemed most effective as a negative weapon. Woodward explained:

> We found that you couldn't use trust in a positive way. A slogan like 'you can trust John Major' just invites people to start discussing Major's credibility in a way that causes as many problems as it solves. Chris Patten and I decided that you could use it positively in speeches but not in advertising. We tested 'You can't trust Labour' and time after time people's first response was 'yes, that's true'. When we tried to pin it down to specific reasons people always said Kinnock. When we tried to pin it down further it came down to the economy and taxation.[27]

Both the issue terrain – economy and tax – and the campaigning style – the negative onslaught on Labour's trustworthiness – were heavily influenced by the media experts. Moreover John Major's professed disdain for the image-makers deserves to be thoroughly debunked. This may be easy enough with hindsight, especially after Chancellor Norman Lamont's post-resignation speech to the House of Commons (June 1993) when he accused pollsters and party managers of dictating government policy. But before the election few media commentators had read the signals and Major rejoiced in a plain-as-pump-water, honest image which was deliberately fostered to contrast with the over-protected, packaged Kinnock. For careful observers, however, the signs were already there. Major's leadership campaign had enlisted help from Mrs Thatcher's favourite media advisers, Sir Tim Bell and Sir Gordon Reece, according to the *Sunday Times* (2 December 1990). Public relations consultants, Shandwick, were engaged to advise Major on media relations during the Gulf War, and thereafter the Shandwick connection prospered. *Campaign* reported (20 December 1991) that Peter Gummer, Shandwick's chairman and brother of Agriculture Minister, John Gummer, was Major's 'informal public relations adviser'. Shandwick also 'loaned' one of its directors, Mary Bartholomew, to replace Christine Wall at CCO, and act effectively as Woodward's deputy.

As the election approached, a few commentators began to notice that Major was less than careless of his image. John Simpson, assigned by the BBC to cover Major's tour, noted that Major was highly sensitive to media criticism, far more than Mrs Thatcher (28 March 1992, *Spectator*). Barbara Amiel's profile in the *Sunday Times* (29 March 1992) suggested, perhaps prophetically, that Major's greatest weakness was 'his obsession with the media'.

Labour: The Increasing Influence of Media Specialists

Labour offered the clearest example of political marketing yet seen in Britain, involving not merely slick presentation but, more significantly, sustained post-1987 efforts to change its policies according to public opinion.

Research conducted after the 1987 defeat, under the auspices of the Shadow Communications Agency (SCA), concluded that Labour's extremist, divided image, lack of economic credibility and unilateral defence policy had cost some 7 per cent in public support since 1964.[28] The leadership instituted the Policy Review to transform the party programme in line with this research, culminating in the abandonment of 'extremist' commitments: unilateralism, nationalisation and the commitment to wholesale reversal of Tory trade union legislation.

The Policy Review was the key instrument in Labour's 'repositioning', to borrow the marketing term much used by Labour strategists. To quote Patricia Hewitt, it was 'a central component in the task of positioning Labour for the next general election', helping to shed the negative, extremist reputation, while also promoting the positive image of a modern party.[29] Labour mounted public relations exercises, particularly 'Labour Listens' (1987/8), to broadcast the the message that the party was becoming more responsive to ordinary people and less dominated by the doctrinaire. The point was emphasised when the final report of the Policy Review was launched in July 1989 under the title *Meet the Challenge, Make the Change*, – a slogan written by advertising adviser Barry Delaney.

In the celebrated 'prawn cocktail' offensive, Shadow Chancellor John Smith and his shadow Treasury team dined with key City figures and businessmen to reassure them of Labour's new commitment to the free market and prudent approach to public spending and taxation. 'We can't spend what we haven't earned' was Smith's oft-repeated message. At the same time, the party moved to divest itself of lingering left-wing taint and the purge of Militant members intensified, including MPs Dave Nellist and Terry Fields. Tony Benn was crushed in the leadership election of autumn 1988, gaining only 11 per cent of electoral college votes, compared to Kinnock's 89 per cent.

Labour's transformation was accompanied by a concentration of power in the leadership. It assumed new powers to select by-election candidates and took measures to reduce the potentially disruptive input of the party conference. The findings of the Policy Review were presented to conference as packages to be accepted or rejected in their entirety, effectively limiting debate on particular items. A new body, the Policy Forum, was established in 1990 to provide 'rolling consultation' on policy matters, reducing conference, in the eyes of critics, to the status of US-style conventions.[30] The annual conference became less a forum for debate and more, akin to the Conservatives, a golden opportunity for public relations. Opinion polls suggest that Labour was largely effective in shedding its most damaging negatives and by 1989 it was no longer regarded as extreme or divided. Indeed, by the summer of 1989, it was Mrs Thatcher's Conservatives who were seen as extreme. According to MORI, 58 per cent rated the Tories as extreme right, while 37 per cent thought Labour extreme left.[31]

Labour's metamorphosis came to be synonymous with communications director, Peter Mandelson. Labour's hard Left, in particular, elevated Mandelson to quasi-mythical status by dispensing on him the kind of odium reserved for historic class traitors.[32] Mandelson was the Machiavellian powerhouse behind the new rightward-drifting Labour, considered more influential than the NEC or even the general secretary, Larry Whitty. Heffernan and Marqusee's *Defeat from the Jaws of Victory*, by far the most compelling left-wing account of Labour in the period, suggests that 'marketing' was merely the rationalising cloak to drape Kinnock and Mandelson's conventionally right-wing project. Their view provides a cynical corrective to the temptation to see Labour's remodelling as 'pure' marketing. Their theory has some support from one of Labour's advertising advisers, who noted that Mandelson would tend to ignore market research when its results did not suit him.[33] 'Quite right, too,' the same source added, 'because the quality of a lot of Labour's research was very poor.'

The Left may exaggerate the importance of Mandelson, partly out of dislike of his right-wing views and partly perhaps because of the residue of distaste at the morality of marketing for an ostensibly socialist party. However it is indisputable that the media experts, the 'marketers', were far more prominent in the Labour Party than ever. This trend continued even after Mandelson left Walworth Road in June 1990 to become prospective parliamentary candidate for Hartlepool. But it was the SCA, headed by Philip Gould and Patricia Hewitt, rather than Mandelson's successors John Underwood and David Hill, who became the key figures in Labour's communications strategy.

Heffernan and Marqusee argue that Underwood's appointment was a rare NEC triumph for the soft Left over the Kinnockite Right, whose preferred candidate was Colin Byrne, Mandelson's deputy, who was engaged to Kinnock's press secretary, Julie Hall. Once he was in place, Underwood's authority was undermined by Kinnock's private staff. There was a clear power struggle but neither Underwood nor Byrne emerged as clear victors.[34] Matters came to a head when

Underwood insisted, with the backing of Whitty, that Byrne be removed as chief press and broadcasting officer. Kinnock supported Byrne, and Underwood felt compelled to resign. He was replaced in June 1991 by the compromise candidate and the man he had beaten for the post a year earlier, David Hill, formerly Roy Hattersley's aide and adviser.

Hill makes the point that the churning within Walworth Road's communications department created a vacuum which the SCA attempted to fill:

> Peter Mandelson went, John Underwood came and clearly found problems and conflicts here. He then went and there was a further interregnum. I then arrived and during that 18-month period – from Peter Mandelson leaving to my first months here – there was a vacuum and the SCA were under massive pressure to fill it, and they were able to provide the communications directorate with a sense of continuity at a time when there was quite a lot of friction. This period was close to the election period, so that when the election actually came the postition of the SCA was formalized and they were very much at the centre of what was going on.[35]

Thus the post-Mandelson friction served further to enhance the role of the media experts of the SCA, who, in the eyes of many on the NEC and at Walworth Road, had become an independent power base answerable only to Kinnock.

Scapegoating of Labour campaign managers was inevitable after Labour's general election failure. This was perhaps an even more crushing blow than 1987 because at last Labour had genuine reason for optimism, in the midst of a deep recession and with promising opinion polls. For many in the party defeat came to be pinned to a series of campaign blunders, most notably the Jennifer's Ear PEB, the complacent triumphalism of the Sheffield Rally – claimed to be the most expensive political rally ever held in Britain – and the decision to raise the issue of proportional representation (PR) in the last few days of the campaign.

These errors were attributed largely to the excessive influence of the SCA – particularly Gould and Hewitt – and lack of input from the experienced politicians. Transport spokesman John Prescott, for instance, claimed repeatedly that the campaign had been hijacked by outsiders – the SCA – and that he had effectively been barred from a high profile.[36] A post-election report prepared by Jim Parish, head of the Propaganda Unit at Walworth Road, also blamed many campaign failures on the 'wholesale takeover' of day-to-day strategy by the SCA.[37] These views were typical of many in the party, regardless of position on the left–right spectrum. It was no surprise, therefore, when the new party leader John Smith and his deputy Margaret Beckett dismantled the SCA, following the October 1992 party conference.[38]

Critics from the Left argued that marketing itself was part of the problem; the party had pushed to the centre in pursuit of the opinion polls, abandoned principles, smothered political argument with public relations and ultimately alienated its basic, grassroots appeal.[39] It had left the party without a clear identity and open to the Tory taunt that it would do virtually anything to garner votes.

There is some force in the Left argument. Labour doffed its 'unelectable' commitments and in doing so relinquished the very policies which made it stand apart from the crowd. It tried but failed to find what Patricia Hewitt called 'symbolic policies' which would both radiate the new progressive Labour image and provide vote-winning appeal, much as council house sales had for Thatcher's Tories.[40] It ended up looking moderate but little different from Major's 'caring' Conservatives, and seemed to be relying more on anti-Tory feeling than on pro-Labour enthusiasm. Even the *Guardian*, Fleet Street's only Labour supporter apart from the *Mirror*, protested in its opening election leader column, 'for a party of change and idealism they are pathetic'.[41]

There can be no doubt, however, that Labour had no choice but to remould itself if it desired electoral credibility. There is no evidence either from the election result or any known opinion research that the party would have fared better under a bolder left-wing banner. But the net result was that the two main parties were divided by little except personality, a factor that the Tories milked for every possible advantage.

The Liberal Democrats: Disciplined at Last

The Liberal Democrats were determined not to repeat the fiasco of 1987. Yet they began campaign planning from their weakest position in ten years. The post-1987 events had taken their toll. The Alliance parties' poll standing plummeted amid the public bloodletting over the SDP/Liberal merger. There followed the continuing muddle about a name for the new party – the Social and Liberal Democrats, the Democrats, and eventually, the Liberal Democrats. The ultimate humiliation came in the European parliamentary elections of 1989, when they were beaten into fourth place by the Greens, who secured more than twice the SLD's derisory 6 per cent. Financial crisis compounded the misery: the Euro-elections left the party with a projected year-end deficit of £600 000.

Paddy Ashdown took over as leader in July 1988 and presided over a remarkable transformation of fortunes. The breakthrough came at the Eastbourne by-election in October 1990. Eastbourne had been a rock solid Conservative seat whose MP, Ian Gow, commanded a 17 000 majority in 1987. The by-election was called after Gow was blown up in his car by an IRA bomb – circumstances which, looked at cynically, should have favoured the Conservative candidate. Yet the Lib Dems gained the seat on a stunning 20-point swing. That achievement was bettered at Ribble Valley (7 March 1991) where Mike Carr won with a 24.7 per cent swing to the Liberal Democrats. Throughout 1991 the Lib Dems averaged 14 per cent in the MORI polls, a considerable improvement upon previous years.

Nevertheless, when Des Wilson was appointed campaign manager in February 1990, the prospects were still gloomy. Wilson described his task as rather akin to Labour's in 1987: to establish the party's credibility, secure it as *the third force* in British national politics and see off the last of the diehard SDP and Liberal rumps.[42] Mindful of the lack of discipline in 1987, caused largely by the difficulties of uniting the parties under the two Davids, Owen and Steel, Wilson was determined to run a tight ship. The command structure involved a strategy group and a planning group which would run the campaign once the election was announced. Wilson insisted on full authority over both and, even though there were at least eight regular members of the strategy group, final decisions were kept strictly within his remit in consultation with Ashdown.[43]

Wilson's dictatorial approach and his high campaign profile prompted some internal discontent among members who felt that authoritative figures, particularly Shirley Williams, Roy

Jenkins and David Steel, should have been used more prominently. According to one Liberal source, however, Steel's relative absence from the screens was less a strategic decision and more a clash of personality: 'Steel refused to come south during the campaign because of "that bastard" Wilson'.[44]

Wilson determined early on to run a highly presidential campaign around Paddy Ashdown, partly because Ashdown was a convincing performer on television and a vigorous campaigner on the trail. Ashdown was a relatively new leader of a new party and he needed to establish himself clearly with the electorate. He was also a fresh face and colourful figure amid the grey of Major and Kinnock. Revelations towards the end of 1991 of Ashdown's affair with his former secretary may even have boosted his popularity, given the dignified demeanour of Ashdown, his wife and, indeed, his former secretary.

Ashdown and Wilson decided to highlight the party's single most distinctive policy commitment – electoral reform – under the slogan 'Fair Votes' which was translated to 'My Vote' in the campaign proper. Wilson was critical of the Alliance failure to push electoral reform in 1987, diverted, in his words, 'by opinion polls that told us people were more concerned about *practical* issues, such as health and education, housing and unemployment. We were advised by the advertising men that it made no sense to appeal to people on issues that did not seem to them a priority'.[45] This time around, Wilson determined to force this core Liberal issue to the forefront, regardless of its salience according to the opinion polls. This approach makes good 'marketing' sense within the context of the Lib Dems' rather limited strategic aims of re-establishing credibility and winning back the support that had slipped since 1987. It would have been less sensible in 1987, when the Alliance needed to broaden its appeal to capitalise on a genuine opportunity to push Labour into third place.

It also reflects Wilson's own background as a pressure group campaigner, with single-issue causes such as Shelter, Friends of the Earth and more lately the Campaign for Freedom of Information. Wilson's whole experience was based on raising the profile of little-known issues and influencing the media agenda. It was not surprising, therefore, that he should express scepticism at the advertisers' follow-the-polls wisdom. The party did hire an agency, TBWA Knight, Holmes, Ritchie, in

May 1991. Wilson wanted a contract, rather than less easily disciplined volunteers, and TBWA were prepared to run the account at a loss.[46] But the agency's input was strictly limited to technical matters; it drew up the posters but Wilson's planning committee made the decision that posters would be preferred to newspaper advertisements, and then only selectively in major towns.[47]

The Permanent Campaign

The pre-campaign – which has come to be known as the *near-term* or *long* campaign – was waged with an unprecedented intensity in 1992. Both Conservative and Labour pre-campaigns could be traced with ease to the autumn of 1991 and the party conferences, in Labour's case well before. From January 1992 on the parties held press conferences almost daily,[48] the themes on which the election would be fought were mapped out clearly, and when the election was finally called the campaigns moved seamlessly into the final four weeks – the campaign-proper.

The pre-campaign is not unique in British electioneering: 1959, 1964, 1979 and 1987 all furnished examples. The case of 1992 was remarkable in that *all three* major parties mounted pre-campaigns with a rigour and discipline rarely, if ever, witnessed. Of course, the pre-campaigns were made virtually inevitable by John Major's decision to let the parliament run to close to its full five-year limit. Not coincidentally, two of the four earlier pre-campaigns (1964 and 1979) were also triggered by near full-length parliamentary terms. However it may not be premature to talk in terms of the 'permanent campaigns' of US experience. The necessity for pre-campaigns had become a fundamental piece of wisdom in both Conservative and, following its example, Labour camps, based on the correct belief that the four-week campaign-proper was too short a period to change voters' minds. According to Shaun Woodward, the long campaign is *the* key lesson that British political marketers have learned from the USA.[49]

Party Advertising

Historically, advertising is a fairly peripheral part of British election campaigns which are geared primarily to influencing the television news agenda. However advertising raised a higher profile in this campaign than any since the war. This was only partly due to increased campaign expenditure:

	1987	1992
Con	£9.0m	£10.1m
Lab	£4.2m	£7.1m
LDem	£1.9m	£2.1m[50]

Labour spent about £3.3 million on advertising alone, about £1 million more than their 1987 figure, but the Conservatives' advertising spend was slightly less than their 1987 figure of £7 million.

Just as important as expenditure were the Labour and Conservative advertising strategies which were both designed to extract extra mileage from news coverage. They both exploited new tactics to this effect. The first was to hold press conferences at the sites of poster launches. The TV cameras showed posters going up and not infrequently being papered over the moment the press conference ended. Of one such stunt, *Campaign* noted:

> A Labour poster showing four skeletons, warning of the dire consequences of a fourth [Tory] victory, was said by Labour officials at the launch to be appearing on 1000 sites. In fact, it was run on just 50 sites but received widespread coverage on TV news bulletins and in the press. 'We had about £200 000 worth of coverage for only £10 000 worth of poster space,' one Labour party official said this week.[51]

The parties also routinely held press reviews of their PEBs, a tactic pioneered by Labour for the 1987 'Kinnock' broadcast, filmed by *Chariots of Fire* director Hugh Hudson. The involvement of big name film directors – Hudson, Mike Newell (Jennifer's Ear) and John Schlesinger (John Major – The Journey) – ensured added news value.

A second strategy, imported from the USA, was the deliberate injection of near-the-knuckle emotive material – the 'Benetthon strategy' – to provoke hostile reaction from rival politicians and thereby create news. Labour pushed the tactic with vigour on the issue of the NHS. The 'Jennifer's Ear' PEB is the most blatant example, but Labour had offered a taste of things to come with an early campaign newspaper advertisement showing a picture of 18-month-old baby Georgina Norris, who died from a heart ailment after her operation was cancelled. The copyline contrasted government under-funding of the NHS with Tory tax cut 'bribes'.

'Jennifer's Ear', filmed by Mike Newell (*Four Weddings and as Funeral*), was a genuinely ground-breaking political advertisement. The shortest PEB of the campaign at just over four minutes, it was a mini docudrama using actors to tell the story of two little girls requiring ear operations, one waiting in pain for nearly a year on the NHS, the other being treated immediately on payment of £200. At first Labour campaigners were delighted with the Tories' angry reaction. Health Minister William Waldegrave accused Labour of 'Nazi propaganda', which ensured that the PEB topped the news bulletins after its airing on 23 March.

The tactic backfired when the name of Jennifer Bennett, on whom the fictional film was based, leaked to the press and her parents were found to be in open disagreement. Jennifer's father (Labour) attested to the truth of the PEB, her mother and grandfather (Tory) claimed it was a gross distortion. One campaign official claims that Labour's health spokesman Robin Cook first discovered this from Waldegrave as the two men did the rounds of the broadcasting studios the day after the PEB was aired. How on earth could Labour researchers have missed the fact that Jennifer's mother had been a Tory candidate and her grandfather a former Tory mayor, Cook demanded of party campaign officials. 'We received the really alarming reply that, "of course, we knew that, but we didn't think it mattered". There was one clear lesson from that episode, that the glitz and the glamour were not under sufficient political control'.[52]

The fall-out and the hunt for the 'mole' who leaked Jennifer's name overwhelmed TV news, accounting for about half of all election news on the main two channels for three days.[53] The view of some Labour insiders, that Jennifer's Ear was a crucial campaign blunder, did not really harden until after the election result and the inevitable post-mortems. In fact, Labour scored its highest poll leads in the week following the broadcast.

Labour clearly did not lose the election because of Jennifer's Ear but it was a blunder nonetheless. It derailed Labour's carefully planned health assault and greatly embarrassed Cook, who, according to one source, became a great deal less sympathetic to the blandishments of the communications team. It also provided the Tories and their tabloids with the perfect ammunition to attack Labour's and Kinnock's trustworthiness. Most importantly it did nothing to heighten voter dissatisfaction with Tory NHS policy (see below).

The Conservatives' most striking PEB came, not in the campaign proper, but in January. The first 30 seconds of Saatchis' 'tax bombshell' were run almost exactly as an American campaign spot and in use of imagery and sound effects were highly reminiscent of Bush's notorious Dukakis advertisements. The Tories returned with the tax bomb poster during the campaign proper which was supplemented by the 'Double Whammy' (higher prices, higher tax), 'Oh no, it's a tax demand' (Labour manifesto) and the campaign theme, 'You can't trust Labour'.

Saatchis' advertisements were generally better, if less clever, than Labour's. They were aggressive, direct and unified around simple themes of tax and trust. Woodward was determined to produce highly professional advertisements and PEBs, conscious of how badly party worker morale had been affected by Hugh Hudson's outclassing of Tory efforts in 1987. Too much of the SCA's work, as admitted in Larry Whitty's post-election report, was 'too complicated and diffuse'.[54]

THE PRESIDENTIAL CAMPAIGN

The Major Effect

Political scientists conventionally dismiss the role of leaders as an important influence on voting behaviour in Britain. History offers many examples of the less popular leader winning elections. Thatcher herself was considerably less popular than Callaghan in 1979. Yet 1992 may be an exception.[55] Major's leadership transformed the immediate political scene: it buried – temporarily at least – internal differences as the party united around their new leader; it helped push the Tories into an opinion poll lead which they held until the Gulf War ended in

February 1991; and it wrongfooted Labour whose strategy had relied upon the contrast between the new moderate Labour and the increasingly extreme Mrs Thatcher.

Major's conciliatory style could scarcely have been less like Thatcher's and he and the Tories benefited from the comparison. He moved immediately to replace the poll tax, putting Michael Heseltine – its most celebrated Tory opponent – at the Department of the Environment. Major pledged, like Thatcher before him, that the NHS would be safeguarded; unlike Thatcher and the Conservative party generally, he seemed to be trusted on the caring issues, according to the polls.

Major appropriated much of Labour's campaigning territory. As David Hill lated conceded, Brixton-to-Westminster Major was the very embodiment of 'opportunity Britain' – a Labour slogan – more even than Kinnock, who had been to university while Major had not.[56] The launch of the Citizens' Charter (July 1991) to establish consumer quality measures in the public services was close to the 'quality commissions' and 'customer-care contracts' proposed by Labour's Policy Review.

The Tory change in leadership required new strategic thinking from both the Conservative and Labour camps. The Tories solved their new problem – the lack of an identity clearly differentiated from Labour – with the 'branding' strategy, with its heavy emphasis on the prime minister to contrast with 'untrustworthy' Kinnock. For Labour the strategic problems were less easily resolved. Labour had repositioned itself as a pragmatic party in sharp contrast to the ideologically driven Thatcher government. The plan, lampooned as the 'valium strategy', had relied greatly on disenchantment with the Thatcher government to drive voters into Labour's arms.[57] With the Thatcher dragon slain by her own party, Labour seemed unsure how to react. At first, largely at Kinnock's insistence, it tried to portray Major as 'son of Thatcher'. The tack shifted later to 'Major the ditherer', but both attempts failed to dent his popularity.

David Hill admitted later that a serious weakness of Labour's campaign was its total failure to undermine Major's integrity.[58] Crucially they failed to pin the blame on his government for the recession of 1991–2 (Table 7.3).

Table 7.3   Who/what most blamed for state of the economy, 1992

	All %	Con %	Lab %	LibDem %
Thatcher's govt.	46 (47)	12	78	57
Major's govt.	5 (7)	2	7	6
World economy	47 (24)	84	12	34
Not stated	3 (22)	2	3	3

Source: Harris ITN exit poll, 9 April 1992; Harris poll, Sept. 1991.[59]

Labour's efforts were impressively ineffective even with their own voters, who refused to visit the sins of the mother upon 'son of Thatcher'. Liberal Democrat voters either blamed Thatcher, or, ominously for Labour, adopted the argument advanced by the Tories that the world recession, not Major, was responsible for Britain's economic plight. Comparison with a Harris poll of September 1991 shows that the percentage blaming the world recession almost doubled (24 per cent to 47 per cent) over the six months to the election; there was a slight decrease in the percentage blaming Major. 'We probably underestimated the amount of change that people perceived as a result of John Major becoming Prime Minister,' said Hill.[60]

Kinnock: the Achilles' Heel

A vital part of the Tory strategy was to capitalise on voters' contrasting perceptions of Major and Kinnock, and there is some evidence of success. Published and private polls, including Labour's own focus group surveys, confirmed that Neil Kinnock was an electoral weakness. While the parties ran neck-and-neck, Major was by far the favoured candidate for the job of prime minister, leading Kinnock by between 14 and 20 points from January to April 1992, according to ICM. ICM's post-election analysis concluded that Kinnock was a key factor in the late swing to the Conservatives: 'Among the people who subsequently told ICM that they had changed their vote from either Labour or Liberal to the Conservatives, dislike of Neil Kinnock was one of the factors most often mentioned'.[61]

Table 7.4   Main obstacles to voting Labour, 1991–2

	11–12 Sept. 91 (%)	2–3 April 92 (%)	Change
Give unions power	40	29	–11
Don't like Kinnock	38	40	+2
Economic incompetence	30	23	–7
Too extreme	13	11	–2
Too divided	23	9	–14
Tax	n/a	25	

Source: Harris, *Observer* polls.

MORI's final *Sunday Times* panel survey of the campaign found that Kinnock lagged Major (and Ashdown) by 11 points as the 'most capable leader', by 21 points on the question of being good in a crisis, and by 13 points on perceptions of honesty. Harris polls too confirm the 'Kinnock factor'. By the time of the election Kinnock was by some margin the single largest obstacle to voting Labour (Table 7.4), when Labour seemed to have gone some distance to reducing their traditional weaknesses of economic incompetence, trade union power, defence, extremism and disunity. Labour's private campaign research warned that Kinnock might prove a barrier to wavering Liberal Democrat supporters, who had a low regard for his competence. By the middle of the campaign proper, the research reported that the Conservatives' onslaught on Kinnock's 'inconsistency of values' appeared to be working.[62] By every known measure, Kinnock clearly was not a vote-winner for Labour, something that Labour strategists acknowledged by their efforts to promote the front-bench team, especially Smith, Brown (Trade and Industry), Beckett (Treasury Chief Secretary) and Blair (Employment). Labour ran a far less leader-focused campaign than in 1987, when Kinnock beamed from the front cover of the manifesto and Hugh Hudson's 'biopic' PEB was shown twice. Instead Kinnock was packaged through party publicity as the sober head of an able team.

This was sensible, especially since polls showed that Smith

had a higher trust rating than the Chancellor, Norman Lamont – an eight-point advantage according to MORI's panel survey. But it failed to alleviate the Kinnock problem. One Walworth Road campaign official said privately that Labour's solution, much like the Tories', should have been to replace the leader. It was suggested that party research had shown consistently over a long period that Kinnock was Labour's most serious liability, that he should have been told and been urged to stand down in the party's interest. The official believed that Kinnock was protected from the most unflattering research by officials unwilling to confront him with the awful truth.[63]

Towards Presidential Politics?

Party leaders have dominated many, probably most, post-war campaigns but rarely have they been considered an important infuence on voters' behaviour. Why should 1992 have been so different, if indeed it was?[64] One reason may be that offered by, among others, Anthony King, that the leaders' impact on the vote increases when, first, the parties are close in the polls and, second, there is a wide gap in the ratings of the two main leaders. Both conditions were met in 1992. They were not in 1979, when despite Thatcher's personal unpopularity, the Tories entered the race holding a ten-point advantage.

A second reason was the nature of the contest which, more than at any time since the 1950s, was virtually ideology-free. The leader columns of the national broadsheets were unanimous: the parties seemed indistinguishable on most important policy questions. As Major ventured into the Labour territory of caring Britain, so Labour talked the language of free markets and completely dropped the word 'socialism'. With few glaring political differences, the focus would turn almost inevitably to the leaders and their fitness to govern.

The Tories' highly presidential campaign, built almost entirely around 'honest John', was thus an entirely rational response to the particular circumstances. It should be seen in this light and not necessarily as a model for future campaigns. He was 'sold' in a way that Mrs Thatcher never was: his reassuring smile covered the hoardings, newspaper advertising and the manifesto. In 1983 Thatcher had vetoed a biopic PEB made by Tim Bell because she feared it was too presidential. In 1992 two of the Tories' five PEBs were devoted entirely to Major, including John Schlesinger's 'The Journey', showing his ascent from working-class Brixton to Number 10. John Major's amiable personality was the key tool, *the* significant difference both from Thatcher's Tories and Kinnock's Labour. Thus, both in the PEBs and in his speeches, he focused on his personal credo and vision of a classless Britain. Much in the manner of US presidential candidates, he was set above and slightly apart from his party.

Labour, by contrast, adopted an anti-presidential tactic – to promote the team rather than the leader. Given Kinnock's weakness this was also entirely rational. Kinnock, the sober-suited chairman of the board, represented a change in image from earlier efforts to present him as the tough and passionate leader, epitomised by Hudson's 1987 broadcast. However, regardless of intention, it was difficult to maintain the team approach because the media spotlight inevitably focused on the leaders.[65] Nicholas O'Shaughnessy argued, unfairly, that Labour's generally sharp marketing was flawed by its 'American-style presidential' starring role for Kinnock.[66] To the contrary, Labour campaigners were well aware of Kinnock's shortcomings but it simply proved impossible to protect him from the media glare.

David Hill disputes the thesis that the leaders were particularly important at this election. He argues that what people call the 'Kinnock factor' is merely a shorthand description of everything that ailed Labour. 'It is convenient to blame Kinnock rather than the party. It means that people do not have to think in detail about what went wrong.'[67] Post-election research revealed a 'hidden agenda' of a deep-seated, gut feeling of distrust of Labour, according to Hill. The 1980s baggage of extremism, in-fighting and trade union dominance still weighed heavily in the back of many people's minds. As the prospect of Labour victory came closer, so the fears began to re-emerge. When respondents were asked the cause of their anxiety, the word 'Kinnock' sprang most readily to people's lips.

This research is almost identical to the findings of CCO. But one wonders why the Tories could pinpoint 'trust' a year before the election, when Labour only realised its true

significance after the event? Hill is almost certainly correct
that 'Kinnock' is shorthand for a larger problem. But that
does not absolve the Kinnock Factor. It merely raises a new
question of why Kinnock was so closely identified with the
1980s 'baggage'. The Kinnock problem was that he *epitomised*
Labour's weaknesses: its left-wing past, its close ties to the
unions, its general economic incompetence, and lack of clarity
about where it now stood. Kinnock personified Labour's shortcomings, while Major offered strengths where his party was
weak.

Kinnock did not profit personally from the considerable
achievement of making the Labour Party electable once again.
Labour was riven with internal strife and in danger of being
surpassed by the Liberal/SDP Alliance as the second force in
British politics when Kinnock became leader in 1983. In Hill's
words, Kinnock made the party 'respectable' again, defeating
the Trotskyist entrists, who threatened to drag the party away
from its grass roots of the respectable working class. Under
Kinnock's leadership Labour increased its lead over the third
party from two points (1983) to 17 points (1992). Labour
seemed on the brink of becoming the largest party in a hung
parliament in the early months of 1992 and it came out of the
election clearly established as the only credible alternative to
the Tories.

Kinnock's failure to reap any personal reward reflects partly
the limits of marketing and partly flawed marketing. Labour
paid a price in loss of respect as it off-loaded 'unelectable'
policies which were once articles of faith. From a marketing
perspective – that of rational electioneering – the party had no
choice but to change. In doing so it ran the inevitable risk of
appearing to abandon principle. Ironically a flaw of Labour's
marketing was that it appeared far too obviously as *marketing*.
The change of heart, especially after 1987, was achieved with
too little bloodshed to be entirely convincing. Unilateralism,
nationalisation and other 'left' policies, once passionately es-
poused by Kinnock, were jettisoned with the minimum of
acrimony at the rose-scented party conferences. Kinnock's
conference speeches rarely if ever got to grips with the major
issues dividing the party. His call for change relied little on
points of principle and much more on the need for the party

to face electoral reality. He gained a reputation for ruthlessly suppressing disagreement in the NEC and Shadow Cabinet and his failure to meet opponents head-on in open political debate earned him the contempt of the Labour Left, surpassing all Tory loathing.[68]

In political marketing terms, Labour pursued a classic risk elimination strategy. Kinnock scarcely needed to wage a public fight when he was assured of NEC and conference victories on important issues. Had he engaged in debate, he would have taken the risk of rekindling the traditional party weakness of disunity. But, by his avoiding it, the quality both of his leadership and of his personal political conviction were brought under suspicion. He was vulnerable to the charge of poll-chasing. In the end Kinnock looked so rehearsed, packaged and protected that it appeared that even his media minders did not trust him.

THE CAMPAIGN ASSESSED

1987 Revisited

The sounds of 1987 echo through a review of the 1992 campaign. As in 1987, media commentators believed that Labour had 'won' the campaign, only more so. Labour made the Conservatives look like a 'beaten army', said the post-election editorial in the *Independent on Sunday* and few in Fleet Street would have protested. The Tory campaign impressed nobody, to judge by media coverage. Sir David English, editor of the staunchly Conservative *Daily Mail*, declared in his paper's leader that the Tories deserved to be beaten unless they pulled up their socks. As the polls swung towards Labour, so the panicky Tory press erupted with a torrent of often contradictory advice to CCO campaign managers: be more positive (*Express, The Times*), more aggressively negative (*Telegraph*).[69]

We argued earlier that the press misjudged the campaign in 1987 and were over-impressed with Labour's more polished TV performance, while the more significant strategic battle escaped them almost entirely. Shaun Woodward, not surprisingly, has argued that the press were taken in again in 1992, mistaking glitz and glamour for effective campaigning, confusing tactics and presentation with strategy.[70] So which party did wage the more effective campaign?

The Negative Campaign: the Tory Attack

We have seen that Tory attempts to capitalise on Labour's long-term weaknesses (unions, economic incompetence, extremism and internal disunity) failed to make headway in the period from September 1991 to April 1992 (see Table 7.4). As obstacles to a Labour vote these all declined over the period. The one and highly significant exception was dislike of Kinnock (up two points from 38 per cent to 40 per cent). There is also evidence that the Tories' double-barrelled tax campaign – Budget tax cuts coupled with the Labour tax bombshell offensive – paid dividends. The tax bombshell campaign was launched in January and seemed to be making ground by February 1992 (Harris) when tax had leapt from nowhere to become the second most important barrier to a Labour vote at 36 per cent, behind dislike of Kinnock. During the campaign proper its salience seemed to diminish, down to 25 per cent by 2–3 April in third place behind Kinnock (40 per cent) and unions (29 per cent).

However tax may well have been crucial in shaping personal financial expectations. Almost half of the Harris exit sample, and fully 88 per cent of Tory voters and 46 per cent of Liberal Democrats, believed that Labour's tax proposals would leave them worse off (see Table 7.5). Labour's assertion that the Shadow Budget would benefit eight out of ten families was less credible than the 'bombshell' message.

Table 7.5   Would you be better or worse off under Labour's tax and benefit policies?

	Tot %	Con %	Lab %	LibDem %
Better	30	3	64	21
Worse	49	88	9	46
No change	19	8	24	31

Source: Harris ITN exit poll.

There is no strictly comparable question in earlier polls, but we can get an indication of change over time from questions on personal financial circumstances (compare Tables 7.5 and 7.6). Since September 1991 the perceived Labour threat to personal financial health increased by 14 points overall, by 21 points for Tory voters and by 11 points for Liberal Democrats.

Table 7.6   Financial situation in six months if Labour win

	Tot %	Con %	Lab%	LibDem %
Better off	18	4	39	18
Worse off	35	67	6	35
Same	41	26	52	44

Source: Harris, 11–12 September 1991.

Personal economic expectations – the pocketbook theory of voting behaviour – were strongly correlated with voting in 1992. According to David Sanders's analysis: 'around 76 per cent of Labour and Conservative supporters voted in accordance with their pocketbooks, a very strong indication that egocentric voting played an important role in the election'.[71] Thus the Tory tax offensive may well have been decisive in tipping wavering supporters back into the fold.

Labour's post-election analysis of floaters in south eastern marginals confirmed the importance of tax. While the Tories had offered tangible benefits – low taxes, low inflation, the 'right to buy' – Labour represented a risk to personal prosperity. 'Above all, there was a fundamental lack of trust in the Labour Party which allowed Tory attacks, particularly about tax, to strike home. "People have had it hard under the Conservatives . . . we thought it would get worse under Labour." '[72]

Robin Cook admitted after the election that Labour underestimated the tax problem. The Shadow Budget (16 March) 'seemed so successful that it gave us the false impression that we had neutralised the tax issue'.[73] Labour believed that the Tories had played their best card too soon and that the Shadow Budget had countered it. However the Tories stepped up the tax assault following the Shadow Budget, amply assisted by their tabloid henchmen. During 19–31 March, five of 11

Table 7.7 Main obstacles to voting Conservative, 1991–2

	11–12 Sept. 1991 (%)	2–3 April 1992 (%)	Change
Health/NHS	49	30	–19
Not caring	30	20	–10
Education	25	20	–5
Not managing economy well	21	28	+7
Don't like Major	8	13	+5
Unemployment	n/a	31	n/a

Source: Harris polls.

main daily press conferences were devoted to tax and the cost of Labour's spending plans, easily the single most frequent Tory topic of the campaign. Tax also dominated the Tory press agenda; only opinion polls were the subject of more lead stories.[74]

A rueful Labour campaigner noted subsequently that Kinnock, not John Smith, bore the brunt of the defence of Labour's tax proposals after the opening week of the campaign proper. Kinnock presented a more vulnerable target than Smith, enabling the Tories to hitch tax to the more general sense of distrust in Labour's competence.[75]

The Negative Campaign: the Labour Attack

Labour's claim for success comes not from the traditional areas of Tory weakness but on their comparative strength, management of the economy. As an obstacle to a Tory vote it increased by seven points from September 1991 to the election (see Table 7.7). It thus emerged as a bigger barrier to voting Tory than economic incompetence was to Labour. Labour had timed their Shadow Budget at the beginning of the campaign to coincide with a series of official economic indicators (unemployment, trade figures and inflation) which it anticipated correctly would prove bad news for the government. The media were sure to be dominated by the recession that week and

Labour planned 'to run with grain', as David Hill said on a
television interview during the campaign.

> Then on the day after the list of indicators drew to a close
> with the trade figures, we've moved on to health and edu-
> cation, having planned that in advance in the knowledge
> that we'd done well in fighting the Tories on recession and
> taxation and now we can move on to our territories from a
> position of strength.[76]

But Labour failed to extend its advantage on its own territory
of the caring issues, which all declined as obstacles to voting
Tory. Health, the most ferocious cannon in Labour's arsenal,
fell by a spectacular 19 points. Health is not normally considered an important influence on voting, but CCO campaign
staff seemed anxious about its potential impact.[77] They had
been shaken by Labour's health assault at the Monmouth by-
election (16 May 1991). The accusation that the Tories planned
to privatise the NHS had struck a nerve and was widely believed to have cost the Tories the seat. In fact, the CCO was
bracing itself for an NHS counter-attack after it launched the
'tax bomb' in January 1992. 'They should have come back to
us on health every day,' said Shaun Woodward. 'We were surprised that they didn't.'[78] Instead Labour kept the NHS powder dry for phase two of the campaign proper, but the plan to
pin down the Tories on privatisation fell apart amid the
Jennifer's Ear fiasco.

The best that Labour could claim was that the tactic worked
well as an agenda-setter. Health, albeit in the context of
Jennifer's Ear, dominated the airwaves for three days.[79] According to MORI, the NHS had lagged seven points behind
unemployment as the most import issue to voters in January
and February. By the end of the campaign it had become the
top issue. But Labour failed to convert greater salience into
increased dissatisfaction with the Tories. Not only did health
plummet as a barrier to the Conservatives but Labour's NHS
policy lead actually declined by seven points during the campaign (see Table 7.8).

The Agenda-setting Battle

The battle for control of the media agenda dominated all the
major parties' communications strategies. Each party strove to

Table 7.8 Which party has the best policies on each problem?

	18–20 March Survey 2 (%)	25–27 March Survey 3 (%)	1–3 April Survey 4 (%)	Change 1–4 (%)
Health care				
Con	27	30	31	+4
Lab	51	48	48	−3
LibDems	9	11	12	+3
Unemployment				
Con	21	23	23	+2
Lab	46	44	44	−2
LibDems	12	12	15	+3
Education				
Con	31	32	30	−1
Lab	38	36	37	−1
LibDems	15	20	22	+7
Economy				
Con	40	40	40	0
Lab	30	33	35	+5
LibDems	10	11	13	+3
Replacing poll tax				
Con	24	24	27	+3
Lab	39	41	40	+1
LibDems	14	15	16	+2
Taxation				
Con	41	43	42	+1
Lab	31	31	31	0
LibDems	13	13	15	+2

Source: MORI, *Sunday Times* panel (1544 adults).

promote its own strong issues and rivals' weaknesses in the hope that this would filter through to voters as increased salience.

Judged by the agenda-setting standard, Labour's campaign emerged as the clear winner. The top three issues cited in the Harris exit poll were all solid Labour territory (Table 7.9). Four of the top seven issues were Labour's. The Conservatives' main boast is that they managed to force tax onto the agenda, if only at the bottom. However Labour was less successful at

Table 7.9   Two most important issues when deciding
how to vote, 1992

	All %	Con %	Lab %	LibDem %
NHS/Health	32	20	44	39
Unemployment	29	12	45	32
Education	23	14	25	38
Economy	23	35	11	21
Poll tax	18	7	30	19
Price/inflation	15	26	7	7
Tax	12	23	3	6

Source: Harris ITN exit poll.

shifting perceptions of party capabilities. In fact, MORI's panel
surveys show that there was hardly any campaign movement of
any significance when respondents were asked which party had
the best policies to deal with the major issues (Table 7.8).
None of the parties suffered any serious damage or scored any
great success. The best performances were the Liberals on
education (up seven points), Labour on the economy (up five
points) and the Tories on health (four points).

Clearly national agenda success is not sufficient for victory
at the polls, a fact that was also demonstrated at the 1987
election, when unemployment and the NHS were also the top
two issues. Labour could scarcely have hoped for a more promising agenda, yet it wrested few voters away from the Tories.
Table 7.9 shows that Conservative voters' agenda was quite
distinct from that of the nation at large: economy, inflation
and tax were their top three issues. This is where Labour must
make inroads if it is to chip away at that four-election solid 42
per cent Tory vote share.

CONCLUSION

A fourth election victory and a retained 42 per cent vote share
are the Tories' impressive claims to having waged the most
effective campaign. It was not pretty. It was far less slick and
smartly turned out than Labour's. A post-election internal

review listed a string of errors at CCO: the prime minister's tour was poorly planned, the media were not kept properly informed, co-ordination was lacking, there was a failure in many target seats, press conferences in the wake of Jennifer's Ear veered out of control and occasionally CCO descended into chaos.[80]

For all that, the Conservatives' strategic thinking was as sharp as ever, waging an entirely rational campaign around the themes of trust and tax, from which they did not depart except for a brief panic around Jennifer's Ear. The strategic concept was crude: a blatant appeal to fear and greed. The evidence is that it worked and that there was a late surge as the Tories managed to convince half the voters that they would be worse off under Labour. There can be little doubt either that the Tory-supporting tabloids did a robust job for their party in the end, warming to the themes of tax and Kinnock's credibility. One of Major's more memorable speech lines, 'nightmare on Kinnock street', was reportedly handed to him by a friendly journalist before it was pursued over eight pages of the *Sun*.[81]

In his resignation speech, Kinnock quoted Lord McAlpine, former Tory treasurer, who claimed that the election was won by the editors of the Tory tabloids. However this overstates the case; evidence of a late swing is found among *Mirror* readers, as well as Conservative paper readers. The late surge was a national, not a newspaper phenomenon.[82]

Labour committed errors but nonetheless its campaign, over the long term, achieved a great deal. It shed or reduced significantly its most damaging image problems, it restored electoral credibility and it helped crunch the Liberal Democrats into a lonely third place. Labour approached the campaign proper in a rational manner, managing to promote its own 'caring' issues but well aware that the economy would be the decisive terrain. Through John Smith and the Shadow Budget, Labour tackled the economy head-on. It did not run and hide from economic issues as it had in 1987. The Shadow Budget was a bold and positive initiative. However it was also fatally flawed in that it allowed the Tories to target voters earning or anticipating earning the not especially generous salary of £21 000 per year. Sources close to Smith say that he became convinced that his budget cost Labour the election, and clearly it provided the Tories with fresh ammunition for their tax offensive. It is also true that, had Smith not announced specific tax and National Insurance plans, Labour would still have been vulnerable to the tax scare. Perhaps Labour's biggest mistake was not the Shadow Budget itself, but the complacent belief that it had taken the sting out of the tax issue.

The other celebrated blunders, Jennifer's Ear and the Sheffield Rally, pale by comparison. The Sheffield Rally effect is impossible to quantify, although Neil Kinnock clearly believed its over-triumphalist tone hit exactly the wrong note. 'I've cursed myself ever since,' he told David Dimbleby in an interview aired on BBC2 (5 December 1992). Both events were far less important than tax. They were almost certainly less important than proportional representation, which Kinnock raised in the last week of the campaign. It appeared as a crude bribe to Liberal supporters and sparked the Tory retort that a Liberal Democrat vote would let in Labour, an appeal which Liberal campaigners believed caused their late slippage. Worse, having raised the issue, Kinnock then refused to say where he stood on it. Kinnock ended up looking muddled and evasive; Major took advantage, resolutely opposing both PR and electoral pacts.

It is going too far to suggest that Labour grabbed defeat from the jaws of victory. The prospect of a Labour majority was always remote; the party had a mountain to climb from its feeble base of 1987, needing to gain 97 seats on an 8 per cent swing, while the largest swing to any party since 1945 has been 5 per cent (1979). However Labour campaign errors – especially tax – probably cost the half a per cent swing which would have caused a hung parliament. Labour failed its most basic task of all, to increase dissatisfaction with the government.

8 Thatcher's Legacy: The Americanisation of British Politics?

Political marketing is now clearly woven into the fabric of British politics. It has been adopted by right and left of the spectrum, trade unions, pressure groups and charities. Thatcher's Conservative Party led the way with the hiring of Saatchi & Saatchi in 1978 and the incorporation of marketing expertise at high levels of influence in the party organisation. By the late 1980s Labour had become the new marketing leaders, Peter Mandelson its driving force and the red rose its clearest symbol. Where once the Labour leaders had reacted with alarm and contumely to the 'marketing of Margaret', by the early 1990s the tables had turned. The Tories accused Labour of reducing politics to slick and phoney images, John Major renounced the image-makers and Harvey Thomas parted company with Conservative Central Office (CCO) complaining that the party was neglecting fundamentals of communications.

The history of British political campaigning has witnessed this kind of turn-about before. The Conservatives, with their greater affinity for business techniques and more hierarchical organisation, have been the communications pioneers throughout most of the century. But, particularly after periods of opposition, Labour has sometimes nudged ahead in the communications battle. To the Tories belong most of the innovators: J.C.C. Davidson modernised Tory organisation and campaigning between the world wars; Stanley Baldwin was quickest to exploit radio and the newsreels; in the post-war period party chairmen Woolton and Poole imported commercial techniques, market research and advertising; Anthony Eden and especially Harold Macmillan were the first leaders to grasp and take advantage of the potential of television. Labour's moments are mostly post-Second World War: Herbert Morrison capitalised on the machinery of government publicity in a manner not seen again until Thatcher's second administration;

after 13 years of opposition the 1964 Labour campaign was a classic piece of 'political marketing' – or rational electioneering, as it was then called; and Harold Wilson introduced show business into political campaigning in a manner not repeated until Margaret Thatcher became prime minister.

If the use of political marketing this century could be shown on a graph it would not describe an ever-ascending curve. It would be instead a more or less gentle slope with a few troughs and peaks along its length as parties adapted to changing political and technological environments. Politicians and party managers may be expected to adopt the most effective means of communication available and electoral success will most likely ensure that methods will be copied. There have been along the way fluctuations according to the personal taste, energy and inclination of party leaders. Yet in the long term there seems little prospect that political marketing will diminish, either in its strategic concern to temper the product according to the views of the electorate or in the broader sense of presentational and promotional techniques.

The post-1992 election backlash against Labour's Shadow Communications Agency does not signal the beginning of the end for political marketing. The campaign proved once again that glitz and glamour is merely the froth of image-making; designer suits, oak panel sets and a chauffeured Daimler could not suddenly bestow an aura of authority around Neil Kinnock. Endorsements by celebrities – 'luvvies for Labour' as Walworth Road cynics called one much-hyped campaign event – cannot change the basics of party image: trustworthiness and fitness to govern. The merchants of glitz and glamour may find themselves under tighter political control, quite properly. But the more fundamental contribution of marketing to electoral strategy is here to stay. Market research, to paraphrase André Malraux's advice to General de Gaulle, may well be like medicine – not science but more scientific than anything else.[1]

The marketing concept is found under different guises and names since the advent of mass democracy; it is manifested in the pursuit of electoral credibility. The distinguishing features of political marketing rest in its reliance on increasingly acute and precise commercial techniques to discover voters' motivations and desires, coupled with a more specialised and disciplined approach to communications. Marketing offers a rational way to behave in competitive democracies – provided, of course, that electoral credibility is the goal. Logically, true idealists and parties which claim to know the 'objective interests' of their constituents have no need for the marketing concept, although market research would sharpen presentation. But for parties genuinely seeking office, political marketing offers a contemporary model of rational electioneering. This is why political marketing has become a modern phenomenon of competitive democracies the world over and why it is likely to be durable. It is not merely 'designer politics' for an era saturated in the obsessions of style, imagery and packaging – the paraphernalia of post-modernism.

THE CONTRIBUTION OF MARGARET THATCHER

At first sight the study of Margaret Thatcher and political marketing presents a paradox: on the one hand the resolute, conviction, ideologically committed politician; on the other, the packaged, marketed product. One might imagine that Lady Thatcher herself would not like the term 'political marketing' to be too closely associated with her name. Yet she presided over the introduction and intensification of the techniques of marketing and her extraordinary success as the longest continuously serving prime minister this century ensured that her methods were the model to copy.

It is important to state what marketing was *not* with Thatcher. Downing Street was not the equivalent of Reagan's White House where a president obsessed with the need for public approval kept a coterie of pollsters and image-makers as his closest advisers. Both leaders retained powerful and influential press secretaries: Ingham for Thatcher and Larry Speakes, followed by Marlin Fitzwater, for Reagan. But Thatcher had no equivalent of Mike Deaver, a public relations expert, whose office was the one closest to the Oval Office, who sat in on most of the president's meetings, organised the president's schedule and advised continuously on his image.[2] According to Donald Regan, the President's Chief of Staff:

> [Deaver] saw – designed – each Presidential action as a one-minute or two-minute spot on the evening network news, or a picture on page one of the *Washington Post* or *New York*

Times, and conceived every Presidential appearance in terms of camera angles.[3]

Downing Street had no equivalent of the Political Agenda Control System (PACS), a computer programme designed by Dick Wirthlin to analyse and predict public response to every significant presidential action – although CCO hired Wirthlin in Thatcher's last years. Additionally Reagan counted Stuart Spencer, a Californian publicist and lobbyist, among his kitchen cabinet.[4]

By comparison, Mrs Thatcher's association with the image-makers was sparing. Contact with her most trusted image advisers, Sir Gordon Reece and Sir Tim Bell, was intermittent and infrequent outside election times.[5] Their views were by no means always acceptable to Ingham, who resisted attempts which he believed downgraded the Government Information Service, such as the initiative to supply ministers with public relations minders. With these qualifications in mind, however, Thatcher did exploit marketing to a significant degree: in the shaping of the party's political programme, devising electoral strategy and designing communications campaigns. Most importantly the marketing concept shaped the manifesto and electoral strategy in all three elections under Mrs Thatcher's leadership. This is not to say that market research dictated the details of policy but it did suggest the tone and tenor and indicate that certain policy options should be included and that others were electorally out of bounds.

The Marketing Concept and Party Policy

Thatcher's first election as leader, in 1979, provided a near-perfect example of strategy matching the conclusions of market research: she combined a manifesto of mainstream Conservative economic prudence with the rhetoric of strong leadership. There were clear intimations, if not pledges, of a tough stance on issues where the polls showed that the electorate had moved to the right, particularly immigration and law and order. The gulf between Thatcher's uncompromising rhetoric and compromising policies struck commentators at the time; however they sought an explanation, not in terms of political marketing, but in the tension between pragmatism and ideological conviction.

Thatcher's second election in 1983 seemed to offer a superb opportunity to power ahead with truly radical free market, anti-state policies: the Labour Party had split, was in disarray and headed by an unpopular leader; the Conservatives had held a substantial lead in the polls for about a year, Mrs Thatcher had secured complete dominance over her party, was adored in the pro-Tory tabloid press and widely respected as a strong leader. Yet marketing research suggested a steady rather than adventurous programme and, on cue, the Conservatives adopted a manifesto characterised by continuity and notable for its lack of radical zeal. Much to the regret of right-wing think-tanks, with whom she was associated, Thatcher failed to make any radical commitment to dismantle the 'socialist' welfare state and instead pledged that the National Health Service was safe in Conservative hands.[6]

In 1987, once again, the Conservative manifesto and electoral strategy closely followed the analysis of marketing research which warned that 'time for a change' could be a potent appeal unless the electorate could be persuaded that the Tories were the party with the fresh and dynamic ideas. The marketers suggested specific areas where Mrs Thatcher might care to direct her energies, notably health and education (although not local government finance). Marketing analysis played a crucial role in encouraging Mrs Thatcher to push for an energetic manifesto, and this at an apparently risky time when the prospects of victory were far less assured than in 1982. Her willingness to tailor the manifesto in this way suggests that Mrs Thatcher was more of a pragmatist and less of an ideologue than her abrasive, anti-socialist rhetoric might lead one to believe. The chasm between her abrasive stance and the relative sobriety of her policy commitments encourages the view that Thatcherism was not so much an ideology, more a style of leadership and a set of values.[7] Thatcher's use of marketing was in the tradition of rational electioneering; it was not a slavish follow-the-polls policy or a drastic reduction to the lowest common denominator. It seemed, instead, a rational balance between the political aims of the prime minister and her party and the tolerance of the electorate. The surprise may be not that Mrs Thatcher engaged in political marketing but that her opponents were willing to run, even boastful of, their own irrational campaigns.

The Increased Influence of the Marketing and Media Experts

The Thatcher era offered a more central and influential role for the specialists of market research, communication and advertising. At first the differences seemed modest: Saatchi & Saatchi were asked to script as well as produce party political and election broadcasts, which allowed them to import ideas from the commercial world, to use actors, mood music and voice-overs. Previously politicians had prepared scripts themselves and the media experts' role was confined to providing technical advice. In addition to the broadcasts and paid advertising, Saatchi also prepared collateral material, such as leaflets for doorstep delivery. Again this seems a fairly modest development, but it was an important step towards the creation of a disciplined, unified campaign, co-ordinated so that all parts of the communications orchestra were playing in harmony.

Saatchi also pioneered qualitative, attitudinal focus group research which was used relatively little in politics at that time. Focus group research is now undertaken regularly by the Conservatives and Labour in the testing of themes, slogans and advertising. Most significantly, in combination with increasingly sophisticated quantitative polling, it has provided the parties with their most precise tool for understanding voters' motivations and attitudes. It has thus become essential for establishing campaign strategy. Saatchi's expertise in analysing qualitative research ensured their involvement in the political machinery to a degree unprecedented for an advertising agency in Britain. It meant that they were not merely technicians or tacticians but were intimately involved in strategy. The pattern was followed at Labour where the SCA was responsible for the conduct, analysis and interpretation of all qualitative research for the 1992 election. The progression from technician to strategist renders out of date the traditional claim that pollsters do not influence policy but merely highlight parts of an already selected programme.

Marketers have not replaced the politicians in writing the details of policy, but they are not particularly interested in these details; they advise on image, stance and themes which are incorporated into the strategy adopted *prior* to the development of policy. Qualitative research, for instance, led to the Conservative discovery that unemployment was not likely to cause electoral difficulties in 1983, even though most people rated it as the most important national problem. This finding was vital for the 1983 Tory strategy and it is inconceivable that it did not influence Conservative economic policy, if only to confirm the control of inflation as a higher priority than the reduction of unemployment. The passage of years, with about three million jobless, should not be allowed to dull the memory of how startling a discovery this was at a time when conventional wisdom would have expected government survival to be incompatible with mass unemployment.

New Tactics and Techniques of Communication

The 1980s were marked by the intensification of specialisation within the field of communications. Until the mid-1970s parties' teams of specialists would comprise, typically, press officers, usually ex-Fleet Street; speechwriters, often also journalists; pollsters and advertising volunteers or an agency. Thatcher broadened the group significantly. The Conservatives established the first marketing department in British politics in the realisation that the traditional skills of the press officer were no longer adequate for all the demands and opportunies of modern communications. A television specialist, at first Gordon Reece, became essential. Reece encouraged Thatcher to exploit the less political 'human interest' programmes, such as *The Jimmy Young Show, Jim'll Fix It* and the Michael Aspel chat show – against the advice of Bernard Ingham, who thought that too many chat shows would cheapen the office of prime minister.[8] Reece also designed the leader's tour specifically for the television cameras, creating photo-opportunies, in the belief that a minute's coverage on prime-time news was worth the whole of a current affairs programme, and he advised her to limit drastically interviews with 'hostile' presenters.

Harvey Thomas (of Billy Graham's crusades) transformed the staging of political rallies and conferences, exploiting colour co-ordinated scenery, dramatically presented slogans, autocue machines, lighting, video screens, greenery, flags, music and warm-up acts – all designed ultimately to present the right pictures for the TV audience. Direct mail became a major communications tool in 1987 and required a new set of consultants. Public relations professionals were engaged in government policy launches and privatisation campaigns; and with the spectacular progress of new technology, computer experts also became indispensable to the party communications army. Thus specialists in television, rallies, direct mail, computer programming and public relations swelled the corps of experts employed or consulted routinely by the parties.

A feature of the period was the drive for disciplined communications, to weld the various parts of the ensemble into a single, unified image. There was no more clear example of this than the Conservatives' 1986 Bournemouth conference: slogans, stage-setting, advertising, press handouts, publicity material for the audience and ministers' speeches were all carefully coordinated to project the image of a united government geared dynamically to the 'Next Moves Forward'. The triumph of disciplined communications at the party conference proved harder to maintain in the hurly-burly of the next year's election campaign, when unexpected events, unpredictable press conferences and simple gaffes threw plans into disarray or made them irrelevant.

The goal of disciplined communications tends to pressure campaign managers into caution; they restrict opportunities for leading politicians to make chance remarks and mistakes. Gordon Reece set the pattern in 1979: the Tories waged a deliberately short campaign, all-ticket rallies cut down the risk of hecklers, the leader's tour was designed for photo-opportunities and openings for reporters' questions or for public displays of protest kept to a minimum. The 'elimination of risk' approach has been thoroughly incorporated into Labour communications strategy. According to Peter Mandelson, there was probably only one part of the 1987 campaign that was 'left to chance' – 'Leader's question time', a Labour innovation of 1987 in which Kinnock was questioned by school children deliberately *not* vetted for political viewpoint. In 1992 Kinnock's carefully orchestrated campaign was 'vacuum-sealed', in the words of David Hill.[9]

Cautious, risk elimination tactics are a major reason why recent election campaigns appeared dull to experienced commentators: there were few real eccentricities or mistakes, limited opportunities for the more independent party spirits and little real debate. Blandness and excessive caution are ills associated with the political marketer's art in the United States and doubtless the risk of boring students of politics is a cheap price to pay for strong, clear and unified images. Modern marketing has not invented dull campaigns, of course; an acquaintance with history suggests that lively and genuine debate has been the exception rather than the rule. Enoch Powell observed of the 1970 election, for instance, that voters were being asked whether they preferred to be ruled by a man with a pipe or a man with a boat.[10]

Perhaps a more significant concern is the extension of the disciplines of political marketing well beyond the election campaign period into the party conferences and mid-term campaigns. If not yet quite the 'permanent campaigns' of American presidential politics, the Conservatives have waged conscious and co-ordinated pre-campaigns, most obviously in 1978/9 and 1986/7, and by 1992 all the mainstream parties followed suit: the themes, slogans, targets and images of the campaign proper were all clearly mapped out in the preceding months.

Quasi 'permanent' campaigns have meant tighter central control over internal party mechanisms with potential for dissent or public embarrassment: annual party conferences, selection of candidates and (in the Tory case) the provision of speakers for the constituencies. The Labour conference is the most dramatic example, but Conservative conferences, particularly under Thatcher, led the trend. Heath was the first Conservative leader to treat the party conference seriously enough to attend for the entire week, no doubt encouraged by the nearly blanket coverage of television. Under Mrs Thatcher the public relations potential of the conference was exploited to new levels. Debates were stage-managed to eliminate virtually any opportunity for disgruntled representatives to speak from the floor, in marked contrast with other less publicised party gatherings, such as the Conservative Central Council, Young Conservatives, Federation of Conservative Students and Conservative Trade Unionists' conferences.[11] So total appeared the propagandists' control that annual conferences earned the disparaging nickname of 'Nuremberg rallies', and not merely from cynical journalists. The Charter Movement, which campaigns for internal party democracy, complained: 'Applause and standing ovations – or the lack of them – are the only real expressions of democracy left to the constituency representatives.'[12] The only time in 14 years that representatives threatened revolt, ironically, was the annual conference at Blackpool in 1991, when the rapturous reception for Lady Thatcher – by now ex-leader – threatened to destroy the carefully planned conference schedule.

Government Publicity: the Growth of 'Political Advertising'

Government advertising on television in support of controversial policy was one of the most distinctive features of political communications in the Thatcher era. Government appeared at times addicted to advertising – the 'megaphone solution'. Government advertising more than doubled in real terms, from £40 million to £90 million in the years 1976 to 1987. From 1986 until Mrs Thatcher's resignation, the government jockeyed for position as the country's most lavish advertiser alongside multinational corporations Procter & Gamble and Unilever. Significantly the proportion of total spending accounted for by *television* commercials more than doubled, from 25 per cent in 1970 to 56 per cent in 1988. More significantly still, there was a massive proportionate increase in advertising in support of contested social and economic policy: the privatisations, employment measures and health and social service reforms.

In 1970, some 58 per cent of government advertising concerned armed forces recruitment and telecommunications services, two uncontentious, non-party political fields. Spending on the controversial areas, health, trade and industry and employment, accounted for less than 5 per cent. By contrast, in 1988, the armed forces and postal services took just 21 per cent of the advertising expenditure, while trade, health and employment took 46 per cent. The increase in controversial advertising is put into sharper relief against the background of a government which passed legislation – the Local Government Acts of 1986 and 1988 – to forbid councils from issuing publicity material which promotes a point of view readily identifiable with one party and contested by another. The government refused to extend the statutory controls to government publicity spending.

Government had at its disposal the most creative publicity talent in the land and plentiful funds to argue its case. This is accepted as a traditional perk of all governments, along with the resources of the civil service generally, but the Thatcher government use of television has weighted the balance even more heavily in favour of the incumbents. Their extensive use of television adds a new dimension to the old debate because paid-for TV advertising is a resource banned to political parties. They are allowed only limited and infrequent direct access to television through the (five) annual party political broadcasts. The arcane definition of 'political' employed by the IBA (now ITC) permits the government broad leeway to promote its policies. But opposition parties are not allowed to respond in kind to government commercials which implied, for instance, that the entire nation welcomed the sale of British Gas.

The controversy about government publicity was the most sustained and vociferous since the post-war Labour government incensed the Conservatives with the creation of the Central Office of Information. The debate seemed to die with Thatcher and Ingham, however, even though spending remained high, dropping significantly only in the year after the May 1992 election.

THE IMPACT OF MARKETING

It is difficult to gauge the impact of political marketing alongside the many other general and specific factors which influence voters at any one election. There is no satisfactory way to isolate and measure the effectiveness of the various elements of communications campaigns. In that absence marketing may seem of marginal significance set beside the Winter of Discontent in 1978/9, the Falklands victory of 1982, the post-Callaghan turmoil in the Labour Party and divisions in the opposition, and Nigel Lawson's and Norman Lamont's tax-cutting budgets.

It is impossible to be precise, but it is clear that the Conservatives made intelligent use of political marketing to develop rational strategies for all three elections under Mrs Thatcher's stewardship. On each occasion they identified clearly their target voters and their electoral pledges and communications campaigns were tailored to suit. They did not make the elementary strategic errors of investing enormous campaigning energy in factors unlikely to influence the vote, as Labour did in all three elections from 1979 to 1987.

The Winter of Discontent handed the Tories a powerful weapon and they made effective use of it to intensify dissatisfaction with the Labour government, despite Callaghan's considerable popularity advantage over Thatcher. Saatchi's 'Labour isn't working' slogan, the most brilliant and memorable piece of political advertising of the Thatcher era, struck to the heart of Labour's vulnerability on one of its traditional strengths. If, as Gordon Reece believed, Saatchi advertising helped dissuade Callaghan from holding an autumn 1978 election then it made a vital contribution to the Tories' ultimate success.

The 'Next Move Forward' relaunch in the autumn of 1986 also deserves credit for restoring Conservatives' morale after a torrid year, and setting them on course for the election with an image of unity and purpose previously lacking. Despite being out-presented by Labour in the 1987 election, the Tories followed a more effective strategy, pummelling Labour on its vote-losing weaknesses of defence, extremism and economic management and mounting a sustained counter-attack to the time-for-a-change challenge. Labour's prettier campaign, by contrast, was waged on the strategically weaker territory of the caring issues which, as the Tories predicted correctly, converted few votes.

The pattern repeated itself in 1992 and this time the campaign may well have been decisive. The Tories looked disorganised and Labour far more polished and disciplined. Both parties planned around sound strategic themes: trust (Tories) versus change (Labour). But while the Tories never wavered from the theme, Labour confusingly shifted tack from the Sheffield Rally. At the beginning of the campaign Labour marketed itself as the challenger, under the slogan 'It's time for change'. By the end, the challenger was presenting itself virtually as the new government with stunts such as the mock Queen's Speech. Labour's intention was to shift gear and emphasise the image of a bandwagon rolling them inexorably to power. However it was probably a marketing mistake to attempt such an image-transformation in mid-campaign and it certainly diverted attention from the Opposition's attack on the Government's record. The latter is the more important point because, according to political marketing wisdom, the opposition's overriding task is to increase dissatisfaction with the government. Labour's failure in 1992 was in the negative campaign.

Since the 1979 election, the Tories have managed to maintain most of their share of the total vote: 44 per cent in 1979, 42.4 per cent in 1983, 42.2 per cent in 1987 and 41.9 per cent in 1992. Their target voters in 1979 were the skilled working class (C2) (27 per cent of the electorate); women (52 per cent of the electorate); and first-time voters (14 per cent of the electorate). Over the period 1974–87 the swing to Conservative was 5.5 per cent across the total electorate. In the target sectors it was: C2 – 11 per cent; women – 4.5 per cent; and first-time voters – 7.5 per cent.[13] The C2 achievement is clearly considerable, with double the national swing. Tory success with women is less convincing, one point lower than the national swing. The swing was greater among male voters at 7.5 per cent, incidentally.

As long as the Conservatives can hold on to about 40 per cent of the national vote they will almost certainly continue in government while the opposition vote is split. The challenge for the Opposition is to prise away 3 or 4 per cent of the wavering Tory voters. A clue here may be the issue agenda which looks quite different for Tory voters than for the rest of the nation. Whereas other voters overwhelmingly put unemployment and the caring issues top of their concerns, for Tories it was the economy, prices and tax. If Labour wants to make inroads into that Tory 40 per cent, then they would do worse than borrow the slogan pinned to Clinton's campaign 'war room' in Little Rock: 'It's the economy, stupid'.

The Limits of Political Marketing

The greatest single failure of marketing concerned, not Labour, but Mrs Thatcher herself. Any and every account of the marketing of Thatcher will stress the attention to personal details, her voice, clothes, hair-do, television manner and House of Commons delivery. Most accounts also emphasise Sir Gordon Reece's carefully designed photo-opportunities which set out to create a more warm and womanly image for a leader generally perceived as aloof and rather superior. To this end, for example, Mrs Thatcher infamously cuddled a new-born calf, donned work clothes to coat chocolates, and performed a host of other down-to-earth tasks, mingling with sports personalities and welcoming a hug from World Cup hero Paul Gascoigne; she shied away from aggressive television interviewers except when unavoidable, such as at election times, and cultivated warmer, 'human interest' outlets: women's magazines, chat shows and opportunities to display the softer, family side of her personality: for example, interviews with Jean Rook and Miriam Stoppard, and appearances on the Jimmy Young and Michael Aspel shows and *Desert Island Discs*.

However opinion polls across the period of Mrs Thatcher's premiership suggest that none of this personal marketing worked. Her three main image difficulties of April 1979 (talks down to people, out of touch with ordinary people, down to earth) remained negatives throughout. In fact, they tended to increase at election times when she exposed a higher than usual profile (see Table 8.1).

Table 8.1   Profile of Mrs Thatcher: trends, 1979–90 (i)

	April 1979 (%)	May 1983 (%)	June 1987 (%)	Sept. 1990 (%)	High (%)	Low (%)	Change April 79–Sept. 90 (%)
Talks down	31	54	61	56	61	31	+25
Down to earth	24	22	18	8	24	8*	−16
Out of touch	25	49	53	63	25	63	+38

* refers also to Oct. 1985.
Source: MORI.

Her two strengths were that she was seen as a capable leader and good in a crisis (Table 8.2). These images, forged during the Falklands War, owed relatively little to the marketers. Thatcher's best positive and worst negative ratings tended to coincide with elections, which suggests that the more people saw of her the more she was disliked and respected simultaneously. It also suggests that Tebbit, Dobbs and Saatchi were wise, in 1987, to treat Mrs Thatcher as a strong card in the campaigning deck, rather than build the campaign around

Table 8.2   Profile of Mrs Thatcher: trends, 1979–90 (ii)

	April 1979 (%)	May 1983 (%)	June 1987 (%)	Sept. 1990 (%)	High (%)	Low (%)	Change April 79–Sept. 90 (%)
Capable leader	26	62	59	39	62	26	+13
Good in crisis	n/a	62	55	40	62*	31	n/a

* refers to Jan. 1987.
Source: MORI.

her – as Bell and Lord Young advised. Indeed, Dobbs's *Blue Book* argued further that Thatcher should not attempt to cultivate a softer image but should simply play to her strengths; her image by then was set in concrete and was not liable to short-term or even intermediate-term change.

This suggests that the trivia of image-making, the undeniably fascinating details of appearance and style which so obsess the media, have relatively little impact, especially if they attempt to shift hardened opinion. It is difficult to know if the trivia *ever* have much persuasive power, although marketers and even seasoned campaigners will often invest them with such. Heath, for instance, believed that Macmillan's authoritative spin of the globe in a party election broadcast of 1959 turned the election. Peter Mandelson thought the red rose itself was one of the most effective factors in Labour's 1987 campaign: 'without overstating the case, it created a unique harmony and cohesion'.[14] Kinnock will forever curse himself for his exuberant rock'n roll, 'we're all *right*' yell at the Sheffield Rally. Michael Dobbs has suggested that the historic turning-point in Mrs Thatcher's premiership was the seemingly trivial moment when she rushed to the cameras to announce, 'We have become a grandmother'. It 'chilled the hearts of many loyal followers' because it brought the shock of recognition that she had become hopelessly remote and out of touch.[15]

Such moments may sometimes, like the inspired poet, capture and crystallise the general mood, but in Britain, at least, personal image-making is unlikely to have much sustained influence. In situations such as American presidential primaries, where candidates are often unknown previously to the nation at large, and which are judged, in the nature of the contest, on personal qualities, the image-maker's arts have far more scope to influence public perception. In France, too, the personal character of presidential elections offers more potential for effective interventions by advertising and public relations experts. Advertising professional Jaques Seguela, a celebrated French equivalent of Tim Bell, is acclaimed for transforming Mitterrand from an austere 'wolf' to the Tonton (uncle) of the French nation.[16] Seguela persuaded the then (1980) presidential hopeful to doctor his set of ferocious, nicotine-stained canines – 'You will never be elected with teeth like that' – to adopt a statesmanlike upright bearing and swap his dull bankers' suits for the more stylishly cut apparel of the French Left. 'No one will ever know if it was the image-makers who put Mitterrand into power,' Seguela commented. 'But it was certainly Mitterrand who gave power to the image-makers.'

In Britain the influence of personal image-making is more restricted, for two main reasons. First, in the normal course of events, the popularity of the leader seems to have relatively little influence on voters' party choices. In 1945 the people elected Labour by a landslide despite Winston Churchill's great international stature, and in 1970 and 1979 the greater popularity of Labour leaders failed to stop Tory victories. The experience of 1992 seems to be the exception rather than the rule. Second, a new party leader is immediately thrust into the public eye and the media experts have only a short period to mould public opinion before it starts to harden. By the time an election arrives most people will have firm views and the marketers must then work with the grain of existing opinion if they hope to make any impact.

Old Solutions, New Problems

Marketing failed Mrs Thatcher ultimately, in that the difficulties she found herself in 1989/90 were partly created by the solutions accepted in 1986/7. Her marketing-inspired radical manifesto countered the threat of time-for-a-change but equally it exposed her government to the charge of extremism as a succession of controversial and unpopular policies – in education, health and the community charge – were implemented.

The weakness which the Tories had exploited ruthlessly in Labour at the last two elections was starting to backfire.

MORI's perceptual mapping analysis in the summer of 1989 found that the Conservatives were seen as significantly *more* extreme, and Labour *less* extreme than in 1988.[17] A MORI poll found that 78 per cent of their sample considered themselves middle-of-the-road or moderate, while 58 per cent rated the Tories as substantially right or far right, and only 37 per cent thought Labour substantially or extreme left.[18] After ten years of Thatcherism, Britons had not converted to Thatcherite individualistic free enterprise ideals. A majority preferred to live in a country which emphasised social provision of welfare to one in which the individual was encouraged to look after her/himself; a majority also thought that public interests and a managed economy were more important than private interests and the free market. About 55 per cent of MORI's poll thought that the country was heading in the wrong direction and significantly this view was held most strongly (62 per cent) by the 15–28-year-old group – 'Thatcher's children'.

Encouraged by the marketers, Thatcher had pushed well to the right of public opinion and found herself with dwindling space for manoeuvre. She was stuck with an uncaring image which would be difficult if not impossible to budge and after 12 years in government the time-for-a-change appeal was likely to be potent. Yet the counter-attacking option of another energetic and radical manifesto risked moving her further to the right of most voters and liable to wounding accusations of extremism. Mrs Thatcher seemed willing to take that option; her speech at the 1990 Tory conference in Bournemouth indicated yet more radical changes in education with the introduction of vouchers, more privatisation, further tax cuts and easier council house sales.[19] Her parliamentary colleagues, it transpired, were less eager to take the risks.

Michael Dobbs, one of the main architects of the 1987 strategy who had since returned to Saatchis', betrayed no trace of embarrassment at his own responsibility for her predicament when he suggested publicly in 1989 that the party's real solution was to replace Thatcher:

The style of leadership which the party needs for the 1990s is very different from that required to see off Scargill and

Galtieri during the 1980s and Mrs Thatcher has not yet been able to convince even her own party that she has the touch necessary to lead them forward for the next decade.[20]

Marketers cannot be blamed for the details of Thatcher's unpopular policies, of course; nor for the succession of Cabinet resignations which eventually led to the leadership challenge and Thatcher's resignation. These were due to political factors outside their sphere of influence. Nevertheless their strategy and solutions for the problems of 1987 helped create the political crisis which led to her downfall.

THATCHER'S LEGACY

The example of Mrs Thatcher's Conservative Party provides sharp insight into both the strengths and limitations of marketing. Political marketing provided rational strategies which helped Thatcher to become the only leader to win three successive election victories this century. It set the parameters for her political programme, identified the target voters and supplied the appeals and slogans tailored to win them over. The marketers' task was assisted by the adoration of Maggie in the pro-Tory tabloid press, especially the *Sun*, with its high proportion of skilled working-class readers. However marketing did not reduce Thatcher to a slavish follow-the-polls approach to policy; nor did it undermine the obligations of leadership or reduce politics to a bland baby food. These are the undramatic but solid strengths of the marketing approach as employed by a 'conviction' politician.

Media interest in Thatcher the marketed politician waned after 1987 as red rose Labour became the new focus. But this should not mislead one into thinking, as casual media discussion often implies, that the point of marketing is a wholesale redesign of outlook and image. Thatcher made sensible use of marketing in all her three election campaigns. It is a tool, and need not be the master. Ken Livingstone makes the point: following the polls is not only immoral, it is also a marketing mistake:

People become cynical; they rightly become suspicious. Though wary of ideologues, they still like to think that politicians have some basic beliefs . . . Interestingly enough, the opinion polling for the GLC actually discredits the follow-the-poll approach. The results show that if arguments are presented clearly and openly people can be persuaded, minds can be changed. Respect can be earned, even when people disagree with your views on particular issues.[21]

Labour, in its quest to shed its negative extremist and divided image, may have paid a price in loss of respect as it off-loaded 'unelectable' policies which had once been articles of faith. Kinnock was satirised weekly in *Spitting Image* as a man who would do virtually anything to garner votes. Even at the low points of popularity, Mrs Thatcher rated strongly as a capable leader; Kinnock's down-to-earth qualities did not seem able to earn him respect. A MORI poll in October 1990 found that 39 per cent of all voters and 73 per cent of Conservative supporters thought Thatcher a capable leader; only 24 per cent of the total thought the same of Kinnock and, most significantly, only a minority (41 per cent) of Labour supporters judged him a capable leader.[22] Ultimately the 'Kinnock factor' was a deterrent to a Labour vote in 1992; he was Labour's 'trust problem' personified.

Arguably Labour's bland and sanitised image may also have taken its toll on the party's attempts to revive its dwindling membership. A recruitment drive, supported by a substantial marketing effort, newspaper advertising and direct mail, was launched in January 1989 with the goal of one million members by the next election. Two years later Labour's individual membership was about 300 000, well below its 1984 and 1985 figures.[23] Kinnock's new model Labour had become less frightening to the electorate, but equally it failed to inspire enthusiasm and de-energised constituency activists who still have an important role to play in mobilising the vote.[24]

The example of both Thatcher and Kinnock demonstrates the limits of marketing as a manipulator of opinion. It was not able to persuade voters that Mrs Thatcher was warm and caring, nor was it able to convince them that Thatcher's individualistic vision was the best one for Britain. Nor could Kinnock's designer-suited and highly protected performance convince voters that he was prime minister material. This conclusion fits the predominant theoretical view of the 'limited effects' of media upon its audience. It should provide comfort to the school of thought which is alarmed by the array of sophisticated weapons marketing may put at the disposal of an unscrupulous power-seeker.

THE GLOBALISATION OF POLITICAL CAMPAIGNING: COPYING THE USA?

All the significant changes and innovations in the last 14 years have their roots in the USA, the undoubted world leader of political marketing. Many of the trends evident in Britain can also be seen in competitive democracies throughout the world, leading to speculation about the 'Americanisation' of political campaigning.

From Latin America, through Europe to India and Australia, Americanisation is seen in both the vocabulary and the technology of campaigning. The tendency to centralised control of campaigns has been evident everywhere. Professional media consultants have swelled in number and increased in influence, especially in the USA, Latin America and, to a lesser extent, in Germany, Japan and France. Where once electoral strategy was determined by party leaders it is now increasingly influenced by the media professionals, relying on in-depth focus group surveys. This trend reached a new peak in Britain with Labour between 1987 and 1992. Although we do not yet have a corps of paid political consultants to compare with the American experience, it is noticeable that the media advisers of the two major parties now look and sound virtually alike. As one Tory adviser said after 1992, 'Woodward, Gould and Mandelson were almost interchangeable'.

The relatively new technologies of focus group surveys, direct mail and computers offering data banks on membership and electorates, are also trends manifest everywhere, except India, where the use of new technology is mixed and direct mail is used hardly at all. 'Pre-campaigns', despite national legislation governing official campaign periods, look likely to become the norm, fulfilling expectations from American experience that political marketing will lengthen campaigns.

Political advertising has become an increasingly high-profile campaign tool, even in countries such as Britain and France, where paid political commercials are banned on television. Paid TV advertising was until the 1980s confined to the Americas and Australia, but by the late 1980s and early 1990s was permitted also in Germany, Italy and Sweden. As deregulation of European broadcasting systems continues and cable and satellite grow, paid advertising seems sure to spread. The broadcasting revolution is devaluing the currency of free party broadcasts, which is the alternative usually offered when paid advertising is banned. Satellite and cable channels are rarely required by law to carry free party broadcasts – Sky News took them voluntarily in 1992 – and hence their value will diminish as the audience fragments across the new services.

There is certainly no groundswell in Britain in favour of paid advertisements, despite the trend to model party broadcasts on commercial advertising.[25] Nor is there likely to be unless and until Britain follows the lead of much of the rest of democratic world and imposes spending ceilings on national campaigns.

Spiralling campaign costs has been another US-led international trend. Presidential elections were brought under some control in 1976 by the allocation of public funds to the main candidates on condition that they adhere to spending limits, some $50 million in 1992. For a wealthy freelance like Ross Perot, however, who claimed to be willing to put up $100 million of his own money, the only ceiling was his own purse. Perot won 19 per cent of the national vote (compared to Clinton's 43 per cent and Bush's 38 per cent), the best vote for a third party candidate since Teddy Roosevelt in 1912. Clearly his campaign would have been impossible without his personal fortune.

The power of money to swamp the airwaves and 'buy' votes was a major impetus behind the 1970s drive to control campaign spending in the USA. The 100 per cent spending advantage which Republican candidates held over the Democrats in the Nixon era was held to be worth about three percentage points in national vote share.[26] On reflection there were other compelling reasons, especially prosperity, to explain Republican success. However the threat of the power of money to the democratic process has prompted similar initiatives, particularly spending controls and public funding, in many countries. Germany has gone furthest down the public funding

Table 8.3   Labour and Conservative campaign expenditures
compared, 1964–92 (£000)

Year	Lab (1)	Con (2)	(1 as % of 2)
1964	538	1233	44
1966	196	350	56
1970	526	630	83
1974 (Feb.)	440	680	65
1974 (Oct.)	524	950	55
1979	1566	2333	67
1983	2300	3833	60
1987	3800	8900	43
1992	7100	10 100	71

route but, in the 1970s and 1980s, Australia, Canada, Japan, the Netherlands, Norway, Spain, Turkey, the USA and Venezuala all moved in this direction and the trend seems set to continue.

Britain under the Conservatives has stood apart, resisting both public funding and national campaign expenditure limits. Yet it is now clear that there are absurd anomalies in Britain's campaign expenditure laws. Dating from the nineteenth century, they impose strict limits on candidates' expenses in the constituency campaigns but put no ceiling at all on spending on the now far more costly national campaigns waged by the parties' central organisations.[27] Until the end of the 1950s, central party expenditure was relatively small at about one-fifth of all campaign spending. At the last two elections national campaign expenditure was double that in the constituencies. The switch to national spending, fuelled mainly by newspaper advertising, gives a clear edge to the Tories, as the wealthiest party (see Table 8.3).[28] Typically the Liberal/Alliance spends a good deal less than Labour. Ratios of Conservative:Labour: Liberal/Alliance central spending at the last four elections were as follows: 12:7:1 in 1979; 12:7:6 in 1983; 12:6:2 in 1987; and 12:9:2 in 1992. Labour and the Liberal Democrats both support increased state funding for parties, but there is unlikely to be any major change while the Conservatives remain in power.

Globalisation: the Limits of American Influence

It is clear that American influence on political campaigning is considerable in Britain and throughout much of the democratic world. As political marketing becomes more thoroughly incorporated, and campaigns more highly orchestrated, so fears grow about the Americanisation of global politics. 'Americanisation' is a loaded term with respect to political conduct, much as it is in the broader debate about global media development. Its meaning is rarely defined and too often taken for granted as a catch-all condemnation of image-conscious campaigning. 'Americanisation' anxiety, routine at British elections at least since 1960, erupted with new force as the Labour Party moved to elect a new leader after the death of John Smith in May 1994. Writing in the *New Statesman*, Tariq Ali offered a typical, scathing assessment of the 'fatal attraction of Americanisation', which threatened to destroy Labour politics. The leading candidate, Tony Blair, was ridiculed as the 'English Clinton': exactly the type of candidate demanded by Americanisation: 'A shallow person, preferably a family man, a male bimbo who looks good on television, someone who can read an autocue with confidence, but, above all, a person not burdened by the deadweight of ideas; especially not social democratic ideas.'[29]

This is 'Americanisation' as a rhetorical device to belittle a (right-wing Labour) opponent, which was the point of Tariq Ali's piece. However, it is not helpful as either description or explanation of British or global developments in political campaigning. It is to be expected that political campaigners around the world will seek to learn lessons from developments in the USA, the global leader in the field, but the ways in which American models are adopted, adapted and rejected varies according to national political and media systems, cultures, tastes and tolerance of electorates and individual parties and politicians.

We have looked at political campaigning in Britain this century and shown that the drive towards marketing has come from within; a response to changing political and electoral circumstances in Britain and the growth of new communications technology. American techniques have been grafted on (for example, recognition of the importance of television, photo-opportunities, direct mail, telephone canvassing) and rejected (presidential-style debates, paid political advertising on television, campaign spending limits). We have argued that, contrary to popular view, campaigns do not seem to have become more coarse or less serious or, even, more dominated by personality. We have demonstrated the limitations of American-style personal image-making in Britain with regard both to Margaret Thatcher and Neil Kinnock.

The limits of American influence globally may be shown by reference to the apparent and much-criticised trend towards personality politics, with leaders encouraged to by-pass party organisation and appeal directly to electorates via television. Critics argue that this trend has hastened the decline of party politics, encouraging voters to judge candidates (leaders) above and apart from their tainted party machines. There is certainly some truth in this with respect to American campaigns, although as Bartels suggests, the evidence is less clear cut than it at first appears.[30] However, it is highly questionable that this is a global trend.

In France and Japan, for example, the reverse may well be the case. De Gaulle established the presidency as an independent bulwark deliberately set apart from the party squabble. In the de Gaulle and Pompidou eras, presidential candidates appealed independently of parties directly to the electorate. But, since Pompidou's death, party influence has grown such that the major presidential candidates now all seek official nomination by their parties. Japan's indigenous democratic tradition is based on candidate-centred, personalised campaigns. Over the last 20 years it has attempted to break with this past with laws restricting candidate campaigns and encouraging national party activities in an attempt to force Japan into the mould of supposedly modern party politics.[31] The attempt has been only partially successful and Japan remains dominated by personality politics. But this has little to do with the American contagion of presidentialism.

Similarly, in Britain leader-focused campaigns cannot be attributed to American influence; leader domination is neither new nor displaying a clear unidirectional trend. Winston Churchill, under the slogan 'Vote for Him' waged a more presidential campaign than any of Mrs Thatcher's. Harold Wilson pushed his personality to the fore and hijacked control of the campaign from party HQ in far more swaggeringly presidential style than Neil Kinnock. Labour waged a less leader-focused campaign in 1992 than in 1987, while the Tories' unabashed concentration on John Major in 1992 represented, not the peak of a trend, but rather a rational answer to a specific set of campaigning circumstances. If Major is still in place by the next election, it is unlikely that the tactic will be repeated.

Thus there is a native British history of leader-focused campaigns and no evidence that this is an intensifying trend. Moreover, as argued above, leaders seem to have relatively minor influence on British voters' choices compared to other factors, such as social class, party identification and policy. Britain still has a relatively strong party system and this will continue to be a major limitation on the scope for American influence. Thus one cannot blame American influence for personality politics in Britain. Moreover, it is too easy and too glib to dismiss personality as a triviality. As *Washington Post* columnist David Broder said of US races, they may not be beauty contests but they *are* personality duels, with voters deciding who they trust most to stand up to pressure, to take difficult decisions, represent the country abroad and so on. The quality of leadership, even in Britain where party is far more important to voters' choices, is a legitimate question to raise in electoral contests.

The limits of American influence may be shown also by reference to another 'US contagion': attack politics or negative campaigning. Kathleen Hall Jamieson, refreshingly, rounds on the tendency of most media and academic commentators to assume that negative campaigning is *necessarily* harmful to political discourse. On the contrary, she argues it is essential for genuine debate and ensures that policy pledges and politicians' reputations are examined.[32] Campaigns composed of entirely promotional material would not serve the public, flaws would be left unexposed and voters misled, unless the media were willing and able to take on the job of opposition.

There is evidence that American negative campaigning has influenced Britain, although of course there is an indigenous tradition of politicians who need no lessons in how to go for the jugular. However, political marketing tends to prescribe negative campaigns, especially in advertising where it is so much easier to attack than to propound. It is noticeable that since the late 1950s, when advertising became an important part of British campaigning, it has become increasingly dominated by aggressive attacks on opponents. The 1992 election seemed to confirm this trend with Labour's health advertising and the Tories' 'tax bombshell' and the 'double whammy', American slang that needed translation for a British audience. However, there is still remarkably little evidence in Britain of personal slanging, a much-criticised feature of US presidential and, especially, congressional campaigns.[33]

Moreover, an ill-judged negative campaign can backfire. The notorious tactics which defeated Dukakis did not work when Bush tried to repeat the treatment on Clinton. The assault on Clinton's character, his patriotism (Clinton's infamous role in anti-Vietnam War protest while at Oxford) and his record as governor of Arkansas all failed to stem the drift from Bush. The US 1992 example also highlights the difficulty of wholesale transfer of campaign tactics from one country to another. The Bush camp, influenced by British experience and with assistance from CCO, built its campaign around trust and tax. As Clinton's communications director George Stephanopoulos put it, 'They're obviously trying to take a cookie cutter, put it on the Tory campaign and bring it to America.'[34] However, Bush's credibility, unlike Major's at that time, was seriously undermined by his tax rise U-turn. 'Read my lips – no new taxes' helped Bush win in 1988; it returned to haunt him in 1992.

The great fear of attack politics, that the democratic process was being ground down to slick and aggressively negative images with the side-effects of an increasingly cynical and apathetic electorate, was not borne out in the 1992 US presidential race. Voter turnout increased, commentators noted that interest in the substantive issues seemed unusually robust and the media, reacting to the 1988 Bush campaign, carried extensive ad-watch analysis, which may well have helped innoculate audiences against the worst of advertising excesses. Perot's best third candidate showing for 80 years broke nearly all the modern rules, as he fought a campaign of swingeing petrol tax rises with virtually no personal attacks on opponents. His crudely made half-hour 'info-commercials' attracted average ratings of 13 million viewers, more than many network soaps.[35]

POLITICAL MARKETING: THE FUTURE

Information technology and the expanding broadcasting market are the two key factors shaping the future of political communications. Computer technology is capable of revolutionising campaigning, transforming market research into an increasingly precise predictive tool, reviving individual contact with voters through more accurately targeted direct mail and injecting new vigour into constituency activities which have been eclipsed by national television campaigns since the late 1950s. While information technology is brimming with opportunities for political marketers, the broadcasting revolution comes laden with challenges and new tests.

Information Technology

Campaign software has become one of the fastest-growing specialities in political consulting in the United States. In Britain it is still a relative newcomer. By 1992 computers were installed in about half the Conservative and Labour local organisations to perform a variety of tasks: to record the canvass, produce letters for direct mail, keep campaign diaries and produce publicity via desktop publishing packages. Nationally, computers are starting to transform central organisations. Ridiculous as it may seem, the major parties (excepting the SDP, as was) had only rough ideas of how many members they had and less idea of who they were: details were held in constituencies and branches and, until the advent of relatively cheap and powerful computers, it was impossible for the national organisation to keep tabs on the constantly changing names and figures.

Central computers have made possible nationally directed mailshots, fund drives and membership schemes.[36] Parties use computers to download electoral rolls on to disc for the constituency canvass and also to provide databases for the organisation of party conferences and press gatherings. A potentially important new use of computers may be in two-way communication with the constituencies. In 1987 Labour experimented with Telecom Gold to keep the local organisations informed of campaign messages. In 1989 the Conservatives undertook a major overhaul of their information technology equipment and evaluated data transmission and electronic mail services – Telecom Gold, Prestel, Viewdata – to see which would best suit their needs. The uses anticipated for two-way communication include a kind of mass opinion poll as the results of canvass returns and the questions of most concern on the doorstep are fed to the centre for analysis. At the same time party headquarters could supply a political database into which the local workers could dip for all the kinds of information, campaign guides and publicity samples which are now sent through the post.

One might also expect that the Richard Wirthlin-pioneered computer models of opinion poll analysis and prediction will be developed further. Research into target areas of the electorate is still relatively crude in British politics by comparison with the commercial sector. Research tracking voters' reception of individual political communications campaigns is also relatively undeveloped and might be expected to attract marketers' attention.

Another United States innovation, satellite conferencing, was pioneered in Europe by the Conservatives in June 1990. Nearly 2000 party workers in five cities were linked by satellite 'teleconference' to London where Health Secretary Kenneth Clarke held a briefing about the NHS reforms. At a cost of £25 000, it was an initiative that proved too costly for the 1992 campaign but may well be considered for the future.[37]

One old technology which is still a new technique in Britain is telephone canvassing, which began to make headway in by-elections prior to the 1987 campaign and was used by the Tories fairly extensively in 1992. One drawback however is that telephone calls count as an election expense whereas the wear and tear of canvasser's shoe leather does not.

The Broadcasting Revolution

Deregulation is another highly significant piece of Margaret Thatcher's marketing legacy and the greatly expanded broadcast market provides the second major source of change and challenge for political communications. The merger of BSB and Sky testifies to the difficulties of sustaining satellite TV services in the middle of a recession. Yet, while the take-off, particularly of cable, continues to be sluggish, we are certainly headed for far greater television choice.

The combination of fiercer competition and the 'lighter touch' rules of the Broadcasting Act 1990 promises that television will become a tougher, less deferential place for political parties. The satellite and cable channels are obliged to report news and current affairs with due impartiality and accuracy, but they are not bound by the conventions of balance which have traditionally governed ITN and BBC political coverage. The conception of balance and the tradition of public service ensured that the old four-channel closed system was uniquely vulnerable at election times to parties' attempts to influence the news agenda. Typically, television devoted extensive coverage to election campaigns and attempted to ensure that the time allocated to the two major parties was roughly equal. Stories which might not have warranted space if judged by normal news values were sometimes included to maintain a fair balance of coverage as between the three major parties.

It is hard to see how the 'stopwatch' conception of balance will survive into a more competitive media market, and indeed, ITN abandoned the stopwatch in 1992. Interest and entertainment criteria are part of routine news values, and the harder TV companies are forced to scrap for audiences the less keen they will be to risk losing viewers with election overkill in the name of public service. Parties will be forced, rather in the manner of their American counterparts, to fight for prime time on bulletins.

Such an outcome may have welcome effects: it may weaken the political marketers' opportunity to massage the agenda and force-feed the media with a diet of carefully concocted risk-free photo-calls. The new broadcasting market also devalues another traditional party communication tool, the Party Political Broadcast. PPBs are required by law to be broadcast only on the terrestial channels and hence their value to the parties will diminish if and when the audience fragments across the satellite services.

However, it is also certain that as soon as one door closes the political marketers will seek to open another. They will examine and attempt to devise new and more effective ways of putting across their messages. One option currently being suggested is a revamp of the present PPB system of five 10-minute or ten 5-minute PPBs a year. Labour media adviser Barry Delaney favours splitting their total 50-minute annual allocation into much shorter commercial-style slots of about one-minute or 30 seconds. A more radical solution would permit paid party advertising on television, capped within expenditure limits. It would offer the parties greater control and flexibility than PPBs, enabling them to select the channel of choice and target viewers more effectively.[38] Political advertising on television is likely to strike the rawest nerve of concern at the use of political marketing; particularly for Britons it tends to symbolise all that is most objectionable in America's dollar-saturated campaigns. There is no doubt that political marketing and its associated techniques have been put to disreputable purposes in the past and certainly will be again. However, just as in commercial advertising the easiest product to advertise is the best product, so in politics the most effective way to create an image of competence, credibility and unity is by actually being competent, united and believable. Marketing reflects the strengths and weaknesses of the democratic process in which it is engaged. For the most part its tools are neutral: they may be employed by the principled and unprincipled politician alike. They have not created the unscrupulous seeker of power, nor banality nor triviality nor dirty tricks nor virtually any of the evils with which marketing is sometimes associated. If anything, campaigns, monitored so closely now on television, are cleaner than before.

Market research brings reality into the often small, closed world of the typical politician; it informs parties of people's real concerns. The marketing concept drives parties to be more democratic, more responsive to the electorate's wishes. The techniques of communication improve the quality of propaganda, heighten interest and can also play a genuinely informative role in the political process. Margaret Thatcher and the Conservatives gave political marketing status, and their victories established its reputation. There is no doubt that it is here to stay and as the technologies of communication become more complex and sophisticated, so the influence of the media experts will grow. Ultimately the use of political marketing for good or ill depends upon the rules of campaigning, the ethics of politicians, the vigilance of opponents and the media, and the political interest and sophistication of the electorate.

Notes

Introduction: Propaganda and Political Marketing

1 Stanley Kelley, *Professional Public Relations and Political Power* (1956) p. 210.
2 Hugo Young and Anne Sloman, *The Thatcher Phenomenon* (1986) p. 94.
3 Ibid., pp. 94–5.
4 See especially *New Statesman*'s election edition, 10 June 1983.
5 For an account of the programme, see *The Listener*, 16 June 1983.
6 Wendy Webster, *Not A Man To Match Her* (1990).
7 Philip Kleinman, *The Saatchi & Saatchi Story* (1987) p. 32.
8 *Campaign*, 30 November 1990.
9 Martin Harrop, 'Political Marketing', in *Parliamentary Affairs*, July 1990, 43(3).
10 Interview with Peter Mandelson at the Labour Party conference, Blackpool, October 1986.
11 'Party Presence', in *Marxism Today*, October 1989.
12 Harrop, op. cit.
13 The £11 million figure is quoted in Eric Clark, *The Want Makers* (1988) p. 312. For a full account of the GLC campaign and its success in shifting public opinion, see Robert Waller, *Moulding Political Opinion* (1988).
14 *Observer*, 24 December 1989.
15 Richard Rose, *Influencing Voters* (1967) p. 13.
16 See Michael Cockerell, *Live from Number 10*, pp. 280–1.
17 Quoted in H.J. Hanham, *Elections and Party Management: Politics in the Time of Disraeli and Gladstone* (1978) p. 202.
18 Serge Chakotin, *The Rape of the Masses: The Psychology of Totalitarian Propaganda* (1939) pp. 131–3.
19 Ibid., p. 171.
20 Ibid.
21 See Max Atkinson, *Our Masters' Voices* (1988) pp. 13–14.
22 Quoted in Michael Thomas, *The Economist Guide to Marketing* (1986).
23 Michael J. Baker, 'One More Time – What is Marketing?', in Michael J. Baker (ed.), *The Marketing Book* (1991).
24 Nicholas O'Shaughnessy, *The Phenomenon of Political Marketing* (1990) p. 2.
25 Harrop, op. cit.
26 O'Shaughnessy, op. cit., p. 23.
27 Michael J. Baker, op. cit.
28 Tom McBurnie and David Clutterbuck, *The Marketing Edge* (1987) p. 7.
29 See, for example, Roland Perry, *The Programming of the President* (1984).
30 O'Shaughnessy, op. cit., pp. 43–5.
31 See Michael J. Baker, op. cit.

299

32 See Keith J. Blois, 'Non-Profit Organisations and Marketing', in Michael J. Baker (ed.), op. cit.

33 John Ramsden, *The Making of Conservative Party Policy* (1980) p. 3.

34 See Richard Kelly, 'Party Organisation', in *Contemporary Record*, April 1991 4(4).

35 The 1988 AGM of the National Union of Conservative and Unionist Associations accepted a Model Rule which obliged constituencies to select candidates only from a list approved by CCO. Although the centrally approved list existed previously, it had not been formally binding on constituency associations.

36 Michael Cassell, 'Hard left softened up as party leadership scents better times', *Financial Times*, 3 October 1989.

37 See Nick Grant (Labour's publicity director), 'A Comment on Labour's Campaign', in I. Crewe and M. Harrop (eds), *Political Communications: The General Election of 1983* (1986).

38 *The Guardian*, 24 April 1991.

39 For an article which captures well the predominant view of the 'presidential' nature of British campaigns, see Richard Holme, 'Selling the PM', in *Contemporary Record*, Spring 1988, vol. 2(1). See also Bob Franklin *Packaging Politics* (1994).

40 Larry Sabato, *The Rise of Political Consultants: New Ways of Winning Elections* (1981).

41 Ibid., p. 7.

42 For a general introduction to the American party system and the effect of campaign finance rules and primary elections, see M.J.C. Vile, *Politics in the USA* (1983). See also Philip John Davies and Fredric Waldstein (eds), *Political Issues in America Today* (1987).

43 Sidney Blumenthal, *The Permanent Campaign* (1982) pp. 22–6.

44 Quoted in O'Shaughnessy, op. cit., p. 5.

45 Sabato, op. cit., p. 37.

46 Roland Perry, op. cit., pp. 153–74.

47 Ibid., pp. 170–1.

48 O'Shaughnessy, op. cit., p. 247.

49 Joseph A. Schumpeter, *Capitalism, Socialism and Democracy*, 5th edn (1976) p. 283.

50 See Jeffrey B. Abramson, F. Christopher Arterton, and Gary R. Orren, *The Electric Commonwealth: The Impact of New Media Technologies on Democratic Politics*, 1988.

51 Frank Luntz, *Candidates, Consultants & Campaigns* (1988) p. 227.

52 See, for example, Kathleen Jamieson, *Packaging the Presidency* (1984) pp. 446–52.

53 Harrop, op. cit.

54 There is debate about whether the media became less vigorous and critical during the period of Thatcher's governments. The main elements from opposite poles are summarised in two articles in *Contemporary Record*: Hugo Young, 'The Media Under Mrs Thatcher', *Contemporary Record*, April 1990, 3(4); Jeremy Tunstall, 'The Media: Lapdogs for Thatcher?', *Contemporary Record*, November 1990, 4(2).

55 Quoted in Sabato, op. cit., p. 144.

56 O'Shaughnessy, op. cit., p. 154.
57 Harrop, op. cit.
58 Hilde T. Himmelweit *et al.*, *How Voters Decide* (1981).
59 See, for example, A. Heath *et al.*, *How Britain Votes* (1985).
60 John Curtice, 'Interim Report: Party Politics', in R. Jowell *et al.*, *British Social Attitudes: The 1987 Report* (1987).
61 Harrop, op. cit.
62 Interview with Sir Tim Bell.
63 Interview with Patricia Hewitt, June 1990.
64 Quoted in Luntz, op. cit., p. x.
65 Interviews with Conservative Party marketing consultants and members of George Bush's presidential campaign team.
66 D. Kavanagh, *Politics and Personalities* (1990) pp. 1–14.

1 Crusted Agent to Media Expert: The Changing Face of Campaigns

1 Lord Windlesham, *Communication and Political Power* (1966) p. 25.
2 H.J. Hanham, *Elections and Party Management: Politics in the Time of Disraeli and Gladstone* (1978) p. 201.
3 Ibid., p. 238.
4 Ibid., p. 237.
5 Ibid., p. 215. A number of historical studies of American political campaigning make a similar point. See, for example: Kathleen Hall Jamieson, *Packaging the Presidency* (1984); Gil Troy, *See How They Ran* (1991).
6 Interview with Joe Haines.
7 Interview with Sir Tim Bell.
8 Quoted in Sidney Blumenthal, *Permanent Campaign* (1982) p. 33.
9 George Creel, *How We Advertised America* (1920) p. 4.
10 Ibid., p. 5.
11 Harold Lasswell, *Propaganda Technique in the World War* (1927) pp. 220–1.
12 T.H. Qalter, *Propaganda and Psychological Warfare* (1962) p. 66.
13 G. Jowett and V. O'Donnell, *Propaganda and Persuasion* (1986) p. 125.
14 Ibid., p. 137.
15 Henry James Houston and Lionel Valdar, *Modern Electioneering Practice* (1922) p. 9.
16 Interim and Final Reports of the Committee on Party Organisation, April and June 1911. Conservative Party Archives.
17 Ibid.
18 Davidson was the fourth party chairman. A. Steel-Maitland was appointed the first party chairman in June 1911 as a result of the report of the Committee on Party Organisation.
19 See Robert Rhodes James, *Memoirs of a Conservative: J.C.C. Davidson's Memoirs* (1969) pp. 270–2.
20 Ibid.
21 See R.R. James, *Anthony Eden* (1986) p. 191.

22　See Peter Stead, 'The British Working Class and Film in the 1930s', in Nicholas Pronay and D.W. Spring (eds), *Propaganda, Politics and Film 1918–45* (1982).

23　Ibid.

24　This account relies on Keith Middlemas, *Politics in Industrial Society* (1979) pp. 131–2.

25　Quoted in Middlemas, ibid., p. 356.

26　See R.D. Casey, 'The National Publicity Bureau and British Party Propaganda', *Public Opinion Quarterly*, iii (1939) p. 624.

27　See Philip M. Taylor, *Projection of Britain* (1981).

28　J.A. Ramsden, 'Baldwin and Film', in Pronay and Spring (eds), op. cit. (1982).

29　Middlemas and Barnes, *Baldwin* (1969) p. 480.

30　Ramsden, op. cit.

31　J. Ramsden, *A History of the Conservative Party: The Age of Balfour and Baldwin* (1978) p. 235.

32　Reports of the Conservative Party Conferences, 1924 and 1929. Conservative Party Archives.

33　See R.R. James, *Memoirs of a Conservative* (1969), p. 303.

34　BARB Establishment Survey, March 1990, quoted in Saatchi & Saatchi, *Media Yearbook 1990*.

35　Research carried out annually for the Independent Broadcasting Authority (now the Independent Television Commission) confirms this. In 1992, for instance, television was cited by 71 per cent as the main source of world news and 62 per cent for UK news.

36　Joseph Klapper, *The Effects of Mass Communication*, (1960).

37　See Martin Harrop, 'Voters', in Jean Seaton and Ben Pimlott (eds), *The Media in British Politics* (1987), for a good summary of research thinking on media effects and voters. For discussion about the present state of communications research, see *European Journal of Communication*, vol. 5, 2–3, June 1990; for good introductions, see O. Boyd-Barrett and P. Braham (eds), *Media, Knowledge and Power* (1987).

38　The terms 'marketing research' and 'market research' are now used interchangeably, but originally there was a difference. 'Marketing research' was the more comprehensive concept, covering all market investigation, while 'market research' was narrowly limited to research about a particular product.

39　For an introduction to market research, see Peter Chisnall, *Marketing Research* (1981).

40　Letter to *The Times*, 23 April 1965. It should be noted that Hutchinson's comments were almost certainly a criticism of Labour's campaign.

41　Lord Windlesham, op. cit., p. 79.

42　Robert Blake, *The Conservative Party from Peel to Churchill* (1979) p. 259.

43　Ibid., p. 260.

44　See Middlemas, op. cit., p. 355.

45　T.F. Lindsay and Michael Harrington, *The Conservative Party 1918–70* (1974) p. 159.

46　Minutes of the Tactical Staff Committee, 23 July 1947 and 3 September 1947. Archives of the Conservative Party.

47 Ibid., 17 June 1947.
48 Ibid., especially minutes for January and February 1948.
49 Blake, op. cit., p. 262.
50 H.G. Nicholas, *The British General Election of 1950* (1951) p. 122.
51 Ibid., p. 39.
52 Ibid., p. 107.
53 Lord Windlesham, op. cit., p. 36.
54 Ibid., p. 51.
55 See D. Butler and R. Rose, *The British General Election of 1959* (1960) p. 32.
56 House of Commons Debates, *Hansard*, vol. 627, col. 788, 21 July 1960.
57 Lord Windlesham, op. cit., pp. 54–5.
58 Andrew Gamble, *The Conservative Nation* (1974) p. 67.
59 Interview with Enoch Powell, 1986.
60 Quoted in Butler and Rose, op. cit., p. 54.
61 Ibid., p. 26.
62 See Michael Cockerell, *Live from Number 10* (1988) p. 78.
63 Quoted in M. Cockerell, ibid., p. 67.
64 Ibid., p. 71.
65 Ibid., p. 74.
66 Richard Rose, *Influencing Voters* (1967) p. 86.
67 D. Butler and A. King, *The British General Election of 1964* (1965) p. 90.
68 Abrams' survey was based on a 12-page questionnaire answered by 724 people. See M. Abrams and R. Rose, *Must Labour Lose?* (1960).
69 Ibid., p. 71
70 Butler and King, op. cit., p. 70.
71 M. Cockerell, op. cit., p. 87.
72 Sir Robin Day, *Grand Inquisitor* (1989) p. 256.
73 (Sir) G. Pattie, 'Marketing the Tories', *Crossbow*, 12(47) April–June 1969.
74 Quoted in Butler and King, op. cit., p. 92.
75 See Mireille Babaz, *Le Rôle de la Publicité dans les Campagnes Electorales Britanniques* (1977) p. 199.
76 Ibid., pp. 206–8.
77 Interview with Joe Haines.
78 Interview with Lord Fraser of Kilmorack, November 1987.
79 Interview with Joe Haines.
80 D. Butler and M. Pinto-Duschinsky, *The British General Election of 1970* (1971) p. 153.
81 Cockerell, op. cit., p. 158.
82 Andrew Alexander and Alan Watkins, *The Making of the Prime Minister 1970* (1970) p. 170.
83 Ibid., p. 173.
84 Ibid., p. 187.
85 Quoted in Cockerell op. cit., p. 162.
86 Barry Day, 'The Politics of Communication' in R. Worcester and M. Harrop (eds), *Political Communications: The General Election Campaign of 1979* (1982).
87 Ibid.

88 Ibid.
89 For a post-mortem on the 1970 opinion polls, see Butler and Pinto-Duschinsky, op. cit.
90 Ibid.

2 The Rise of Thatcher: Political Marketing's Quantum Leap

1   Norman Tebbit, *Upwardly Mobile* (1989) pp. 171–80.
2   See Nicholas Wapshott and George Brock, *Thatcher* (1983) p. 110.
3   There are many accounts of the leadership race and all the biographies contain versions. The best accounts are to be found in: Wapshott and Brock, op. cit., and Nigel Fisher, *The Tory Leaders: Their Struggle for Power* (1977). For accounts of the tumult about policy see Dennis Kavanagh, *Thatcherism and British Politics* (1987); Hugo Young, *One of Us* (1989); and Jock Bruce-Gardyne, *Mrs Thatcher's First Administration: The Prophets Confounded* (1984).
4   Wapshott and Brock, op. cit., p. 121.
5   Jean Rook, 'Woman of Destiny', in *The First Ten Years* (1989).
6   Max Atkinson, *Our Masters' Voices* (1988) p. 112.
7   In an interview with *TV Times*, some 15 years later, in November 1990, Mrs Thatcher insisted that she still hated seeing herself on television.
8   See Hugo Young, op. cit., pp. 124–6.
9   Barbara Castle, *The Castle Diaries 1974–76* (1980) p. 332.
10 Quoted in Michael Cockerell, *Live from No. 10* (1988) p. 213.
11 Ivan Fallon, *The Brothers* (1988) p. 149.
12 See Michael Cockerell, op. cit., p. 217.
13 Ibid., p. 217.
14 Ivan Fallon, op. cit., p. 150.
15 Ibid., p. 151.
16 Ibid., p. 151.
17 Hugo Young, op. cit., p. 125.
18 Interview with David Boddy, May 1987.
19 Mireille Babaz, *Le Rôle de la Publicité dans les Campagnes Electorales Britanniques de 1964, 1966 et 1970* (1977).
20 Fallon, op. cit., p. 153.
21 Ibid.
22 The account given here relies heavily on Philip Kleinman, *The Saatchi & Saatchi Story* (1987).
23 Ibid., p. 15.
24 Ibid., p. 25.
25 Quoted in Fallon, op. cit., p. 154.
26 Ibid., pp. 147–9.
27 Interview with Tim Bell, October 1986.
28 Tim Bell, 'The Conservative Advertising Campaign', in R. Worcester and M. Harrop (eds), *Political Communications: The General Election Campaign of 1979* (1982).
29 Fallon, op. cit., p. 157.
30 Interview with Bell, October 1986.

31   Quoted in Tim Bell, 'The Conservative Advertising Campaign', in Worcester and Harrop (eds), op. cit.

32   Ibid.

33   Ibid.

34   Unattributable interview with a CCO official.

35   For details of audience reaction to PPBs, see Barrie Gunter *et al.*, *Television Coverage of the 1983 Election* (1986).

36   Interview with Bell, October 1986.

37   Tim Delaney, 'Labour's Advertising Campaign', in Worcester and Harrop (eds), op. cit.

38   Bell, in Worcester and Harrop (eds), op. cit.

39   Ibid.

40   Tony Benn's diary entry for 7 September 1978 details the Cabinet meeting at which Callaghan announced his decision. Callaghan was said to be swayed by factors such as the devolution referendum and polls which suggested that Labour voters did not want an election. See Tony Benn, *Conflicts of Interest: Diaries 1977–80* (1990) p. 334.

41   Fallon, op. cit., p. 160.

42   Lord Whitelaw, *The Whitelaw Memoirs* (1989) p. 159.

43   D. Butler and G. Butler, *British Political Facts 1900–1985* (1986).

44   Bernard Donoughue, *Prime Minister* (1987).

45   Benn, op. cit., pp. 244 and 292.

46   D. Butler and D. Kavanagh, *The British General Election of 1979* (1980), p. 85.

47   Tim Bell, in Worcester and Harrop (eds), op. cit., p. 14.

48   The full text of the advertisement is reproduced in Worcester and Harrop, op. cit.

49   Ibid.

50   For a contemporary assessment, see Tony Benn, op. cit., p. 494; also Butler and Kavanagh, op. cit.

51   Hugo Young, op. cit., p. 128.

52   Butler and Kavanagh, op. cit., p. 78.

53   Ibid., p. 83.

54   Ibid., p. 64.

55   Ivor Crewe and Bo Sarlvik, 'Popular Attitudes and Electoral Strategy', in Zig Layton-Henry (ed.), *Conservative Party Politics* (1980).

56   Unattributable interview with Downing Street aide.

57   Wapshott and Brock, op. cit., pp. 155–6. It should be noted, however, that another biographer, Patrick Cosgrave, disputes this version.

58   Cockerell, op. cit., p. 247.

59   Butler and Kavanagh, op. cit., p. 172.

60   For an account of Labour's campaign, see Tim Delaney, 'Labour's Advertising Campaign', in Worcester and Harrop, op. cit. See also Butler and Kavanagh, op. cit.

61   Cockerell, op. cit., p. 248.

62   See Butler and Kavanagh, op. cit., p. 323.

63   Peregrine Worsthorne, in *Sunday Telegraph*, 14 May 1978.

64   Butler and Kavanagh, op. cit., p. 165.

65   Cockerell, op. cit., pp. 233–5.

66   Patrick Cosgrave, *Margaret Thatcher – A Tory and Her Party* (1978) p. 209.
67   Cockerell, op. cit., p. 248.
68   Ibid., p. 250. Reece's attention to apparently minor detail shocked Roger Bolton, then a young producer for the BBC, who went on to make *Death on the Rock* at Thames TV: Reece would check the colour of the set, the flowers and the furniture, whereas other political press aides pressed for details of the likely questioning; see Cockerell, p. 233.
69   See Barry Day, 'The Politics of Communication', in R. Worcester and M. Harrop (eds), *Political Communication: The General Election Campaign of 1979* (1982).
70   Quoted in Butler and Kavanagh, op. cit., p. 323.
71   The polling figures quoted in this passage are taken from Butler and Kavanagh, op. cit., p. 323.
72   ITN, *British Voting Trends 1979–1987* (1987).
73   Most polls listed these five as the top issues, although not necessarily in this order. The particular value of the Harris exit poll is that it is a measure of people who actually *voted*, when about 25 per cent of those eligible did not.
74   MORI, *British Public Opinion*, June 1987.
75   Interview with a Conservative Party pollster.
76   Donoughue, op. cit., p. 191.
77   Tim Delaney, op. cit., pp. 27–31.
78   Interview with Bell, October 1986.
79   See Butler and Kavanagh, op. cit., pp. 319–20.

3   Marketing Triumphant: Falklands Fallout

1   For an excellent account of the economic difficulties and policies in this period, see Peter Riddell, *The Thatcher Government* (1983).
2   Gallup polls quoted in D. Butler and G. Butler, *British Political Facts 1900–1985* (1986).
3   Some scholars doubt the long-term impact of the Falklands, arguing that it had little effect on voting decisions at the 1983 election. See, for example, Ivor Crewe, 'Why Labour Lost the Election', *Public Opinion*, July 1983.
4   For inside accounts of the early conflicts within the Cabinet, see Jock Bruce-Gardyne, *Mrs Thatcher's First Administration* (1984), James Prior, *A Balance of Power* (1986) and Peter Hennessy, 'The Prime Minister, the Cabinet and the Thatcher Personality', in K. Minogue and M. Biddiss (eds), *Thatcherism* (1987).
5   Denis Healey, *The Time of My Life* (1989) p. 488.
6   Ibid. (Thorneycroft, although party chairman, was not actually a member of the Cabinet. It does not diminish Healey's point, however.)
7   *Daily Mail*, 1 May 1982.
8   Quoted in Hugo Young, *One of Us* (1989) p. 396.
9   Speech at the Conservative Party Annual Conference, Brighton, 10 October 1980.

10 Quoted in Wendy Webster, *Not A Man to Match Her* (1990) p. 156.
11 Ibid.
12 Andrew Thomson, *Margaret Thatcher: The Woman Within* (1989) p. 179.
13 Denis Healey, op. cit., p. 499.
14 Wendy Webster, op. cit., p. 85.
15 David Owen, *Personally Speaking* (1987) p. 199.
16 Margaret Thatcher, speech at a Conservative rally, Cheltenham race course, 3 July 1982, CCO press release.
17 Michael Cockerell, *Live from Number 10* (1988) p. 275.
18 See Wendy Webster, op. cit., pp. 72–3.
19 The MORI poll analysis of the Falklands is taken from Robert Worcester, 'Changes in Politics', in Madsen Pirie (ed.), *A Decade of Revolution* (1989).
20 Ibid. (Opinion eventually became equivocal on the merits of the Suez adventure, but Eden's personal rating remained high. Although he was to resign, owing to ill-health, his party went on to win a landslide in 1959.)
21 Tam Dalyell, *Misrule* (1987) p. 6.
22 For accounts of government information, censorship and media coverage, see Glasgow University Media Group, *War and Peace News* (1985); Robert Harris, *Gotcha!* (1983); Michael Cockerell *et al.*, *Sources Close to the Prime Minister* (1984); D. Morrison and H. Tumber, *Journalists at War*; for accounts of alleged misinformation and deception, see Clive Ponting, *The Right to Know* (1985) and Dalyell, op. cit.
23 Quoted in Michael Cockerell, *Live from Number 10*, p. 272.
24 Ibid., p. 272.
25 Ibid.
26 Bernard Ingham, *Kill the Messenger* (1991) pp. 294–7.
27 See Nicholas Jones, BBC political correspondent, in *The Guardian*, 4 March 1991.
28 Glasgow University Media Group, op. cit., p. 172.
29 Ibid., p. 173.
30 Ibid., p. 174.
31 Ibid., p. 8.
32 Ingham, op. cit., p. 286.
33 House of Commons Defence Committee, *The Handling of the Press and Public Information during the Falklands Conflict*, HMSO, 8 December 1982, vol. II, p. xxxviii.
34 Ibid., vol. II, pp. 66–7.
35 Glasgow University Media Group, op. cit., p. 9.
36 Ingham, op. cit., p. 290.
37 For an account of the battle between Ingham and Cooper, see R. Harris, *Good and Faithful Servant* (1990) pp. 93–100.
38 Ingham, op. cit., pp. 288–9.
39 Quoted in R. Harris, op. cit., p. 99.
40 Ingham, op. cit., p. 284.
41 Defence Committee, op. cit., vol. II, pp. 76–7.
42 Interview with David Boddy, May 1987.
43 See *Sunday Telegraph*, 24 January 1982.

44 D. Butler and D. Kavanagh, *The British General Election of 1983* (1984) pp. 333–4.
45 Interview with David Boddy, May 1987.
46 Ibid.
47 Ibid.
48 Harvey Thomas, *Making an Impact* (1989) p. 177.
49 Ibid., p. 111.
50 For a discussion of the benefits that the sincerity machine can bestow, see Max Atkinson, *Our Masters' Voices* (1988).
51 Thomas, op. cit., p. 15.
52 Interview with Harvey Thomas, July 1988.
53 Thomas, op. cit., p. 15.
54 Unattributable interview with a Thomas aide.
55 Thomas, op. cit., p. 136.
56 Ibid., p. 172.
57 Ibid., p. 144.
58 Butler and Kavanagh, *The British General Election of 1983* (1984), p. 36.
59 Interview with David Boddy, May 1987.
60 Young, op. cit., p. 329.
61 Quoted in Young, ibid., p. 323.
62 See Butler and Kavanagh, op. cit., pp. 38–9.
63 Ibid., p. 62.
64 Nick Grant, 'A Comment on Labour's Campaign', in I. Crewe and M. Harrop (eds), *Political Communications* (1986), p. 82.
65 *Listener*, 16 June 1983.
66 See Tony Benn, *Conflicts of Interest: Diaries 1977–80* (1990); also Robert Harris, *The Making of Neil Kinnock* (1984).
67 For a tabloid-style exposé of the *Sun*'s leading role in the assault on the 'loony left', see Peter Chippindale and Chris Horne, *Stick It Up Your Punter* (1990).
68 Cecil Parkinson, 'The Conservative Campaign', in Crewe and Harrop (eds), op. cit.
69 *Listener*, 16 June 1983.
70 Ibid.
71 Butler and Kavanagh, op. cit.
72 Ibid., p. 269.
73 *Listener*, op. cit.
74 Butler and Kavanagh, op. cit., pp. 208–12.
75 Parkinson, op. cit., p. 60.
76 M. Pinto-Duschinsky, 'Financing the General Election of 1983', in Crewe and Harrop (eds), op. cit., p. 290.
77 Crewe and Harrop, op. cit., p. 81.
78 Quoted in Butler and Kavanagh, op. cit., p. 106.
79 Interview with Sir Tim Bell.
80 Butler and Kavanagh, op. cit., pp. 149–50.
81 Ivan Fallon, *The Brothers* (1988), p. 179.
82 See Butler and Kavanagh, op. cit., p. 151.
83 Ibid., pp. 151–3.

84   For a detailed account of the Alliance's 1983 campaign, see H. Semetko, 'Political Communications and Party Development in Britain: The Social Democratic Party from its Origins to the General Election of 1983' PhD Thesis, University of London, 1987.
85   Butler and Kavanagh, op. cit., p. 155.
86   Ibid.
87   Ibid., p. 276.
88   Nick Grant, op. cit.
89   Ibid.
90   Butler and Kavanagh, op. cit., p. 272.
91   *Listener,* 16 June 1983.
92   For contrasting accounts of the argument about the Alliance leadership, see David Steel, *Against Goliath* (1989), pp. 245–6 and David Owen, op. cit., p. 221.

4   Towards the Permanent Campaign: the 1987 Election

1   Norman Tebbit, *Upwardly Mobile* (1989) pp. 302–3.
2   See D. Butler and D. Kavanagh, *The British General Election of 1987* (1988) pp. 27–9.
3   *Public Opinion Background Note 155,* 29 September 1986, Special Services Department, Conservative Central Office.
4   Rodney Tyler, *Campaign!* (1987) pp. 36–8.
5   Butler and Kavanagh, op. cit., p. 33.
6   Anonymous source.
7   Unattributable interview.
8   Peter Mandelson and Patricia Hewitt, 'The Labour Campaign', in I. Crewe and M. Harrop (eds), *Political Communications: The General Election Campaign of 1987* (1989).
9   John Sharkey, 'Saatchi's and the 1987 Election', in Crewe and Harrop, ibid.
10   Unattributable interview.
11   Norman Tebbit, op. cit., p. 331.
12   Ibid., p. 326.
13   Private sources from both CCO and Downing Street are relied on in this account.
14   The target groups for direct mail are taken from the *Blue Book.*
15   Tebbit, op. cit., p. 313.
16   Interview with Michael Dobbs.
17   'Letter from Kinnock Steel Thatcher Owen', *The Observer Magazine,* 17 May 1987.
18   The British electoral system notoriously squeezes third parties to the advantage of the two major parties. If the third party's vote is spread more or less uniformly across the country, as was the case with the Alliance, it can expect a meagre return in seats. The anomaly was never more clear than in 1983 when Labour won 186 more seats than the Alliance with only a 2 per cent greater share of the vote. For a discussion of the merits and demerits of the British electoral system,

see V. Bogdanor and D. Butler (eds), *Democracy and Elections* (1983) and J. Curtice and M. Steed, 'Proportionality and Exaggeration in the British Electoral System', in *Electoral Studies*, 1986, vol. 5, pp. 209–28.

19   For an analysis of the changing political geography of Britain, see R.J. Johnston *et al.*, *A Nation Dividing* (1988).

20   A joint BBC/ITN study calculated what the result of the 1979 election would have been if conducted under the 1983 boundaries. It concluded that the Conservatives would have won an additional 21 seats, Labour would have lost 10 and the Liberals two. See BBC/ITN, *The BBC/ITN Guide to the New Parliamentary Constituencies* (1983).

21   Interview with Paul Medlicott, media adviser to David Steel.

22   *Financial Times*, 12 May 1987.

23   Unattributable interview with a Downing Street aide.

24   Unattributable interview.

25   *In Touch* was a leaflet designed by CCO for local adaptation and doorstep delivery. Based on the Liberal community leaflets, it was devised by David Boddy.

26   *The Blue Book*, December 1986 draft, p. 106.

27   Interview with Tom Arnold, September 1987.

28   See Butler and Kavanagh, op. cit., pp. 139–62.

29   See Barrie Axford and Peter Madgwick, 'Indecent Exposure?', in Crewe and Harrop, op. cit.

30   See Colin Munro, 'Legal Controls on Election Broadcasting', in Crewe and Harrop (eds), *Political Communications: The General Election Campaign of 1983* (1986).

31   *The Economist*, 13 June 1987. See also Blumler *et al.*, 'The Earnest Versus the Determined: Election Newsmaking at the BBC, 1987', in I. Crewe and M. Harrop (eds), *Political Communications: The General Election Campaign of 1987* (1989).

32   See Sharkey, 'Saatchi's and the 1987 Election', in Crewe and Harrop, ibid.

33   See Norman Tebbit, op. cit., pp. 323–5.

34   Interview with a leading campaign official.

35   Interview with Patricia Hewitt.

36   Butler and Kavanagh, op. cit., p. 159.

37   Ibid., p. 217.

38   Pardoe called the 1987 election campaign the 'most dispiriting experience of my political life'. See John Pardoe, 'The Alliance Campaign', in Crewe and Harrop, *Political Communications* (1989).

39   In Butler and Kavanagh, op. cit.

40   Wall was the Downing Street officer who set up a photo-opportunity of the prime minister running along a beach with a King Charles spaniel named Polo while on holiday in Cornwall. The resulting news pictures much impressed CCO and Mrs Thatcher's personal team, and effectively established Wall's reputation with them.

41   Lord Young, *The Enterprise Years* (1990) p. 210.

42   Norman Tebbit, speaking to the Political Communications Conference, University of Essex, 23 October, 1987.

43 Interview with campaign official.
44 Rodney Tyler, op. cit., p. 190.
45 Lord Young, op. cit., p. 217.
46 Interview with CCO official.
47 Terry Coleman, *Thatcher's Britain*, p. 37. Coleman's book is a superb colour-piece commentary of the 1987 campaign (1987).
48 Unattributable interview.
49 Sharkey speaking at the University of Essex, Political Communications Conference, October 1987.
50 Newspaper circulation and partisanship since 1945 is examined in D. Butler, *British General Elections since 1945* (1989).
51 See Brian MacArthur, 'The National Press', in Crewe and Harrop, *Political Communications* (1989).
52 See Butler and Kavanagh, op. cit., p. 183.
53 Ibid., p. 141.
54 I. Crewe and M. Harrop (eds), *Political Communications: The British General Election of 1987* (1989), p. 47.
55 Lord Young, op. cit., pp. 224–5.
56 This account of campaign costs relies on M. Pinto-Duschinsky, 'Financing the British General Election of 1987', in Crewe and Harrop *Political Communications* (1989) and Media Expenditure Analysis Ltd.
57 Pinto-Duschinsky, ibid., p. 16.
58 Ibid., p. 280.
59 *The Guardian*, 15 June 1987.
60 Pre-campaign activities differ from mid-term campaigns in that they are specifically and consciously interwoven with the general election campaign strategy; mid-term campaigns may be discrete events usually concerned with single issues.
61 The proportion of the electorate professing party partisan identity declined from 80 per cent in 1964 to about 70 per cent in 1983. The proportion who declare strong allegiance tumbled more steeply from 44 per cent in 1964 to 26 per cent in 1983. The process of dealignment results in increasing voter volatility, especially in by-elections and mid-term opinion polls, and the growth of the minor parties. See B. Sarlvik and I. Crewe, *A Decade of Dealignment* (1983). Himmelweit *et al.* (1985) dispute that volatility is increasing and argue instead that floating voters constituted about one-third of the electorate consistently throughout the 1970s and 1980s. See also A. Heath *et al., Understanding Political Change* (1991).
62 There is not space here to do justice to the Alliance campaign. For inside accounts of the campaign's many tensions and mistakes, see John Pardoe, op. cit.; Des Wilson, *Battle for Power* (1987); David Steel, *Against Goliath* (1989); and David Owen, *Personally Speaking* (1987).
63 Interview with Paul Medlicott, June 1987.
64 See M. Scammell, 'The Impact of Marketing and Public Relations on Modern British Politics: The Conservative Party and Government under Mrs Thatcher', PhD, University of London, 1991.
65 See *Campaign*, 3 July 1987.

66   Margaret Thatcher, *The Downing Street Years* (1993) pp. 580–1.

67   P. Hewitt and P. Mandelson, 'The Labour Campaign', in Crewe and Harrop, *Political Communications* (1989) p. 54.

68   The figure of 16 per cent was quoted by Peter Mandelson at press briefings in the days following the PEB.

69   Mandelson confirmed that he had been approached, but did not appear to take the offer too seriously, believing that it would be impossible for someone of his political persuasion to work successfully for an agency noted for Conservative clients. Interview with Mandelson, September 1987.

70   Quoted in *Campaign*, 7 August 1987.

71   Labour ran 22 different press advertisements during the campaign. These concentrated on health, education, unemployment, poverty and crime. Only one, concerning Britain's investment record, might be said to be a purely 'economic' advertisement.

72   John Curtice, 'Interim Report: Party Politics', in R. Jowell, S. Wither-spoon and L. Brook (eds), *British Social Attitudes: The 1987 Report* (1987).

73   Interview with Patricia Hewitt, June 1990.

74   Norman Tebbit, *Upwardly Mobile*, p. 332.

75   Unattributable interview with former Number 10 aide.

76   There are a number of stories about Bell which have wide circulation within the advertising world. In one, Bell, at a party for Kenny Everett at the restaurant Chez Gerrard, began to tell ribald anecdotes about Mrs Thatcher and make derisory comments about her 'twit' son Mark. The comments appeared in the press verbatim because a journalist, unknown to Bell, joined the table with a tape recorder. See Ivan Fallon, *The Brothers* (1988) p. 177.

77   Margaret Thatcher, op. cit., p. 354. See also Ian MacGregor, *The Enemies Within* (1986) pp. 255–8.

78   Hart's guests at these annual meetings have included Bell, Lord Young, Richard Perle, former White House defence adviser and Michael Forsyth, former chairman of the Conservative Party in Scotland. Cecil Parkinson has been billed as guest speaker but not appeared.

79   See Fallon, op. cit., pp. 169–84.

80   See Lord Young, op. cit., pp. 218–24.

81   Ibid., p. 222.

82   Unattributable interview with member of the Lowe Howard-Spink & Bell agency, August 1987.

83   Unattributable interview.

84   Butler and Kavanagh, *The British General Election of 1987*, p. 28.

85   Among the rumours reaching the prime minister was one that Norman Tebbit had approached Geoffrey Howe to talk about unseating Mrs Thatcher. Unattributable sources for this thesis confirmed that such a rumour was circulating and was indeed picked up in Downing Street, although it was not given much credence.

86   Lord Young, op. cit., p. 191.

87   Unattributable interview with a CCO official.

88   Unattributable interview with CCO official.

89   *New Statesman*, 24 July 1987.

5 Government Publicity: Managing the News

1 For accounts of these issues, and government secrecy generally, see Clive Ponting, *Right to Know* (1985) and *Whitehall: Tragedy and Farce* (1986); Michael Cockerell *et al.*, *Sources Close to the Prime Minister* (1984); Peter Hennessy, *Whitehall* (1990); and Peter Golding *et al.* (eds), *Communicating Politics* (1986).

2 See Valerie Adams, *The Media and the Falklands Campaign* (1986); Glasgow University Media Group, *War and Peace News* (1985); D. Morrison and H. Tumber, *Journalists at War* (1988); Carla Garapedian, 'Media Coverage and Government Policy Presentation' (1987); and J.E. Wentz, 'A Comparative Study of Mass Media Operations' (1988).

3 See, for example, Michael Leapman, *The Last Days of the Beeb* (1987); Michael Cockerell, *Live from Number 10* (1988); and Roger Bolton, *Death on the Rock* (1990).

4 Sir Fife Clark, *Central Office of Information* (1970) p. 157.

5 See William Crofts, *Coercion or Persuasion?* (1989) p. 218.

6 Ibid., p. 219.

7 Interview with Ross Barr.

8 Harold Wilson, *The Governance of Britain* (1976) p. 119.

9 John Ramsden, *The Making of Conservative Party Policy* (1980) pp. 5–6.

10 See, for example, 'The Word According to Whitehall', in *The Independent*, 10 May 1989.

11 Bernard Ingham, *Kill The Messenger* (1991) pp. 348–9.

12 Ingham's irritation with *Today* presenter, the late Brian Redhead, caused him to refuse all the programme's requests for interviews with the prime minister: ibid., p. 354.

13 Ibid., p. 356.

14 Roger Bolton, 'The Problems of Making Political Television', in P. Golding *et al.* (eds), *Communicating Politics* (1986).

15 Roger Bolton, *Death on the Rock* (1990).

16 *The Independent*, 17 May 1989.

17 Bernard Ingham, speech to the Guild of British Newspaper Editors, Cardiff, May 1983.

18 Christine Wall went to CCO before the 1987 general election and later became CCO Director of Information; Rose Padwick, Ingham's secretary, left Downing Street to become Christine Wall's secretary in September 1989; and former Downing Street press officer Alex Pagget served as chief press officer in the Conservative Scottish office.

19 For a discussion of the guiding philosophy of the Civil Service and the effect of the Thatcher Factor, see Peter Hennessy, *Whitehall* (1990).

20 Ingham, op. cit., p. 225.

21 Interview with Bevins shown on 'Good and Faithful Servant', *Dispatches*, Channel 4, November 1990.

22 Ingham, op. cit., p. 199.

23 Interview on *Frost on Sunday*, TV-am, 12 May 1991.

24 Ingham, op. cit., p. 351.

25 Ibid., p. 364.

26 Ibid., pp. 198–9.
27 Ibid., p. 343.
28 For accounts of Ingham's background in the Yorkshire provincial press, the *Guardian* and in the GIS, see Robert Harris, *Good and Faithful Servant* (1990), and Ingham, op. cit.
29 Harris, ibid., pp. 2–3.
30 Ingham, op. cit., p. 115.
31 According to Harris, James failed to win Thatcher's confidence and the lobby soon found him a 'complete disaster'. Harris, op. cit., p. 71.
32 Ibid., pp. 70–73.
33 Powell was seconded to Number 10 from the Foreign Office in 1984. He was retained at Number 10 by John Major until 1991.
34 For a comparison between Ingham and previous press secretaries, see Colin Seymour-Ure, 'The Prime Minister's Press Secretary', *Contemporary Record*, Autumn 1989, 3(1).
35 See Marcia Williams, *Inside Number 10* (1972) pp. 219–29.
36 Interview with Sir Tom McCaffrey.
37 Ingham, op. cit., p. 169.
38 Lord Donoughue, *Prime Minister* (1987) p. 165.
39 P. Dunleavy *et al.*, 'Prime Ministers and the Commons: Patterns of Behaviour, 1868–1987', *Public Administration* (1990).
40 *Scotland on Sunday*, 30 July 1989.
41 See D. Butler, *British General Elections Since 1945* (1989) Table 10.1, pp. 93–4.
42 Murdoch's Sky channels were not regarded as domestic television because they were transmitted from a foreign-owned satellite. For an inside account of the tussle to take over *The Times* and *Sunday Times*, see Harold Evans, *Good Times Bad Times* (1983); see also William Shawcross, *Murdoch* (1992).
43 James Prior, *A Balance of Power* (1986) p. 134.
44 Ingham, op. cit., p. 236.
45 Ibid., p. 357. The proposals referred to were contained in the white paper, *Broadcasting in the '90s*, November 1988.
46 For example, Haines is credited by Donoughue with persuading Wilson to accept a voluntary rather than statutory pay policy. Haines also tried to persuade Wilson to adopt a policy of selling council houses to tenants. See Donoughue, *Prime Minister* (1987) pp. 68–9, 106–7; also Joe Haines, *The Politics of Power* (1977).
47 Interview with McCaffrey.
48 Ingham, op. cit., p. 162.
49 Interview with McCaffrey.
50 See Seymour-Ure, op. cit.
51 Ibid.
52 Ingham, op. cit., pp. 368–9.
53 The IPCS lodged 'fundamental objections in principle to the post of Head of Profession . . . being vested in the holder of a post which has such a close political identification with the Prime Minister . . .': Elizabeth Jenkins, Assistant Secretary of the IPCS, to Barry Sutlieff, Head of Information, Department of Employment, 27 April 1989.

54 Jean Caines (Environment and latterly DTI), Brian Mower (Home Office and latterly FCO), Jim Coe (Agriculture and latterly Education), and Romola Christopherson (Health). Additionally Hugh Colver (Defence) and Mike Granatt (Energy) both did stints at the Number 10 press office.
55 Ingham, op. cit., pp. 370–71.
56 Harris, op. cit., p. 119.
57 Ingham, op. cit., p. 368.
58 Jenkins to Sutlieff, op. cit.
59 Quoted in *The Times*, 7 May 1990.
60 Tyler, *Campaign!* (1987) p. 16.
61 Unattributable interview.
62 Ingham, op. cit., p. 319.
63 Ibid., pp. 322–3.
64 Interview, *Dispatches*, Channel 4.
65 Quoted in the *Financial Times*, 3 February 1989.
66 *Hansard*, 28 April 1986, col. 762.
67 Ingham, op. cit., pp. 325–8.
68 Ibid., p. 319.
69 Ibid., p. 335. For an alternative account of the Westland leak, written without benefit of Ingham's explanation, see Harris, op. cit., pp. 128–42.
70 Ingham, op. cit., p. 331.
71 Ibid., p. 332.
72 Harris, op. cit., p. 163.
73 Ingham, op. cit., p. 320.
74 Interview with Chris Moncrieff, January 1986. *The Guardian*'s Ian Aitken affectionately likened Ingham to a 'gingery Father Bear' and said he was probably the best press secretary since Harold Evans served Harold Macmillan: *Guardian*, 16 May 1991.
75 Ingham, op. cit., pp. 368–9.
76 Neville Taylor, 'Behind the Whitehall Curtain', *British Journalism Review* (1989) 1(1).
77 Interview with Boddy.
78 *Mail on Sunday*, 22 November 1987.
79 Private conversation.
80 Ingham, op. cit., p. 394.
81 Marcia Williams, *Inside Number 10* (1972) p. 222.
82 Seymour-Ure, op. cit.
83 Ibid.
84 Francis Williams, *Parliament, Press and the Public* (1946) pp. 136–7. Williams was press secretary to Clement Attlee.
85 Peter Hennessy, *Whitehall* (1990) p. 365.
86 See Jeremy Tunstall, *The Westminster Lobby Correspondents* (1970).
87 *Secrets*, newspaper of the Campaign for Freedom of Information, May 1989, no. 17.
88 Minutes of the Lobby Inquiry Meetings: Owen and Steel, 15 November 1984.
89 Steel to David Hughes, Honorary Secretary of the Parliamentary Lobby Journalists, 17 November 1986.

90   Lobby Inquiry minute, 4 December 1984.
91   Report of the Inquiry into Lobby Practice, 10 December 1984.
92   Report of the Inquiry into Lobby Practice, December 1986.
93   Jon Hibbs, submission to the Lobby Inquiry, 18 November 1986.
94   David Rose, submission to the Lobby Inquiry, 5 November 1986.
95   Colin Seymour-Ure, *The Press, Politics and the Public* (1968) p. 210.
96   Hibbs, op. cit.
97   Cockerell *et al.*, op. cit., p. 33.
98   Hibbs, op. cit.
99   Anthony Bevins, 'The Crippling of the Scribes', *British Journalism Review*, Winter 1990, 1(2).
100 David Broder, *Behind the Front Page* (1987) p. 238.

6   Government Advertising: Information or Propaganda?

1   Central Office of Information, *Annual Report and Accounts 1992–93* (1993).
2   See Digby Anderson, *The Megaphone Solution: Government Attempts to Cure Social Problems with Mass Media Campaigns*, Social Affairs Unit, 1988.
3   See Sir Fife Clark, *Central Office of Information* (1970) p. 92.
4   Figures taken from COI, *Client Services*, March 1990.
5   Frank Dobson, then Shadow Leader of the House of Commons, press release, 11 April 1989.
6   Quoted by Frank Dobson, *Hansard*, 16 May 1989, vol. 153, no. 106, col. 181.
7   National Audit Office, *Publicity Services for Government Departments*, 1 December 1989, p. 5.
8   Using government data (Supply Estimates and COI annual reports) the only direct comparisons that can be made over this time period are on expenditure routed through the COI. There are two main weaknesses with the data: lack of detail – there is no way of examining expenditure on individual campaigns or the form of the spending (for example, advertising, TV, press, direct mail); an absence of details about non-COI departmental expenditure, of which there is often a substantial amount. We have used Register-MEAL estimates for costing of individual advertising campaigns.
9   National Audit Report, op. cit., pp. 32–5.
10 Andrew Grice, 'Selling Ads to Whitehall', *Campaign*, 22 January 1988.
11 COI, *Annual Accounts*, 1989–90.
12 The effectiveness of the GLC's campaign in changing attitudes is chronicled in Robert Waller, *Moulding Political Opinion* (1988).
13 Sir Fife Clark, op. cit., p. 14.
14 Marjorie Ogilvy-Webb, *The Government Explains* (1965).
15 Treasury and Civil Service Committee, Seventh Report 1987–88, *Public Expenditure and Estimates*, 13 July 1988.
16 Government response to the 7th Report of the Treasury and Civil Service Select Committee, in NAO 1989 report, op. cit., Annex 3.

17 W. Crofts, *Coercion or Persuasion?* (1989) pp. 229–31.
18 *Hansard*, 16 May 1989, vol. 153, no. 106, col. 183.
19 The IBA (now ITC) is disallowed by law from broadcasting advertisements from political organisations or which have a political end. The criteria of 'political end' are: (1) an advertisement whose purpose is to change the law; (2) an advertisement seeking to influence the way people vote; and (3) an advertisement seeking to press the government or MPs to take action.

By way of interest, advertisements submitted by the Friends of John McCarthy were turned down under point (3), because they urged people to write to their MPs.
20 Interview with Stuart Patterson, IBA spokesman.
21 IBA Annual Report, 1988–9.
22 Interview with Stuart Patterson.
23 Committee of Public Accounts, Nineteenth Report, *Publicity Services for Government Departments*, 1989–90.
24 Bernard Ingham, *Kill the Messenger* (1991) p. 374.
25 COI, *Annual Accounts*, 1989–90.
26 COI, *Annual Report and Accounts*, 1992–3.
27 Lord Young, *The Enterprise Years* (1990) p. 159.
28 Appendix to the Committee of Public Accounts, Nineteenth Report, op. cit.
29 Bundles of 'Action for Jobs' pamphlets were stacked at CCO awaiting distribution during the 1987 general election campaign.
30 Transcript of *Panorama*, BBC1, 4 September 1989.
31 Lord Young, op. cit., p. 188.
32 Various associations of businessmen and women were formed as a result of the Jobs breakfasts initiative. The best-known were Business in the Community, of which Tim Bell was a leading force, and the Per Cent Club.
33 Interview with Neville Taylor.
34 Unattributable interview with DTI official, 22 September 1987.
35 NAO report, op. cit., p. 15.
36 See Committee of Public Accounts, Nineteenth Report, op. cit., p. 6.
37   Figures taken from a letter from the director general of the COI to the clerk of the Treasury and Civil Service Committee, Seventh Report, 1987/8, op. cit., p. 28.
38 Ibid., p. 31.
39 Ibid., p. vii.
40 Law Report, 17 May 1989, *The Independent.*
41 MEAL figures quoted in 'Privatisation Advertising: A report by Tony Blair MP, Shadow Energy Secretary', April 1989.
42 Sources: National Audit Office Reports of the flotations (1984–5) HC no. 495, and (1987–8) HC nos 22, 37, 243 and 312; Supply Estimates 1988–9, *Hansard* Written Answer 6 February 1989.
43 Alison Turner, 'British Gas Flotation: How Advertising Helped Extend Popular Share Ownership', in Paul Feldwick (ed.), *Advertising Works 5* (1990) pp. 310–42.
44 Ibid., p. 316.

45 John Major, 16 May 1989, *Hansard*, vol. 153, no. 106, cols 197–8.
46 Taken from a DMB&B strategy document quoted in Tony Blair, 'Privatisation Advertising', op. cit.
47 *Hansard*, 16 May 1989, op. cit., cols 200–201.
48 *British Public Opinion Newsletter*, MORI, November 1989.
49 Quoted in Tony Blair, 'Privatisation Advertising', op. cit.
50 Marjorie Ogilvy-Webb, op. cit., pp.78–9.
51 Digby Anderson, *The Megaphone Solution*, op. cit.
52 Lord Young, op. cit., p. 208.
53 See Michael J. Baker (ed.), *The Marketing Book* (1991) p. 364.
54 See Peter Hennessy, *Whitehall* (1990).

7 The Image-Makers Unbound: Marketing in the Post-Thatcher Era

1 Interestingly Des Wilson and the Liberal Democrats emerge as the most determined bullies, something which Wilson said he would deny were it not for the fact that he takes considerable pride in it. See International Press Institute, 'Potholes on the Campaign Trail' (June 1992).
2 Ibid.
3 See Holli Semetko *et al.*, *The Formation of Campaign Agendas* (1991) for a comparative analysis of party and media roles in recent American and British elections.
4 Senior Conservative Central Office officials Sir John Lacy and Mark Fullbrook were sent to Washington to assist the Bush campaign. See 'Republicans take a tax bomb from the Tories', *Sunday Times*, 11 October 1992.
5 A Channel 4 *Dispatches* programme, 'Nine Days in April' (25 September, 1992) argued that campaign errors, especially raising the issue of PR, cost Labour the election.
6 *Interim Report of the Market Research Society Inquiry into the Performance of the Opinion Polls in the 1992 General Election*, 12 June 1992.
7 See A. Heath *et al.*, *Labour's Last Chance* (1994). P. Clifford and A. Heath argue that the campaign made little difference and that there was a systematic bias in favour of Labour in the opinion polls throughout the campaign.
8 John Wakeham, PSA Conference on the 1992 General Election, University of Essex, 18 September 1992.
9 Interview with Harris researchers, March 1992.
10 John Wakeham, 'The Conservative Campaign', in Ivor Crewe and Brian Gosschalk (eds), *Political Communications: The General Election of 1992* (forthcoming).
11 The Summer Heat on Labour campaign of 1990 argued that Labour's new policy initiatives were merely a 'series of PR exercises to market an unsellable proposition': *Labour Behind the Mask*, CRD, Summer, 1990.

12   Interview with Harvey Thomas, ITN 12.30 News, 21 May 1991.
13   See D. Butler and D. Kavanagh, *The British General Election of 1992*
      (1992) p. 27.
14   *Income and Expenditure Account: Year Ended March 31 1991*, Conservative
      Central Office.
15   John Jenkins (ed.), *John Major: Prime Minister* (1990) p. 7.
16   Butler and Kavanagh, op. cit., p. 32.
17   Ibid., pp. 36–7.
18   Brendan Bruce, *Images of Power* (1992) p. 86.
19   Interview with Shaun Woodward, 19 September 1992.
20   Ibid.
21   'Saatchis pitched for Labour', *Campaign*, 28 June 1991.
22   Shaun Woodward, speech to the IPA, 21 September 1992.
23   Shaun Woodward, ibid.
24   The brothers took the extraordinary step of bringing in an 'outsider',
      Robert Louis-Dreyfus, as chief executive to rationalise the company
      and placate the stock market. Its year end figures to December 1991
      showed pre-tax losses of £58 million compared to a £35 million pre-
      tax profit for the previous year.
25   See Butler and Kavanagh, op. cit.
26   Interview with Robert Waller, 29 September 1992.
27   Interview with Shaun Woodward, 30 September 1992.
28   *Labour and Britain in the 1990s*, The Labour Party, May 1988.
29   Patricia Hewitt, *Policy Review – Note for Discussion* (1988).
30   See, for example, Michael Cassell, 'Hard left softened up as party
      leadership scents better times', in *Financial Times*, 3 October 1989.
31   *British Public Opinion*, June 1989.
32   Richard Heffernan and Mike Marqusee's *Defeat from the Jaws of Victory*
      (1992) offers a brilliant if uncompromisingly partial account of
      Mandelson's contribution.
33   Private sources.
34   Heffernan and Marqusee, op. cit., pp. 227–30. Butler and Kavanagh
      also support this account of Underwood's departure from Walworth
      Road. See Butler and Kavanagh, op. cit., p. 60.
35   Interview with David Hill, July 1992.
36   Prescott's views are cited at length in Steven Barnett, 'Hi-jacked! –
      television and politics during the election', in *British Journalism Review*
      (1992) vol. 3(2) pp. 17–19.
37   Quoted in Ivo Dawney, 'Mirror cracks as the Left regards its voters',
      Financial Times, 11 June 1992.
38   See 'New Labour team seeks ad agency', *Campaign*, 9 October 1992.
39   The post-election struggle to reshape Labour's identity was cast by
      media commentators as a fight between modernisers and tradition-
      ists about the 'Clintonisation' of the party. Clintonisation, according
      to its critics, was an attempt to move Labour further to the right, to
      become a British version of the US Democrats, solidly centrist and
      smothered in public relations gloss. Clare Short, for instance, spoke of
      the 'Mandelson project', by stealth and administrative manoeuvre, to
      shift Labour down the Democratic route (interview on BBC Radio 4,

World at One, 10 January, 1993). The argument between modernisers and traditionalists ran particularly strongly in the early weeks of 1993 in the pages of the *Guardian* and the *New Statesman*. See especially Tony Benn, 'The battle over Labour plc', *Guardian*, 7 January 1993; 'Clinton team identifies targets for success', *Guardian*, 11 January 1993; Philip Gould, 'The American Dream: Lessons for Labour', *New Statesman*, 15 January 1993, pp. 21–2.

40　Patricia Hewitt, *Policy Review – Note for Discussion*.

41　See M. Harrop and M. Scammell, 'A Tabloid War', in Butler and Kavanagh, *The British General Election of 1992*, p. 198.

42　Des Wilson, speaking to the Political Communications 1992 Election Conference, University of Essex, 18 September 1992.

43　Private sources.

44　Interview with a member of the planning group.

45　Des Wilson, *Battle for Power* (1987) p. 314.

46　'TBWA wins the Democrats' vote', in *Campaign*, 17 May 1991.

47　Stephen Ingle, 'The Liberal Democrats and the 1992 Election', a paper presented to the PSA conference on the 1992 election, University of Essex, 18 September 1992.

48　See Dennis Kavanagh and Brian Gosschalk, 'The Changing Role of Election Press Conferences', in Crewe and Gosschalk (eds) *Political Communications: the General Election of 1992* (Cambridge University Press, forthcoming).

49　Interview with Shaun Woodward, September 1992.

50　These are the parties' own estimates of national campaign expenditure, quoted in Butler and Kavanagh, op. cit., p. 260.

51　*Campaign*, 13 March 1992.

52　Unattributable interview, September 1992.

53　See T.J. Nossiter, M. Scammell and H. Semetko, 'Old Values Versus News Values' (forthcoming).

54　Quoted in *Campaign*, 26 June 1992.

55　I. Crewe and A. King dispute that Major had an important pro-Tory influence on 1992 voting behaviour. Crewe and King, 'Did Major Win? Did Kinnock Lose' in Heath *et al.* (eds), op. cit.

56　Interview with David Hill, July 1992.

57　*Guardian*, 5 October 1989.

58　Interview with David Hill, July 1992.

59　We make no apologies for relying on the Harris exit poll. Voting intention figures for the poll were as follows: Con – 41 per cent; Lab – 36 per cent; LibDem – 18 per cent. These figures were all within two points of the actual result (41.9; 34.4; 17.8), well within the pollsters' normal plus-or-minus-3-points 'health warning' and the most accurate of the campaign.

60　Interview with David Hill, July 1992.

61　*ICM Review No. 8*, January–June 1992.

62　Private sources.

63　Private sources.

64　The importance of the Major/Kinnock contest to the vote seems to have become the accepted wisdom of politicians, campaign officials, media pundits, indeed virtually everyone apart from political scientists who are still awaiting conclusive proof.

65 See Nossiter *et al.*, op. cit. . . .
66 *Independent on Sunday*, 12 April 1992.
67 Interview with David Hill, July 1992.
68 See, for example, Tony Benn, *The End of an Era: Diaries 1980–1990* (1992); Heffernan and Marqusee, op. cit.
69 For an assessment of the press in the campaign, see Harrop and Scammell, 'A Tabloid War', op. cit.
70 Shaun Woodward, speaking at the PSA 1992 General Election conference, University of Essex, 18 September 1992.
71 David Sanders, 'Why the Conservative Party Won Again', in Anthony King (ed.), *Britain at the Polls* (1992).
72 Giles Radice, *Southern Discomfort* (1992) Fabian Pamphlet 555. The research involved focus group discussions with wavering voters, all white-collar and skilled manual workers (C1s and C2s), in five south eastern marginal seats: Slough, Stevenage, Gravesham, Luton South and Harlow.
73 Robin Cook, speaking at the PSA Conference on the 1992 General Election, University of Essex, 18 September 1992.
74 See Harrop and Scammell, op. cit., p. 201.
75 Anonymous source.
76 David Hill, interviewed on *Dispatches*, Channel 4, 8 April 1992.
77 Interview with Shaun Woodward, September 1992.
78 Ibid.
79 See Nossiter *et al.*, op. cit.
80 Reported in *Sunday Telegraph*, 3 May 1992.
81 See Nicholas Jones, *Election 92: The Inside Story of the Campaign* (1992).
82 Harrop and Scammell, op. cit., p. 209.

8 Thatcher's Legacy: The Americanisation of British Politics?

1 André Malraux, *Antimémoires* (1967), i.122.
2 Donald Regan tells the bizarre story that Deaver organised the president's schedule only after consultation with Nancy Reagan and the First Lady's 'friend', a San Francisco astrologer. See Donald T. Regan, *For the Record* (1988) pp. 73–5.
3 Ibid., p. 248.
4 Ibid., p. 57.
5 Private sources.
6 Ralph Harris and Arthur Seldon, in a publication by the right-wing Institute of Economic Affairs, argued that Mrs Thatcher's reluctance to tackle the NHS resulted from 'ill-considered advice based on defective measurement of public opinion': Ralph Harris and Arthur Seldon, *Welfare without the State* (1987).
7 See Michael Biddiss, 'Thatcherism: Concept and Interpretations', in K. Minogue and M. Biddis (eds), *Thatcherism* (1987).

8   Bernard Ingham, *Kill The Messenger* (1991) p. 352.
9   Interview with David Hill, September 1992.
10   Patrick Cosgrave, *The Lives of Enoch Powell* (1989) p. 17.
11   The only criticism of the government at the 1986 conference con-
     cerned, ironically enough, the presentation of government policy.
     There was no objection to government policies from any of the floor
     speakers. See Richard Kelly, *Conservative Party Conferences* (1989) p.
     155.
12   *Charter News*, 1990 Party Conference, Issue 1.
13   Source: MORI, *British Public Opinion*, April/May 1992.
14   Peter Mandelson, 'Marketing Labour', *Contemporary Record*, Winter 1988
     1(4).
15   'Can Mrs Thatcher Survive?', *Evening Standard*, 27 October 1989.
16   See The Sunday Review in the *Independent on Sunday*, 5 May 1991.
17   MORI's perceptual mapping computer analysis is derived through a
     multi-comparison technique whereby each party is plotted on a graph
     according to its score on a number of attributes relative to each other
     and to other parties' scores. See *British Public Opinion*, September 1989.
18   MORI's study on public attitudes to mark Mrs Thatcher's ten years at
     Downing Street is the source for this account. See *British Public Opin-
     ion*, June 1989.
19   Mrs Thatcher, speech to the Conservative Party Conference, 12 Octo-
     ber 1990.
20   'Can Mrs Thatcher Survive?', *Evening Standard*, 27 October 1989.
21   Quoted in Robert Waller, *Moulding Political Opinion* (1988) p. 106.
22   MORI poll analysis, December 1990.
23   The figures come from NEC Annual Report, 1991.
24   See Patrick Seyd and Paul Whitely, *Labour's Grass Roots* (1992) pp.
     207–11.
25   For a discussion of this issue see Margaret Scammell and Holli A.
     Semetko, 'Compaign Advertising on British Television in Lynda Lee
     Kaid and Christina Holz Bacha (eds), *Political Advertising in Western
     Democracies* (Sage, forthcoming).
26   See Larry M. Bartels, 'The Impact of Electioneering in the United
     States', in David Butler and Austin Ranney (eds), *Electioneering: A Com-
     parative Study of Continuity and Change* (1992).
27   The Representation of the People Act 1989 set the limits on candi-
     dates' expenses at parliamentary elections as follows (by-elections in
     brackets): county constituency: £3648 plus 4.1p per elector (£14 592
     plus 16.4p per elector); borough constituency: £3648 plus 3.1p per
     elector (£14 592 plus 12.4p per elector).
28   Table 8.3 is derived from Keith Ewing, *Funding of Political Parties in
     Britain* (1987) p. 90; Michael Pinto-Duschinsky, 'Funding the British
     General Election of 1987', in Crewe and Harrop (eds), *Political Com-
     munication: The General Election Campaign of 1987* (1989).
29   Tariq Ali, 'The British Clinton', *New Statesman and Society*, 20 May 1994.
30   Bartels, op. cit.
31   See Gerald L. Curtis, 'Japan' in Butler and Ranney (eds), op. cit.
     (1992).

32   Kathleen Hall Jamieson, *Dirty Politics*, p. 220.
33   See Scammell and Semetko, op. cit.
34   Quoted in *Sunday Times*, 'Republicans take a tax bomb from the Tories', 11 October 1992.
35   Bill Carter, 'Perot gave networks a race at any rate', *New York Times*, 3 November 1992.
36   Constituency associations are less than convinced that centrally directed mail increases total funds to the party; rather, many think it may divert funds from the constituencies to the centre.
37   *Conservative Newsline*, June 1990.
38   For an argument in favour of paid political advertising see M. Scammell, 'Political Advertising and the Broadcasting Revolution', in *Political Quarterly*, April 1990, 61(2).

Select Bibliography

Books

Abrams, Mark, and Richard Rose, *Must Labour Lose?*, Harmondsworth: Penguin, 1960.

Abramson, Jeffrey B., F. Christopher Arterton and Gary R. Orren, *The Electronic Commonwealth: The Impact of New Media Technologies on Democratic Politics*, New York: Basic Books, 1988.

Adams, V. *The Media and the Falklands Campaign*, Basingstoke: Macmillan, 1986.

Alexander, Andrew, and Alan Watkins, *The Making of the Prime Minister 1970*, London: Macdonald, 1970.

Atkinson, Max, *Our Masters' Voices*, London: Routledge, 1988.

Axford, Barrie, and Peter Madgwick, 'Indecent Exposure' in Ivor Crewe and Martin Harrop (eds), *Political Communications: The General Election Campaign of 1987*, Cambridge: CUP, 1989.

Babaz, M., *Le Rôle de la Publicité dans les Campagnes Electorale Britanniques de 1964, 1966 et 1970*, Paris: University of Lille, 1977.

Baker, Michael J. (ed.), *The Marketing Book*, Oxford: Chartered Institute of Marketing/Butterworth-Heinemann, 1991.

Baker Michael J., 'One More Time – What is Marketing?' in Michael J. Baker (ed.), *The Marketing Book*, Oxford: Chartered Institute of Marketing/Butterworth-Heinemann, 1991, pp. 3–9.

Bartels, Larry, 'The Impact of Electioneering in the United States' in David Butler and Austin Ranney (eds), *Electioneering: A Comparative Study of Continuity and Change*, Oxford: Clarendon, 1992.

Bell, Tim, 'The Conservative Advertising Campaign' in R. Worcester and M. Harrop (eds), *Political Communications: The General Election Campaign of 1979*, London: Macmillan. 1982, pp. 11–25.

Benn, Tony, *Against the Tide: Diaries 1973–76*, London: Hutchinson, 1989.

Benn, Tony, *Conflicts of Interest: Diaries 1977–80*, London: Hutchinson, 1990.

Benn, Tony, *The End of an Era: Diaries 1980–90*, London: Hutchinson, 1992.

Biddiss, M. 'Thatcherism: Concept and Interpretations' in K. Minogue and M. Biddiss (eds), *Thatcherism*, London: Macmillan, 1987.

Blake, Robert, *The Conservative Party from Peel to Churchill*, London: Fontana, 1979.

Blois, Keith J., 'Non-Profit Organisations and Marketing' in Michael J. Baker (ed.), *The Marketing Book*, Oxford: Chartered Institute of Marketing/Butterworth-Heinemann, 1991.

Blumenthal, S. *The Permanent Campaign*, New York: Simon and Schuster, 1982.

Blumler, Jay G., Michael Gurevitch and T.J. Nossiter, 'The Earnest versus the Determined: Election Newsmaking at the BBC, 1987' in Ivor Crewe and Martin Harrop (eds), *Political Communication: the General Election Campaign of 1987*, Cambridge: CUP, 1989, pp. 157–74.

Bogdanor, V. and D. Butler (eds), *Democracy and Elections*, Cambridge: CUP, 1983.

Bolton, Roger, 'The Problems of Making Political Television: A Practitioner's Perspective' in P. Golding *et al.* (eds), *Communicating Politics*, New York: Holmes & Meir, 1986, pp. 93–112.

Bolton, Roger, *Death on the Rock*, London: W.H. Allen, 1990.

Boyd-Barrett, O. and P. Braham (eds), *Media, Knowledge and Power*, Beckenham, Kent: Croom Helm, 1987.

Broder, David, *Behind the Front Page*, New York: Simon & Schuster, 1987.

Bruce, Brendan, *Images of Power*, London: Kogan Page, 1992.

Bruce-Gardyne, Jock, *Mrs Thatcher's First Administration: The Prophets Confounded*, London: Macmillan, 1984.

Butler, David, *British General Elections Since 1945*, Oxford: Basil Blackwell, 1989.

Butler, David, and Gareth Butler, *British Political Facts 1900–1985*, London: Macmillan, 1986.

Butler, David, and Dennis Kavanagh (eds), *The British General Election of February 1974*, London: Macmillan, 1974.

Butler, David, and Dennis Kavanagh (eds), *The British General Election of October 1974*, London: Macmillan, 1975.

Butler, David, and Dennis Kavanagh (eds), *The British General Election of 1979*, London: Macmillan, 1980.

Butler, David, and Dennis Kavanagh (eds), *The British General Election of 1983*, London: Macmillan, 1984.

Butler, David, and Dennis Kavanagh (eds), *The British General Election of 1987*, London: Macmillan, 1988.

Butler, David and Dennis Kavanagh (eds), *The British General Election of 1992*, London: Macmillan, 1992.

Butler, David, and Anthony King, *The British General Election of 1964*, London: Macmillan, 1965.

Butler, David, and M. Pinto-Duschinsky, *The British General Election of 1970*, London: Macmillan, 1971.

Butler, David, and Austin Ranney, *Electioneering: A Comparative Study of Continuity and Change*, Oxford: Clarendon, 1992.

Butler, David, and Richard Rose, *The British General Election of 1959*, London: Macmillan, 1960.

Castle, Barbara, *The Castle Diaries 1974–76*, London: Weidenfeld & Nicolson, 1980.

Chakotin, Serge, *The Rape of the Masses: The Psychology of Totalitarian Propaganda*, London: Routledge, 1939.

Chippendale, Peter, and Chris Horne, *Stick It Up Your Punter*, London: Heinemann, 1990.

Chisnall, P., *Marketing Research*, 2nd edn, Maidenhead, Berkshire: McGraw-Hill, 1981.

Clark, Eric, *The Want Makers*, London: Hodder & Stoughton, 1988.

Clark, Sir Fife, *Central Office of Information*, London: Allen & Unwin, 1970.

Cockerell, Michael, *Live from Number 10*, London: Faber & Faber, 1988.

Cockerell, Michael, P. Hennessy and D. Walker, *Sources Close to the Prime Minister*, London: Macmillan, 1984.

Coleman, Terry, *Thatcher's Britain: A Journey through the Promised Lands*, London: Bantam, 1987.

Cosgrave, P. *Margaret Thatcher – A Tory and Her Party*, London: Hutchinson, 1978.

Cosgrave, P. *The Lives of Enoch Powell*, London: Bodley Head, 1989.

Creel, George, *How We Advertised America*, New York: Harper & Row, 1920.

Crewe, Ivor, and Brian Gosschalk (eds), *Political Communications: The General Election Campaign of 1992*, Cambridge: CUP (forthcoming).

Crewe, Ivor, and Martin Harrop (eds), *Political Communications: The General Election Campaign of 1983*, Cambridge: CUP, 1986.

Crewe, Ivor, and Martin Harrop (eds), *Political Communications: The General Election Campaign of 1987*, Cambridge: CUP, 1989.

Crewe, Ivor, and Anthony King, 'Did Major Win? Did Kinnock Lose?' In A. Heath, R. Jowell and J. Curtice (eds), *Labour's Last Chance? The 1992 Election and Beyond*, Aldershot, Hampshire: Dartmouth, 1994.

Crewe, Ivor, and Bo Sarlvik, 'Popular Attitudes and Electoral Strategy' in Zig Layton-Henry (ed.) *Conservative Party Politics*, London: Macmillan, 1980, pp. 244–75.

Crofts, William, *Coercion or Persuasion?* London: Routledge, 1989.

Curtice, John, 'Interim Report: Party Politics' in R. Jowell *et al.*, *British Social Attitudes: The 1987 Report*, Aldershot: Gower, 1987.

Curtis, Gerald L. 'Japan' in David Butler and Austin Ranney (eds), *Electioneering: A Comparative Study of Continuity and Change*, Oxford: Clarendon, 1992.

Dalyell, Tam, *Misrule*, London: Hamish Hamilton, 1987.

Day, Barry, 'The Politics of Communication' in R. Worcester and M. Harrop (eds), *Political Communications: The General Election Campaign of 1979*, London: Macmillan, 1982, pp. 3–10.

Day, Sir Robin, *Grand Inquisitor*, London: Weidenfeld & Nicolson, 1989.

Davies, P.J., and Fredric Waldstein (eds), *Political Issues in America Today*, Manchester: Manchester University Press, 1987.

Delaney, Tim, 'Labour's Advertising Campaign' in R. Worcester and M. Harrop (eds), *Political Communications: The General Election Campaign of 1979*, London: Macmillan, 1982, pp. 27–31.

Donoughue, Lord Bernard, *Prime Minister*, London: Jonathan Cape, 1987.

Evans, Harold, *Good Times Bad Times*, London: Weidenfeld & Nicolson, 1983.

Ewing, K. *The Funding of Political Parties in Britain*, Cambridge: CUP, 1987.

Fallon, Ivan, *The Brothers*, London: Hutchinson, 1988.

Feldwick, Paul (ed.), *Advertising Works 5*, London: Cassell, 1990.

Fisher, Nigel, *The Tory Leaders: Their Struggle for Power*, London: Weidenfeld & Nicolson, 1977.

Franklin, Bob, *Packaging Politics: Political Communications in Britain's Media Democracy*, London: Edward Arnold, 1994.

Gamble, Andrew, *The Conservative Nation*, London: Routledge & Kegan Paul, 1974.

Glasgow University Media Group, *War and Peace News*, Milton Keynes: Open University Press, 1985.

Golding, Peter, Graham Murdock and Philip Schlesinger (eds), *Communicating Politics*, New York: Holmes & Meir, 1986.

Grant, Nick, 'A Comment on Labour's Campaign', in I. Crewe and M. Harrop (eds), *Political Communications: The General Election Campaign of 1983*, Cambridge: CUP, 1986, pp. 82–7.

Gunter, B., M. Svennevig and J.M. Wober, *Television Coverage of the 1983 General Election*, London: Gower, 1986.

Haines, J. *The Politics of Power*, London: Hodder & Stoughton (Coronet), 1977.

Hall, Stuart, and Martin Jacques (eds), *New Times*, London: Lawrence & Wishart, 1989.

Hanham, H.J., *Elections and Party Management: Politics in the Time of Disraeli and Gladstone*, 2nd edn, Hassocks, Sussex: Harvester, 1978.

Harris, Robert, *Gotcha!* London: Faber & Faber, 1983.

Harris, Robert, *The Making of Neil Kinnock*, London: Faber & Faber, 1984.

Harris, Robert, *Good and Faithful Servant*, London: Faber & Faber, 1990.

Harrison, Martin, 'Broadcasting' in D. Butler and D. Kavanagh (eds), *The British General Election of 1983*, London: Macmillan, 1984, pp. 147–74.

Harrison, Martin, 'Broadcasting' in D. Butler and D. Kavanagh (eds), *The British General Election of 1987*, London: Macmillan, 1988, pp. 139–162.

Harrop, Martin, 'Voters' in J. Seaton and B. Pimlott (eds), *The Media in British Politics*, Avebury: Gower, 1987.

Harrop, Martin, 'Press' in D. Butler and D. Kavanagh (eds), *The British General Election of 1987*, London: Macmillan, 1988, pp. 163–90.

Harrop, Martin, and Margaret Scammell, 'A Tabloid War' in D. Butler and D. Kavanagh (eds), *The British General Election of 1992*, London: Macmillan, 1992, pp. 180–210.

Healey, Denis, *The Time of My Life*, London: Michael Joseph, 1989.

Heath, Anthony, Roger Jowell and John Curtice, *How Britain Votes*, Oxford: Pergamon Press, 1985.

Heath, Anthony, John Curtice, Geoff Evans, Roger Jowell, Julia Field and Sharon Witherspoon, *Understanding Political Change*, Oxford: Pergamon Press, 1991.

Heath, Anthony, Roger Jowell and John Curtice (eds), *Labour's Last Chance? The 1992 Election and Beyond*, Aldershot, Hampshire: Dartmouth, 1994.

Hebdige, Dick, 'After the Masses' in S. Hall and M. Jacques (eds), *New Times*, London: Lawrence & Wishart, 1989, pp. 76–93.

Heffernan, Richard and Mike Marqusee, *Defeat From the Jaws of Victory: Inside Kinnock's Labour Party*, London: Verso, 1992.

Hennessy, Peter, 'The Prime Minister, the Cabinet and the Thatcher Personality' in K. Minogue and M. Biddiss (eds), *Thatcherism*, London: Macmillan, 1987, pp. 55–71.

Hennessy, Peter, *Whitehall*, London: Fontana, 1990.

Hennessy, Peter, and Anthony Seldon, *Ruling Performance: British Governments from Attlee to Thatcher*, Oxford: Basil Blackwell, 1987.

Hewitt, P., and P. Mandelson, 'The Labour Campaign' in I. Crewe and M. Harrop (eds), *Political Communications: The General Election Campaign of 1987*, Cambridge: CUP, 1989, pp. 49–54.

Hill, Dr. Charles (Lord), *Both Sides of the Hill*, London: Heinemann, 1964.

Himmelweit, Hilde T., Patrick Humphreys, Marianne Jaeger and Michael Katz, *How Voters Decide*, London: Academic, 1981.

Houston, Henry James, and Lionel Valdar, *Modern Electioneering Practice*, London: Charles Knight, 1922.

Hughes, C., and P. Wintour, *Labour Rebuilt*, London: Fourth Estate, 1990.

Ingham, Bernard, *Kill The Messenger*, London: Harper Collins, 1991.

James, Robert Rhodes (ed.), *Memoirs of a Conservative: J.C.C. Davidson's Memoirs*, London: Weidenfeld & Nicolson, 1969.

James, Robert Rhodes, *Anthony Eden*, London: Weidenfeld & Nicolson, 1986.

Jamieson, Kathleen Hall, *Packaging the Presidency*, Oxford: Oxford University Press, 1984.

Jamieson, Kathleen Hall, *Dirty Politics: Deception, Distraction and Democracy*, New York: Oxford University, Press.

Jenkins J. (ed.) *John Major: Prime Minister*, London: Bloomsbury, 1990.

Johnston, R.J., C.J. Pattie and J.G. Allsopp, *A Nation Dividing: The Electoral Map of Great Britain 1979–1987*, London: Longman, 1988.

Jones, Nicholas, *Election 1992: The Inside Story of the Campaign*, London: BBC, 1992.

Jowell, Roger, Sharon Witherspoon and Lindsay Brook, *British Social Attitudes: The 1987 Report*, Aldershot: Gower, 1987.

Jowett, Garth S., and Victoria O'Donnell, *Propaganda and Persuasion*, Newbury Park, California: Sage, 1986.

Kavanagh, Dennis, *Thatcherism and British Politics*, Oxford: OUP, 1987.

Kavanagh, Dennis, *Politics and Personalities*, London: Macmillan, 1990.

Kelley, Stanley, *Professional Public Relations and Political Power*, Baltimore: Johns Hopkins, 1956.

Kelly, Richard, *Conservative Party Conferences*, Manchester: Manchester University Press, 1989.

Klapper, J., *The Effects of Mass Communication*, Glencoe, Illinois: Free Press, 1960.

Kleinman, P., *The Saatchi & Saatchi Story*, London: Weidenfeld & Nicolson, 1987.

Lasswell, H., *Propaganda Technique in the World War*, New York: Knopf, 1927.

Layton-Henry, Zig (ed.), *Conservative Party Politics*, London: Macmillan, 1980.

Leapman, Michael, *The Last Days of the Beeb*, London: Hodder & Stoughton (Coronet), 1987.

Lindsay, T.F., and Michael Harrington, *The Conservative Party 1918–70*, London: Macmillan, 1974.

Luntz, Frank, *Candidates, Consultants and Campaigns*, Oxford: Basil Blackwell, 1988.

MacArthur, Brian, 'The National Press' in Ivor Crewe and Martin Harrop (eds), *Political Communications: The General Election Campaign of 1987*, Cambridge: CUP, 1989.

MacGregor, Ian, *The Enemies Within*, London: Collins, 1986.

Mandelson, Peter, and Patricia Hewitt, 'The Labour Campaign' in Ivor Crewe and Martin Harrop (eds), *Political Communications: The General Election Campaign of 1987*, Cambridge: CUP, 1989.

Malraux, André, *Antimémoires*, Paris: Gallimard, 1967.

McBurnie Tom and David Clutterbuck, *The Marketing Edge*, London: Penguin Books, 1987.

Middlemas, Keith, *Politics in Industrial Society*, London: Andre Deutsch, 1979.

Minogue, K., and M. Biddiss (eds), *Thatcherism*, London: Macmillan, 1987.

Morrison, D., and H. Tumber, *Journalists at War*, London: Sage, 1988.

Munro, Colin, 'Legal Controls on Election Broadcasting' in Ivor Crewe and Martin Harrop (eds), *Political Communications: The General Election Campaign of 1983*, Cambridge: CUP, 1986.

Nicholas, H.G., *The British General Election of 1950*, London: Macmillan, 1951.

Nossiter, T.J., Margaret Scammell and Holli A. Semetko, 'Old Values Versus News Values' in Ivor Crewe and Brian Gosschalk (eds), *Political Communications: The General Election Campaign of 1992*, Cambridge: CUP (forthcoming).

Ogilvy-Webb, Marjorie, *The Government Explains*, London: Allen & Unwin, 1965.

O'Shaughnessy, Nicholas J., *The Phenomenon of Political Marketing*, London: Macmillan, 1990.

Owen, David, *Personally Speaking*, London: Weidenfeld & Nicolson, 1987.

Pardoe, John, 'The Alliance Campaign' in I. Crewe and M. Harrop (eds), *Political Communications: The General Election Campaign of 1987*, Cambridge: CUP, 1989, pp. 55–9.

Parkinson, Cecil, 'The Conservative Campaign' in I. Crewe and M. Harrop (eds), *Political Communication: The General Election Campaign of 1983*, Cambridge: CUP, pp. 59–64.

Patten, C. 'Policy-Making In Opposition' in Zig Layton-Henry (ed.), *Conservative Party Politics*, London: Macmillan, 1980.

Perry, Roland, *The Programming of the President*, London: Aurum, 1984.

Pinto-Duschinsky, M. 'Financing the British General Election of 1983' in I. Crewe and M. Harrop (eds), *Political Communication: The General Election Campaign of 1983*, Cambridge: CUP, 1986, pp. 283–93.

Pinto-Duschinsky, M. 'Financing the British General Election of 1987' in I. Crewe and M. Harrop (eds), *Political Communications: The General Election Campaign of 1987*, Cambridge: CUP, 1989, pp. 15–28.

Pirie, M. (ed.), *A Decade of Revolution*, London: Adam Smith Institute, 1989.

Ponting, Clive, *The Right to Know: Inside Story of the Belgrano Affair*, London: Sphere, 1985.

Ponting, Clive, *Whitehall: Tragedy and Farce*, London: Hamish Hamilton, 1986.

Prior, James, *A Balance of Power*, London: Hamish Hamilton, 1986.

Pronay, N., and D.W. Spring, *Propaganda Politics and Film 1918–45*, London: Macmillan, 1982.

Pym, Francis, *The Politics of Consent*, London: Hamish Hamilton, 1984.

Qualter, T.H., *Propaganda and Psychological Warfare*, New York: Random House, 1962.

Ramsden, John, *A History of the Conservative Party, Vol. 3: The Age of Balfour and Baldwin*, London: Longman, 1978.

Ramsden, John, *The Making of Conservative Party Policy: The Conservative Research Department since 1929*, London: Longman, 1980.

Ramsden, John, 'Baldwin and Film' in N. Pronay and D.W. Spring (eds), *Propaganda, Politics and Film*, London: Macmillan, 1982.

Regan, Donald T., *For the Record*, London: Hutchinson, 1988.

Riddell, Peter, *The Thatcher Government*, Oxford: Martin Robertson, 1983.

Rook, Jean, 'Woman of Destiny' in *The First Ten Years*, London: CCO, 1989.

Rose, Richard, *Influencing Voters*, London: Faber & Faber, 1967.

Saatchi and Saatchi, *Media Yearbook 1990*.

Sabato, Larry, *The Rise of Political Consultants: New Ways of Winning Elections*, New York: Basic Books, 1981.

Sanders, David, 'Why the Conservative Party Won Again' in Anthony King (ed.), *Britain at the Polls*, New Jersey: Chatham House, 1992.

Sarlvik, B. and Ivor Crewe, *Decade of Dealignment: The Conservative Victory of 1979 and Electoral Trends in the 1970s*, Cambridge: CUP, 1983.

Scammell, Margaret and Holli A. Semetko, 'Party Advertising in the 1992 British Election' in Lynda Lee Kaid and Christina Holz-Bacha (eds) *Political Advertising in Western Democracies*, Sage (forthcoming).

Schumpeter, Joseph A., *Capitalism, Socialism and Democracy*, 5th edn, London: Unwin, 1976.

Seaton, J., and B. Pimlott, *The Media in British Politics*, Avebury: Gower, 1987.

Semetko, Holli A., Jay G. Blumler, Michael Gurevitch and David H. Weaver, *The Formation of Campaign Agendas: A Comparative Analysis of Party and Media Roles in Recent American and British Elections*, Hillsdale, New Jersey: Lawrence Erlbaum, 1991.

Seyd, Patrick and Paul Whitely, *Labour's Grass Roots*, Oxford: Clarendon, 1992.

Seymour-Ure, Colin, *The Press, Politics and the Public*, London: Methuen, 1968.

Seymour-Ure, Colin, *The Political Impact of Mass Media*, London: Constable, 1974.

Sharkey, John, 'Saatchis and the 1987 Election' in I. Crewe and M. Harrop (eds), *Political Communications: The General Election of 1987*, Cambridge: CUP, 1989, pp. 63–71.

Shawcross, William, *Murdoch*, London: Chatto & Windus, 1992.

Stead, Peter, 'The British Working Class and Film in the 1930s' in N. Pronay and D.W. Spring (eds), *Propaganda, Politics and Film 1918–45*, London: Macmillan, 1982.

Steel, David, *Against Goliath*, London: Weidenfeld & Nicolson, 1989.

Taylor, Philip M., *Projection of Britain: British Overseas Publicity and Propaganda 1919–1939*, Cambridge: CUP, 1981.

Tebbit, Norman, *Upwardly Mobile*, London: Futura, 1989.

Thatcher, Margaret, *The Downing Street Years*, London: Harper Collins, 1993.

Thomas, Harvey, *Making an Impact*, Newton Abbot, Devon: David & Charles, 1989.

Thomas, Michael, *The Economist Guide to Marketing*, Oxford: Basil Blackwell, 1986.

Thomson, Andrew, *Margaret Thatcher: The Woman Within*, London: W.H. Allen, 1989.

Troy, Gil, *See How They Ran*, New York: Free Press, 1991.

Tunstall, J., *The Westminster Lobby Correspondents*, London: Routledge & Kegan Paul, 1970.

Turner, Alison, 'British Gas Flotation: How Advertising Helped Extend Popular Share Ownership' in P. Feldwick (ed.), *Advertising Works 5*, London: Cassell, 1990.

Tyler, Rodney, *Campaign!*, London: Grafton, 1987.

Vile, M.J.C., *Politics in the USA*, London: Hutchinson, 1983.

Wakeham, John, 'The Conservative Campaign' in I. Crewe and B. Gosschalk (eds), *Political Communications: The General Election of 1992*, Cambridge: CUP (forthcoming).

Waller, Robert, *Moulding Political Opinion*, London: Croom Helm, 1988.

Wapshott, Nicholas and George Brock, *Thatcher*, London: Futura, 1983.

Webster, Wendy, *Not A Man To Match Her*, London: The Women's Press, 1990.

Whitelaw, Lord, *The Whitelaw Memoirs*, London: Aurum, 1989.

Williams, Francis, *Parliament, Press and the Public*, London: Heinemann, 1946.

Williams, Marcia, *Inside Number 10*, London: Weidenfeld & Nicolson, 1972.

Wilson, Des, *Battle for Power*, London: Sphere, 1987.

Wilson, Harold, *The Governance of Britain*, London: Sphere, 1976.

Windlesham, Lord, *Communication and Political Power*, London: Jonathan Cape, 1966.

Worcester, Robert, 'Changes in Politics' in Madsen Pirie (ed.), *A Decade of Revolution*, London: Adam Smith Institute, 1989.

Worcester, Robert and Martin Harrop (eds), *Political Communications: The General Election Campaign of 1979*, London: Allen & Unwin, 1982.

Young, Lord (David), *The Enterprise Years*, London: Headline, 1990.

Young, Hugo, *One of Us*, London: Macmillan, 1989.

Young, Hugo and Anne Sloman, *The Thatcher Phenomenon*, London: BBC, 1986.

Articles, Pamphlets and Theses

Anderson, D., *The Megaphone Solution: Government Attempts to Cure Social Problems with Mass Media Campaigns*, Social Affairs Unit, 1988.

Barnett, Steven, 'Hi-jacked! – Television and Politics during the Election', *British Journalism Review*, 1992, 3(2) pp. 17–19.

Bevins, A., 'The Crippling of the Scribes', *British Journalism Review*, Winter 1990, 1(2): 13–17.

Campbell, B., 'Party Presence', *Marxism Today*, October 1989.

Casey, R.D., 'The National Publicity Bureau and British Party Propaganda', *Public Opinion Quarterly*, 1939, 3(4): 623–34.

Crewe, Ivor, 'Why Labour Lost the Election', *Public Opinion*, July 1983.

Curran, James, 'The New Revisionism in Mass Communication Research: A Reappraisal', *European Journal of Communication*, June 1990, 5(2–3): 135–64.

Curtice, John, and Michael Steed, 'Proportionality and Exaggeration in the British Electoral System', *Electoral Studies*, 5, 1986, pp. 209–28.

Dunleavy, Patrick, George Jones and Brendan O'Leary, 'Prime Ministers and the Commons: Patterns of Behaviour, 1868–1987', *Public Administration*, April 1990, 6(1).

Garapedian, Carla, 'The Relationship between Media Coverage and Government Policy Presentation', University of London, PhD thesis, 1987.

Harris, Ralph, and Arthur Seldon, *Welfare Without the State*, London: Institute of Economic Affairs, 1987.

Harrop, Martin, 'Political Marketing', *Parliamentary Affairs*, July 1990, 43(3): 277–91.

Holme, Richard, 'Selling the PM', *Contemporary Record*, Spring 1988, Vol. 2(1).

IBA, *The IBA Code of Advertising Standards and Practice*, London: IBA, 1989.

ITN, *British Voting Trends 1979–1987*, 1987.

Kelly, Richard, 'Party Organisation', *Contemporary Record*, April 1991, 4(4).

Mandelson, Peter, 'Marketing Labour', *Contemporary Record*, Winter 1988, 1(4).

Media Expenditure Analysis Limited, *Monthly Digest 1970–1989*, MEAL.

Pattie, G., 'Marketing the Tories', *Crossbow*, April–June 1969, 12(47).

Radice, Giles, *Southern Discomfort*, Fabian Pamphlet 555, 1992.

Scammell, Margaret, 'Political Advertising and the Broadcasting Revolution', *Political Quarterly*, April–June 1990, 61(2): 200–13.

Scammell, Margaret, 'The Impact of Marketing and Public Relations on Modern British Politics: the Conservative Party and Government under Mrs Thatcher', University of London, PhD thesis, 1991.

Semetko, Holli A., 'Political Communications and Party Development in Britain: The Social Democratic Party from its Origins to the General Election of 1983', University of London, PhD thesis, 1987.

Seymour-Ure, C., 'The Prime Minister's Press Secretary', *Contemporary Record*, Autumn 1989, 3(1).

Taylor, Neville, 'Behind the Whitehall Curtain', *British Journalism Review*, Autumn 1989, 1(1): 29–33.

Tunstall, J., 'The Media: Lapdogs for Thatcher?', *Contemporary Record*, November 1990, 4(2).

Wentz, J.E., 'A Comparative Study of Mass Media Operations during 1986 at the UK Ministry of Defence and the US Department of Defence', University of London, LSE, PhD thesis, 1988.

Young, Hugo, 'The Media Under Mrs Thatcher', *Contemporary Record*, April 1990, 3(4).

Index